BTEC NATIONAL
FOR IT PRACTITIONERS

OPTIONS

MARK FISHPOOL
BERNADETTE FISHPOOL

HODDER
EDUCATION

PART OF HACHETTE LIVRE UK

Orders: please contact Bookpoint Ltd, 130 Milton Park, Abingdon, Oxon OX14 4SB. Telephone: (44) 01235 827720. Fax: (44) 01235 400454. Lines are open from 9.00 to 5.00, Monday to Saturday, with a 24-hour message-answering service. You can also order through our website www.hoddereducation.co.uk

If you have any comments to make about this, or any
of our other titles, please send them to
educationenquiries@hodder.co.uk

British Library Cataloguing in Publication Data
A catalogue record for this title is available from the British Library

ISBN: 978 0 340 968 376

This Edition Published 2007
Impression number   10 9 8 7 6 5 4 3 2 1
Year   2012 2011 2010 2009 2008

Hachette Livre UK's policy is to use papers that are natural, renewable and recyclable products and made from wood grown in sustainable forests. The logging and manufacturing processes are expected to conform to the environmental regulations of the country of origin.

Microsoft product screen shot(s) reprinted with permission from Microsoft Corporation. Adobe product screen shot(s) reprinted with permission from Adobe Systems Incorporated.

Cover photo from © ImageSource/Punchstock.
Typeset by Pantek Arts Ltd, Maidstone, Kent.

Printed in Italy for Hodder Education, an Hachette Livre UK Company, 338 Euston Road, London NW1 3BH.

Contents

Introduction		vi
Units covered by this book and CD-ROM		viii
Assessment and Grading		ix
Unit 4	IT Project	1
Unit 5	Advanced Database Skills	47
Unit 6	Advanced Spreadsheet Skills	101
Unit 10	Client-side Customisation of Web Pages	152
Unit 19	Web Server Scripting	237
Unit 23	Installing and Upgrading Software	306
Unit 24	Digital Graphics and Computers	344
Unit 25	Object-oriented Programming	378
Braincheck and Activity Answers		429
Index		449

Unit 13, Human–Computer Interaction and Unit 21, Website Production and Management are covered on the accompanying CD-ROM.

HODDER
EDUCATION
The Expert Choice

What does 'the expert choice' mean for you?

We work with more examiners and experts than any other publisher

● Because we work with more experts and examiners than any other publisher, the very latest curriculum requirements are built into this course and there is a perfect match between your course and the resources that you need to succeed. We make it easier for you to gain the skills and knowledge that you need for the best results.

● We have chosen the best team of experts – including the people that mark the exams – to give you the very best chance of success; look out for their advice throughout this book: this is content that you can trust.

More direct contact with teachers and students than any other publisher

● We talk with more than 100 000 students every year through our student conferences, run by Philip Allan Updates. We hear at first hand what you need to make a success of your A-level studies and build what we learn into every new course. Learn more about our conferences at **www.philipallan.co.uk**

● Our new materials are trialled in classrooms as we develop them, and the feedback built into every new book or resource that we publish. You can be part of that. If you have comments that you would like to make about this book, please email us at: **feedback@hodder.co.uk**

More collaboration with Subject Associations than any other publisher

● Subject Associations sit at the heart of education. We work closely with more Associations than any other publisher. This means that our resources support the most creative teaching and learning, using the skills of the best teachers in their field to create resources for you.

More opportunities for your teachers to stay ahead than with any other publisher

● Through our Philip Allan Updates Conferences, we offer teachers access to Continuing Professional Development. Our focused and practical conferences ensure that your teachers have access to the best presenters, teaching materials and training resources. Our presenters include experienced teachers, Chief and Principal Examiners, leading educationalists, authors and consultants. This course is built on all of this expertise.

Acknowledgements

For Norman Hardy – teacher, mentor and much-missed friend.

The author and publishers would like to thank the following for permission to reproduce copyright material:

Figure 4.19 (p. 21) with kind permission of ACAS, www.acas.org.uk; Figure 10.44 (p. 208) courtesy of Adobe Systems; Figure 19.53 (p. 283) with kind permission of www.2shared.com; Figure 23.22 (p. 326) copyright © 1995–2008 RealNetworks, Inc. All rights reserved. RealPlayer is the registered trademark of RealNetworks, Inc.; Figure 23.23 (p. 328) © WIBU-SYSTEMS AG, www.wibu.com; Figure 24.4 (p. 347) © iStockphoto.com/216Photo; Figure 24.5 (p. 348) © iStockphoto.com; Figure 24.6 (p. 349) © graficart.net/Alamy; Figure 24.9 (p. 350) © Helene Rogers/Alamy; Figure 24.10 (p. 350) courtesy of Epsom UK Ltd; Figure 24.11 (p. 351) with kind permission of Hewlett Packard; p. 396 © Keith Morris/Alamy.

Microsoft product screen shots reprinted with permission from Microsoft Corporation. Adobe product screen shots reprinted with permission from Adobe Systems Incorporated.

Every effort has been made to trace and acknowledge copyright. The publishers will be happy to make arrangements with any copyright holder whom it has not been possible to contact.

Introduction

Welcome to Edexcel's BTEC National family of qualifications!

For over 20 years, the BTEC National family of Computing and IT qualifications have represented **the** practical, vocational-oriented alternative to GCE A-Level study.

During 2006 Edexcel revised their 2003 BTEC National qualification for IT practitioners, taking into consideration invaluable feedback from various professional bodies, schools, colleges and employers.

Both its academic and vocational themes have been thoroughly revised to more appropriately reflect the changing needs of employers in the IT sector and the expectations of learners both in schools and colleges. Accordingly, part of its revised structure includes a mixture of vendor units from Microsoft, Cisco and CompTIA.

The new BTEC National qualification (encompassing an Award, Certificate and a Diploma) links firmly to its sector's National Occupational Standards (NOS) and is supported by its Sector Skills Council (SSC).

All qualifications have been accredited to the National Qualifications Framework (NQF) at level 3.

Academic pathways

The new BTEC National scheme has four pathways which define occupational routes in the modern IT Industry. These are:

✓ IT and Business
✓ Software Development
✓ Systems Support
✓ Networking

Although each pathway has a number of common units (e.g. Unit 1 – Communication and Employability Skills for IT), they each contain a combination of specialist units which can make the learning experience truly unique. Usually your school or college will select **which** specialist units will be included on your course. Most units require 60 hours of study but Unit 4 (IT Project), due to its complexity and breadth of learning opportunities, is a double unit, having 120 hours of study.

BTEC National Award for IT Practitioners

In order to achieve the BTEC National Award (BNA) for IT Practitioners you should pass units which total 360 Guided Learning Hours (GLH). This is equivalent to six units of study, including four specialist units. The award has no pathway options.

This is roughly equivalent to studying one GCE A-Level.

BTEC National Certificate for IT Practitioners

In order to achieve the BTEC National Certificate (BNC) for IT Practitioners you should pass units which total 720 GLH. Usually this is equivalent to 12 units of study, including a maximum of eight specialist units. The Certificate is available in all four vocational pathways listed above.

This is roughly equivalent to studying two GCE A-Levels.

BTEC National Diploma for IT Practitioners

In order to achieve the BTEC National Diploma (BND) for IT Practitioners you should pass units which total 1080 Guided Learning Hours (GLH). Usually this is equivalent to 18 units of study, including a maximum of 12 specialist units. As with the Certificate, the Diploma is available in all four vocational pathways.

This is roughly equivalent to studying three GCE A-Levels.

What's in this book

This book has been written to act as a companion to the previous volume which covered the core units of the BTEC IT Practitioners programme. **Together** they represent a very comprehensive support aid and learning tool for both teachers and students.

This volume includes material which is designed to help you study (and complete) the **most popular specialist units** of the BTEC National Award, Certificate or Diploma for IT Practitioners, no matter which route you eventually follow.

Icons used in this book

 A light overview of the unit's content and purpose.

 Complex topics made easy for you.

 Key term which you should understand in order to succeed in the unit.

 An activity – something to get you working on aspects of the unit, may be practical or theoretical.

 An opportunity to test your memory and understanding of the unit's content.

 A case study concerning a select number of realistic businesses that want to use IT but who may no know how. Your task will be to solve their problems.

 Where related material can be found.

 How to achieve the prize (completing the unit).

 A list of extra resources that can be found on the CD.

 Other books, some recommended by Edexcel, which contain useful reading for the unit.

Units covered by this book

This **book** covers the following **10** units marked as specialist on all versions of the qualification:

Specialist Units	GLH	BTEC National Award	IT and Business		Software Development		Systems Support		Networking	
			Certificate	Diploma	Certificate	Diploma	Certificate	Diploma	Certificate	Diploma
Unit 4 IT Project	120	✗	✓	✓	✓	✓	✓	✓	✓	✓
Unit 5 Advanced Database Skills	60	✓	✓	✓	✓	✓	✓	✓	✓	✓
Unit 6 Advanced Spreadsheet Skills	60	✓	✓	✓	✓	✓	✓	✓	✓	✓
Unit 10 Client-Side Customisation of Web Pages	60	✓	✓	✓	✓	✓	✗	✓	✓	✓
Unit 13 Human–Computer Interaction	60	✓	✓	✓	✓	✓	✓	✓	✓	✓
Unit 19 Web Server Scripting	60	✗	✗	✗	✓	✓	✓	✓	✗	✓
Unit 21 Web Production Management	60	✓	✓	✓	✓	✓	✓	✓	✓	✓
Unit 23 Installing and Upgrading Software	60	✓	✓	✓	✓	✓	✓	✓	✓	✓
Unit 24 Digital Graphics and Computers	60	✓	✓	✓	✓	✓	✓	✓	✓	✓
Unit 25 Object-Oriented Programming	60	✗	✗	✗	✓	✓	✓	✓	✗	✓

Assessment and Grading

Assessment for this qualification is undertaken through a series of coursework-based assignments. Your tutors may use assignments developed by Edexcel, or will write assignments for you to do that meet grading criteria. These assignments, and the work you provide, are marked and checked by your own centre and are then checked through external verification activity with a representative from Edexcel.

This qualification will now be awarded on a points system, although your certificate will show achievement at Pass, Merit or Distinction. To monitor your own progress as you undertake the course, each unit has a monitoring sheet for you to use. A full set of master grids that you can print off and use is included on the companion CD.

Each time you complete an assignment, your tutor will identify which **grading criteria** you have been awarded. You can tick off your achievement on the relevant unit sheet. Using this mechanism you will be able to identify which grading criteria you still have outstanding at each level (Pass, Merit and Distinction). **You must always remember** that to achieve a particular grade you must have been awarded **all the grading criteria available within a grade**. For a Pass, all **Pass** criteria must have been achieved. For a **Merit** grade, all **Pass** and all **Merit** criteria must have been achieved. For a **Distinction** grade, all **Pass**, all **Merit** and all **Distinction** criteria must have been achieved.

Once a unit has been completed you will then be awarded a number of points. This will be dependent on the size of the unit and the grade you achieved. Please see the following points table:

Size of Unit (GLH)	Pass Grade	Merit Grade	Distinction Grade
30	3	6	9
60	6	12	18
90	9	18	27
120	12	24	36

Table reproduced from the Edexcel Qualification Specification

The points score for each individual unit is reported to Edexcel at the end of your course. The points are then added together to give a **total score**. This will be the overall grade that you achieve for the qualification. It is known as your **qualification grade**.

Qualification grade

The qualification grade boundaries and UCAS points (as at 1 January 2007) are shown below and represent information about how your grade will be calculated, based on the number of points you have achieved in the selection of units you studied (N.B. **All** tables shown here have been reproduced from the Edexcel Qualification Specification):

Grade boundaries BTEC National Award	Overall grade BTEC National Award		UCAS points
36–59	Pass	P	40
60–83	Merit	M	80
84–108	Distinction	D	120

Grade boundaries BTEC National Certificate	Overall grade BTEC National Certificate	UCAS points
72–95	PP	80
96–119	MP	120
120–143	MM	160
144–167	DM	200
168–216	DD	240

Grade boundaries BTEC National Diploma	Overall grade BTEC National Diploma	UCAS points
108–131	PPP	120
132–155	MPP	160
156–179	MMP	200
180–203	MMM	240
204–227	DMM	280
228–251	DDM	320
252–324	DDD	360

Further information can be found on the Edexcel website at www.edexcel.org.uk. For example, you can look at the unit specification and guidance given to your tutors. Your centres have been advised by Edexcel to keep up to date with the latest guidance provided on the website.

Unit 4

IT Project

Capsule view

In order for IT professionals to identify and effectively implement technical solutions to business and organisational problems, the process needs to have a coherent structure and guidelines so that any risks to the project can be minimised.

IT projects must thus be carefully managed, implemented and documented to ensure that they provide the solution to meet the needs of the organisation. Formalising this process also enables project teams to review the success of the project after implementation.

In this 120-hour IT Project unit, you will be shown a complete project process by walking through a virtual problem. Drawing heavily on the concepts of the Systems Analysis unit (Unit 7 in the Core Text) you will be guided through the project process using the same case studies defined in the *BTEC National for IT Practitioners: Core* book by the same authors. These case studies are defined in this unit, immediately following the unit learning aims.

It is likely that this double unit will be studied in the second year (or towards the end) of your programme as it draws heavily on your understanding of concepts covered in the core units. In order to recommend and develop a solution, whether it is a software solution, business solution or technical solution, this unit anticipates that you have already achieved skills and understanding in these areas.

Learning aims

1 Understand how **projects** are **specified** and **managed**.
2 Be able to **plan** an IT project.
3 Be able to **implement** an IT project.
4 Be able to **test**, **document** and **review** an IT project.

Case Studies

Lee Office Supplies is a small stationery and office equipment supplier trading with our other two organisations, **Frankoni T-shirts Limited** and **KAM (Kris Arts & Media) Limited**.

Frankoni T-shirts Limited is a national company with outlets in larger towns. They specialise in producing personalised T-shirts on demand, using iron-on designs that they buy in from other companies, but particularly from KAM Limited. The T-shirts themselves can be purchased from a range of alternative suppliers.

KAM (Kris Arts & Media) Limited is primarily a graphic design company. The company specialises in taking photographic images for use in advertising and other artistic pursuits, along with hand-drawn and computer-generated images, particularly used in T-shirt design. Trading from only one location, KAM's artistic reputation has seen a vast increase in their customer base.

The three companies seen here will again be used throughout this text to underpin activities and to provide a contextual framework for some of the concepts you will meet.

1 Understand how projects are specified and managed

1.1 Project specification

Identification of stakeholders

Key Terms

A **stakeholder** is an individual or a group of individuals who have a **direct interest** in something because they **use** it, have **invested** in it, or are **affected by** it in some way. This 'something' could be more or less anything although the term is most frequently used when referring to those who are interested in tangible items such as products, services or project outcomes.

One of the fundamental reasons why projects don't fully succeed is because analysts and IT professionals fail to recognise some of the stakeholders in the project and so the stakeholders themselves, and thus their input and views, are effectively ignored. This means that some of the stakeholders may not buy in to the project and in some extreme cases they could actively try to sabotage the project and what the project is trying to achieve.

Successful IT projects fully identify and include all stakeholders at some level, whether this is asking for information that will enhance and inform the project, asking for their opinions on what the outcomes should be, or asking them to be involved in the testing of the product.

In general there are always project stakeholders and many of these are obvious – others less so and the level to which they will be allowed to have an input in a project will vary, depending on the project itself. In general, stakeholders include those shown in Figure 4.1.

In terms of an IT-related project, many of these will not have any involvement – for example, it is unlikely that environmental groups will be asked to have an input. This is largely because they will not be interested in the project itself, or the outcomes of the project. Equally the same may be true of local residents.

However, it is likely to affect:

◆ **employees** – who will have to use the outcome of the project;
◆ **legal bodies** – for example compliance with laws like the Data Protection Act;
◆ **suppliers** – the project outcome may mean that the purchasing process might be changed;

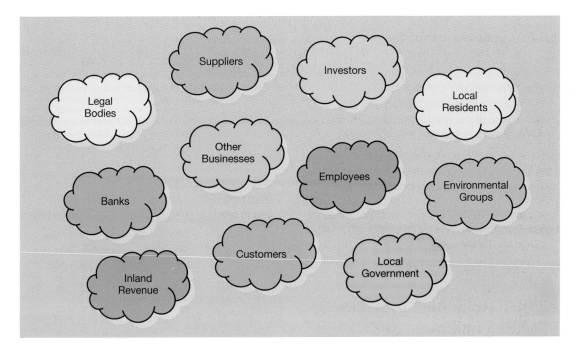

Figure 4.1 Possible project stakeholders

◆ **customers** – again the outcome might mean changes in the way that customers place orders, for example as a result of the project they might now be able to order online, rather than just by telephone.

It is the responsibility of the project team to ensure that all relevant stakeholders are not only identified, to set the level of influence that these individuals and groups should be allowed to have, but also to ensure that these stakeholders remain informed about the project and its progress.

Business case requirements

To make sure that ultimately the project solution will fully meet the requirements and needs of the business, it is essential that these requirements are identified.

In addition, because some aspects may be more keenly sought than others, it is most likely that the project stakeholders will wish to set different priorities to different requirements. Using a documentation technique frequently referred to as a PRL (Problem and Requirements List) or Requirements Catalogue, the document is designed to reflect all the stakeholders' requirements/objectives for the project, from a business perspective – the question it is set to address is: 'What are the problems and how will the resolutions actually benefit the organisation or business?'

To complete the PRL:

◆ Each requirement/objective is specified by
  ◆ identifying the user;
  ◆ identifying the nature of the problem or requirement;
  ◆ giving the problem or requirement a priority relative to the others in the list (and to the objectives of the organisation as a whole):
    ◆ E – requirements/objectives felt to be **essential** and without which the project will be deemed to have failed.

- ◆ D – requirements/objectives felt to be **desirable** and which really should be there if the project is to be considered a success.
- ◆ N – **non-essential** aspects that would be nice that but are not essential to the success or failure of the project (and could be added later).
- ◆ Providing a brief explanation of the business case (how resolving the requirement or objective will benefit the organisation).
- ◆ Eventually, later in the project, the Solution column will be completed to reflect how the designers believe the remedy will be achieved.

PRL (PROBLEM and REQUIREMENTS LIST)				
System:		System Component:		Date:
User	Problem/Requirement	Priority	Business Case	Solution

Figure 4.2 Problem and requirements list template

A completed PRL might look something like that shown in Figure 4.3.

PRL (PROBLEM and REQUIREMENTS LIST)				
System: Finance		System Component: Customer Account Management		Date: 5th August 2008
User	Problem/Requirement	Priority	Business Case	Solution
Admin	Invoice generation	E	Faster generation and distribution of customer invoices to improve cash flow	
Admin	Statement generation	E	Automated generation of statements to improve cash flow	
Credit Controller	Exceptions list	D	To facilitate better credit control	
Managers	Period/Trend analysis	D	To establish whether there are identifiable trends to debtor or creditor status	

Figure 4.3 Partially completed PRL for the Customer Account Management function within the Finance System

Here four important aspects of the Customer Account Management function have been identified. You will notice that in this instance none of the requirements are listed as N. This is because it is expected that all of these objectives will be met in the final solution. The first two are essential to the organisation. The last two are also required, but are less critical.

Specific objectives or deliverables

Once a series of PRLs have been developed to show the objectives and business requirements for all aspects of the system, the combination of these will provide a list of specific objectives for the system. Known as the system deliverables, it is the job of the project team to make sure that these objectives are met as part of the problem resolution.

Also, having these formalised as a list will provide all stakeholders with a focus against which to review the success or failure of the project.

Benefits and success factors

While the list of potential business benefits the system will provide could be extensive, they can be grouped into two main categories:

◆ **Indirect benefits** – this could include improved customer service or better access to information.
◆ **Direct benefits** – for example, reduced costs (less labour expense) or faster response times.

The typical **benefits** that the organisation may see could include:

◆ reduction in staff costs;
◆ savings in other operating costs that the organisation experiences, such as consumables;
◆ better sales as marketing information and data analysis improves;
◆ improved cash-flow position because invoices and statements go out faster;
◆ better stock control;
◆ enhanced customer service;
◆ happier staff;
◆ better quality and quantities of information for managers.

As for the relative success of the project, it will be dependant on how many of the identified benefits are implemented during the execution of the project. Let's use a simple example – say that 12 potential benefits have been identified. Only seven of these are actually achieved. The project would then be said to have moderate success. On the other hand, if there were 12 potential benefits and all were actually achieved, then the success factor would be considered very high indeed.

Project boundaries or scope

Before any formal activity on a project can begin, it is important that the problem, as understood by all, has been agreed and written down, as this will form a record and provide boundaries for the subsequent activities. Although the boundaries and scope of the project might be modified during the life cycle of a project, if this is not done formally there is potential for a misunderstanding between users, analysts and developers about **what** was identified as being **needed** and what has subsequently been **developed**.

Defining the scope of the project by writing the requirements specification will ensure that all those involved in the project will have no doubts about what the system **will** and **will not** do.

Case Study

ITRemedies4U Limited has been asked by Lee Office Supplies to develop a stock handling system that is dynamically linked to an invoicing system. The idea is that items will automatically be removed from stock as they are invoiced. As part of the invoice process the VAT due is calculated and added to the sub-total before the invoice is printed.

The project scope/boundaries were given as: Develop a stock control and invoicing system to handle day-to-day sales activities.

However, after the system has been completed, the managers of Lee Office Supplies expect the system to also be capable of automatically outputting the combined VAT data required quarterly for a tax return.

Discuss the following with your tutor or a fellow student: 'Are the managers' expectations fair?'

Answer

While the system may well be capable of generating this information because the data is calculated and is being stored within the system, there is nothing in the originally defined boundaries or scope to specify that this functionality is required. While it is true that this functionality can be added at a later date, its absence at the first point of review cannot be considered when measuring the success or failure of the project. It wasn't asked for, so the fact that it was not there should not be a seen as a detrimental factor and, as such, the managers' expectations that it should already be present in the system are unfair.

Constraints

The most common constraints on any project are time, skills, technology and money, although skills and technology in themselves are often reliant on the availability of money!

Time

Most projects have time constraints. This can be a number of weeks, months or, in the case of a very large project, this could be in excess of a year. Either way, part of the project management process is to effectively manage whatever time you have been given.

If you are asked to specify how long you think you need for the completion of a project, it is always sensible to overestimate rather than underestimate, as there may well be penalties for not completing the project in the timescale specified.

While you will often be able to negotiate the amount of time you will be given, there will be times when a deadline is prescribed by the client in order to meet their needs, and if you do not feel able to meet the imposed deadline, you may well have to withdraw from the project.

Skills

In reality it is unlikely that you would be asked to complete an entire project on your own. This is because most projects would probably be too big for a single person to complete. Working with others, on the other hand, does have its advantages and disadvantages.

If you or your project team have any skills gaps you have two main choices:

◆ Buy in the skills you lack.
◆ Undergo training to acquire the skills.

Both of these options, however, rely on you having the time and/or money to pursue these as a possible solution.

Teamwork scorecard

+ The larger the team, the wider the range of available skills is likely to be.
+ There will probably be more ideas to choose from as each person may have different ideas on how a solution could be facilitated.
+ There will be more people to share the overall burden of the project.
− You find yourself having to rely on others and so you can, at times, be let down.
− Sometimes the fact that the group is made up of a number of individuals with conflicting ideas may result in lots of discussion with little work actually being done.

Working-alone scorecard

+ You have greater control over the whole project.
+ You can work at times to suit you so the whole project can be more flexible.
+ You have greater autonomy.
− You have fewer people to share ideas with.
− You have to be more disciplined as there are no others around you ensuring you meet your deadlines.
− It can be very isolating.
− The learning curve to acquire any skills you lack, but which you need for the project, is likely to be steep.

Technology

The constraints on technology can come from two perspectives:

◆ You have to use the technology the organisation already has (there is no budget for any more).
◆ The technology you would ideally use for the project is outside the budget you have been set.

In order to establish the technological constraints you will need to investigate the current system. You will need to understand what components the system has and how they are configured.

While accessing the information may be different in other operating systems, in Windows XP it is accessed through the Start Menu, as can be seen in Figure 4.4.

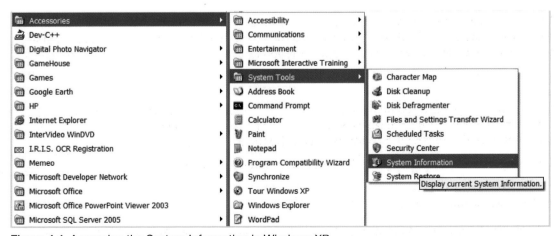

Figure 4.4 Accessing the System Information in Windows XP

Once the interface has been accessed, there is a menu of different aspects of the system that can be individually accessed to provide the relevant detail:

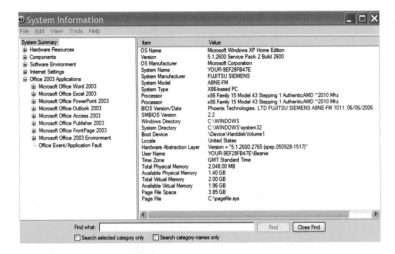

Figure 4.5 System Information

Carefully investigating the existing technology will give you a much better understanding of what you have to work with. It might, after all, not necessarily be the case that the whole system needs upgrading – it might just be one or two components and the operating system.

In any case, you will be expected to be able to justify any expense you identify.

Money

Most organisations don't have a bottomless purse to fund projects. It is likely, therefore, that if you undertake a commercial project you will be given an absolute budget. In some instances you can negotiate, but you must bear in mind that if you fail to meet the project deadlines you may face stiff financial penalties.

Consideration of options

In most situations there are three potential solutions to the problem:

◆ bespoke solution
◆ off-the-shelf solution
◆ tailored solution.

These solutions are normally electronic in nature, although another normal replacement is always possible and should not be discounted without consideration.

Each of the above has **advantages** and **disadvantages** for the organisation and the project team.

Bespoke solution

A bespoke solution is one that is **created from scratch**. This means that the solution will not accommodate any existing systems.

Bespoke solution scorecard:

+ The organisation will get a system that completely meets its needs.
− This is likely to be an expensive solution, in which case it might be outside the financial scope of some organisations.
− It will take a significant amount of time to develop, so the organisation will have to wait.
− The developer will need the right level of programming skill in all the relevant areas.

At times there is no option other than to create a bespoke solution, usually because no current off-the-shelf solution exists, and a tailored solution might still not provide all the functionality that is required by the system users.

Off-the-shelf solution

An off-the-shelf solution is one that is easily facilitated because it can simply be purchased and installed – for example the installation of a wireless router, network cards and associated software to create a computer network.

Off-the-shelf solutions are ideal in most situations where a specific type of application is required.

If the organisation requires functionality that isn't included in a solution, they might need to purchase further hardware, peripherals or software. In these circumstances, there could be a compatibility issue between systems and, as a result, problems sharing information and resources.

Off-the-shelf solution scorecard:

+ No development time needed (this really is an instant solution!).
− Can be expensive, particularly if the solution is software reliant and it requires organisations to buy and maintain **site licences**.
− Might not have **all** the functionality needed.

Tailored solution

A tailored solution uses a generic system or package or a range of pre-existing technology to build a solution.

A tailored solution, therefore, is always developed from something that can be purchased and easily adapted, modified or tweaked to provide the necessary functionality.

For the purposes of a project, there should be documented evidence that alternative solutions were at least considered. This will reassure the client that the solution that was ultimately recommended was the right one for the situation.

Tailored solution scorecard:

+ Little development time needed.
+ Less expensive than a bespoke solution and can be adapted to include at least the most important functional requirements of the solution.
− As with a completely off-the-shelf solution, this can be expensive, particularly if the solution is software reliant and it requires organisations to buy and maintain **site licences**.
− Might not have **all** the functionality needed.

Unit Link

For more on alternative solutions to business problems, see the companion **Core Text**, **Unit 7 – Systems Analysis and Design**, section 2.2 (particularly in relation to software development projects) – see pages 162 to 166.

Other, e.g. ethical issues, sustainable issues, understanding consequences of failure to hit deadlines or produce product

Although less likely, other constraints on projects may also exist – for example, ethical or sustainability constraints.

Key Terms

Ethical constraints are constraints that exist because the project or its outcomes would not be considered right or moral for some reason. For example, would it be ethical for a company to invest in a system that ultimately would damage the environment? Possibly not.

Sustainability constraints is about whether there are any constraints that will prevent the project or project outcome from being maintained on a long-term basis – for example the system might require a resource that may not remain easily available in the longer term.

When it comes to commercial projects particularly, because they are contract dependant, it is quite usual for there to be some type of penalty clause that sets out how the client will be compensated should the project fail to finish on time, or should the project outcome not be fully delivered as specified. These penalties can be extremely steep.

Risks and risk mitigation

There are a number of risks to any project, some of which will now be listed here, along with a potential way to reduce the relevant risk. The main risks are:

◆ projects that run over budget;
◆ projects that run over deadline;
◆ projects that have not been successful in delivering the required product.

Successfully managed projects have a better chance of being successful; for example, **projects are better managed** and therefore potential risks are reduced when formalised meetings and deadlines have been agreed at the start. These are usually recorded in a project plan that should contain:

◆ **Specific milestones** – these will be points in the project where tasks should have been completed.
◆ **Team meetings** – regular team meetings where progress is reviewed should also be planned, as an opportunity for members of the project team to **get together** and **discuss** any issues that are arising. However, this can become **unproductive** unless the meetings are kept short and to the point.
◆ **Interim review dates** – where the team and the client get together to review progress and discuss any issues.
◆ The **final handover date** – this should reflect the date previously agreed with the client.

It is not uncommon for a contract to contain a heavy penalty for each day that a project runs over the deadline.

In the eventuality that you discover that the project is going to cost the client more than originally anticipated, it is your responsibility to inform the client of this immediately. The client can, after all, refuse to pay any more, in which case the project might be cancelled. Similarly, if you are unable to deliver the agreed product, this can have very serious consequences and it should be discussed with the client as soon as possible.

Project planning – useful things to remember

When planning a project, ensure that you allow **sufficient time** to undertake **all aspects** of the project, from analysis, through design to building, testing, implementation and review.

A **novice analyst** is likely to **underestimate** the **time** it **actually** takes to **build** and **test** the system. In reality, **testing alone** can take as much as **50 per cent** of the **total development time**.

1.2 Project life cycles

While *Core Text Unit 7 – Systems Analysis and Design* contains a full range of project life cycles, a simplified model can also be used (see Figure 4.6).

This model consists of five main stages, each of which will be explained below.

Unit Link

For more on life cycle models, see the companion **Core Text, Unit 7 – Systems Analysis and Design**, pages 137 to 185.

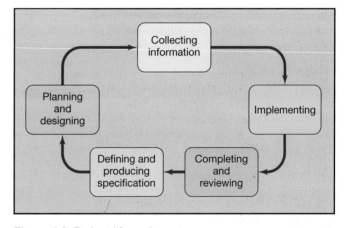

Figure 4.6 Project life cycle

Defining and producing specification

Firstly the problem (or problems) must be carefully described. In reality this is often done by the managers of an organisation, although it is sometimes preferable to speak directly to the users of the system who may be better placed to explain the exact nature of the problem! The problem is then defined in writing and is agreed by both the project team (or representative) and the client or their representative. If you are unable to get a signature from your client, then send them an email and ask them to confirm by return. That way you will have a formal record of agreement.

The specification is then defined as a set of actual deliverables that will be achieved through the project.

Case Study

Problem definition for Frankoni T-shirts

Frankoni T-shirts Limited are having difficulties keeping track of their T-shirts and iron-on designs and they are frequently running out of the most popular T-shirts and designs because they are not aware that stocks have been low. In addition, now that they are increasingly selling goods via their own website, they would like to automate the invoicing system.

The specification focuses on what the new system will **need to do** to enable users to carry out their individual tasks from a **functional perspective**. Once the functionality of the system has been established, the necessary inputs can be identified, the processing requirements can be established and the outputs predicted. At this stage, however, there are no suggestions on how the functionality will be achieved.

Case Study

Functional specification for Frankoni T-shirts

A stock system including minimum stock reordering levels.

Automated invoicing system.

Alternatively, rather than a functional specification, this could be a technical specification for a network or other technical solution.

The specification will contain a list of any identified hardware or software requirements, or anything else that will be needed to facilitate the solution (for example network cabling, desks and chairs, four PCs with wireless connections and a wireless router, security software for these machines etc.).

Planning and designing, collecting information

Although on Figure 4.6 these two parts of the life cycle are shown as consecutive steps, with planning and designing appearing to occur before collecting information, it is fair to say that they more or less happen simultaneously, with each part providing information that might tweak another aspect of the process.

The project itself will be planned, including identifying review points and other milestones, and consideration of what resources will be needed, how much money will be required to see the project through to completion and what deadlines are required.

While this is going on, information about the existing system and its processes is being collected, collated and analysed – after all, you cannot design a solution if you do not understand what you have already! For further information on collecting information, see section 2.2 later in this unit where a number of information-gathering techniques will be discussed.

Implementing

While many project teams assume that implementation is solely about creating the project product, they should remember that the implementation part of the life cycle also includes any testing that needs to be undertaken. It is very common for project teams to drastically underestimate how much time will be needed for this phase. It is far better to heavily overestimate than to underestimate and thereby not carry out effective testing.

Completing and reviewing

Once the project is complete, the product is activated or brought to life and is tested again in situ. The whole team involved in the project then get together to review its success, using the original functional specification or technical specification to provide a list of performance criteria against which the success or failure of the project can be judged.

The review will probably highlight a number of aspects that will require either immediate resolution (something in the product doesn't work as it should and that needs to be addressed), or an additional wish list of enhancements that will make the product even better. In the event that the client wants or needs additional enhancements, in a commercial project there will probably be an opportunity to charge extra for the additional work.

1.3 Project management tools

In order to ensure that projects stay on track, there are a number of techniques that can be used to help the planning process. Application of these techniques will enable managers to control the development of projects by providing a framework against which progress can be measured. These techniques are either business-practice driven (and many were created before the advent of software solutions), like Gantt and PERT charts; others have been developed as part of the expanding range of specialist software. In fact, many of the older techniques have now been incorporated as part of dedicated project development packages, such as Microsoft Project®. What follows here is an overview of these concepts.

General planning and scheduling tools, e.g. Gantt and PERT charts

Gantt charts are used for sequencing processes, particularly where there is a necessity for some activities to take place before other activities may begin. On the other hand, if processes can take place at the same time because they are not reliant on other actions, then these can be shown as simultaneous.

In a sequence, for example, you need to boil the kettle before you attempt to make a cup of tea. However, you could, simultaneously be feeding the cat at the same time that the kettle is boiling.

If we were to apply the technique to the investigation phase of the Frankoni project, a manually created Gantt chart might look something like this:

Case Study

Gantt chart for Frankoni T-shirts project

Investigation phase for Frankoni T-shirts stock and invoicing system project.

The current stock system and current invoicing system must be investigated, and the investigation written up (usually in report format). Then a planning meeting will take place.

		Mon	Tue	Wed	Thu	Fri	Mon	Tue	Wed	Thu	Fri	Mon	Tue
Investigate current stock system	8 days												
Write up report	2 days												
Investigate current invoicing system	5 days												
Write up report	3 days												
Planning meeting	2 days												

Figure 4.7 Simple Gantt chart

What can you see when you look at this Gantt chart and what assumptions can you make?

a The investigations of both existing systems are being undertaken at the same time, therefore they cannot be being done by the same individuals.

b The team investigating the current invoicing system will have nothing to do for two days because the stock system investigation team need longer (this is not unusual if one process is more complex than another).

Everyone will be available for the Planning Meeting because all the other processes will have been finished.

The same processes are represented in a Gantt chart created in Microsoft Project® in Figure 4.14.

A PERT (Programme Evaluation and Review Technique) chart is also based on the identification and definition of task-oriented concepts, but goes further by recognising that there is an element of probability because some tasks may not take the amount of time or the resources first estimated (the tasks may take more time or require more than the anticipated resources or they may take less) – so PERT charts are created incorporating probability theory.

The simplest planning technique is to annotate a simple calendar that shows which activities happen when.

If adopting this planning method, the calendar can be used in two different ways. In the first instance (Figure 4.8) the blocks have been coloured to highlight different types of activity:

◆ investigation in blue
◆ written reports in green
◆ planning in yellow.

An alternative would be to colour the blocks differently, as can be seen in Figure 4.9.

In this instance, a whole process has shared a single colour – all activities focusing on the stock system are shown in blue blocks, all activities around the invoicing system are shown in green.

Whichever method is chosen, what should be noted is that planning shown visually is often easier to understand and more obvious than a simple list of tasks where it can be hard to see how the whole process is put together:

Investigate current stock system	8d	Mon 12/11/07	Wed 21/11/07
Write up report	2d	Thu 22/11/07	Fri 23/11/07
Investigate current invoicing system	5d	Mon 12/11/07	Fri 16/11/07
Write up report	3d	Mon 19/11/07	Wed 21/11/07
Planning meeting	2d	Mon 26/11/07	Tue 27/11/07

Figure 4.8 Using a simple calendar to plan activities (version 1)

Figure 4.9 Using a simple calendar to plan activities (version 2)

Critical path methods

The critical path method (often simply referred to as CPM) is another visual technique that uses diagrams, but which is different from what you have already seen here because in this instance the relationship between the activities is identified. In fact, the method looks for the route through the activities where there is the least flexibility.

It is centred on the concepts of logic and efficiency.

As with Gantt charts, however, it accepts that there will be some activities that must be carried out sequentially (known as a series) and others that can be executed simultaneously (known as parallel).

The basis for the method is attempting to answer a set of questions:

1 How long will it take to fully complete the project?
2 Which activities are inflexible and thus help to fix the project time?
3 Which activities can be shortened (if at all possible), or should we give more resources to?

These questions are answered by addressing the following:

a Identify the tasks that need to be undertaken.
b Identify the resources needed to achieve the project.
c Establish the priority of the individual tasks.
d Establish the sequence of activities and how long each should take.
e Decide where there is a possibility for activities to be carried out in parallel.
f Calculate the shortest time in which the project can be completed allowing for all the necessary activities to have been undertaken.

Figure 4.10 represents a network diagram. For the purposes of this diagram the actual nature of the tasks is not relevant, only the time and sequencing of the events is important.

In order to identify the critical path, we now need to calculate the longest path through the project:

Path 1   A, B, F, G   or   2 + 6 + 2 + 1   = 11 days

Path 2   A, C, F, G   or   2 + 3 + 2 + 1   = 8 days

Path 3   A, D, E, F, G   or   2 + 4 + 7 + 2 + 1   = 16 days

Thus the critical path is Path 3.

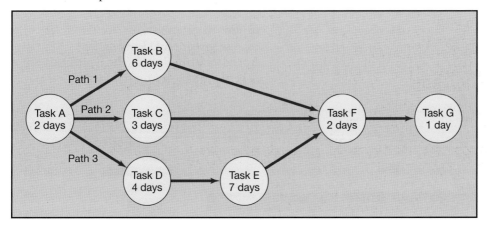

Figure 4.10 Network diagram

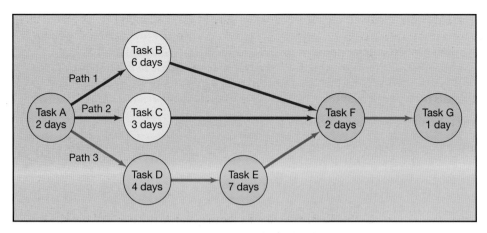

Figure 4.11 The Critical Path highlighted on the network diagram

If we now wish to shorten the project, we would need to look carefully at tasks D and E to see whether they can be shortened, either by being more efficient or by giving the tasks more resources to get them done more quickly for example.

Specialised software packages, e.g. Microsoft Project®

In the development of Microsoft Project®, Microsoft included functionality that allows the user to input the tasks and allocate times and resources, but then view the project in a number of different ways.

Using the same scenario as shown in Figures 4.7, 4.8 and 4.9, we will now replicate the project using the specialised software.

First we list the tasks and how long we estimate each will take:

	Task Name	Duration
1	Investigate current stock system	8 days
2	Write up report	2 days
3	Investigate current invoicing system	5 days
4	Write up report	3 days
5	Planning meeting	2 days

Figure 4.12 Task list

We now allocate a start date for the project. Because we have not identified any dependencies, the bars for the Gantt chart will all be at the same starting point:

	Task Name	Duration	Start	Finish	12 Nov '07	19 Nov '07
					F S S M T W T F	S S M T W T F
1	Investigate current stock system	8 days	Mon 12/11/07	Wed 21/11/07		
2	Write up report	2 days	Mon 12/11/07	Tue 13/11/07		
3	Investigate current invoicing system	5 days	Mon 12/11/07	Fri 16/11/07		
4	Write up report	3 days	Mon 12/11/07	Wed 14/11/07		
5	Planning Meeting	3 days	Mon 12/11/07	Wed 14/11/07		

Figure 4.13 Gantt chart bars

The dependencies are identified by allocating predecessor activities. These can simply be typed in, or the physical bars can be moved into position. If using the drag and drop technique the system will prompt you to ask whether the activity should be linked to the one before it:

Figure 4.14 Completed Gantt chart

Once completed, the user can now use the View menu to view the project in a number of different ways, in effect replicating the earlier charts at the touch of a button.

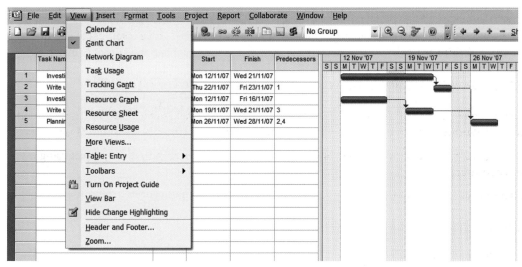

Figure 4.15 View menu showing the diagram options

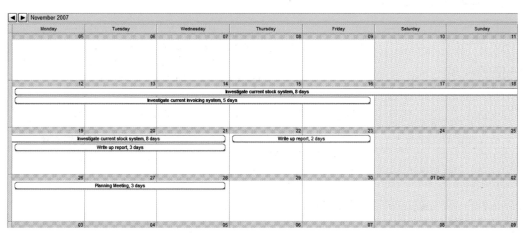

Figure 4.16 Calendar view

Figure 4.17 Microsoft Project® version of a network diagram

	Task Name	Duration	Start	Finish	Predecessors	12 Nov '07	19 Nov '07	26 Nov '07
1	Investigate current stock system	8 days	Mon 12/11/07	Wed 21/11/07		2/11 ▬▬ 21/11		
2	Write up report	2 days	Thu 22/11/07	Fri 23/11/07	1		22/11 ▬ 23/11	
3	Investigate current invoicing system	5 days	Mon 12/11/07	Fri 16/11/07		2/11 ▬ 16/11		
4	Write up report	3 days	Mon 19/11/07	Wed 21/11/07	3		19/11 ▬ 21/11	
5	Planning Meeting	3 days	Mon 26/11/07	Wed 28/11/07	2,4			26/11 ▬ 28/11

Figure 4.18 Microsoft Project® version of a critical path diagram highlighting the critical path in red

Clearly there are other menu options that can be investigated at your leisure.

There is functionality that will allow users to allocate project resources (particularly, but not exclusively, people).

1.4 Resources

When it comes to providing resources for a project, there are four main categories to be considered.

Information

In this instance, information is data. What data can be made available to the project team? Here are some examples that might be required to facilitate the Frankoni project:

Customer, Supplier, Stock, Price

This is not the investigation; this is just an overview of the data that is broadly required to facilitate the project.

People (expertise and responsibilities), e.g. project managers, product developers, programmers, systems analysts

The people (the human resources) also need to be analysed. The team needs to establish the skills and expertise that each person has, as it is obviously best if each person in the team can do what they do best! Frequently this is done by way of a skills analysis – where all the activities that the project requires are listed and the individuals carry out a self-evaluation on how experienced and capable they feel they are in each of the categories. This analysis also often leads to a natural dissemination of responsibilities.

Typical areas of responsibility include:

◆ **Project manager** – usually a single individual controls the whole project, although sometimes the sub-areas also have supervisors.

- ◆ **Analyst** – often a team of individuals with sound analytical skills who will take responsibility for investigating the existing system and making recommendations about the types of solution that might be appropriate; in most cases the analysts will also develop the specification about what the system will need to do.
- ◆ **Designer** – designers will take the specification and design a solution in terms of data and how it will be structured, and what physical aspects of the system will be required (how many computers, configuration, network requirements, peripherals etc.).
- ◆ **Programmer/developer** – here the design is taken and implemented; this could be by a programmer for a solution in Visual Basic® or Visual C#®, or a website created in Dreamweaver®; it could be a database solution developed in Microsoft Access®, or it could be the installation of a hardware solution or a network.
- ◆ **Tester** – with some systems, the programmers or developers will undertake the task of testing the system, but with others specially trained testers could be used.
- ◆ **Documenter** – every developed system should be documented so that others can understand how it is put together; sometimes this will be done by the development team, while in other instances it will be done by a documentation specialist.

If a project is being undertaken by a single person, they will effectively have to have as many as possible of the skills listed above, as they will need to be able to take on many, or even all, of the roles described.

Equipment or facilities, e.g. software, hardware

The project team must consider what equipment or facilities already exist and should establish which aspects the client wishes to retain – for example, the client may state that while new computers can be purchased, the existing ones should be upgraded if necessary, not simply replaced. Alternatively, there may be a particular piece of software that will need to work with the developed system, either because the systems will share data, or because some of the functionality already exists in other software owned by the organisation – so why replicate the processes if the systems can be developed to work side by side.

Money

It is usual for organisations to have decided how much they can make available for a project before any activities are undertaken. However, sometimes the organisation will have no idea about how much a new system will cost, and they will set an initial study in motion to establish the likely costs of implementing a solution to their problems.

The actual amount to be spent will be negotiated and agreed before the project begins and it is the job of the project team to ensure that the project costs do not ultimately exceed the budget they have been given. If, at any point, it appears that there could be a problem, it is the duty of the project team to highlight the issues to the client.

1.5 Other issues

In addition there could be other considerations that need to be taken into account, and factors that the project manager and team need to manage.

Effects of changing external factors

A key to ensuring that a project is ultimately successful is to be aware of the external environment – for example this could be making minor adjustments to the project to respond to activities of customers, suppliers or competitors.

Case Study

External factors that could affect the Frankoni T-shirts project

The following are examples of external factors that could need to be taken into account in the development of a system:

Customers or suppliers moving to EDI (Electronic Data Interchange) systems, which could impact on how orders are placed or invoices are distributed.

Competitors have started to offer bulk-buying discounts, so the system being developed for Frankoni might need additional functionality that allows Frankoni staff to apply a discount structure for its customers.

Sometimes companies choose to be proactive, rather than waiting to be reactive when it comes to project development. In reality Frankoni might decide to ask its customers or suppliers whether they intend to make any changes to the way they do business with the company, which might have a bearing on how the project solution is put together.

Monitoring progress

Having planned the project and created a series of review points and milestones, the project manager(s) will carefully monitor the progress of the project and, should any difficulties be experienced, the client will need to be advised as soon as possible.

It is not acceptable to know that there are problems and to effectively ignore them as failure to meet the final deadlines, or to produce the intended project outcome, can result in heavy penalties.

Taking corrective actions where necessary

The project manager(s) will need to take any steps to correct any failures in the project – they will need to support the project team, sometimes making additional resources available to ensure that the project comes back on track.

Communications

Effective communication is probably the most important aspect of successful project management. This not only includes communications within the project team and with supervisors and managers, but also includes communications with the client and/or their representatives.

Unit Link

For more on effective communication, see the companion **Core Text, Unit 1 – Communication and Employability Skills in IT**, pages 1 to 44.

Communication can take place in many forms – through writing, speech, body language and images, and because it is a fundamental aspect of working in the IT sector, an entire unit has been written about it.

Working within relevant guidelines (internal and external) and legislation

Other project constraints have to be managed – for example, any newly developed projects should always comply with up-to-date legislation. In fact, the project team should also investigate legislation that is under development to ensure that they will not find themselves having to make amendments to the system in the medium term.

They should also be mindful of any guidelines that exist, either internal 'house' guidelines about what systems should or should not have, or external guidelines such as those that might exist for the sector or environment in which they operate.

Dealing with conflict

It is unlikely that a project will be seen through from beginning to end without conflict situations occurring. These must be quickly dealt with and carefully managed to ensure that the project is not detrimentally affected.

The most important steps in resolving a conflict are:

◆ Identify the nature and cause of the conflict.
◆ Decide how you will manage the conflict.
◆ Find a way to get those in conflict together to begin the resolution process.
◆ Enable the discussion, ensuring that each person involved has an opportunity to share their concerns, thoughts and feelings.
◆ Help them to move towards a resolution – this will usually involve them agreeing to some sort of action plan and may well involve a significant amount of compromise.
◆ Once agreement has been reached, make sure that the actions are carried out.

For further information on managing conflict in the workplace, see the following website:
www.acas.org.uk

If, in managing your own project, you find you need support in dealing with conflict situations, you should make sure you tell your tutor or project supervisor.

Impact of project outputs on other systems, e.g. staff, organisational structures

The effect of the implementation of a project may be more far-reaching than just affecting direct users of the system. These are some common issues:

Figure 4.19 ACAS website

◆ **Staff might need to change working methods.** This could be because some processes need to change with the implementation of the new solution – different working patterns (times of the day), processes might need to be carried out in a different way, processes might have been eliminated, some staff might require new skills to work with the system.
◆ **Organisational structures might change.** There could be redundancies where staff skills are no longer required, staff could be transferred to different areas of the organisation to be retrained, new departments or functional areas could be created that require new staff, managers etc.

All aspects of the system's implementation should have been considered as part of the project.

1.6 Project methodologies

As we have seen, both here and in *Core Text, Unit 7 – Systems Analysis and Design*, there are a number of methodologies that could be adopted to give a project structure and to make it more likely that ultimately the project outcomes are achieved.

Benefits and drawbacks of formal methodologies

Methodologies scorecard:

+ Adopting a formal methodology to support a project will give the project a **recognisable framework** within which the team can operate.
+ It will enable the team to **identify** all **required steps**, which should ensure that the project will ultimately be successful.
− Sometimes having a framework can be too **limiting** because too many **constraints** are often said to **diminish creativity**.
− Some steps required by a methodology might be detrimental to the project. For example, SSADM is a methodology best suited to the development of data dependant systems – entity relationship modelling and data flow diagramming techniques, which are required as part of the SSADM process, would not be relevant to projects like websites (if there are no data needs) or to a hardware/network solution – but leaving out steps might compromise the effectiveness of the project overall.

Examples, e.g. Prince2, Sigma, company specific

Additional examples included here include Prince2 and Sigma:

Prince2

For almost 20 years Prince2 has been seen as one of the leading methodologies for IT project management, although its concepts can be equally applied to non IT-based projects. The diagram shown in Figure 4.20 gives an overview of the concepts.

Unit Link

For more on formal methodologies, see the companion **Core Text**, **Unit 7 – Systems Analysis and Design**, pages 137 to 140.

The steps in the Prince2 framework are explained as follows:

1 **Directing a project** – within this methodology it is expected that the business/corporate managers will start the project and offer support and guidance, but that they will not be excessively committed to the project as a whole.
2 **Starting up the project** – involves setting up a project management team that includes individuals to represent the interests of those with a stake in the project, e.g. users.
3 **Initiating a project** – decisions are made about how to make certain that the project will meet its objectives. This can often be a process of ensuring that all members of the organisation commit to the project.

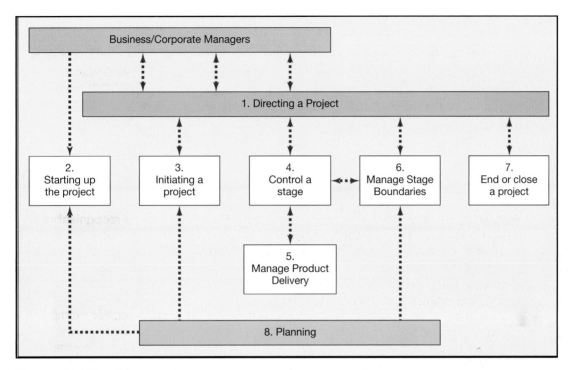

Figure 4.20 Prince2 framework

4 **Control a stage** – ongoing management of the project by the project manager, involving managing the day-to-day activities and workload, reacting as appropriate to internal and external events, and reporting any major issues to the corporate and business managers as needed.

5 **Manage product delivery** – this defines the processes that will take place to facilitate reporting on progress and delivery of completed work.

6 **Manage stage boundaries** – preparing for reviews where progress is examined, future plans are discussed and any out-of-tolerance situations (those on or just beyond the stage boundaries) are resolved.

7 **End or close a project** – deciding how to end the project, how to manage any follow-up activities including the project review.

8 **Planning** – defines how to plan, regardless of when the planning is done.

Prince2 methodology scorecard:

+ Widely understood and recognised methodology.
+ Structured method that incorporates well-established good business practices.
+ Facilitates control in how the project is managed, how resources are used and how risk is diminished.
− Does not give guidance about managing the people involved in the project team.

Sigma

Sigma, or more appropriately **Six Sigma**, is a methodology that organisations use to improve business processes, thereby enhancing organisational performance, reducing waste and thus improving product quality, profits and employee morale.

Sigma has two basic process definitions that define the activities in the process.

The DMAIC version identifies the processes as:

◆ define
◆ measure
◆ analyse
◆ improve
◆ control.

This improvement system constantly looks for opportunities within processes where step-by-step or incremental improvements can be implemented to enhance overall quality.

The alternative, DMADV, identifies the processes as:

◆ define
◆ measure
◆ analyse
◆ design
◆ verify.

This system, which is more like the simple project life cycle shown in section 1.2 (see Figure 4.6), is designed to be used in the development of new products or processes that need to be of very high quality. This system, as described, appears to focus on the development of completely new products or processes, but this does not mean that it must be excluded as a methodology for existing systems where it can be successfully used, particularly when seeking to develop systems that need more substantial improvements.

Company-specific methodologies

A whole range of company-specific methodologies also exist – for example:

◆ ABC Methodology (see **www.gemsconsult.com/abc_methodology.html**)
◆ Epsilon Project Methodology (see **www.epsilonconcepts.com/company/our-methodology/**)
◆ DataX Methodology (see **www.datax.com.ua/company/methodology/**).

These methodologies do have common concepts with many of the standard methodologies, but have variations in how they are applied to specific project problems.

2 Be able to plan an IT project

2.1 Project plan

Purpose

The purpose of the project plan is to identify the tasks and activities that will need to be carried out as part of the project. Usually this is a list of functionality that will need to be implemented. Using project techniques such as Gantt charts or PERT charts, or software such as Microsoft Project®, the plan will formalise the activities and give the whole project structure.

Braincheck – Project management crossword

Complete the project management crossword. A solution is provided on page 429.

Clues:

ACROSS

4 The components needed to supply the project
6 The process of watching the development of the project
7 The expected outcome of a project
8 A project solution made from scratch

DOWN

1 An individual or group of individuals that have a direct interest in something
2 The most important aspect needed to ensure the success of a project – could be in written or verbal form
3 _____ Path (the technique used to determine the longest route through a project)
5 The absolute limits of a project

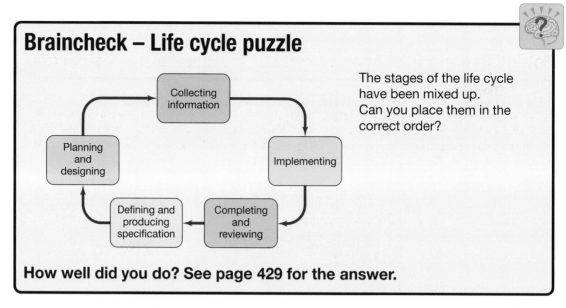

Braincheck – Life cycle puzzle

The stages of the life cycle have been mixed up.
Can you place them in the correct order?

How well did you do? See page 429 for the answer.

Content, e.g. identification of phases and activities, timescales

The plan content will include the identification of the activities, their nature, how they will be resourced, and deadlines indicating when phases should be complete.

Sensible project plans also include some **recovery** time – these are odd days or weeks where no activities are planned so that in the event that the project hits problems, taking longer than necessary to complete an activity will not have a detrimental affect on the whole project. The positive effect of this is that if the time is not then used, the project will be able to finish early.

Review points

It is good practice to plan a series of review points – some with users, some with managers and some with other project team members.

This will ensure that all interested parties are kept informed about the project and how it's progressing; they will be able to ask questions to clarify their understanding of any aspects of the project and, in some cases, will be able to help identify any issues that could have a detrimental effect on the completion of the project.

Use of appropriate and available software, e.g. project management packages, spreadsheets, drawing packages, graphics, databases

As suggested in section 1.3, there are a series of project management packages available, although other packages can be used just as effectively to make diagrams, graphs or tables of project information.

Because, with some software, you may need training to become familiar with the program's functionality, there might be times when it would be more expedient to use the alternatives, such as Microsoft Excel®, CorelDRAW® or Microsoft Access®, because the extra time it takes to create the diagrams would ultimately be less than the time that would be spent in training for the project software. A trade-off maybe, but an important consideration when time or money are limited.

2.2 Detail of activities

Potential for parallel or sequential processes, resources needed for each activity

As described in sections 1.3 and 1.4 above, the tasks and activities will be defined and decisions will be made about which activities need to be undertaken in sequence, which can be run in parallel and what sort of resources are required. In Figure 4.21 we see an additional column now added to the Microsoft Project® Gantt chart: Resource Names.

	Task Name	Duration	Start	Finish	Predecessors	Resource Names	12 Nov '07	19 Nov '07	26 Nov '07
1	Investigate current stock system	5.33 days	Mon 12/11/07	Mon 19/11/07		Ranjit,Sam,Dave		19/11	
2	Write up report	2 days	Mon 19/11/07	Wed 21/11/07	1	Ranjit,Dave		19/11 — 21/11	
3	Investigate current invoicing system	3.33 days	Mon 12/11/07	Thu 15/11/07		Emma,Mary,Paul	15/11		
4	Write up report	3 days	Thu 15/11/07	Tue 20/11/07	3	Emma,Mary	15/11	20/11	
5	Planning Meeting	3 days	Wed 21/11/07	Mon 26/11/07	2,4	All		21/11	26/11

Figure 4.21 Human resources identified

By separating the names of the individuals involved with a comma, an additional view in Microsoft Project® will now allow you to charge for their time as individuals. Accessing the Resource Information view, and adapting the costs (basic pay, overtime rates etc.), you can build up a profile of how much the project is actually costing.

Review points, e.g. milestones, checkpoints, deadlines

Here a full one-day review has been added as part of the project plan.

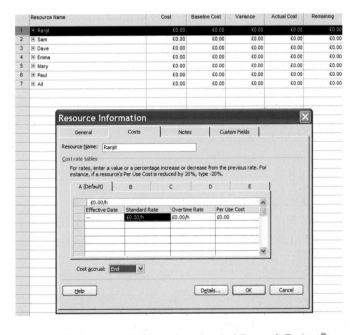

Figure 4.22 Resource Information view in Microsoft Project®

	Task Name	Duration	Start	Finish	Predecessors	Resource Names	12 Nov '07	19 Nov '07	26 Nov '07
1	Investigate current stock system	5.33 days	Mon 12/11/07	Mon 19/11/07		Ranjit,Sam,Dave		19/11	
2	Write up report	2 days	Mon 19/11/07	Wed 21/11/07	1	Ranjit,Dave		19/11 — 21/11	
3	Investigate current invoicing system	3.33 days	Mon 12/11/07	Thu 15/11/07		Emma,Mary,Paul	15/11		
4	Write up report	3 days	Thu 15/11/07	Tue 20/11/07	3	Emma,Mary	15/11	20/11	
5	Planning Meeting	3 days	Wed 21/11/07	Mon 26/11/07	2,4	All		21/11	26/11
6	Team Review	1 day	Mon 26/11/07	Tue 27/11/07	5	All			26/11 — 27/11

Figure 4.23 Project review points added

Collecting information

There are a variety of investigation techniques available to the project team, any of which could be used to help in the information-gathering process.

These techniques include:

◆ interview
◆ questionnaire
◆ data analysis – examination of records
◆ meetings
◆ document analysis – examination of existing documents
◆ observation.

Each method has very different uses, and consequently has advantages and disadvantages when applied to analysis activities. How appropriate a specific technique is will depend on a number of factors:

◆ size of the organisation
◆ number of staff employed (and who could be potential users of the system)
◆ location
◆ distribution.

Interview

An interview is a process where a member of the project team will meet with a user or group of users to discuss the **functional roles**. This is usually **pre-arranged** at a **convenient time**. In order to ensure that the user(s) will supply the correct information when interviewed, a **checklist** of **points** and **questions** should be created in advance.

Questionnaire

While lists of relevant questions formatted as a questionnaire are an exceedingly useful investigation tool, the success rate in acquiring the right information is lower than for most other techniques. This is because with most other techniques there is either an element of face-to-face contact, or physical documents or records will be used, which will ensure that information gained will be reliable.

Analysis of existing data

What is required with this technique is that the project will **examine** the organisation's **existing records**, from a **data** rather than a **documentation perspective**. These records could be in many forms. If the organisation currently has a manual system it will be likely that they will be **ledgers**, **record cards**, **files of invoices**, **statements** and **orders**.

If the system is already computerised, even in part, there will be **electronic data** to consider – possibly using software that is unfamiliar to you.

Meetings

Meetings are a useful way of **effectively** interviewing a **large number of people simultaneously**. As with the one-to-one interview, this will usually take place at a **pre-arranged time** that is **convenient** for **all** those attending.

Document analysis

This requires the physical examination of any relevant documents the organisation holds. If current procedures and processes are well documented then these will provide a convenient source of useful information. The types of source documents that the analyst might be offered include:

◆ sales invoices
◆ delivery notes
◆ purchase orders
◆ statements
◆ purchase and sales ledgers
◆ customer record cards
◆ supplier record cards
◆ HR (human resource) documents
◆ production documents.

Braincheck – Planning word search

```
U E E J D A T A Z R A L L W Z O R R O H
P K T U M A V O X T S I N L B H P G R P
X S A F J O A X G D R O C E R R L N H W
H C I H U X X F Q Q P L A N N E B T E P
M R V E G N T W H D L I A R Z M C E F H
J M J S T H C P Y X F M C G B E N O F X
X S E Q P M T T A U U R U H J N O W E B
Q I L I C S X B I Q D N S O J O I P C H
H N A L D P Y X P O S S R H N T T A T D
O Q M Z Z P S X Q I N P A E A S A A I K
T I R G I D K Y B I O A U B V E M N V H
B Y I N T E R V I E W W L S L L R A E W
R A O P R W Q V X A P F R V O I O L U G
M W P A Q Q W L E L L A R A P M F Y Y S
O B S E R V A T I O N V U K G R N S C H
F R Y E S A H P C H T Z I I F Z I I E T
M A E T U L G R A H I R D G J Y B S U E
S W M Y O K A W D Z E M F E Q Y Z B F Q
C M Y U P F D S E Q U E N T I A L O H Y
T E R I A N N O I T S E U Q A V F Y K P
```

The following terms have been hidden in the word search grid above.
Can you find them all?

INTERVIEW	PROJECT	INFORMATION	RECORD
FUNCTIONAL	SEQUENTIAL	PARALLEL	EFFECTIVE
PHASE	TEAM	PLAN	OBSERVATION
QUESTIONNAIRE	ANALYSIS	DATA	MILESTONE

A solution is provided on page 430.

The analysis of these documents can help the project team to develop an understanding of how the information flows through the organisation.

Observation

Like interviews, observations can be extremely informative. One of the main reasons why is that during an interview, or even on a questionnaire, a system user will probably have no difficulty recalling and **describing activities** that they do on a **regular basis**. What is likely, however, is that **irregular tasks** may be forgotten, but these might also be important to the project.

Unit Link

For more on information gathering techniques (including an investigation into their strengths and weaknesses as techniques), see the companion **Core Text, Unit 7 – Systems Analysis and Design**, section 2.1, pages 156 to 161.

3 Be able to implement an IT project

3.1 Design

This is the creative part of the project. Drawing on combined expertise and skills, the project team needs to find the best way of facilitating the solution.

As with the planning and investigation parts of the project life cycle, the design phase also needs some structure.

Use of appropriate methods to design a solution to the problem and design documentation

Depending on the nature of the project, a number of tools exist to help the project team to communicate their vision to the client, users and each other.

As such, it is likely that a series of diagrams (usually supported by written descriptions) will be developed to explain the proposed solution.

The design is usually said to have physical and logical aspects and, usually, the design phase begins with the design team creating a logical representation of the new system. The type of diagrams used will depend on the solution that has been identified.

Entity Relationship Models (ERM) and **Data Flow Diagrams** (DFD) are used to express the **logical** design of systems that contain data.

The ERM will provide a design for the tables that will store the system's data in a Microsoft Access® database for example. This design tool is fully explored in *Unit 7 – Systems Analysis and Design*, section 3.1, pages 169 to 176.

In addition a series of DFDs would be developed that would represent the functional areas of the organisation and that would show how the data is **used**, **processed** and ultimately **output** by the system.

In the event that the solution is (or requires) a network, a **network diagram** will be created that represents the various aspects of the network, for example:

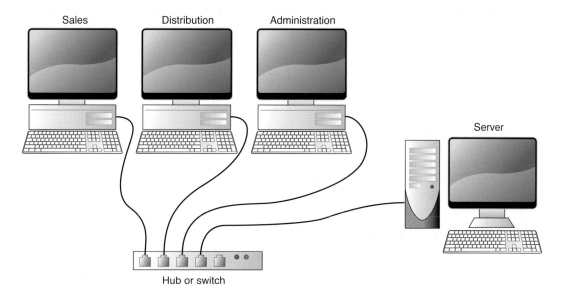

Figure 4.24 Proposed network diagram

The **logical** design will usually be supported by the **physical** design that will include the following information:

For data-intensive systems:

◆ a data table, which is a simple grid containing the names and data types for each piece of data and showing how data links together;
◆ details of how the data will be sorted or indexed;
◆ how the data will be stored (and backed up);
◆ how each output will be designed (for example a management report – the title, data included, any calculations required will be identified and recorded);
◆ drawings of the user interface.

Where computer programming is involved, there are a range of techniques that may be used to support the design of a programmed solution:

◆ **Jackson Structured Diagrams** (JSD) are used to represent solutions that will be coded using a procedural language such as Pascal or C (For more on JSD, see *Unit 18 – Principles of Software Design and Development*, section 2.2, pages 278 to 280).
◆ **Pseudo code** (or the Use of Structured English), which is laid out like programming code, can be used, again to support procedural languages (for more on Pseudo code, see *Unit 7 – Systems Analysis and Design*, section 3.1, pages 178 and 179).
◆ **Storyboards** are used to represent programs that will be written in visual languages such as Visual C++® and Visual Basic®.

For network-based solutions:

◆ proposed **locations** of equipment
◆ **lengths** of **cabling**
◆ **network connectivity**

- **IP addresses**
- **security proposals.**

These formal techniques, supported by descriptive text, form the basis for the design documentation. This documentation should be sufficiently clear that any developers should be able to use it to implement a working solution.

Also, the documentation will be useful when it comes to reviewing the project as there will be an opportunity to fully investigate the design process and identify any particular successes or failures within the process.

3.2 Implementation tools

The choices made in terms of the selection of implementation tools will need to be **justified** not only to the remainder of the project team (if there was disagreement about which tools were favourable), but also to the **client** and the **users** of the system.

Appropriate choices made

When it comes to the choice of implementation tools, the preferences of the project team and their experience of the success or failure of different options will be an important consideration in how the selections are made.

Ultimately, whatever decisions have been made will need to be explained and justified when the project is reviewed.

Use of appropriate software or hardware

Whether or not the use of a particular piece of hardware or of a software solution can be considered appropriate will depend on the success of the project. At times you will be constrained by what you may and may not use, depending on what is available or what the project budget will allow. Equally there are times when, for just a little bit extra, the level of functionality gained will make it worth the extra expense.

3.3 Deliverables

Product, e.g. software application, service, system

The outcome or product of the project could take many forms:

- **Software application** – as suggested earlier in this unit, the application could be developed as a bespoke solution (totally from scratch), purchased as an off-the-shelf solution, or tailored by adapting a generic application such as Microsoft Access®.
- **Service** – the actual deliverable could also be a service; for example the project might have been to develop a technical team to support a computerised manufacturing process.
- **System** – or, as a final option, the outcome could have been the installation of a network or a stand-alone PC.

Either way, the product would need to be fully complete and functioning in order for the project to be considered successful.

Other deliverables, e.g. user training

Other deliverables will also be expected by the client and/or users. This will probably include training, in which case there are a number of alternative strategies for training staff to use the new system:

◆ **Individual** training – this is where each individual user will be trained in the aspects of the system they are going to be using. While this would certainly be the training strategy of choice for most users because they will feel that the training has been tailored to meet their personal needs, it is obviously going to be a very expensive way of training staff.

◆ **Small group** training – often carried out within departments, this can be a very successful way of helping users to understand the processes in the context of what happens in their own work areas. Clearly this will be less expensive than individual training.

◆ **Cascade** training – this is likely to be the most realistic training strategy, where some users come for formal training, in order to take the training back into their own organisations.

In addition to user training, some organisations also require project teams to provide ongoing maintenance, over and above the maintenance strategy agreed as part of the initial contract. This additional requirement often forms an ongoing maintenance contract.

Technical and user documentation

No project is considered truly complete without the production of technical and user documentation.

Theorists believe that **technical** documentation is best written after the system has been fully completed so that all testing activities can be included. Depending on the product of the project, the documentation may include any, or all, of the following:

For data-intensive systems:

◆ menus
◆ data structure information (record structures or variable types)
◆ dataflow diagrams of the completed system to explain the system's processes
◆ entity relationship diagrams that explain how data elements are linked together
◆ details about screen layouts
◆ software solutions will usually have annotated code listings.

For hardware or networked solutions:

◆ network diagrams
◆ IP addresses
◆ system configurations and settings
◆ password protocols.

The technical documentation will be used as a reference manual for any maintenance activities or further development work.

User documentation may contain aspects of the technical documentation, but will be targeted at helping users work with the system. It might cover:

◆ directory structures
◆ accessing files or programs
◆ simple troubleshooting
◆ explanations of functional aspects of the system.

Unit Link

For more on user documentation see **Unit 18 – Principles of Software Design and Development**, section 4.2, page 286 in the **Core Text**.

While it is safe to assume that the technical document will be read by individuals with an understanding of the technical issues, and so it can make use of technical language, more care should be taken when developing the user guide or document to ensure that the language used is appropriate for the level of the users' understanding.

Effective user guides usually contain a series of images or screen shots supported by text.

3.4 Monitoring

Routine communications with stakeholders and interim reviews

As part of the project implementation there will need to be a series of monitoring activities with a range of stakeholders – how often these take place will be considered as part of the planning. There is likely, for example, to be a requirement to have some level of **routine communications with stakeholders**. This could be in the form of weekly, biweekly (once a fortnight) or monthly **emails**, or maybe a short update **newsletter**. It could be a **podcast**, a series of **telephone calls**, an update on the company's **intranet** or it could take any one of a number of other forms.

More in-depth **interim reviews** will also be planned into the project schedule. These will often be undertaken as a group meeting where all stakeholders can be simultaneously informed about the progress of the project; they will be able to answer any questions that the project team has and, equally, will be able to share their thoughts about progress so far. At such meetings it is not unusual for the team to demonstrate the most recent versions of the solution to get immediate feedback.

The key here is that the **stakeholders** are being kept fully **informed** about the project and thus they will feel that they are involved. This is a good tactic if you want to maintain interest in the project and reduce the likelihood of resistance when the solution is fully implemented.

Use of logbooks

The best way to monitor a project is to create a logbook of activities. This can be done by each member of the team to reflect their individual input into the project, or it can be done as a single logbook, with combined entries made against each task by the whole project team.

Either way, this document is useful in supporting the monitoring process and it can also be made available at the end of the project in the final review activity.

A logbook can take almost any form (an example can be found in Figure 4.25).

In this logbook the tasks are defined, the deadline is stated, any resources described, and you will notice that in this example the developer has identified a skills gap, expanded comments are included, then the monitoring column is completed indicating further action when required.

Eventually, when the further work had been completed, the 'Yes' in the final column would be eliminated.

Monitoring progress is part of the reason why the development plan was created in the first place. This document, as it is completed, effectively becomes a **work log** that, in addition, the project manager may well find useful for charging out the time spent on the project.

However, even considering the other positive aspects, monitoring progress is actually essential for three reasons:

Task	By When	Resources needed	Comments	Monitoring	Further action required?
Create an input form as a template for individual stock items	End of week 7		Check tab order of input boxes and alignment	Still some alignment problems, and tab order on two boxes needs reversing	Yes
Create validation routine on minimum stock levels	End of week 15		Validate to ensure that the number in stock can not fall below the minimum stock level without a warning message being displayed	Validation routine did not work and I needed tutor help to fix the problem – this has put the project behind schedule	Yes
Create a query that allows the user to search for all stock items obtained from a particular supplier	End of week 24		This will need an input box to enable the user to key in which supplier he/she wishes to search on	This task has been completed without problems	

Figure 4.25 Logbook

1 The developer and team can see whether they are staying on schedule.
2 The developer and team will be able to use this information during ongoing evaluation activities.
3 At a later date the developer and team can look back at this documentation to remind themselves of past mistakes so that these can be avoided when undertaking future projects.

As mentioned earlier in this unit, the project plan will have been created to include interim review points with your client, users or your project supervisor. When taking part in an interim review or in a routine progress report, make sure that you make your comments positive rather than negative. Too many 'problems' shared or other negative comments will undermine stakeholder confidence in the project.

And lastly, in the **logbook** shown in Figure 4.25 the developer has included comments about problems experienced with the creation of the validation routine. One of the most important aspects of the development of any solution is to ensure that the system has been properly tested. As such, it would be very useful to record any actions taken to resolve problems including screen captures as these will provide excellent evidence of interim testing, particularly if the images also include the relevant error messages.

Routine updating of plan where necessary, e.g. accessing additional resources where necessary, reacting to unforeseen circumstances

While the project plan or schedule will have been created at the start of the project, the plan is actually a living document and it is likely that it will need to be updated from time to time, possibly to add additional tasks, or even to remove tasks that are not required because some aspects of the plan have become unnecessary. Ultimately, the review points and deadlines will be unaffected, even if some tasks move within the plan itself.

At times you and the project team will have to react to unforeseen circumstances – maybe because you can only get delayed access to a resource, the resource will not now be available, you have long-term sickness within the team, or access to the client and users becomes more difficult.

Managing a project well is about being flexible, being able to react when necessary and, most importantly, knowing when to ask for help because things are not going as they should. Remember, for the purposes of this unit's assessment you will have a project supervisor who will assist you should any major problems arise.

4 Be able to test, document and review an IT project

Good practice will have dictated that as part of the design process the project team will have created a testing strategy, which you now need to implement at the end of the project. As such the final element in this unit is to consider the last part of the life cycle.

Why test the product? There are two main reasons for testing:

1   It will allow the project team to confirm that the functionality in the product meets the original system specification.
2   The team can make sure that the user is happy with the end product (acceptance testing).

4.1 Completing process

Testing

In terms of testing, there are two main strategies that will be adopted depending on the type of solution implemented.

Black box

Black box testing is a strategy that tests the developed system for functionality. As such, the testing process will check that the solution does everything it was expected to do by comparing what it actually does with a checklist of the functionality the system is intended to have, taken directly from the specification.

In addition to checking for functional presence, however, it is also important to remember that the term **functionality** also includes:

◆   **checking calculations** (comparing results calculated by the system to results calculated by other means);
◆   **checking** the results of running **queries**;
◆   **checking** the output from **reports**;
◆   **checking** that any files are correctly created/updated as required.

Black box testing can be recorded using any effective recording mechanisms, but evidence by way of screen shots will make proving testing activities much easier.

White box

White box testing is not concerned with checking for functionality or presence of functionality, but is concerned

Unit Link

For more on testing, see the companion **Core Text, Unit 7 – Systems Analysis and Design**, section 4, pages 180 to 183. For more on testing documentation see **Unit 18 – Principles of Software Design and Development**, section 4, pages 283 to 286.

with ensuring that all logic within the system works. In this instance the test plan will look at validation routines, menu systems and pathways to make sure that each possible action that the system could take has been checked to be working as it should.

Documentation

The documentation that is developed to support the product will include, for example, the technical documentation and user guide as discussed in section 3.3.

In addition, documentation should be available to the client that provides a full and complete record of the activities undertaken to test the system. This may include any of the following record types:

◆ test plan or schedule
◆ trace tables, as described in *Unit 18 – Principles of Software Design and Development*
◆ screen shots
◆ development logbook.

This documentation will be used as part of the review process as evidence that can be analysed. If, for example, problems were experienced during development, these questions should be asked in each case:

◆ What was the problem experienced?
◆ Why was this problem experienced?
◆ Could this have been prevented?
◆ How?

As already suggested in this unit, it is often through the post-implementation discussion that many important lessons will be learned.

Review

In reality, the review will usually be undertaken as a group meeting, with the project team and all stakeholders present (or representatives from some stakeholder groups, as it is unlikely, for example, that all users would be present).

The purpose of the meeting is to walk through the entire project process, by stepping through each part of the project life cycle and discussing what went badly, what went well and whether any actions are still required to resolve any outstanding issues.

Before reviewing the process, however, the team will need to check the product developed against the original specification.

The review could result in the development of an action plan that may include any of these maintenance strategies:

◆ **Corrective** maintenance – this is where any last bugs in the system are fixed. Sometimes the developers are unaware of errors, as they do not surface until the users begin to use the system within normal parameters. Corrective maintenance is usually carried out quickly.
◆ **Perfective** maintenance – this is where the system does actually work quite well, but with a little extra time or expense, it could have some additional functionality that would be keenly sought after by the client – for example, new reports or different views of data. If perfective maintenance is required, any activity is usually carried out in the medium term (within about six months, say).

- **Adaptive** maintenance – this is future driven and is the process of constantly checking the system to make sure that it still meets the needs of the organisation – for example, the project may have seen the installation of a single PC or a pair of networked PCs. After 12 months it is clear that more PCs are required to provide a multi-user system. Alternatively, new technology has been developed that could be successfully (and beneficially) incorporated into the system.

The review is extremely important to make sure that any lessons to be learned from the completion of this project have indeed been learned!

Handover and sign off

The final part of implementing the product or system is for the project team to hand the product or system over to the client and/or users and for them to sign it off by confirming that, from their perspective, the project is complete and the project team does not have to have any further input.

It is quite normal for the last payment against the contract to be withheld until after the handover point.

If there are a large number of system users it is likely that you will need to create a questionnaire as a means of gathering user feedback as, if there are any problems, the developers will then have a formal record of any problems found, which will make perfective maintenance easier to achieve.

Other, e.g. arranging support

While the project may indeed be complete at this point, this may not be the final contact that the project team has with the client. If you go into a shop like PC World and you purchase a product, the product will be under warranty for a given length of time after purchase. In this period, it is the responsibility of the shop (or in some cases the manufacturer of the product you purchased through the shop) to repair the item for free in the event that it fails. In the same way, it is likely that the project team, or at least a member of it, will remain on call to resolve any last issues for an agreed period after handover.

After that point, a further longer-term maintenance contract might be negotiated (although there will obviously be a charge for this level of ongoing support).

4.2 Functional testing of the product

As suggested in section 4.1, functional product testing will check not only for presence of functional aspects of the system, but will also check the results of calculations, queries and reports.

In order to do this, data will need to be made available. This data might be dummy data (made up by the project team) or might be provided by the client and the users.

Test data

The data that is chosen and used for the purposes of testing the system or product should be carefully selected to ensure that it is sufficient in quantity, and the quality of spread covers the range required to facilitate effective testing:

- **Normal data** – this is data that would be considered to be **within** a **sensible range** – the type of data that would be expected to be input when the system is being used normally.
- **Extreme data** – this data, while still within a sensible range, is **less likely** to be input. For example, an age over 104 is not actually impossible but it is unlikely!

♦ **Erroneous data** – is data that cannot be considered either normal or sensible! It is data that is intentionally incorrect. The data will contain **values outside valid ranges** and could also contain **incorrect types of values** (e.g. characters where numbers are expected and vice versa).

In many cases the data will, in the first instance, be dummy data – data that is made up by the project team for the purposes of testing the system. Subsequently, the team should ensure that real 'live' data is used. This is provided by the client or users.

Structured walkthroughs

A structured walkthrough as part of the testing procedure can be undertaken formally (with managers also present) or informally with the project team. Either way, it should be taken seriously as there could be a potential for issues to be rubber stamped as approved, just to show the process has been carried out. So, a sense of shared responsibility is crucial to ensure that the process can be got through without minor squabbles.

The purpose of the walkthrough is to use the test data to trigger any problems with the system. As with any testing, the process should have been planned to ensure that all the relevant parts of the system will have been tested. In many respects, it is a confirmatory process – if testing has taken place during development, then this really should be a straightforward process.

Test plan or schedule

The test plan, formulated to ensure that the testing will cover functionality and accuracy (black box), and every possible logic pathway (white box) can be simply put together, but using a template, like the one shown below, formalises the process.

Unit Link

The sample test plan has been taken from the **Core Text**, where it appears in **Unit 7 – Systems Analysis and Design**. For more on the components of a test plan, see section 4.3, pages 182 and 183.

The columns shown with a ● are completed by the project development team while the system is being designed, and the remaining columns are completed during implementation and/or during final testing.

Test plan template

Test#	Purpose of test	Test values (or data source)	Expected results of test	Actual results of test	Action required
●	●	●	●		

Figure 4.26 Sample test plan

There is no hard and fast rule about what the test plan or schedule should look like, but the version here will be particularly useful in software development projects.

4.3 Review

The first part of the review is to look at the success or failure of the product that the project produced.

Against specification

As suggested earlier, the first aspect of the review is to carry out a systematic check to confirm that the functionality that has been produced by way of the product matches the original specification and thus meets the expectations of the user.

Identification of potential additional development

The second aspect is to identify maintenance needs – to fix bugs that still exist in the system and to make minor modifications to expand functionality.

4.4 Review of project management

The latter part of the review is an examination of how the project was actually managed. As a novice project developer, you will have a significant amount to consider in terms of how well you managed your time and your resources, and how well you chose the tools you used in development. Your investigation of your management of the project will form a basis for evaluation of the project process as a whole. You should consider aspects such as:

Actual dates achieved for milestones compared to planned dates with reasons for difference

Dates when milestones were achieved will be compared with the planned achievement dates and reasons for early or late completion will be discussed. It is clear that there will be situations where it was impossible to predict particular occurrences – and other occasions where it will simply be a case that aspects were overlooked, or the level of effect of a situation might not have been accurately predicted.

Actual use of resources compared with planned resources needed

It is quite unusual for projects to use the exact quantity of predicted resources. The two resources often incorrectly estimated are time and skills. This is partly why it was suggested earlier in this unit that 'catch-up' or 'slack' time be built into the project plan to give a little breathing space if things do not go as expected.

Others, e.g. unanticipated external factors that affected the project

Unanticipated external factors could include a number of issues that could have a positive, but more likely detrimental, effect on the project. Some of these might include:

- expectations of other customers or clients
- activities of competitors
- natural disasters such as flooding
- other disasters such as fire or theft
- difficulties experienced by external contractors who are supporting the project.

These are really difficult to predict and manage. For this reason responding effectively to these types of factors is something that becomes easier with experience.

Validity of the tools used

Assessing the validity of the tools used in a project comes from two perspectives:

- The tools used to develop the solution may need to be justified, particularly if there were problems during development or if there have been problems since. For example, was Microsoft Access® the right database program to use as the basis for the solution, or should the product have been developed using MySQL® instead? Would a different router have been more appropriate than the one that was actually used because compatibility issues with existing systems were experienced? The project team will need to justify the decisions made.
- The project management tools used should also be reviewed for their validity. For example, the use of data flow diagramming for a system that has no data would clearly have been a poor decision. Equally the use or non-use of project management software like Microsoft Project® or the open source dotProject would be discussed and justified.

All the decisions made as part of the life cycle and subsequent product development can be, and should be, analysed for their validity.

4.5 Technical documentation

Documentation as appropriate to the particular project chosen

As you will have seen throughout this unit, there are a whole host of different documentation tools that you, or a project team, can use to document the product of a project.

Which are used and which are ignored will be dependant on a **single factor**, which is that the combination of the **documents should ultimately explain the system**. For example, it is unlikely that you would use programming documentation tools like JSD diagrams if it is a hardware solution – similarly, you would not use a network diagram to explain a database.

4.6 User guide

Instructions on how to use the product or service

Over the years you will, without doubt, have seen many user guides. Guides for computer software, computer games, electronic equipment: the list is endless. The images in Figures 4.27 to 4.29 are different examples of user guides.

The first image (Figure 4.27) shows part of the installation instructions for a D-Link® KVM Switch. You will notice instantly that it contains both photographic images and supporting text. This is a good

Figure 4.27 User guide for the installation of a KVM Switch

example of a user guide because the text beside each image is used to provide further information about the image. Similarly, you could argue that the image is in fact supporting the text, giving the user visual confirmation of what is being read.

In fact, you could possibly use either the text or the images only to achieve the installation, but providing them together ensures success.

The second example (Figure 4.28) is taken from a software guide and uses screenshots of the software being used to guide the user through the creation of a form in Microsoft Access®.

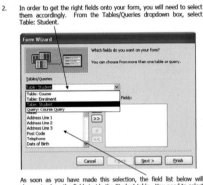

Figure 4.28 Part of a user guide for using Form Wizard in Microsoft Access®

As with the first example the text and image used together will help the user achieve success, although on this occasion, while the user could probably also achieve using only the text, it is unlikely that the image alone would have been of sufficient use. In this instance, therefore, the text is essential to the image, but the image is not necessarily essential to the text!

Finally, the snapshot of the user guide shown in Figure 4.29 is solely textual.

C #

Saving edited source code programs (1.2.2)

You should get into the practice of saving your source code at an early stage. It is also advisable, as suggested earlier, that you save back-up copies of your developed programs as losing your hard work can be very frustrating! Saving your work can be undertaken by using the "Save as" function, or the "Write to" function if you are making an additional copy. This is, however, not the same on all compilers and you will need to refer to your compiler's help system if you are in any doubt about the process.

Retrieving and correcting source code files when compilation errors occur (1.2.3)

Retrieving a saved source program is done using the "File", "Open" functions in your compiler.

Once your program has been edited or corrected it should be saved as normal.

Figure 4.29 Part of a user guide on saving files in C#

This is probably the least useful of the three examples because, for the user, there is a significant amount to read. For a novice who is learning about programming and the programming environment, this might be quite daunting.

Getting help

In addition to technical documents and user guides, online FAQs can be very useful for obtaining information.

Figure 4.30 (Source: **www.microsoft.com/ uk/office/ preview/programs/access/ faq.mspx**) provides an example of the FAQ screen for Microsoft Access® support.

It is a good example of an FAQ because it sets each part of the content out as a question, along with its answer.

In terms of the user guide you develop to support your project, you should include an FAQ with some of the questions you think inexperienced users are more likely to ask.

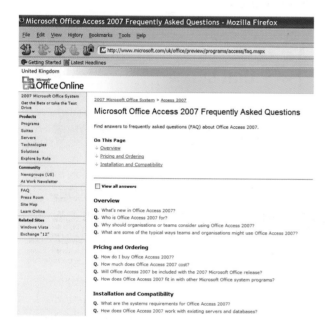

Figure 4.30 Microsoft Access® FAQ

Also, you might like to include some suggestions about other avenues of getting help that your client or users could explore, such as technical staff or websites.

Known bugs

If there are any bugs in your solution that have not been resolved, you should make sure that these are listed in the user guide. This does not necessarily mean that your product doesn't work, but you may have found that it has some incompatibilities with other software packages, particular operating systems or peripherals.

Any issues that could affect the working of the product should be highlighted.

Gaining and using feedback

It is good practice to give your users an opportunity to feed back to you and/or the project team. This could be as simple as including an email address in your user guide and asking for any relevant feedback to be forwarded.

This may result in additional material for an online FAQ!

Other, e.g. hardware or system requirements

The final part of the user guide will include a list of the minimum system requirements that are needed to correctly run the solution – for example:

OS	Windows 2000 Professional
	Windows XP Home Edition
	Windows XP Professional
CPU	Intel® Pentium® III at least 700 MHz
	(Intel® Pentium® 4 at least 2 GHz recommended)
RAM	At least 256 MB (512 MB recommended)
Free hard disk space	At least 250 MB for installation
Connector	USB 2.0
Display	Must be capable of displaying 1024 x 600 dots
Miscellaneous	Internet Explorer® 6 or later
	DirectX® 9.0 or later

Activity

Find three different user guides and compare them. Decide on the following:

◆ Which is more informative?
◆ Which is easier to use?
◆ Which do you prefer?
◆ Why?

Discuss your thoughts with a tutor or fellow student.

Unit Links

Unit 4 is an optional unit on all of the BTEC National Certificate and Diploma for IT Practitioners pathways, but is not available on the BTEC National Award.

In addition this unit chapter has identified direct links with:

Unit 1 – Communication and Employability Skills in IT

Unit 7 – Systems Analysis and Design

Unit 18 – Principles of Software Design and Development.

Achieving success

In order to achieve each unit you will complete a series of coursework activities. Each time you hand in work, your tutor will return this to you with a record of your achievement.

This particular unit has 22 criteria to meet: 11 Pass, 7 Merit and 4 Distinction.

For a **Pass**:

You must achieve **all** 11 Pass criteria.

For a **Merit**:

You must achieve **all** 11 Pass and **all** 7 Merit criteria.

For a **Distinction**:

You must achieve **all** 11 Pass, **all** 7 Merit **and** 4 Distinction criteria.

So that you can monitor your own progress and achievement in each unit, a recording grid has been provided (see below). The full version of this grid is also included on the companion CD.

Assignment	Assignments in this unit			
	U4.01	U4.02	U4.03	U4.04
Referral				
Pass				
1				
2				
3				
4				
5				
6				
7				
8				
9				
10				
11				
Merit				
1				
2				
3				
4				
5				
6				
7				
Distinction				
1				
2				
3				
4				

Help with assessment

With a large number of **Pass** criteria to be met, this unit needs you to demonstrate a full understanding of project management techniques and further requires you to show that you have mastered these skills by implementing the whole of the project life cycle.

Merit grades will require you to show a deeper understanding of the process and use additional techniques not required at Pass. You will need to show that you can adapt to accommodate the unexpected and that you can communicate on all levels.

For a **Distinction** you will need to provide evidence that you can assess your own performance, evaluate the effectiveness of the project and its impact on the wider business systems, and that you can justify your decisions.

Online resources on the CD

Key fact sheets
Electronic slide show of key points
Multiple choice self-test quizzes

Further Reading

Dawson, C., 2005, *Projects in Computing and Information Systems: A Student's Guide*, Addison Wesley, ISBN 0321263553.

Maylor, H., 2005, *Project Management and Microsoft Project CD*, FT Prentice Hall, ISBN 0273704311.

Yeates, D. and Cadle, J., 2004, *Project Management for Information Systems*, FT Prentice Hall, ISBN 0273685805.

Unit 5

Advanced Database Skills

Capsule view

As a highly practical 60-hour unit, Advanced Database Skills will help you to develop a range of skills that will be highly valued by employers. This is because databases play a pivotal role in the recording of business transactions.

Used to store large quantities of information about an organisation's activities and stakeholders, manipulation of the data through the database software's own utilities will also enable organisations to view its own data from different perspectives to help managers make informed decisions.

On the completion of this unit you will be able to design, implement and test a multi-table database.

As part of the learning process the Frankoni T-shirts database referred to in the examples in this unit (and used in many of the activities) has been provided for you on the companion CD. Clearly to make use of this you will need to copy it to your own system.

Learning aims

1 Understand the purpose and features of relational databases.
2 Be able to create, populate and test a multiple database.
3 Be able to use advanced features of a database and test functionality.

Braincheck – What do you know?

As with the Spreadsheets unit (Unit 6), the title of this unit contains the term Advanced. Thus it will be assumed that you already understand many of the basic concepts that will be developed here.
To check your understanding prior to starting the unit, complete the following grid and check your answers against those provided.

▶

Term	Explanation
Database object	
Table	
Record	
Field	
Format	
AutoNumber	
Structure	
Data integrity	
Validation	
Naming conventions	
Design view	
Datasheet view	
Form	

How well did you do? See page 431 for answers.

Seek further information for any terms that you did not know or where your explanation was incorrect.

Unit Link

For more on the basic concepts of databases see **Unit 9 – Database Software** on the CD included in the following text:

BTEC First for ICT Practitioners course text by McGill, Fishpool & Fishpool (2006), published by Hodder Education.

1 Understand the purpose and features of relational databases

Until the introduction of relational database technology, all databases were effectively files containing a single table of data. Consider the data shown in Figure 5.1, which is an extract from Frankoni's purchase data for September 2007.

FRANKONI T-SHIRTS

Purchase Records for September 2007

Date	Supplier Name	Address	Quantity	Description	Price
01/09/2007	Kavana Shirts	14 North Road, Bristol, BS14 9FM	100	T-shirts Blue XL	4.52
01/09/2007	Ramises	Button Business Park, Cardiff, CF4 1MP	30	T-shirts Red L	3.44
04/09/2007	Maximum Ideas	Frayer Building, Corsham Road, Swindon, SW4 4PM	45	Assorted Band logos	0.60
06/09/2007	Kavana Shirts	14 North Road, Bristol, BS14 9FM	200	T-shirts Black L	4.70
07/09/2007	Kavana Shirts	14 North Road, Bristol, BS14 9FM	150	T-shirts Black XL	4.60
10/09/2007	Addisons Imports	Hansworth Industrial Estate, Hinkley, Leicestershire, LE7 1UP	190	T-shirts Blue L Long-sleeved	5.60
15/09/2007	Kavana Shirts	14 North Road, Bristol, BS14 9FM	60	T-shirts Blue XL	4.52
21/09/2007	Maximum Ideas	Frayer Building, Corsham Road, Swindon, SW4 4PM	15	Assorted Band logos	0.60
22/09/2007	Kavana Shirts	14 North Road, Bristol, BS14 9FM	55	T-shirts Red L	3.70
22/09/2007	Lataski Logos	Unit 4, Pullman Court, Manchester, M19, 6MQ	50	Assorted Band logos	0.70
22/09/2007	Ramises	Button Business Park, Cardiff, CF4 1MP	40	T-shirts Blue L Long-sleeved	5.30
25/09/2007	Kavana Shirts	14 North Road, Bristol, BS14 9FM	140	T-shirts Blue S	4.12
27/09/2007	Ramises	Button Business Park, Cardiff, CF4 1MP	10	T-shirts Red XL Long-sleeved	5.10
28/09/2007	Kavana Shirts	14 North Road, Bristol, BS14 9FM	15	Assorted Band logos	0.80
30/09/2007	Ramises	Button Business Park, Cardiff, CF4 1MP	25	T-shirts Blue XL	4.60

Figure 5.1 Flat database

In this extract, over the period of September, five suppliers have been used to provide T-shirts and logos for the business: Kavana Shirts, Ramises, Addisons Imports, Maximum Ideas and Lataski Logos.

To record this information, the whole address for each supplier has been keyed in by the user. The problem with repeating data input in this way is that it is prone to errors. Had the user accidentally keyed in 13 North Road instead of 14, the record would be incorrect. A postcode could have been changed, or any of the words in the address could have been incorrectly spelt.

To resolve this, it would have been more sensible to create a relational database where each supplier's actual record was only stored once, and it was then referred to via its Primary Key:

Supplier ID	Supplier Name	Address
S101	Kavana Shirts	14 North Road, Bristol, BS14 9FM
S102	Ramises	Button Business Park, Cardiff, CF4 1MP
S103	Maximum Ideas	Frayer Building, Corsham Road, Swindon, SW4 4PM
S104	Addisons Imports	Hansworth Industrial Estate, Hinkley, Leicestershire, LE7 1UP
S105	Lataski Logos	Unit 4, Pullman Court, Manchester, M19, 6MQ

Figure 5.2 Supplier table

Now, instead of keying in the full name and address of each supplier in the purchases table, the supplier will be referred to by their Supplier ID.

Date	Supplier ID	Quantity	Description	Price
01/09/2007	S101	100	T-shirts Blue XL	4.52
01/09/2007	S102	30	T-shirts Red L	3.44
04/09/2007	S103	45	Assorted Band logos	0.60
06/09/2007	S101	200	T-shirts Black L	4.70
07/09/2007	S101	150	T-shirts Black XL	4.60
10/09/2007	S104	190	T-shirts Blue L Long-sleeved	5.60
15/09/2007	S101	60	T-shirts Blue XL	4.52
21/09/2007	S103	15	Assorted Band logos	0.60
22/09/2007	S101	55	T-shirts Red L	3.70
22/09/2007	S105	50	Assorted Band logos	0.70
22/09/2007	S102	40	T-shirts Blue L Long-sleeved	5.30
25/09/2007	S101	140	T-shirts Blue S	4.12
27/09/2007	S102	10	T-shirts Red XL Long-sleeved	5.10
28/09/2007	S101	15	Assorted Band logos	0.80
30/09/2007	S102	25	T-shirts Blue XL	4.60

Figure 5.3 Purchases table modified to require only the Supplier ID code input

Further limiting the amount of data input by, for example, requiring the user to choose the supplier from a drop-down list, will additionally reduce the potential for data being input incorrectly.

This unit will show you how to successfully design and create multi-table relational databases, and use in-built techniques and user-defined validation and verification routines to ensure that the database is accurate, valid and reliable.

1.1 Relationships

Key Term

The term **relationship** is used to identify the link between two tables. The link itself is established by creating a record that contains the primary key from its own table and a copy of the primary key from another table! Confusing? – look at the image below:

```
Order ID              Supplier ID
Supplier ID           Name
Date                  Address
Quantity              Postcode
Item                  Telephone Number
Price

TblOrder              TblSupplier

Order Table           Supplier Table

         RELATIONSHIP
```

To link an order to a specific supplier, the supplier's ID code is stored within the order. Notice that none of the remaining supplier information is included.

Being able to identify and create the links between tables is the most fundamental requirement for database developers as failing to set accurate relationships will have a detrimental effect on the efficiency and functionality of the final product.

There are many formal methods for identifying the relationships between tables (or entities). These include Entity Relationship Modelling (using ERDs – Entity Relationship Diagrams) and Normalisation.

Creating ERDs is a quick way to identify the main database table objects. This is because the diagrams are made up of a few simple components – primarily they are made up of two components:

 A symbol representing an **entity** (which will become a database table)

A symbol representing a **relationship** (which will provide the link)

The point of an ERD is to show how all of the **data items** stored in tables in a system **relate to each other** and to establish how the different parts of the data will link together in a logical way.

Let's consider a basic database for Frankoni T-shirts. We have already established a relationship between orders and suppliers. Now consider how else data might be linked:

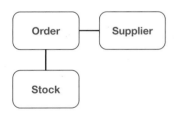

Orders are used to buy goods – so they will be sent to **Suppliers**. Thus there is a direct link.

One link established

What are orders for? **Orders** are for **Stock** items. So here we have another link. Orders are linked to Stock.

Two links established

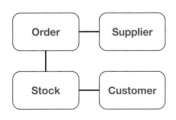

What happens to Stock? **Stock** is sold to **Customers**.

Three links established

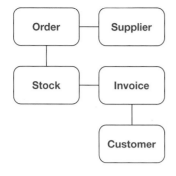

But is the stock merely given to the **Customer**, or is there some sort of documentation (in the same way that) there is an order for the **Supplier**. In this instance the **Customer** doesn't receive the **Stock** without paying for it – on an **Invoice**.

Four links established

So we have now created a simple model of data tables that would be needed to create a basic database for Frankoni. We have not yet, however, decided the **type** of relationship there is between each of the tables.

One-to-one, one-to-many and many-to-many relationships

In concept a relationship will be **one** of **three** types:

——— **One** to **one**

———< **One** to **many** (or **many** to **one**, if drawn the other way)

>——< **Many** to **many**

A successful database requires all relationships to be defined as one to many (or many to one). Any many to many must be resolved until they become one to many (or many to one) and with one-to-one relationships you are likely to find that one set of data probably belongs to the other in the link (it is therefore an attribute).

We need to work through each linked pair of tables and decide how they are linked.

The first pair is Order and Supplier.

Which of the following is likely to be true?

a **One** Order will have **one or many** Suppliers.
b **One or many** Orders will be received by **one** Supplier.
c **One** Supplier will receive one **Order**.

The answer is b) because the other two would not be logical.

Answer a) suggests that more than one supplier will fill a single order. This is highly unlikely as an order is only ever raised to one supplier at a time. It would not be good business practice to have many suppliers trying to fill a single order at the same time!

Answer c) suggests that one supplier will only ever receive a single order. Hardly likely to keep them in business.

We now modify the annotation to reflect how we have resolved the relationship.

(One or many Orders will be received by one Supplier.)

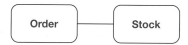

While a single order could contain many stock items, it is also equally likely that an item of stock will appear on many orders. This will create our first many-to-many relationship.

Maybe, to get an answer, we should look at an order form.

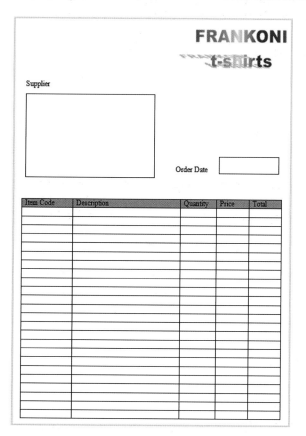

FRANKONI
t-shirts

Supplier

Order Date

Item Code	Description	Quantity	Price	Total

Figure 5.4 Frankoni order form

Here you will see that a single order contains the opportunity to input a number of different stock items in a single document, with each item appearing on its own order line. One order, many order lines. Equally, a single piece of stock can appear on many order lines (in many different orders). We need to add a link table between Order and Stock. This forms our relationship.

And the next pair of tables:

As with the order, it might be useful to look at the document!

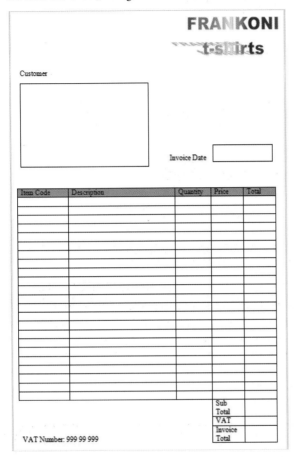

Figure 5.5 Frankoni invoice form

See the similarity? As with Order and Stock we would have a many-to-many relationship that would need to be resolved. This we would do by adding a link table between Invoice and Stock.

And finally – the last two tables:

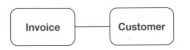

Question: Can a customer receive more than one invoice? Yes. Can a single invoice be sent to more than one customer? No. Therefore, as with the supplier and the order, the relationship will be one to many.

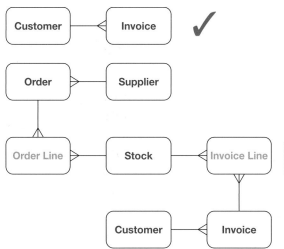

We now need to combine all the ticked tables/relationships.

Now to complete the modelling process and to give a full structure for the database, you would work through each table as shown above and decide what data items you would want to hold for each one.

Unit Link

For more on Entity Relationship Modelling, see the companion **Core Text**, **Unit 7 – IT Systems Analysis and Design**, section 3.1, pages 167 to 179.

Many-to-many (removal through normalisation)

There is an alternative way to approach the removal of many-to-many relationships – through the process of normalisation (see the section that now follows).

Normalisation (first, second and third normal forms)

'Normalisation' is a structured technique developed from an idea originally conceived by E F Codd in 1970. The technique helps you to correctly design relational databases by following a set of rules. It is designed to:

◆ remove repeating data (so makes the data stored more efficient);
◆ remove redundant data;
◆ remove many-to-many relationships;
◆ help identify the **keys** (primary key and foreign key).

Key Terms

Keys (primary and foreign)
Using keys in database tables serves two purposes:

Firstly it provides a unique piece of reference data in a record that users will be able to use to separate one record from another:

ID	First Name	Last Name	Date of Birth
F101	John	Davies	01/06/1987
F102	Barbara	Davies	19/05/1992
F103	John	Matthews	19/05/1992

In the above table we can see that a First Name can be repeated (there could also be more individuals with the name Barbara in the database), and so the field will not provide a good unique reference point.

Similarly, the Last Name and Date of Birth have the same information in more than one record.

The only field or column that does not is the ID column because each record has been given a unique ID number.

This means that if there were two people called John Davies with the same date of birth, through having different IDs they would be considered completely different records.

The second purpose of keys is to provide the link fields between tables. A primary key can only be used once in a table – it cannot, under any circumstances, be repeated.

When used as a foreign key in another table (it's foreign because the key has been used in a table it does not belong to), the data (and the key) can be repeated.

Customer Invoice

Customer ID (Primary Key) Invoice Number (Primary Key)

Name   Customer ID (Foreign Key)

Address   Date

Postcode   etc.

In terms of data that would enable the following:

Customer table inputs:

(15983) John Smith   The House   The Town MF10 7MH

Invoice table inputs:

I12345 15983 01/12/2007

I12972 15983 07/12/2007

I13466 15983 19/12/2007

The customer's ID is only present once in the customer table, but can be repeated in the invoice table as they purchase more and more items on further invoices.

One useful thing to remember is that when linking the two tables through the use of primary and foreign keys, the end of the relationship containing the primary key is the **one** end and the end of the relationship linked to the table containing the foreign key will be the **many** end.

For more on keys see section 1.4.

However, in different publications you may see the normalisation rules applied slightly differently, which will have a bearing on the outcome of the process. How can this be the case? Firstly, it depends whether you normalise all forms at the same time (which can be a major task) or whether you normalise all the documents separately and then find where the results of normalisation overlap. In this instance we will use the second approach and normalise the two Frankoni forms separately.

Firstly the rules:

Step 1 (known as Un-Normalised Form or UNF)
List all the **data items** (known as attributes) and annotate which repeat and which do not.
Step 2 (known as First Normal Form or 1NF)
Separate data that **repeats** from data that does not (by moving to a separate table)
Step 3 (known as Second Normal Form or 2NF)
Move any **data** that has a **part-key dependency** (by moving to a separate table)

Step 4 (known as Third Normal Form or 3NF)

Move any **data** that has a **non-key dependency** – does not belong with the key it sits with (by moving to a separate table).

This probably sounds complicated – so let's work through an example for the Frankoni invoice form.

Step 1 – UNF

1 Identify ALL the attributes/fields/data items on the form (ignoring any logos or other bits of company information) – these are the items where data can be input.
2 Put them in a list.

Your list should contain the following attributes/fields, taken directly from the form:

Customer
Invoice Date
Item Code
Description
Quantity
Price
Total
Sub Total
VAT
Invoice Total

Is there anything vague about this list? Yes – the customer information, what is actually required here, is not specified. Rather than attempting to do this after normalisation has been completed, it is best to add any additional data items before the process starts. So, how shall we define the customer information?

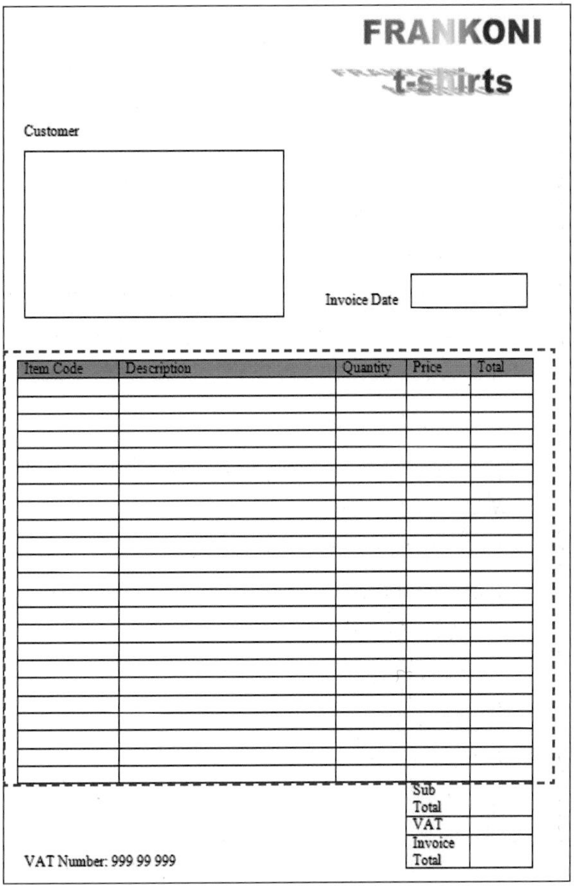

Figure 5.6 Frankoni invoice for normalisation

Customer Name	)	
Customer Address	)	This is the data that comes readily to mind
Customer Postcode	)	

Invoice Date
Item Code
Description
Quantity
Price
Total
Sub Total
VAT
Invoice Total

This now gives us a full list to work with:

Customer Name
Customer Address
Customer Postcode
Invoice Date
Item Code
Description
Quantity
Price
Total
Sub Total
VAT
Invoice Total

This list is still not in Un-Normalised Form (UNF). To achieve this, we need to identify the repeating data and mark it with brackets, to show that it repeats (this is where the user will be able to input multiple items that are similar). What are these? Item Code, Description, Quantity, Price, Total (see the area highlighted with a blue rectangle in Figure 5.6).

Customer Name
Customer Address
Customer Postcode
Invoice Date
[Item Code]
[Description]
[Quantity]
[Price]
[Total]
Sub Total
VAT
Invoice Total

Now reorganise the list so that all the items in brackets are together at the end of the list (it will make the next step more obvious). This is UNF:

Customer Name
Customer Address
Customer Postcode
Invoice Date
Sub Total
VAT
Invoice Total
[Item Code]
[Description]
[Quantity]
[Price]
[Total]

Step 2 – 1NF (First Normal Form)

Working with the UNF list, we now need to separate the repeating data from the non-repeating data. Let's put some space between the two halves of the data – the non-repeating data (data that only has a single input each time) stays at the top, and the repeating data (where we can enter multiple stock items) moves down and, once done, we can remove the brackets:

Customer Name	)	
Customer Address	)	
Customer Postcode	)	
Invoice Date	)	Invoice
Sub Total	)	
VAT	)	
Invoice Total	)	
Item Code	)	
Description	)	
Quantity	)	Invoice Lines (containing Stock)
Price	)	
Total	)	

Each part will now form a different table. The top half will be the remaining **Invoice** information, and the bottom will contain the invoice lines that will ultimately hold the **Stock** items sold information.

Now that we've separated the repeating from the non-repeating data, is there anything to link the two halves of the list now? Not yet.

Let's look at what we've got and ask some questions:

Is any data item in the **Invoice** table unique? No. So we need to make a field or data item that will be absolutely unique to each record. It's an invoice, so let's make it an **Invoice Number**. Once the number is in place, we need to make the link by copying the Invoice Number into the new table also.

But this is not enough to complete the process of 1NF – we don't have anything unique in the bottom list. Is there anything obvious we can use? Yes. The bottom half of the list has an **Item Code** – remember, a unique piece of data for each stock item.

Invoice Number	**Invoice Number**
Customer Name	**Item Code**
Customer Address	Description
Customer Postcode	Quantity
Invoice Date	Price
Sub Total	Total
VAT	
Invoice Total	

We now have something unique about each record in the lower list too.

Step 3 – 2NF (Second Normal Form)

We now ignore the upper half of the list and work with the lower half only. Why? Because for 2NF we have to identify and resolve any part-key dependency and *only* the lower half of the list has a key in two parts.

Looking at the lower half of the list (Invoice Lines table), we need to decide which attributes/fields belong to only one of the keys, not *both* together.

Question: Would the **Description** of the item exist if an item had not been sold? Yes – the stock would still exist even if it had not been sold, it would be in the warehouse.

Question: Would the **Quantity** exist if an item had not been sold? No, because the quantity sold is obviously dependant on there having been a sale in the first place.

Question: Would the **Price** of an item exist if no item had been sold? That depends. If the item is always sold at a standard list price then, yes, it would have existed; if each customer could be charged a different price then, no, it would not have existed. In this instance we will say no.

Question: Would the **Total** exist if an item had not been sold? No, because the total is dependant on the quantity sold, and if none were, then this would not exist either! So:

Invoice Number	**Key**
Item Code	**Key**
Description	Yes
Quantity	No
Price	No
Total	No

We now separate the Yes items from the No, leaving the No behind and moving any Yes items to a new table with the key they belong to – in this case Item Code.

The list now looks like this:

Invoice Number	)	
Customer Name	)	
Customer Address	)	
Customer Postcode	)	Invoice
Invoice Date	)	
Sub Total	)	
VAT	)	
Invoice Total	)	
Invoice Number	)	
Item Code	)	
Quantity	)	Invoice Lines
Price	)	
Total	)	
Item Code	)	Stock
Description	)	

Notice that at 2NF we have not created anything new.

Step 4 – 3NF (Third Normal Form)

We're nearly home.

At 3NF we look at all the tables/entities we have created, and we check whether there is anything we have not yet dealt with. We need to identify and resolve the non-key dependency. This is where there are attributes or fields that don't naturally belong to the table in which they exist. Let's work from the bottom of the list now.

Look at the following:

Item Code	)	Stock
Description	)	

Do all the attributes belong naturally to the key? Yes.

Look at the next table:

Invoice Number	)	
Item Code	)	
Quantity	)	Invoice Lines
Price	)	
Total	)	

Do all the attributes belong naturally to the combined key? Yes! Quantity, Price and Total will exist when an item has been sold on an invoice!

And finally, we look at the Invoice table:

Invoice Number	)	
Customer Name	)	
Customer Address	)	
Customer Postcode	)	Invoice
Invoice Date	)	
Sub Total	)	
VAT	)	
Invoice Total	)	

Do all the attributes belong naturally to the key? Not all of them – which do and which do not, and what shall we do with those that do not?

Let's have a look:

Invoice Number	This is the key so is not included in our deliberations
Customer Name	Would a customer name exist if there had been no invoice? Yes
Customer Address	Would a customer address exist if there had been no invoice? Yes
Customer Postcode	Would a customer postcode exist if there had been no invoice? Yes
Invoice Date	Would an invoice date be needed if there had been no invoice? No
Sub Total	Would a sub-total be needed if there had been no invoice? No
VAT	Would VAT be applied if there had been no invoice? No
Invoice Total	Would an invoice total be calculated if there had been no invoice? No

We now need to separate those data items we believe belong to the invoice and those we feel belong to the customer. And finally, we need to ensure that there is a link between the table that the data items *were* in and the table they are in *now*. So we create a new (sensible) key, which we add to the new table and we leave a copy behind in the original location.

We end up with a list that looks like this:

Invoice Number	)	
Customer ID	)	
Invoice Date	)	Invoice
Sub Total	)	
VAT	)	
Invoice Total	)	
Customer ID		
Customer Name	)	
Customer Address	)	Customer
Customer Postcode	)	

So we can now combine all the tables identified through the normalisation process into one list as follows:

Invoice Number	)	
Customer ID	)	
Invoice Date	)	Invoice
Sub Total	)	
VAT	)	
Invoice Total	)	
Invoice Number	)	
Item Code	)	
Quantity	)	Invoice Lines
Price	)	
Total	)	
Item Code	)	Stock
Description	)	
Customer ID		
Customer Name	)	
Customer Address	)	Customer
Customer Postcode	)	

It might have been easier to have used a spreadsheet and copied and pasted the data items from column to column and cell to cell as follows:

	A	B	C	D
1	UNF	1NF	2NF	3NF
2				
3	Customer Name	**Invoice Number**	**Invoice Number**	**Invoice Number**
4	Customer Address	Customer Name	Customer Name	Customer ID
5	Customer Post Code	Customer Address	Customer Address	Invoice Date
6	Invoice Date	Customer Post Code	Customer Post Code	Sub Total
7	Sub Total	Invoice Date	Invoice Date	VAT
8	VAT	Sub Total	Sub Total	Invoice Total
9	Invoice Total	VAT	VAT	
10	[Item Code]	Invoice Total	Invoice Total	**Customer ID**
11	[Description]			**Item Code**
12	[Quantity]	**Customer ID**	**Customer ID**	Quantity
13	[Price]	**Item Code**	**Item Code**	Price
14	[Total]	Description	Quantity	Total
15		Quantity	Price	
16		Price	Total	**Item Code**
17		Total		Description
18			**Item Code**	
19			Description	**Customer ID**
20				Customer Name
21				Customer Address
22				Customer Post Code

Figure 5.7 Frankoni invoice normalisation

Normalisation is only really a useful technique if you have documents that you can use to apply the process to. If the system has no existing documents you would have three choices: use similar documents maybe from other organisations, create documents for the new situation to normalise, or do not use the technique.

Before moving on, you now need to normalise the second Frankoni form (the order).

Activity – Normalisation – Frankoni

Normalise the form shown in Figure 5.4.

Try not to cheat!

How well did you do? See page 433 for answers.

You will now have two sets of normalisation, one for each of the forms. We will use these again later in section 1.4 to discuss **keys**.

Before we move on, however, we will briefly combine the list of table names that have occurred as a result of the normalisation activities:

Invoice, Invoice Line, Stock and Customer from the Invoice List

Order, Order Line, Stock and Supplier from the Order List

Removing any duplicates (stock – because it's actually the same data, used in a different way), this leaves us with:

Customer, Invoice, Invoice Line, Stock, Order Line, Order, Supplier

You have seen these before as the diagram shown earlier, on page 55.

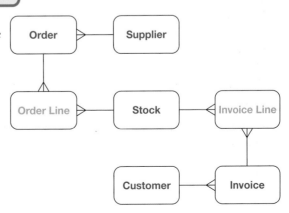

Creating and modifying relationships

Once identified, the individual tables, with the fields as identified through the normalisation process, would be created (for a reminder on how to do this see section 1.3 entitled Creation and Modification) and then the links established.

With the tables in place, you must ensure that you have identified (and activated) the primary key in each table. Activating the primary key is simple. Open the Table in Design View, click on the field or data item you wish to use as the primary key and click on the key symbol on the toolbar (see Figure 5.8).

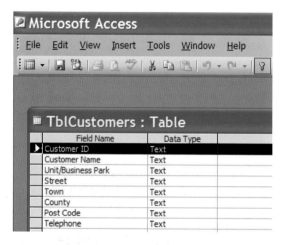

Figure 5.8 Setting the primary key

Figure 5.9 Relationships form

Having checked that all the primary keys are in place, you need to click on the **Relationships** menu on the main toolbar to open the relationships form (see Figure 5.9).

As you can see, the tables have not appeared automatically. To place the relevant tables in the form, you need to click on **Show Table**. A list of available tables will then appear as shown in Figure 5.10.

To make the tables available for linking they need to be added one by one.

Notice that the primary key in each table is emboldened. The foreign keys in each table are not.

To establish the links, it is now a simple case of clicking and dragging the primary key in the one table onto the foreign key in the other. When you perform this action, the **Edit Relationships** dialogue box appears (see Figure 5.12).

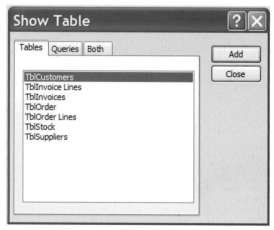

Figure 5.10 Tables list

Figure 5.11 Tables added ready for linking

The dialogue box is telling you that you are about to link the **Customer ID** in **TblCustomers** to the **Customer ID** in **TblInvoices**.

If this is indeed your intention, you can check the box labelled **Enforce Referential Integrity**. The final step is to **Create** the link.

The same process now needs to be undertaken for all the links.

Note – the primary key must be the **AutoNumber** – in the table containing the foreign key it must be defined/typed as a simple **Number**.

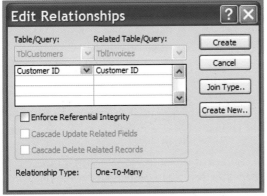

Figure 5.12 Editing Relationships

You **cannot** enforce referential integrity unless the datatype defined in each key field being used to establish the link is the same.

The main error that novice developers experience is when working with number fields. The error occurs when both the primary and foreign keys are created as AutoNumbers.

As can be seen in Figure 5.13, once the relationships have been established, the view can become messy and confusing. It is therefore sensible at this stage to reorganise the tables and relationships to make the diagram more readable.

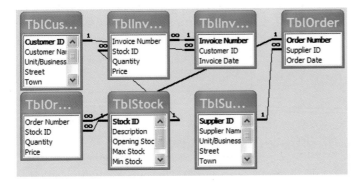

Figure 5.13 Established relationships

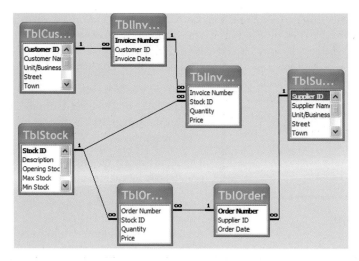

Figure 5.14 Reorganised for readability

Once established, the relationships can be reviewed and edited at any time. They can even be removed and re-established if needed.

Benefits of the relational model

As we saw early in this unit, the predecessor to relational databases was the flat file alternative, which by its very nature required significant data duplication.

The main advantage therefore of relational databases is that in general, apart from duplicated keys to link tables, most items of data are only stored once.

Cascading updates and deletes

When working with the dialogue box shown in Figure 5.12 you will have noticed that when you checked the **Enforce Referential Integrity** box, the two **Cascade** boxes below became available.

What do these do?

If checked, the **Cascade Update Related Fields** function enables the user to change the primary key in the main table if needed, and it will then automatically change the foreign key versions that exist in related records. For example, if you were to change the Supplier ID in the Supplier table, all the orders that exist in the Order table that contain the same Supplier ID will be automatically updated with the new Supplier ID.

Similarly, if **Cascade Delete Related Records** is checked, should the record in the main table containing the primary key be deleted, all the records in related tables linked through their foreign key would be automatically deleted. Using our Supplier/Order example, this would mean that if a Supplier was deleted, all orders that were raised for that particular Supplier would be removed from the database.

⚠️ Microsoft Access® will automatically delete or update the records in the related tables **without displaying any further warnings**. Invoke **Cascade** functionality with care as any deleted records can not be recovered.

1.2 Field properties

Data types and properties of different field types

Each data field must be **typed**. This means that decisions need to be made at the outset as to whether the data item to be stored will be a number, date, text item, logical field etc. Choosing the right data type will ensure that the users will be able to manipulate the data successfully using other database functionality. A computer cannot, for example, add two pieces of text. If the field contains numeric data, it is thus sensible to store the data as a number, so that users will be able to use it in calculations. However, a telephone number is also numeric data, but if this is stored as a number, all leading 0s that form part of the STD code will be removed. In this instance it is more suitable to store the data as text because firstly, this will ensure that the leading 0s are stored, and secondly, the user is unlikely to need the telephone number as a field to calculate with! The data types available in Microsoft Access® are shown in Figure 5.15.

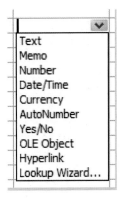

Figure 5.15
Available data types

Data type	Description
Text (known in programming as a String)	A combination of characters, numbers and/or symbols. The maximum text size in a Microsoft Access® database is 255 characters. The minimum is one character.
Memo	A text field where the size of the field does not need to be defined. It might be tempting to use this data type in preference to a text field as both can be similarly formatted. The problem will only be when viewing the data in a memo field because it is easy for the amount of text input to be far greater than the size of the box provided to view the data (so some might not be visible and may be missed).
Number – Integer (whole number)	A number that does not contain any decimal parts. This data type must always be selected as the foreign key data type where an AutoNumber has been used as the primary key data type at the other end of the relationship.
Number – Floating point (decimal)	This number does contain a decimal part and will probably need to be formatted to make it store/display a consistent number of digits after the point.
Date/Time	The advantage of being able to select one of a range of date and time formats is that it then does not matter how the date is input, it will be reformatted and displayed in the chosen style. You should take great care, however, with date formats, particularly US/European and UK formats because in the US and in many European countries the months are displayed before the days. In the UK it is the other way around.
Currency	A number field with a decimal part, which also benefits from having the currency symbol displayed (such as £, € or $).
AutoNumber	The AutoNumber is a number data type that increments automatically as each record is created to provide a unique number. It is possible to start the sequence at alternative start points (see section 1.4).
Yes/No	This data type is a logical one that offers the opportunity to store values such as Yes/No or True/False. This can be input as words or as a tick in a check box.

Data type	Description
OLE Object	Choosing this data type will allow you to insert an object in a field, such as a picture, a sound file or a graph (among others).
Hyperlink	The hyperlink type can either be a URL, or it can be a directory or file path. This then becomes an active link that, when clicked, will open the website, directory or file.
Lookup Wizard	Probably one of the most useful data types, the Lookup Wizard is used to provide a drop-down menu of input choices – the example here is Status (e.g. Mr, Mrs etc). Mr Mrs Miss Doctor Rev Other **Figure 5.16** List created using Lookup Wizard Using this feature where possible also reduces the opportunity for incorrect data input, as the user chooses from a list rather than keying in data manually.

It is unlikely that, in most cases, primary and foreign key fields will be anything other than text or integer numbers (including AutoNumbers).

1.3 Creation and modification

Tables

The process of creating tables is a very simple one.

For each data item that is to be stored in a record, a field needs to be established and that field then needs to be defined with a data type (see previous section).

To create a table, click on **Tables** then on **New**. This opens the Tables dialogue.

Figure 5.17 Creating tables

You will see that there are three methods for creating tables. You can create tables:

◆ in Design View
◆ by using a wizard
◆ by entering data.

Choosing the Design View option opens the table structure. You will now need to enter each of the data fields, one at a time, selecting an appropriate data type in each case. As each one is chosen the **General** tab contents change for additional formatting choices.

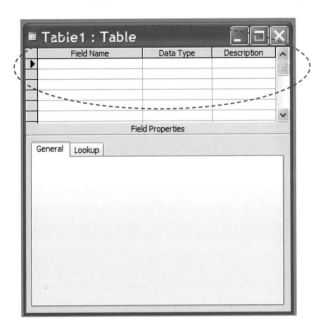

Figure 5.18 Table in Design View

The Description column is also useful and sufficient detail should be included here to ensure that another developer can understand what the field was for.

Using the wizard makes the process easier because the developer simply has to make decisions and follow a set of pre-existing steps.

Using the buttons highlighted, the developer simply clicks to move the selected sample field to become one of the chosen fields in the new table. The >> symbol will move all sample fields across for inclusion in the new table, the > symbol moves only the highlighted sample field. Similarly the < symbol will remove one of the chosen fields back to the sample fields list and << will remove them all.

Once the process is completed, the developer will still need to view the fields in Design View and check the general formatting defaults for each one.

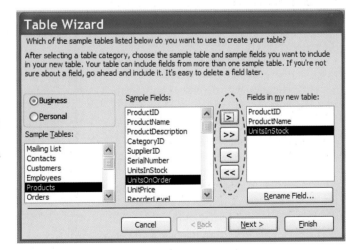

Figure 5.19 Creating a table using the wizard

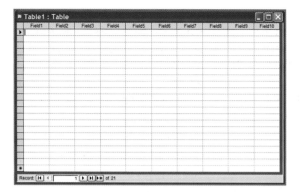

Figure 5.20 Creating a table by entering data (in DataSheet View)

The final method for creating a new table is to create it by entering data. This choice will open the DataSheet View of the table and will allow the developer to simply start keying in the data (see Figure 5.20).

While this can be a useful technique if you are copying and pasting data from another package that is already organised into rows and columns, once the data has been input, the developer will still need to switch to Design View to add field names and check what data types the system has **chosen** for each field. Also, the field sizes will need to be checked, as with any other formatting options.

Queries

A database query is effectively a method of filtering the records by extracting records based on one criterion or a range of criteria. The developer/user will be able to decide which fields they actually want to include in the query, and they will be able to apply sorting on one or more fields, various grouping options etc.

Queries are created using one of two methods:

◆ in Design View
◆ by using a wizard
◆ by using SQL.

When choosing the Design View option, the developer will first need to identify which tables to include (see Figure 5.21).

The area indicated in Figure 5.21 has a number of variables that can be manipulated for each field selected in the query. This is what they do:

Sort   Sorts the whole table by this field either in ascending (A to Z) or descending (Z to A) order. (Remember to exercise caution when sorting as it can be problematic when trying to sort more than one field at the same time.)

Show   The user/developer has the choice of a field used in the manipulation of the data to be displayed. A tick in the **Show** check box will mean that the field is included. Left blank you will be able to sort on the field, filter etc., but the data in the field itself will not be included in the display view.

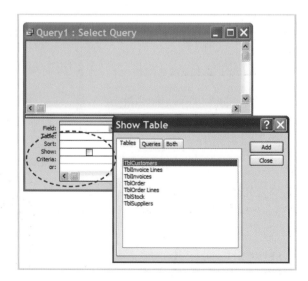

Figure 5.21 Creating a query in Design View

Criteria   The criteria option is used to extract records based on specific search criteria – for example < 16 on a field containing student ages would return only those records where the students' ages are less than 16. Similarly, using the search criteria 'Josie' on a list of learner names will only return the records for any learners named Josie.

Combining the two criteria with an AND will return all learners named Josie who are also under 16. Using combined criteria with OR will return any learners named Josie (regardless of age) and all learners under 16 (regardless of name).

More information about using criteria to extract records through queries will follow in section 2.3.

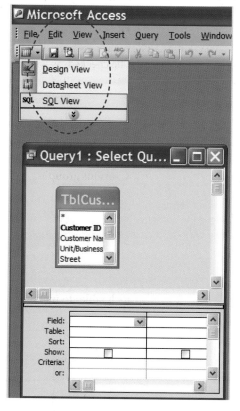

Figure 5.22 Accessing the SQL View option

Look at the list – how many stock items come in the colour Blue?

Answer: four.

The SQL that would extract the four relevant records would look like that shown in Figure 5.24.

But what does this syntax actually mean?

> **SELECT** the **Stock ID** and **Description**
> **FROM** the **TblStock** table
> **WHERE** the **Description** includes the text **Blue**

Creating queries using SQL (Structured Query Language) is a little more complex. Using SQL to develop queries is almost like writing programming code. To access this interface you would first need to create a query in Design View and then click on the SQL View in the switch menu (indicated in Figure 5.22).

The query is developed using a set of key words such as SELECT, UPDATE, FROM and WHERE. Let's look at an example. Examine the data in Figure 5.23.

Stock ID	Description
A101	Assorted Band logos
T101	T-shirts Blue XL
T102	T-shirts Red L
T103	T-shirts Black L
T104	T-shirts Black XL
T105	T-shirts Blue L Long-sleeved
T106	T-shirts Blue S
T107	T-shirts Red XL Long-sleeved
T108	T-shirts Green L
T109	T-shirts Yellow S
T110	T-shirts Purple M
T111	T-shirts Black S
T112	T-shirts Blue XL

Figure 5.23 Data extract from the Stock table in the Frankoni database

Figure 5.24 SQL query to extract all stock items that are Blue

Notice the use of the * (asterisk) on both sides of the word Blue. These are the wildcard symbols and it means that when the search is executed the system will extract all records where Blue forms **part** of the description. This is because in the description field there is text before and after the word Blue. Failure to include the asterisks will return a nil result because no description has only the word Blue in it.

The query result can be seen in Figure 5.25.

Stock ID	Description
T101	T-shirts Blue XL
T105	T-shirts Blue L Long-sleeved
T106	T-shirts Blue S
T112	T-shirts Blue XL

Query1 : Select Query

Record: 5 of 5

Figure 5.25 SQL query result showing four Blue stock items

Case Study

The system for Frankoni T-shirts has invoice and ordering capabilities through an invoice and an order form. The user is able to raise an invoice as goods are sold, or create an order to reflect goods coming in from suppliers.

We now need to add functionality to these forms to automatically update the stock levels.

Firstly we need to create the SQL to Add to stock levels and to Reduce stock levels.

Answer

Add

UPDATE TblStock SET [Stock Level] = [Stock Level]+

[FrmOrderLines Subform].Quantity

WHERE TblStock.[Stock ID]=[FrmOrderLines Subform].[Stock ID];

In English: Update the stock table by finding the stock level and adding the quantity in the OrderLines subform, where the Stock ID in the stock table is the same as the Stock ID in the current line on the OrderLines subform.

Remove

UPDATE TblStock SET [Stock Level] = [Stock Level]–

[FrmOrderLines Subform].Quantity

WHERE TblStock.[Stock ID]=[FrmOrderLines Subform].[Stock ID];

In English: Update the stock table by finding the stock level and deducting the quantity in the OrderLines subform, where the Stock ID in the stock table is the same as the Stock ID in the current line on the OrderLines subform.

Each of these code sequences will need to be placed in a macro.

To create a macro, simply click on the Macro tab, name the macro (something sensible like **Macro Add Stock**), then you need to select a single **Action**. To do this, click on the drop-down box and select **RunSQL**.

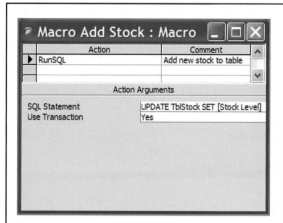

Figure 5.26 Adding SQL to a macro

you to add an **Event**. As an **On Exit** event the macro will run after the data has been input and as the user moves to the next field to input the Price (see Figure 5.27). The user will then be prompted that one record in the stock table is being changed.

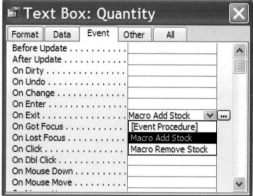

The entire SQL statement shown under the heading **Add** needs to be keyed into the **SQL statement input box** as indicated in Figure 5.26.

When the macro has been saved and closed it needs to be linked to the relevant field in the Order form. To do this you would need to have the Order form open in **Design View** revealing the **Quantity** field in the order lines.

Right clicking and then selecting the **properties** option will open the dialogue box that allows

Figure 5.27 Linking the macro to the field

Once this has been done, the exact same process will need to be undertaken creating a second macro to remove the stock, and adding it as an Event on the Invoice form.

Reports, e.g. changes to a table, adding or deleting fields, changing field characteristics

As with the other objects, there are two ways of creating reports. Reports can be created:

◆ in Design View
◆ by using a wizard.

Choosing to create a report in Design View is actually quite difficult, particularly for an inexperienced developer or user. This is because when you choose this option absolutely nothing is prepared for you (see Figure 5.28) and you will need to begin by identifying which query or table you want to use, and then it will require you to drag and drop the relevant objects onto the report design.

Figure 5.28 Creating reports in Design View

Most users (even experienced ones) tend to use the Report Wizard (see Figure 5.29) in the first instance and modify the report through the Design View when the main structure is in place.

Using the wizard is straight forward – the user simply selects the fields to include by choosing the relevant tables/queries and moving the available fields into the selected fields box.

Once all the relevant fields have been chosen you can click on Next and follow the remaining steps.

Although coverage of this topic is not required in this unit, one real advantage of using the wizard is that if you select fields from more than one table or query (where they are linked) the wizard will add some extra steps that allow you to create a grouped combination, such as a list of all invoices for a particular customer.

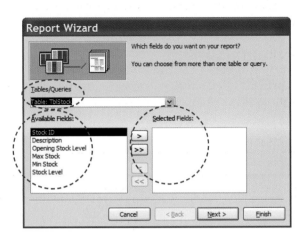

Figure 5.29 Using the Report Wizard

Figure 5.30 Creating a grouped report

In the example shown in Figure 5.30 we have selected fields from the Customers table and from the Invoices table.

The report will then show all customers and any invoices that have been raised for them (see Figure 5.31).

In addition to the techniques already discussed in the development of tables, queries and reports, additional techniques will be covered later in this unit.

TblCustomers

Customer ID	Customer Name	Invoice Number	Invoice Date
C101	Jones, Jones and Lambert		
		7	06/09/2007
C102	Matthew Franks		
		3	01/09/2007
C104	Euston Limited		
		8	07/09/2007
		1	01/09/2007
C105	8 Group PLC		
		5	05/09/2007
C106	Marcus Marlwood Associates		
		4	04/09/2007
C107	Badminton Developments		
		6	05/09/2007
		2	01/09/2007

Figure 5.31 Grouped report

1.4 Key fields

Earlier in the unit chapter we started to discuss the concept of key fields. Here they are explained in more depth.

Primary keys

A **primary key** is a data item within a record that is unique and which can be used to identify a record with certainty. Consider the following data:

First Name	Last Name	Date Of Birth
John	Davies	01/06/1987
Barbara	Davies	19/05/1992
John	Matthews	19/05/1992

Look at the data in each field (column). Is any single piece of data unique?

First Name: **John**, Barbara, **John**
Last Name: **Davies**, **Davies**, Matthews
Date of Birth: 01/06/1987, **19/05/1992**, **19/05/1992**

No field contains truly unique data as in each field data is repeated at least once.

ID	First Name	Last Name	Date Of Birth
F101	John	Davies	01/06/1987
F102	Barbara	Davies	19/05/1992
F103	John	Matthews	19/05/1992

While the remaining data is the same, the ID column has three pieces of data: F101, F102 and F103. None of these is repeated. Thus, it is essential that this column is used to provide a primary key.

The primary key is then copied into the link table so that the relationship can be created. There it is called a foreign key.

The **AutoCounter** mentioned above is often used to provide a primary key.

Foreign keys

A foreign key is the copy of a primary key placed in another table to make a link between two database objects.

To understand how this actually works, we will now use the results of the normalisation on the Frankoni order and invoice forms that were undertaken earlier in this unit (see Figure 5.32).

As suggested earlier in the unit, when the two sets of normalised results are placed in a single list, the Stock table appears twice (once in each list). Clearly a stock table is a stock table, and had one of the stock tables

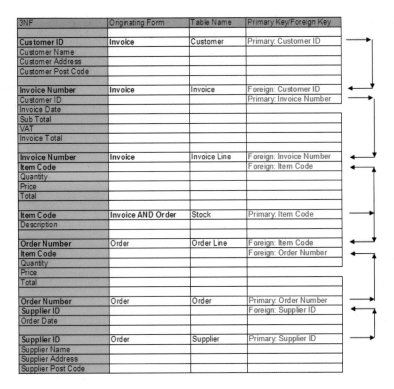

3NF	Originating Form	Table Name	Primary Key/Foreign Key
Customer ID	Invoice	Customer	Primary: Customer ID
Customer Name			
Customer Address			
Customer Post Code			
Invoice Number	Invoice	Invoice	Foreign: Customer ID
Customer ID			Primary: Invoice Number
Invoice Date			
Sub Total			
VAT			
Invoice Total			
Invoice Number	Invoice	Invoice Line	Foreign: Invoice Number
Item Code			Foreign: Item Code
Quantity			
Price			
Total			
Item Code	Invoice AND Order	Stock	Primary: Item Code
Description			
Order Number	Order	Order Line	Foreign: Item Code
Item Code			Foreign: Order Number
Quantity			
Price			
Total			
Order Number	Order	Order	Primary: Order Number
Supplier ID			Foreign: Supplier ID
Order Date			
Supplier ID	Order	Supplier	Primary: Supplier ID
Supplier Name			
Supplier Address			
Supplier Post Code			

Figure 5.32 Combined normalisation results from the order and invoice forms

had different data items to the other, through the combination process you would have sought to include the fields from both stock tables (but ensuring that none of the data items are repeated).

Referential integrity

When we created the relationships in the database between the tables we did so to enforce referential integrity – but what does that actually mean?

It means the process of checking that the values that will ultimately be used as keys in other tables are indeed present at both ends of the relationship. It thus seeks to ensure that consistency is present between linked tables.

However, while the system is capable of finding some integrity errors, it may not find them all and, in the event that a problem arises, the developer will need to do some manual checks.

Auto-incremented keys

We have already suggested that in order to create an auto-incremented unique identifier for a table, we can use the AutoNumber data type and it would be correct to do so. However, when a new field is declared as an AutoNumber in a table, the sequence always begins with the number one.

It is possible, however, to change the initial or opening value of a number sequence by using an Append query. This is how it's done.

1 Create a new table with a **single field**. The field must be set as a **Number** and the field size must be set to **Long Integer**. It is also a good idea to give the only field in the table the **same name** as the incremented value it will replace in its final destination table (see Figure 5.33). Save as **Temp Table** and switch to the Datasheet View.

2 Key a single value into the first record making sure that the value is one below the number you wish to start with. For example, if you want to start the AutoNumber sequence at 1000, you need to set the single value as 999 (see Figure 5.34).

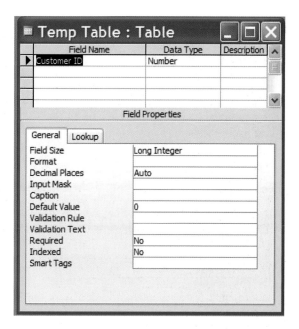

Figure 5.33 Temp Table structure

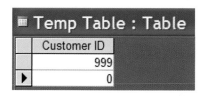

Figure 5.34 Opening value for the new AutoNumber

3 Create the new main table for Customers containing at least two fields – the **Customer ID** field and, say, the **Customer Name**. The Customer ID field must be set to **AutoNumber** and the Customer Name to **Text**.

4 Create a new query, selecting the Temp Table and the only field within it, then click on **Query** and on **Append Query** (see Figure 5.35).

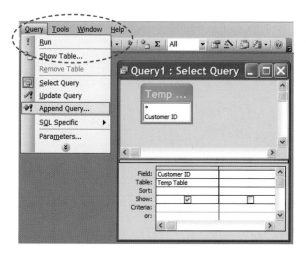

Figure 5.35 Setting up the Append Query

5 A dialogue box will now have appeared asking you to specify which table you wish to append to. Select the **Customer table** (see Figure 5.36).

6 Click on **OK**. You now need to run the query. This can be done either through the Query Menu (Query + Run), or by clicking on the red exclamation mark icon on the toolbar (see the annotation on Figure 5.35).

Figure 5.36 Choosing the table to append to

The system will now tell you it is about to append one record. Click **Yes**.

7 Close the Query (you can actually delete the Query – it is no longer required).
8 Open the Customer table.

Customer : Table

Customer ID	Customer Name
999	
(AutoNumber)	

Figure 5.37 Starting value for the Customer ID sequence

9 In the Customer Name field, to the right of the AutoNumber, key in a first Customer Name. Press Enter.
10 Delete the record containing Customer ID 999.

Customer : Table

Customer ID	Customer Name
1000	Yvonne Crago
1001	Liz Hancock
(AutoNumber)	

Figure 5.38 New customer records

The new AutoNumber sequence will continue incrementally.

Clearly it would be very straightforward to use this method in each table to have an alternative starting value to the default value of one.

1.5 Errors

Identification of typical errors, e.g. different data types in related tables

Errors in databases can be difficult to resolve, which is why it is always so important to try and get the structure right in the first place.

The most common error in a database is linking two fields in different tables that have been defined with different data types.

Firstly it should be easy to spot the problem when you try to establish the link in the first place and enforce referential integrity – at this point you should receive an error message.

Another common error is trying to implement a piece of functionality designed for one data type on a field that has been defined with a different data type (for example trying to add two pieces of text, or a number and a Yes/No field).

Sometimes the error is not obvious until the user or developer attempts to run a query or a report based on a table that contains errors.

Errors can also occur on data input, which is why it is useful to include input masking and data validation where possible (see section 2.1).

A frustrating error that often occurs is where a developer has created a series of queries and reports based on a particular table or combination of tables. The problem is triggered by the fact that someone then deletes a field in a table, which is actually represented in the query or report. If this occurs, every time the linked query or report is opened after the point of deletion, an input box will pop up requesting that the user input the missing data or values. If this occurs, simply putting the field back in the table will not resolve the problem. It might therefore be more appropriate to delete the data items on the query or report concerned.

Rectification of errors

As a general rule, when attempting to rectify errors you should begin by going back to basics and checking the tables involved: check data types, field lengths (if data is truncated – shortened – it is because the developer did not create a field size large enough to accommodate the user input).

Check that the relationships have been implemented correctly.

Then check the query or report design and any calculated expressions (see section 2.3).

If having to make adjustments to primary keys you might need to break (remove) the relationship(s) until the changes have been made and then re-implement them.

Poor design

It is very difficult to produce a fully working and efficient database based on a poor design.

If problems cannot be overcome, you might have to export the data tables into a new database, having created a clean new structure beforehand.

Inconsistent normalisation

Take great care with normalisation. It was suggested earlier that although there is only one set of normalisation rules, they can have different interpretations. Make sure that only one interpretation is applied.

Also, make sure you are not careless when copying and pasting field names as part of the normalisation process. It is very easy to accidentally exclude a field at, say, 1NF, which then remains missing all the way through the process and is not present in the final list.

2 Create, populate and test a multiple database

2.1 Data entry forms

Creating data entry forms is essential if you expect less technical users to competently use your database. Doing this is very straightforward as you simply need to click on the **Forms** tab on the main menu and then either create the form in Design View or using the wizard. As with reports, more developers tend to begin by using the wizard, they then switch to the Design View and make adjustments.

Using the wizard will also ensure that the **tab order** (the order in which each input box is accessed as the user navigates the form) will be the same as in the original table. If, however, you need to change the tab order, switch to the Design View of the form, make sure that **Detail** is clicked, then right click to reveal the **Tab Order** option. When clicked you will be presented with a second dialogue box that lists the fields in the current tab order. To change the order, see the instructions in the box (see Figure 5.39).

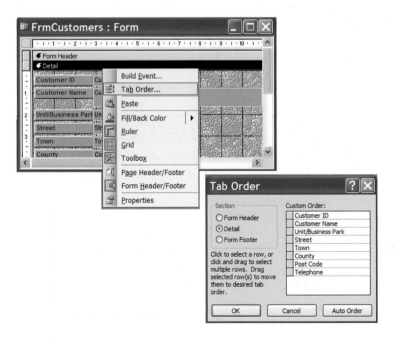

Figure 5.39 Changing the tab order in a form

Verification and validation routines

Input masking

An input mask (whether applied on a form or on the main table) can be used to make the input conform to an expected sequence or combination of values.

This is how it works:

Using a series of symbols the user inputs a sequence into the **Input Mask** box. The key is ensuring that the right symbols are input.

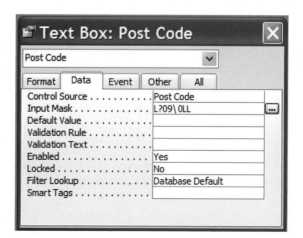

Figure 5.40 Applying an input mask to a Post Code field

Symbols used in input masking can be found in the following table:

Symbol	What it does
L	Requires a character input and entry is compulsory
?	Requires a character input but entry is optional
0	Requires a number input and entry is compulsory
9	Requires a number input and entry is optional
>	Automatically forces the input into upper case
<	Automatically forces the input into lower case

Let's look at that Post Code input mask again:

L?09\0LL

This means:

Letter + Optional Letter + Number + Optional Number + Space + Number + Letter + Letter

Why do we need to accommodate optional input?

While most postcodes follow the format AA1 1AA – others have only one leading letter as in A1 1AA and others still have an additional number in the first half as in AA11 1AA.

Using the sequence of symbols ensures that whatever the combination, the user will be able to input the postcode.

Similar input masks could be placed on the number of characters required on an input, on a telephone number or on a date of birth (although with a date of birth you would probably use the date/time data type in the first place).

Checks for completeness

As suggested in the previous section an input mask could be used to force a required number of input characters (all codes for example must contain five characters – this would be defined as LLLLL, or maybe as a letter, two numbers then two letters, defined as L00LL).

Also as already suggested, if not using an AutoNumber to generate a primary key, failure to include a value will automatically be challenged by the system. However, the actual value input will not be challenged unless it already exists. As such, using an input mask to ensure a substantial and valid primary key is a useful consideration.

The most common check for completeness is to prompt the user to make one last visual check before the record is set in the database. Clearly if an error is found later it is still possible to edit the record.

Data consistency and visual prompts

Sometimes, to ensure that multiple users or a single user using the system many times will input data in a consistent way, it is essential to understand that users can interpret issues differently. For example:

You have been asked to

Input height:

How will you input the information that you are 1.65 metres tall?

1.65 metres
1.65 (and hope that the measurement is in metres)
1.65 m
165 cm
65 inches (you are not sure if a metric or imperial measurement is expected)
5 ft 5 inches
5 ft 5

Might it not have been better to give the user an indication of what is expected? Let's try this again:

Input height in metres (e.g. 1.47):

This will leave the user(s) in no doubt about how to enter the information. You should ensure, however, that these prompts are as brief as possible and you should only add them if you think that there is a vagueness about the input instruction.

Data redundancy

Data is redundant if it is already being stored elsewhere in the database. This is one of the potential problems that techniques like normalisation seek to resolve (by avoiding them in the first place).

If, however, you subsequently find that you have redundant data – simply delete the columns in the table, which will delete the redundant data at the same time. However, be careful to ensure that any queries and reports that use the table will not be adversely affected (see section 1.5).

Drop-down or combo boxes

Limiting how the data is input is often one of the best ways to reduce the potential for data entry errors. If the user cannot input the value, because they simply need to select a value from a list, then the user will not be able to introduce typographical errors.

As mentioned in section 1.2, the lookup wizard that produces lists of available data items from which the user can choose is probably one of the most useful data types. In Figure 5.41 the marital status input has been limited to those items shown in the list. Remember, if you do use such a list it might be useful to include an *Other* option in case the options you have included do not cover the input required.

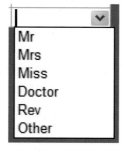

Figure 5.41 Drop-down or combo box used to limit data input

Activity – Validation

The following is an exercise that gets you to develop a simple but effective validation routine on dates. Simply follow the process through!

You are creating a database that records the allocation of visas to individuals wishing to travel abroad. In order to be allowed to travel, these individuals must have received inoculations at least 21 days before departure date. As such, when entering the Travel Date, it needs to immediately validate against the date of the inoculation to ensure that the full 21 days have elapsed. Here's how you do it.

1 Create a database with a single table. The table will contain two fields as shown below. Both must be set as dates (format of your choice) – see Figure 5.42.

Name the table VisaRequest (no spaces otherwise we'll have problems with the code later. Similarly, do not put spaces in the field names and ensure your spelling of field names is the same as that shown in Figure 5.42).

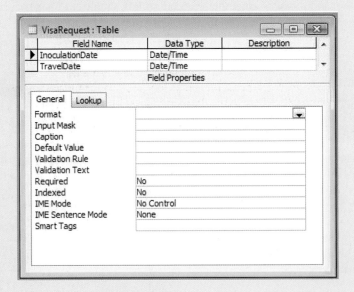

Figure 5.42 VisaRequest table

2 Create a straightforward input form on this table using the wizard, and selecting both fields – the style of the form you use is not important. Name the form Visa Request Form.

3 Go to the Design View of the form.

4 Click on the Travel Date input box, then right click and click on Properties.

5 Select the Event tab, and click into the Before Update box, and click on Event Procedure.

6 Once the **Event Procedure** is in the box itself, click on the button to the right of the drop-down box (a square containing three dots).

7 Key in the code shown in Figure 5.43 **exactly as listed**.

```
Date validation - Form_VisaRequest (Code)

TravelDate                                    ▼   BeforeUpdate                          ▼

    Private Sub TravelDate_BeforeUpdate(Cancel As Integer)
       If (TravelDate < InoculationDate + 21) Then
          Cancel = True
          MsgBox ("Error - Travel date must be 21 days or more after date of Inoculation")
       End If
    End Sub
```

Figure 5.43 Code needed to provide the validation activity

8 Once completed, this will save automatically. Click the close button in the top right-hand corner, so that you can return to the Design View of your form.

9 Click for the input or form view and test your system. Input a date into the InoculationDate field. Now click into the TravelDate field and put in another date (say the following day). Check the validation rule runs (don't forget to test boundaries).

10 If the validation functions as intended you will see an error message as shown in Figure 5.44.

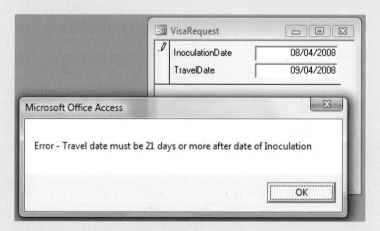

Figure 5.44 Working validation routine

Don't forget that if you don't put in a date that is 21 days or more after the date of inoculation, the system won't allow you to store the record – so, for your traveller, no permission to travel.

2.2 Importing data

Import data from external sources, e.g. other databases, spreadsheets, text files

Data can be imported from other Microsoft Access® databases, other databases (providing that the data has been saved in a compatible format), spreadsheets or text files. It can be imported and appended to an existing table, or it can be made into a new table.

If importing and appending data you must ensure that the fields receiving the data are in the same order as the columns in the source location, and that there are the same number of fields.

To import from an external source, you access the functionality through the **File** menu and then by clicking on **Get External Data** and **Import** (see Figure 5.45).

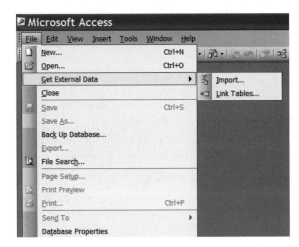

You can then specify the name of the file to import.

The alternative (and often simpler) solution is to copy and paste the data from one location to another. In the event that there are compatibility issues, you might need to use an intermediary program such as Microsoft Excel® to create a .csv file to import.

Unit Link

For more on file formats (such as .csv) see **Unit 6 – Advanced Spreadsheet Skills** in this publication, section 2.4 pages 122 to 124.

Figure 5.45 Importing data from an external source

2.3 Query design

Selection of data types to facilitate querying

To ensure that the criteria you will need to apply in a query will work with the data in the relevant fields, you must ensure that the data types are correct. As often suggested, you cannot calculate with text fields!

One useful thing you can do in a query, however, is create new fields as expressions.

Let's consider our normalisation of the invoice form earlier in this unit. The subsequent invoice lines table included a total field to capture the line total (quantity × price). In fact, it is not necessary to store something that can be calculated when needed.

Figure 5.46 contains an example of creating an expression to provide that total.

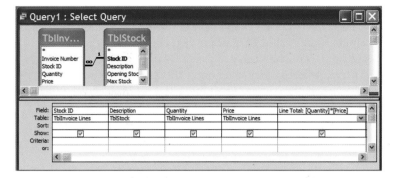

Figure 5.46 Calculated expression field added in the query

The Line Total has been calculated by multiplying the Quantity and the Price.

Using **Line Total:** automatically generates the field title that will be present when you switch to the datasheet view.

Note – although the brackets around Quantity and Price are not technically required, it is useful to get into the habit of using them simply because if a field has a two- or three-part name the brackets are compulsory to indicate to the system that all three words together form the title of the field to use (e.g. [Stock ID], because there is a space between the two parts of the name).

The main operators that are used as filter criteria include the following:

Operator	Function
<	Less than operator (used with numbers)
<=	Less than or equal to operator – notice that there is no space between the two symbols (used with numbers)
>	Greater than operator (used with numbers)
>=	Greater than or equal to operator – again notice that there is no space between the two symbols (used with numbers)
Like	Like, used with asterisks around the search term (e.g. *Cheshire*) will find and display all records where the term Cheshire exists as part of the data in the field, even if there is data before or after the term itself. As such, the following records would be included: Cheshire North Cheshire North East Cheshire Cheshire West Cheshire South West As you can see, it accepts one or more words before or after the search term.
Between	Between is a date operator that is particularly useful if you wish to search for records that have dates that fall between to boundary values – for example: #04/09/2007# And #05/09/2007# When used, the user will simply key in **Between 04/09/2007 And 05/09/2007** The hash symbols that appear in the final version will have been included by the software.

Figure 5.47 Parameter query

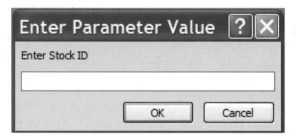

Figure 5.48 User prompt

As part of query design, you have an additional option, which is to create a query known as a parameter query that requires the user to input a search value. This means that, once created, the user will be able to use the same query to search for different records. In Figure 5.47 you will see a parameter query on the Stock ID in the Stock table, where the criteria [**Enter Stock ID**] has been added. When the query is then run, the user will be prompted to provide an input (see Figure 5.48).

Use of logical operators

The **Between** operator uses the logical operator **AND** to create a condition where both criteria have to be met for the records to be included in the result. In this instance, the records must exist between 04/09/2007 and 05/09/2007 inclusive.

Unit Link

For more on logical operators see **Unit 6 – Advanced Spreadsheet Skills** in this publication, section 3.2 pages 130 to 135.

2.4 Exporting data

Query and report results to other applications

Just as you can import tables of data from other applications, you can also export data to other applications such as other databases (both Microsoft Access® versions and others), or you can export to spreadsheet or word processing applications. Again, it is a simple process. You can either copy and paste the records manually, or you can use the **Export** function to create a file of the data.

To do this you choose the **Export** option from the **File** menu (see Figure 5.49).

Do not forget that as part of the procedure you can choose from a range of destination file types that include spreadsheet and html options.

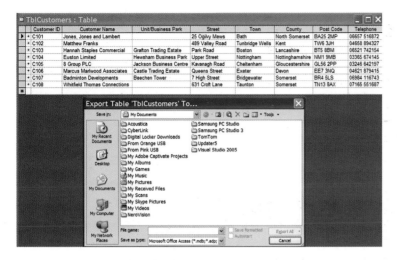

Figure 5.49 Exporting data

3 Use advanced features of a database and test functionality

3.1 Ensuring and maintaining integrity

Use of software features such as update and delete

This topic has already been considered in some depth in section 1.1, **Cascading updates and deletes**. But just as a reminder:

The **Cascade Update Related Fields** function enables the user to change the primary key in the main table if needed, and it will then automatically change the foreign key versions that exist in related records.

Cascade Delete Related Records is used to remove related records in other tables if the parent record in the main table is deleted.

3.2 Creating styles

Forms and reports

To make a database look professional, experienced developers create an interface where each form or report has a similar style or theme. There are a series of automated formats available. To access these, open the form or report in **Design View** then select **AutoFormat** from the **Format** menu (see Figure 5.50).

You will notice that there is also an option to create a customised format.

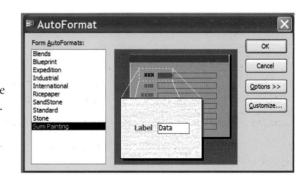

Figure 5.50 Using AutoFormat to promote consistency in style

To create your own format, which you can then add to the list and use across all forms, simply create your form, then click on **Design View** then **AutoFormat, on Format** and then finally on **Customize**. You then simply either click on **Create** and **OK** (this will take all the formatting from the open form and store the information so that the format can be selected when creating other forms) or, if the format already exists and you need to modify it, you will need to select the **Update** option from the list and click **OK**.

Figure 5.51 Creating a customised format for input forms

Style as appropriate to user need and with consistency

One of the first units you will have studied as part of your National Diploma will have been the compulsory unit (Unit 1 – Communication and Employability Skills for IT) where section 2 considered how to make communications appropriate for particular user groups or individuals.

We would all agree that the appearance of any object, be it a document, presentation, spreadsheet or database, should be professional. This is achieved by first making appropriate choices for fonts, colours, images and formats, and by applying these choices consistently.

Unit Link

For more on communicating in a way that is suitable for an audience, see the **Core Text, Unit 1 – Communication and Employability Skills for IT**, section 2, pages 12 to 31.

3.3 Customising

Menus and toolbars, e.g. use show/hide functionality, add buttons to toolbars

Using the show/hide functionality is not the same in Microsoft Access® as it is in Microsoft Excel® and so will be discussed here.

Once a database has been developed, and to ensure that users only access forms, queries or reports that you need them to, Microsoft Access® provides functionality that hides tables and queries. This means that users will be unable to *accidentally* delete columns of data from the main tables, or change the structure of queries. As a developer you need to identify what will be visible in the final database and what will not.

Unit Link

Adding and modifying menus and toolbars is the same in Microsoft Access® as it is in Microsoft Excel® and this topic has thus already been covered in depth.

For information and instructions on adding buttons and menus see **Unit 6 – Advanced Spreadsheet Skills**, section 3.1 (under the heading **Configuring the user interface**, pages 128 to 129) and section 4.5 (under the heading **Customisation**, pages 144 to 146) in this publication.

When you have decided which tables and queries you wish to hide, the process is simple.

With the database open, and the Tables tab selected, the developer will simply need to right click on the table chosen to be hidden and select **Properties** from the bottom of the list. This opens the Properties dialogue box as shown in Figure 5.52.

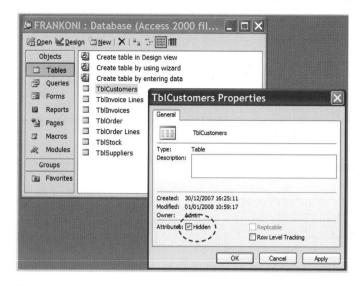

Figure 5.52 Hiding tables

Check the **Hidden** option and then click on **Apply**. Once this has been applied, the icon beside the table to be hidden will appear much fainter than the icons for the other tables that have not yet been selected (compare Figure 5.52 with Figure 5.53).

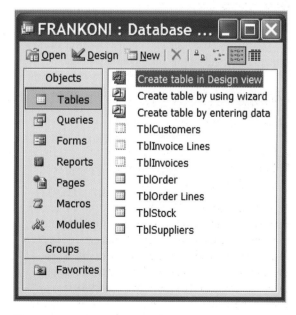

Figure 5.53 First three tables selected for hiding

Activating the hiding option is simple. Select **Options** from the **Tools** menu to reveal the dialogue box shown in Figure 5.54 and ensure the **View** tab is selected.

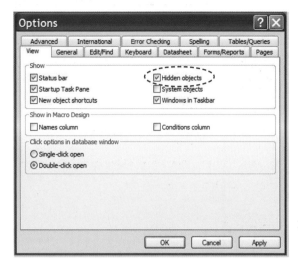

Figure 5.54 Activating hiding

Uncheck the **Hidden Objects** box and click on **Apply**. This will mean that the selected tables will no longer be visible on the main **Tables** tab (see Figure 5.55).

The same process applies to any of the objects on any of the tabs that you might choose to hide. Furthermore, if Show Hidden Objects (as in Figure 5.53) is already unchecked when further objects are hidden, they will simply disappear automatically. Obviously all objects can be recalled by choosing to check the Show Hidden Objects option.

3.4 Automation

Programmed routines, e.g. macros, scripts, program code

Automating actions and processes in the database certainly enhances and simplifies the experience for users and this unit already contains examples of program code (see Validation Activity in section 2.1) and using macros (see the Case Study in section 1.3).

Figure 5.55 Demonstrating absence of hidden tables (compare with Figure 5.53)

As seen in the case study, macros can be attached to events so that they are activated as a field or record is, for example, entered or exited.

Macros can also be attached to command buttons. One of the most common macros that developers create is a print macro that can be run to print a specific number of copies (see Figure 5.56).

The main advantage of creating macros rather than creating script or program code is that most of the work is done for you. In the macro shown in Figure 5.56 all the user needs to do is select the action from a drop-down list and then decide what to print, how many copies to print and the print quality.

Once created the macro is then attached to a command button. To create a button, simply open the chosen form in design view, then click on the **Command Button** icon in the **Toolbox** (see Figure 5.57).

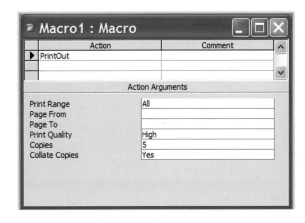

Figure 5.56 Print macro

Figure 5.57 Command button icon

Once clicked, you can draw a command button on the form (see Figure 5.58).

This will automatically open the **Command Button Wizard** where clicking **Miscellaneous** will reveal a number of actions from which you can choose. Select the **Run Macro** option and click **Next**.

The system will now present you with a list of available macros. Choose the one you wish to attach to the button by clicking on it, then click on **Next**. You will now be able to choose either to place a caption on the button (for example, Print) or pictures from which you can choose. Make your choice and click on **Next** and rename the button if you wish, or click on **Finish**.

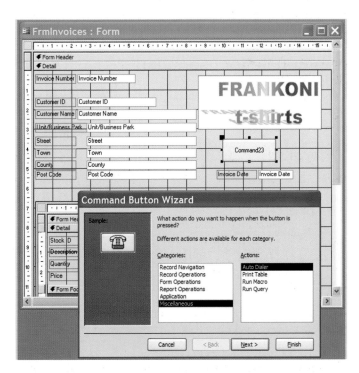

Figure 5.58 Adding a command button to activate the macro

When the user now switches to Form View, the button is visible and clicking on it will activate the macro that prints five copies of the form (see Figure 5.59).

Figure 5.59 Working form with print macro added

Clearly there are many actions that can be automated if required using whichever technique is more appropriate.

3.5 Evaluation criteria

Appropriate for user need

To be able to evaluate your database from any perspective, including whether or not the final solution is appropriate for user need, you will have a set of criteria against which you can carry out the evaluation. It will then usually require you to ask the user (or users) for feedback on the solution – its functionality, ease of use, efficiency, overall appearance etc.

Unit Link

If the database has been developed as part of a project, you will also need to evaluate the development process. For more on this topic see **Unit 4 – IT Project** in this publication.

3.6 Testing

Prior to beginning development, you will have been given a list of functionality in terms of user requirements that your final database would need to have.

Functionality

Functional aspects such as calculated fields, results of queries and reports, activation and actions of any macros, script or code should be carefully checked to make sure it works as intended.

A structured approach to this is needed and testing should have been planned at the outset.

Usually functionality testing will occur at two points – in real time as each piece of functionality is developed, then again when the whole system is tested.

Completing a testing log is essential to keep track of testing activities.

To ensure that the testing activities are as true to real use as possible, data used in the testing process should be carefully selected.

Unit Links

For more on planning testing, selecting test data and recording the results of testing, see the following units:

Unit 7 – Systems Analysis and Design, section 4, pages 180 to 184 of the **Core Text**.

Unit 4 – IT Project, section 4, pages 36 to 45 of this book.

Unit 18 – Principles of Software Design and Development, section 4, pages 283 to 289 of the **Core Text**.

Against user requirements

The user requirements list created at the start of the database development also needs to be checked against the functionality that is actually contained in the finished product.

Any omissions should be addressed.

Customer acceptance

Getting customer acceptance for your database solution at the end of your project is also essential. In the real world, final payment for the product may depend on your users confirming their acceptance of your solution.

Obtaining user acceptance usually requires the developer to carry out a series of interviews with an individual user, all users or selected users if the user group is extensive. In order to obtain the opinions of a very large group of users you would usually do this through a targeted questionnaire.

Some developers choose to use a questionnaire even with a small number of users as, if any problems have been found with the product, the developer will then have a formal record of the problems which will make maintenance easier to achieve.

Braincheck – Crossword

Complete the Database crossword. A solution is provided on page 434.

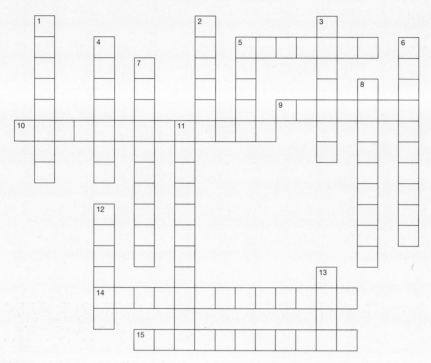

ACROSS

5 Automatic process for deleting or updating a record in a linked table when main record deleted or changed
9 The unique key in the linked table
10 The technique for organising data for a database, developed by Codd
14 The link between two tables
15 The S in SQL

DOWN

1 What a list does so that you can choose an input
2 Send data into another program or location
3 Coded contols that affect how data is input into certain fields
4 The unique key in a main table
5 Modify an interface
6 A relationship type that needs to be resolved
7 Code to check the correctness of inputs
8 A query type that requires a search term to be input by the user
11 An automated numeric key that changes incrementally
12 Bring data into a program from another location
13 Conceal

Activity – Normalisation – Safe Kitty Cattery

Normalise the form shown below.

Try not to cheat!

SAFE KITTY CATTERY

BOOKING FORM

Customer name ....

Address ....

Town ....

Telephone ....

Emergency Number ....

Start Date	End Date	Breed	Cat's Name	Inoculation Dates	Additional Information	Kennel Number

How well did you do? See page 435 for answers.

Activity – Normalisation – Great Tickets

Normalise the form shown below.

Try not to cheat!

GREAT TICKETS

Order Form

Order Number: [   ]   Order Date: [   ]

Customer Name   ....

Address   ....

                               ....

                               ....

                               ....

Postcode   ....

Telephone Number   ....

Despatch Method: [   ]   Payment Method: [   ]

Date Order Processed: [   ]   Processed by: [   ]

Event/Concert Name	Event Location	Date	Adult Tickets	Child Tickets	Concession Tickets	Total Number of Tickets

How well did you do? See page 436 for answers.

Achieving success

In order to achieve each unit you will complete a series of coursework activities. Each time you hand in work, your tutor will return this to you with a record of your achievement.

This particular unit has 13 criteria to meet: 6 Pass, 4 Merit and 3 Distinction.

For a **Pass**:

You must achieve **all** 6 Pass criteria.

For a **Merit**:

You must achieve **all** 6 Pass and **all** 4 Merit criteria.

For a **Distinction**:

You must achieve **all** 6 Pass, **all** 4 Merit **and** 3 Distinction criteria.

So that you can monitor your own progress and achievement in each unit, a recording grid has been provided (see below). The full version of this grid is also included on the companion CD.

Assignment	Assignments in this unit			
	U5.01	U5.02	U5.03	U5.04
Referral				
Pass				
1				
2				
3				
4				
5				
6				
Merit				
1				
2				
3				
4				
Distinction				
1				
2				
3				

Help with assessment

To **Pass** this unit you will be expected to demonstrate an understanding of the concepts of relational databases – what they are and what features they possess (why are they different from their flat file alternatives). You will need to show that you can design and implement a working relational database of at least five tables, setting up relationships, queries and reports, and demonstrating validation techniques and verification routines. You must demonstrate that you can import and export data to and from external locations. Finally you will be expected to carry out the modification of a previously implemented database by adding an additional table.

The **Merit** criteria further require you to explain the concepts of referential integrity and the purpose of primary keys in building the relationships between tables. You will be required to automate a function (this could be through a macro, script or code) and show that you understand the concept of cascade updating and deletion of records.

For a **Distinction** you will need to analyse errors in the design and construction of a database and explain how these errors could have been avoided. You will need to customise the user interface to meet the needs of a defined user or group of users and, finally, you will evaluate a database against required user needs.

Online resources on the CD

Key fact sheets
Electronic slide show of key points
Frankoni database

Further Reading

Hernandez, M., 2003, *Database Design for Mere Mortals: A Hands-on Guide to Relational Database Design*, *2nd Edition*, Addison Wesley, ISBN 0201752840.

Kroenke, D., 2004, *Database Concepts*, *2nd Edition*, Prentice Hall, ISBN 0131451413.

Ponniah, P., 2006, *Database Design and Development: An Essential Guide for IT Professionals: Visible Analyst Set*, John Wiley & Sons Inc., ISBN 0471760943.

Ritchie, C., 2002, *Relational Database Principles*, Thomson Learning, ISBN 0826457134.

Advanced Spreadsheet Skills

Capsule view

Advanced Spreadsheet Skills is a 60-hour unit that is designed to introduce you to some of the advanced features and functions of spreadsheets, particularly in relation to how spreadsheets are used to support organisational activities. The assumption is that you already understand the basic concepts of spreadsheets – that you understand terminology such as row, column, cell, range, and that you can use in-built formulae and can build basic formulae.

As a practical unit, there will be a significant emphasis on the hands-on use of spreadsheet software, with a consideration of spreadsheet technologies, such as the use of comma-separated value (csv) formatting to enable import and export of data into other files or applications.

A range of utilities that enhance the usefulness of spreadsheets will also be explored.

Learning aims

1 Understand how spreadsheets can be used to solve complex problems.
2 Be able to create technically complex spreadsheets that are well structured and fit for purpose.
3 Be able to use functions and formulae to solve complex problems.
4 Be able to create efficient automated and customisable spreadsheets that enable easy analysis and interpretation.

Braincheck – What do you already know?

The title of this unit is Advanced Spreadsheet Skills. As a progression unit that is intended to develop skills, this means that basic concepts will not be covered. You will be expected to understand some of the terminology already. To demonstrate your understanding, complete the following grid:

Term	Explanation
Row	
Column	
Cell	
Operators	
Formulae	
Function	
Parenthesis	
BODMAS	
Condition	
Simple Logical Operators	
Format	
Alignment	
Merge	
Range	

How well did you do? See pages 437 to 441 for answers.
Seek further information for any terms that you did not know or where your explanation was incorrect.

Unit Link

For more on the basic concepts of spreadsheets see **Unit 10 – Spreadsheet Software** in the following text:

BTEC First for ICT Practitioners course text by McGill, Fishpool & Fishpool (2006), published by Hodder Arnold, pages 232 to 275.

1 Understand how spreadsheets can be used to solve complex problems

Although computers have been doing calculations since they first came into existence, VisiCalc was in fact the first commercial spreadsheet program. Released in 1979, the technology grew quickly with more versions of spreadsheet software becoming available containing increasingly more complex functionality.

1.1 Uses of spreadsheets

So what are spreadsheets used for?

Manipulation of complex, mainly numeric data

Spreadsheets have changed the ways in which data can be manipulated and the speed with which calculations can be executed. Prior to the advent of spreadsheets, data users had to physically work with the numbers to calculate the answers and then had to decide how they would present the information. This could mean typing out tables of information on a typewriter, with the possibility of numbers being transposed or simply being typed incorrectly. There are a number of advantages to using spreadsheets:

◆ A simple change to a data item will mean that all numbers affected by the change will be automatically updated.

◆ Spreadsheets can be linked so that a change in one spreadsheet will automatically update numbers in another.

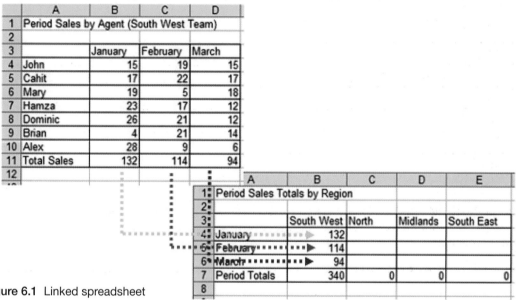

Figure 6.1 Linked spreadsheet

Figure 6.2 Updated linked spreadsheet

Two numbers are now changed – Brian's figure of four in January has risen to 17 and Cahit's figure of 17 in March has fallen to eight. The changes have been made in the Period Sales by Agent (South West Team) spreadsheet and have automatically updated the period Sales.

In a real situation, similar spreadsheets or files would have been developed for the North, Midlands and South East that would be similarly linked into the Period Sales Totals by Region file.

Although the range of functionality that can be applied to non-numeric data is more limited, as can be seen below, the agents in the first spreadsheets have been ordered alphabetically on the click of a button.

	A	B	C	D
1	Period Sales by Agent (South West Team)			
2				
3		January	February	March
4	Alex	28	9	6
5	Brian	17	21	14
6	Cahit	17	22	8
7	Dominic	26	21	12
8	Hamza	23	17	12
9	John	15	19	15
10	Mary	19	5	18
11	Total Sales	145	114	85

Figure 6.3 Alphabetical sort

Presentation of data to suit user and audience requirements

Note: care should be taken when sorting rows of figures, to ensure that the corresponding data on the remaining part of the row is also included in the sort when executed, otherwise the data will no longer be attributed to the correct agent (see highlighted area in Figure 6.4).

	A	B	C	D
1	Period Sales by Agent (South West Team)			
2				
3		January	February	March
4	Alex	28	9	6
5	Brian	17	21	14
6	Cahit	17	22	8
7	Dominic	26	21	12
8	Hamza	23	17	12
9	John	15	19	15
10	Mary	19	5	18
11	Total Sales	145	114	85

Figure 6.4 Selecting the data to sort

When preparing data using spreadsheets, it is the responsibility of the person generating the spreadsheet to ensure that the information is presented in such a way that it will suit the requirements of the audience.

In simplest terms, this might be adjusting font sizes to ensure that all the information is legible for someone with a visual impairment. It could require that the data be presented as a comparative chart like the one shown in Figure 6.5.

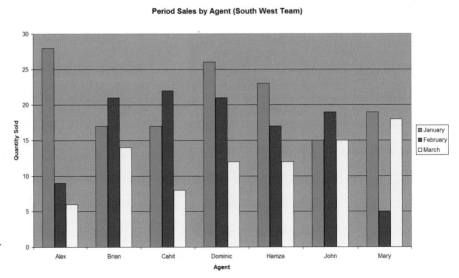

Period Sales by Agent (South West Team)

Figure 6.5 Comparison bar chart

Alternatively, the data users might wish to see a **comparison** of the total quantities sold between the various regions (see Figure 6.6).

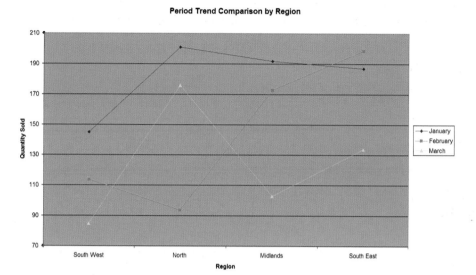

Figure 6.6 Trend comparison chart

Notice that the Y (vertical) **axis scale** has been adjusted to have a maximum value of 210 and a minimum of 70. This is so that more efficient use is made of the visual display area. To effect this, simply click on the axis itself and select **Format Axis** from the menu. Change the values in the **Minimum** and **Maximum** boxes as required.

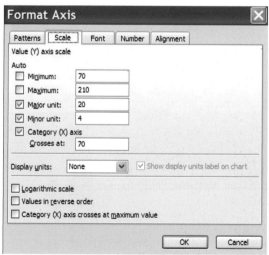

Figure 6.7 Format Axis dialogue box

The default Y axis values on this occasion had been set to a Maximum of 250 and a Minimum of 0 by default. How the graph would have looked had the Y axis scale not been changed can be seen in Figure 6.8.

Considering the needs of the audience is one of the most important skills that a spreadsheet developer needs to master. Reading more information about the principles of effective communication will help you to make important decisions about the presentation of spreadsheets.

Unit Links

For more on the principles of effective communication, see the companion **Core Text, Unit 1 – Communication and Employability Skills for IT**, section 2.1, pages 12 to 16. For more on making charts fit for purpose, see **Unit 3 – Information Systems**, also in the companion **Core Text**, section 1.1, pages 91 to 99.

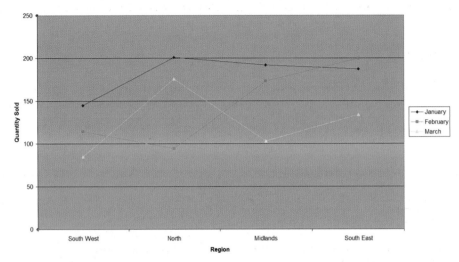

Figure 6.8 Trend comparison chart

Providing timely and accurate information to support decision making

In order for managers to be effective in making decisions about the organisation, they must be able to access information about the organisation and how it has been operating. They might also need to have information about the activities of competitors or stakeholders.

The types of decisions that the information will need to support are operational issues such as monitoring and controlling the organisation's activities or helping the organisation analyse the past and plan for the future.

Whatever the intended use of the information, its preparation should have been **timely** (to ensure that the data would be available for use at the right time) and **accurate** (correct and containing an appropriate level of detail; see section 2.2 later in this unit chapter).

Unit Link

For more on understanding how organisations use business information see **Unit 3 – Information Systems**, in the companion **Core Text**, section 2.1, pages 105 to 110.

How can the use of a spreadsheet help in the process?

Analysis of data

Being able to compare data sets from different operational periods, the same periods from different years or comparing performance against that of a competitor is vital in ensuring that an organisation is able to stay ahead.

Viewing the data in different ways can highlight discrepancies in performance because unusual occurrences can be easier to spot in a graph or chart than if they are merely numbers represented in a table. Look again at the table of data in Figure 6.4. Is it easy to spot that Mary had the lowest monthly quantity and Alex had the highest? Look again at the chart of the same data in Figure 6.5. Is it easier to spot this detail in the chart?

Being able to manipulate tables of data, whether this is making charts and graphs, ordering, sorting, filtering or summarising the data (see later in this unit chapter), makes data analysis a relatively simple process and enables users to understand their information in much more depth.

Goal seeking

This is part of the what-if analysis functionality and is a term that is almost contradictory because what you are using the spreadsheet for is to find a value that contributes to the calculation rather than simply calculating an end result. When using Goal Seek you are able to find one value by making alterations to another value. What does this really mean? The best way to understand it is possibly through the use of an example.

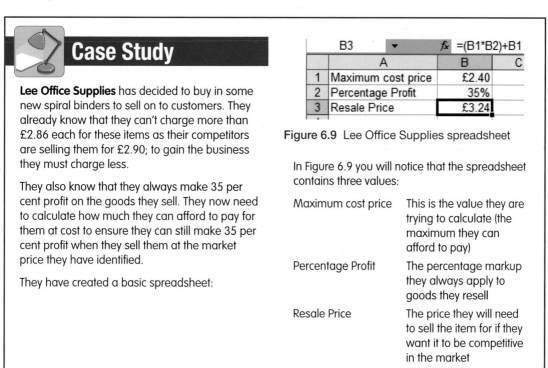

Case Study

Lee Office Supplies has decided to buy in some new spiral binders to sell on to customers. They already know that they can't charge more than £2.86 each for these items as their competitors are selling them for £2.90; to gain the business they must charge less.

They also know that they always make 35 per cent profit on the goods they sell. They now need to calculate how much they can afford to pay for them at cost to ensure they can still make 35 per cent profit when they sell them at the market price they have identified.

They have created a basic spreadsheet:

Figure 6.9 Lee Office Supplies spreadsheet

In Figure 6.9 you will notice that the spreadsheet contains three values:

Maximum cost price	This is the value they are trying to calculate (the maximum they can afford to pay)
Percentage Profit	The percentage markup they always apply to goods they resell
Resale Price	The price they will need to sell the item for if they want it to be competitive in the market

The only formula in the spreadsheet is in cell B3, which is

   (B1*B2)+B1

or (Maximum cost price * Percentage Profit) plus Maximum cost price

So far they have guessed at a number of maximum cost price figures that they thought could give them the actual resale price of £2.86. However, they haven't found the right value as yet.

They now decide to use the Goal Seek function. To do this, click on **Tools** then on **Goal Seek**. The following dialogue box appears:

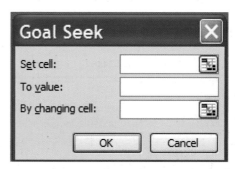

Figure 6.10 Goal Seek dialogue box

The figures and cell references now need to be completed. This is how to interpret the values to enter into the dialogue box:

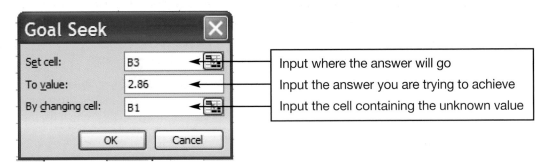

Figure 6.11 Inputting values into the dialogue box

Once these values have been input, click **OK**. The computer will now work incrementally through possible values until it finds a value for Maximum cost price that, when multiplied by the Percentage Profit will give the desired Resale Price.

Click **OK** to leave the Maximum cost price that has been calculated visible in cell B1.

While there are other ways to calculate the missing value without using Goal Seek, this is an easy-to-use, user-friendly interface that can quickly resolve these kinds of queries.

Figure 6.12 Solution found by the Goal Seek function

Case Study

Lee Office Supplies has been advised by its landlords that the rent on the business premises is set to rise by 20 per cent as from 1 April.

The spreadsheet, prior to the anticipated change is shown in Figure 6.13.

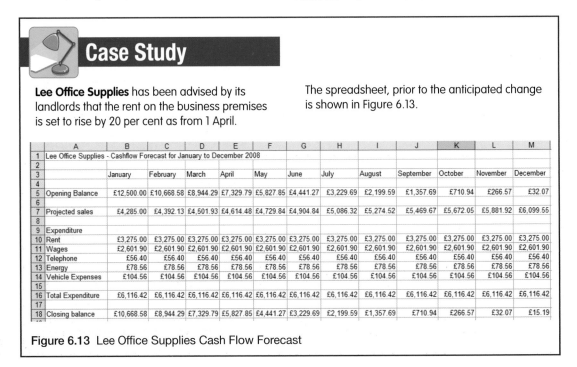

	A	B	C	D	E	F	G	H	I	J	K	L	M
1	Lee Office Supplies - Cashflow Forecast for January to December 2008												
2													
3		January	February	March	April	May	June	July	August	September	October	November	December
4													
5	Opening Balance	£12,500.00	£10,668.58	£8,944.29	£7,329.79	£5,827.85	£4,441.27	£3,229.69	£2,199.59	£1,357.69	£710.94	£266.57	£32.07
6													
7	Projected sales	£4,285.00	£4,392.13	£4,501.93	£4,614.48	£4,729.84	£4,904.84	£5,086.32	£5,274.52	£5,469.67	£5,672.05	£5,881.92	£6,099.55
8													
9	Expenditure												
10	Rent	£3,275.00	£3,275.00	£3,275.00	£3,275.00	£3,275.00	£3,275.00	£3,275.00	£3,275.00	£3,275.00	£3,275.00	£3,275.00	£3,275.00
11	Wages	£2,601.90	£2,601.90	£2,601.90	£2,601.90	£2,601.90	£2,601.90	£2,601.90	£2,601.90	£2,601.90	£2,601.90	£2,601.90	£2,601.90
12	Telephone	£56.40	£56.40	£56.40	£56.40	£56.40	£56.40	£56.40	£56.40	£56.40	£56.40	£56.40	£56.40
13	Energy	£78.56	£78.56	£78.56	£78.56	£78.56	£78.56	£78.56	£78.56	£78.56	£78.56	£78.56	£78.56
14	Vehicle Expenses	£104.56	£104.56	£104.56	£104.56	£104.56	£104.56	£104.56	£104.56	£104.56	£104.56	£104.56	£104.56
15													
16	Total Expenditure	£6,116.42	£6,116.42	£6,116.42	£6,116.42	£6,116.42	£6,116.42	£6,116.42	£6,116.42	£6,116.42	£6,116.42	£6,116.42	£6,116.42
17													
18	Closing balance	£10,668.58	£8,944.29	£7,329.79	£5,827.85	£4,441.27	£3,229.69	£2,199.59	£1,357.69	£710.94	£266.57	£32.07	£15.19

Figure 6.13 Lee Office Supplies Cash Flow Forecast

Scenarios

What-if scenarios can also be modelled using spreadsheet software. In this instance the values on the spreadsheet can be changed in order to forecast what will happen as a result of values changing.

As you can see, the previous projections show that the company will more or less break even if all goes as expected (without the increase in rent). Also, there is no evidence of a bank overdraft being required.

Now we modify the spreadsheet to reflect the change in rent from April with a 20 per cent rise from £3,275 to £3,930.

	A	B	C	D	E	F	G	H	I	J	K	L	M
1	Lee Office Supplies - Cashflow Forecast for January to December 2008												
2													
3		January	February	March	April	May	June	July	August	September	October	November	December
4													
5	Opening Balance	£12,500.00	£10,668.58	£8,944.29	£7,329.79	£5,172.85	£3,131.27	£1,264.69	-£420.41	-£1,917.31	-£3,219.06	-£4,318.43	-£5,207.93
6													
7	Projected sales	£4,285.00	£4,392.13	£4,501.93	£4,614.48	£4,729.84	£4,904.84	£5,086.32	£5,274.52	£5,469.67	£5,672.05	£5,881.92	£6,099.55
8													
9	Expenditure												
10	Rent	£3,275.00	£3,275.00	£3,275.00	£3,930.00	£3,930.00	£3,930.00	£3,930.00	£3,930.00	£3,930.00	£3,930.00	£3,930.00	£3,930.00
11	Wages	£2,601.90	£2,601.90	£2,601.90	£2,601.90	£2,601.90	£2,601.90	£2,601.90	£2,601.90	£2,601.90	£2,601.90	£2,601.90	£2,601.90
12	Telephone	£56.40	£56.40	£56.40	£56.40	£56.40	£56.40	£56.40	£56.40	£56.40	£56.40	£56.40	£56.40
13	Energy	£78.56	£78.56	£78.56	£78.56	£78.56	£78.56	£78.56	£78.56	£78.56	£78.56	£78.56	£78.56
14	Vehicle Expenses	£104.56	£104.56	£104.56	£104.56	£104.56	£104.56	£104.56	£104.56	£104.56	£104.56	£104.56	£104.56
15													
16	Total Expenditure	£6,116.42	£6,116.42	£6,116.42	£6,771.42	£6,771.42	£6,771.42	£6,771.42	£6,771.42	£6,771.42	£6,771.42	£6,771.42	£6,771.42
17													
18	Closing balance	£10,668.58	£8,944.29	£7,329.79	£5,172.85	£3,131.27	£1,264.69	-£420.41	-£1,917.31	-£3,219.06	-£4,318.43	-£5,207.93	-£5,879.81

Figure 6.14 Lee Office Supplies Revised Cash Flow Forecast

The picture now is very different, with the company slipping into overdraft in July 2008. By the end of the financial year the situation is far more serious, with a deficit of nearly £6,000. The organisation now has a number of choices:

◆ sell more products;
◆ reduce expenditure (this could mean reducing staff for example);
◆ refuse to accept the 20 per cent rise in rent;
◆ look for alternative accommodation.

Scenario-based forecasting is one of the most powerful tools to help managers make decisions about future actions.

Key Terms

Data mining is a term applied to software applications that help users drill down into their data to find exceptional events.

The graph in Figure 6.15 was produced from organisational data.

At a glance it is possible to see that something very unusual happened in August 2001 when production seemed to fall uncharacteristically low.

Using data-mining software, users are not only able to identify unusual events, but they can **drill down** into the data on increasing levels to find out why the data appeared to be so different to the expected normal parameters.

It could be that the company unusually closed down for two weeks in August, or that there was a natural disaster, or they were unable to get the raw materials to support widget production. Through

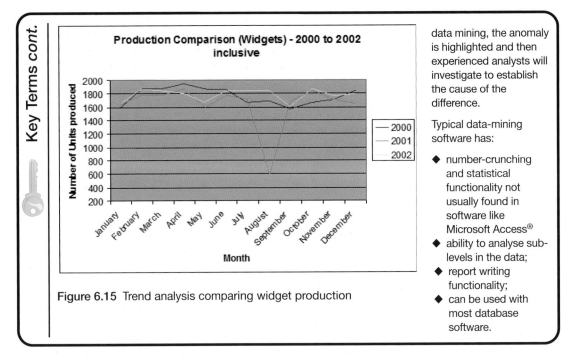

Figure 6.15 Trend analysis comparing widget production

data mining, the anomaly is highlighted and then experienced analysts will investigate to establish the cause of the difference.

Typical data-mining software has:

◆ number-crunching and statistical functionality not usually found in software like Microsoft Access®
◆ ability to analyse sub-levels in the data;
◆ report writing functionality;
◆ can be used with most database software.

1.2 Problem solving

With the advent of spreadsheets came the opportunity to set up templates to undertake a wide range of problem-solving tasks that would have previously been done by human beings using calculators, pens and paper. The following business problem-solving techniques are just some of the range of processes that can be automated using spreadsheet software.

Cash-flow forecasting

As shown in Figures 6.13 and 6.14, cash-flow forecasts are used to predict how certain events will impact on an organisation's financial situation. Simply by changing one or more of the variables, it is possible to see the effect that changes will have.

However, cash-flow forecasting often relies on best guesses, although with experience and historic information to support these hypotheses some guesses are likely to be more accurate than others.

Cash-flow forecasts are commonly done for a quarter, half year, whole year or a number of years. You should remember that the further into the future you attempt to forecast, the less likelihood of accuracy. This is because the further from the present you get, the more uncertainty there is because less is known about the future events.

Budget control

Another common use of spreadsheets is budget monitoring and control.

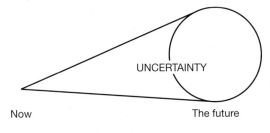

Figure 6.16 Predicting the future

The spreadsheet in Figure 6.17 shows the Temporary Staff Budget, controlled by the HR Manager at Lee Office Supplies. The year began with an opening budget allocation of £5,000 and a number of transactions have seen the balance fall to £1,255.05. This is the remaining amount available for the rest of the year. In the event that further temporary staff cover is needed, the HR manager will now have to make some decisions about whether to use all or some of the remaining budget, or try to make do without staff cover to retain the budget in the event that there is a more urgent need later in the year.

Figure 6.18 shows the formula view of the spreadsheet with the total for each line reduced by the cost on each subsequent line.

What-if scenarios

While the budget control spreadsheet is an example of dealing with **actual events** (things that really have happened), the power of spreadsheets is obvious when applying its techniques to extrapolate the results of what-if scenarios. Cash-flow forecasting shown earlier in this unit chapter is one example of using a spreadsheet to work out what will happen in the event that a certain criterion or set of criteria occurs.

But what-if scenarios can be used in other ways too that don't necessarily have anything directly to do with money. Here is an example:

Using a simple formula, the spreadsheet would be used to monitor the activity on the budget, recording the transactions and providing information about how much of the budget remains unspent. The example shown in Figure 6.17 is an example of a **reducing balance** spreadsheet.

A little like a bank statement, the budget period will begin with an **opening value**, then each transaction or budget allocation will be itemised, reducing the **balance remaining** accordingly.

Lee Office Supplies

1st January 2007 to 31st December 2007 - Temporary Staff Budget

Date	Nature of spend (and circumstances)	Cost	Balance
1st January 2007	Budget allocated		£5,000.00
11th April 2007	3 days to cover staff absence for training (Mike Kidd)	£684.99	£4,315.01
9th July 2007	10 days to cover key staff holiday (Alicia Franks)	£1,766.40	£2,548.61
20th August 2007	5 days to cover key staff holiday (Jack Cahalit)	£837.45	£1,711.16
11th October 2007	2 days to cover staff sickness (Ruth Gibbons)	£456.11	£1,255.05

Figure 6.17 Reducing balance budget control

	A	B	C	D
1	Lee Office Supplies			
2				
3	1st January 2007 to 31st December 2007 - Temporary Staff Budget			
4				
5	Date	Nature of spend (and circumstances)	Cost	Balance
6				
7	1st January 2007	Budget allocated		5000
8	11th April 2007	3 days to cover staff absence for training (Mike Kidd)	684.99	=D7-C8
9	9th July 2007	10 days to cover key staff holiday (Alicia Franks)	1766.4	=D8-C9
10	20th August 2007	5 days to cover key staff holiday (Jack Cahalit)	837.45	=D9-C10
11	11th October 2007	2 days to cover staff sickness (Ruth Gibbons)	456.11	=D10-C11
12				=D11-C12
13				=D12-C13
14				=D13-C14
15				=D14-C15
16				=D15-C16
17				=D16-C17
18				=D17-C18
19				=D18-C19
20				=D19-C20
21				=D20-C21
22				=D21-C22
23				=D22-C23
24				=D23-C24
25				=D24-C25
26				=D25-C26
27				=D26-C27
28				=D27-C28
29				=D28-C29
30				=D29-C30
31				=D30-C31

Figure 6.18 Reducing balance budget formula print

Question: If we adjust or change the formulation of our product (for whatever reason), how will our customers respond?

Here, the quantities of different components that make up the product could be changed. The spreadsheet would be used to record how the formulation of the product is changed and then to analyse the results of the post-change customer testing questionnaire.

Within the functionality of Microsoft Excel® is a **scenario** function that allows you to change figures in designated cells and see the results of changing the numbers.

Case Study

KRIS Arts and Media wishes to launch a new range of media products and services and has decided to put on a corporate event to introduce the developments, with an exhibition and a keynote speaker.

They have asked five different venues to provide information that they will now compare so that they can decide which of the venues to use for the event.

The venues and offers are:

Hellaby Hall

Cost of venue £800
Number of delegates 250
Cost per delegate for catering (optional) £5.40

ARMCC Centre

Cost of venue £710
Number of delegates 205
Cost per delegate for catering (optional) £5.30

Mitton Villa Conference Rooms

Cost of venue £1050
Number of delegates 275
Cost per delegate for catering (optional) £6.15

Bentham Meeting Centre

Cost of venue £890
Number of delegates 195
Cost per delegate for catering (optional) £6.55

JPF Suite

Cost of venue £685
Number of delegates 245
Cost per delegate for catering (optional) £5.70

When making a simple visual comparison it is difficult to decide which offer would be the most beneficial to KRIS Arts and Media. Initially, the JPF Suite is interesting because it has the lowest venue cost. But it isn't the lowest when it comes to the costs of catering.

Using the spreadsheet scenario functionality will help to compare these offers. This is how it's done.

Activity

This activity will walk you through using the **What-if** functionality.

1 Open a blank worksheet in Microsoft Excel®.

2 Now begin by entering the information for Hellaby Hall. See Figure 6.19.

	A	B
1	Venue	
2	Hellaby Hall	
3		Cost
4	Cost of Venue	£800.00
5	Number of delegates	250
6	Cost per delegate for catering	£5.40

Figure 6.19 Details for Hellaby Hall

3 In cell B8, calculate the Total Cost by taking B4 and adding the result of B5 multiplied by B6.

=B4+(B5*B6)

	A	B
1	**Venue**	
2	**Hellaby Hall**	
3		Cost
4	Cost of Venue	£800.00
5	Number of delegates	250
6	Cost per delegate for catering	£5.40
7		
8	Total cost	£2,150.00

Figure 6.20 Total Cost for Hellaby Hall

Figure 6.20 shows the total cost for Hellaby Hall. Save the file.

4 You are now going to use the scenarios functionality. With the spreadsheet still open, click on **Tools** then on **Scenarios** as shown in Figure 6.21.

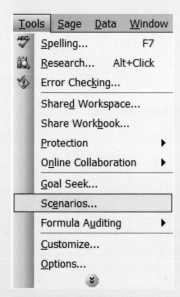

Figure 6.21 Finding the Scenarios function

5 This activates the **Scenario Manager** shown in Figure 6.22.

Figure 6.22 Scenario Manager

At present there are no defined scenarios, so we need to use this interface to process the details for each of the five offers from venues.

6 You must now select **Add** so that you can begin to add each of the offers (including Hellaby Hall). The Add dialogue box is shown in Figure 6.23.

Figure 6.23 Add Scenario dialogue box

a) Give the Scenario a name (best practice would be to give it the venue name, e.g. Hellaby).

b) You now need to click into the Changing cells box and click one by one into each of the cells that will change, separating them with a comma (remember the name of the venue will also be one of the values that will need to change and the total cost), see Figure 6.24.

Figure 6.24 First scenario is added (notice five cells will change)

Once you have done this, click on **OK**. The details for Hellaby Hall will appear, click immediately on **OK** as you need to retain the details originally entered for this venue, see Figure 6.25.

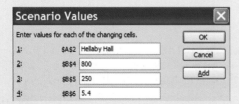

Figure 6.25 Figures entered for Hellaby Hall

Now click on **OK**.

7 The dialogue box will now change and will show the first of the scenarios you have added, as shown in Figure 6.26.

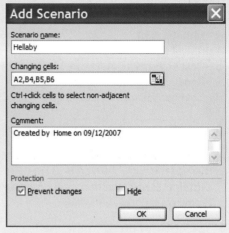

Figure 6.26 First scenario added

8 Repeat the process for the remaining four venues. The Scenario Manager will now look like the image in Figure 6.27.

Figure 6.27 All scenarios added

9 To view all scenarios simultaneously, click on **Tools**, then on **Scenarios** and finally on **Summary**. Make sure that the **Scenario summary** report type is selected.

So that the totals are visible on the comparative summary, in the **Results cells** key in the position of the totals calculation – B8.

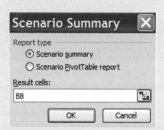

Figure 6.28 Set up the summary

Click on **OK**. You will now notice that the spreadsheet has gained an additional worksheet named **Scenario Summary**.

10 Open this spreadsheet, adjust the columns accordingly – hiding any data you do not wish to be seen on the print, adjusting column widths and alignment as required.

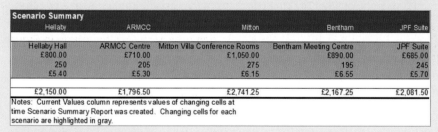

Scenario Summary				
Hellaby	ARMCC	Mitton	Bentham	JPF Suite
Hellaby Hall	ARMCC Centre	Mitton Villa Conference Rooms	Bentham Meeting Centre	JPF Suite
£800.00	£710.00	£1,050.00	£890.00	£685.00
250	205	275	195	245
£5.40	£5.30	£6.15	£6.55	£5.70
£2,150.00	£1,796.50	£2,741.25	£2,167.25	£2,081.50

Notes: Current Values column represents values of changing cells at time Scenario Summary Report was created. Changing cells for each scenario are highlighted in gray.

Figure 6.29 Summary view

It is now easy to compare the venue offers and the anticipated costs. However, this does not take into account how many delegates KRIS Arts and Media believe will attend their event.

Sales forecasting

Forecasting future sales usually uses the results of analysing historical data and using it to predict the future. It could also incorporate the results of marketing activities or national statistics on anticipated growth. The potential for activity in the housing market, for example, is predicted based on how interest rates are expected to behave, which affects the cost of borrowing and thus the individual's ability to get a mortgage.

Let's consider a simpler example:

An ice cream manufacturer uses historic customer buying patterns to establish that the sale of ice cream is higher than the monthly average at Easter, again at Christmas, and is higher still in the summer months of June to August (inclusive). The graph in Figure 6.30 shows how this might look.

Based on this historic data, if the organisation now feels that, through the introduction of new product lines, it will be able to increase sales to in excess of £2m in January, applying the same expected buying patterns will place sales in the summer months to well over £3m at their peak.

Forecasting is one of the most useful tools an organisation has to support it in planning its future activities.

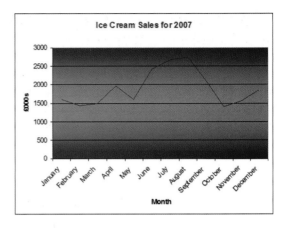

Figure 6.30 Ice cream sales analysis

Payroll projections

Organisations generally pay staff in two ways:

◆ Some staff work set hours each week or month and their pay does not change. In this instance the organisation will always know in advance how much it will need to pay its employees and when.
◆ In some organisations some or all of the employees are paid a variable amount each week or month. This might be linked to production or sales performance, requirements for overtime to cover particular jobs or job roles, special projects and so on.

For most organisations, payroll will be a combination of both of the above. We should not forget, however, that there may be times when an organisation needs to buy in the services of temporary staff – to enable a specific project or support increased activity for example.

In terms of projecting the payroll requirements for those staff that are variably paid, spreadsheets that calculate pay against expected sales or production, for example, will help organisations plan and ensure that there is sufficient money in the bank to pay employees when necessary.

Statistical analysis

While a range of statistical functions such as STDEV (Standard Deviation) are readily available in Microsoft Excel® to help you carry out routine statistical analysis, there are also a series of Data Analysis tools that provide additional analytical functionality and that can be made available in Microsoft Excel® through loading the Analysis ToolPak. This is not usually included with a standard installation, but can be added later.

Trend analysis

As with forecasting, trend analysis uses historical data to make decisions about past events, enabling managers to apply lessons learned to future situations. Data mining, as suggested earlier, uses data to analyse trends and highlight unusual or exceptional events. Further analysis is then possible to establish the reasons behind particular situations.

2 Create technically complex spreadsheets that are well structured and fit for purpose

The key to ensuring that spreadsheets are fit for purpose is making sure that all rows and columns are fully readable, that they have appropriate headings and that where a series of linked spreadsheets are used the formats used are consistently applied across all worksheets. This means that they should share common fonts, font sizes, headings and layout.

2.1 Complexity

Multiple pages and cells linked between pages

Earlier in this unit we suggested that values in one spreadsheet could be dynamically linked to values in another spreadsheet in the same workbook, or even with another workbook. In Figure 6.31 the formula for the North production totals is in fact a value that exists in a file named Linked Workbook 2.xls, on Sheet 1, in cell B15.

B2		f_x	='[Linked Workbook 2.xls]Sheet1'!B15

	A	B	C	D	E	F
1		Production				
2	North	43315				
3	South					
4	East					
5	West					
6	Midlands					

Figure 6.31 Spreadsheet drawing a value from a linked workbook

Any values that are linked **within** a **workbook** will be **immediately updated** when the values they are linked to change.

With values **linked** in **other workbooks**, these will be **updated when** the workbook is **opened**, at least the user has the option to update or not update (to see the data without any changes having been made).

Figure 6.32 Excel's warning regarding linking to another workbook

If the user does select to update the spreadsheet, they will need to save again on exit to make sure the updates are retained.

Complex formulae

Over the years there has been significant disagreement about what constitutes a complex formula. In defining the word complex you may find any of the following phrases used: complicated, multiple parts, related components.

In general, a simple formula can be considered to have one or maybe two parts. A complex formula will have at least two parts.

Example of a simple formula:

Invoice total = Quantity purchased * price + VAT

Example of a complex formula:

Invoice total = (quantity purchased * price) – discount (if conditions met) + VAT

Large data sets

When you consider that a single worksheet contains 256 columns and 65,536 rows, this multiplies out to 16,777,216 cells in a single worksheet, although it is unlikely that all of these cells would contain values. Some columns and rows are left blank to enhance the appearance of the spreadsheet.

Examples of large data sets could include the following:

◆ a sheet of wage calculations for 2000 employees in a factory including gross figures and deductions;
◆ a stock printout for all items held in stock containing the current stock totals, cost price and overall stock values;
◆ sales information from a supermarket's checkouts at the end of each day;
◆ the results of marketing surveys.

In the real world you will find many more examples.

2.2 Accuracy

Check spreadsheets, e.g. user testing, correct calculations with results displayed at appropriate level of detail

One important part of spreadsheet development is checking the spreadsheet.

First, columns should be made wide enough to accommodate all headings and the numbers themselves. Ensure that columns are not made so narrow that a leading digit is masked by the column to the left. If columns are not wide enough to accommodate the data within them, the numbers are shown as hashes. Widening the column will bring the values back into view.

The results of calculations should also be carefully checked. Using alternative means of calculating the answers, such as a pen and paper or a calculator, is necessary to formally test the spreadsheet to ensure that formulae and functions are working as they should.

	A	B	C	D	E	F	G
1	Lee Office Supplies - Cashflow Forecast for January to December 2008						
2							
3		January	February	March	April	May	June
4							
5	Opening Ba	######	£10,668.58	######	£7,329.79	######	######
6							
7	Projected sa	######	£4,392.13	######	£4,614.48	######	######
8							
9	Expenditure						
10	Rent	######	£3,275.00	######	£3,930.00	######	######
11	Wages	######	£2,601.90	######	£2,601.90	######	######
12	Telephone	£56.40		£56.40	£56.40	£56.40	£56.40	£56.40
13	Energy	£78.56		£78.56	£78.56	£78.56	£78.56	£78.56
14	Vehicle Exp	£104.56		£104.56	£104.56	£104.56	£104.56	£104.56
15							
16	Total Expen	######	£6,116.42	######	£6,771.42	######	######
17							
18	Closing bala	######	£8,944.29	######	£5,172.85	######	######

Figure 6.33 Hashes indicate columns should be widened

In addition, developers need to make decisions about the level of detail required in the numbers that are displayed.

With spreadsheets containing British currency, for example, there may be little point in displaying numbers to three decimal places – for example £15.947 – because no physical currency exists for 0.7 pence. On the other hand, there will be instances where it is appropriate to display values to five or more decimal places.

Lifesavers

Before using a spreadsheet, or passing it to someone else for use, check the following:

Does the spreadsheet have an appropriate heading?
Are the columns the correct width to display all headings and values?
Are the number of decimal places displayed appropriate?
Are the number of decimal places displayed consistent over the spreadsheet?
If colours are used, do they enhance presentation?
Are colours, fonts, other enhancements etc. consistent throughout the spreadsheet?

2.3 Structure and fitness for purpose

You should be aware that when working in industry or commerce, some organisations will have their own templates or house styles that dictate the way spreadsheets (and other organisational documents) are constructed and presented.

While studying your BTEC National, unless specified, the choice of structure is yours. However, be prepared to justify your choices!

Formatting, e.g. integer, real, date, currency, text

Whichever format you choose for numbers, dates textual displays, you should ensure consistency in the use of the format. Here, we will briefly look at some format choices that you could make.

Format choice	Description
Integer	An integer is a whole number with no decimal parts – for example the numbers 7, 63 or 1507. Sometimes, particularly when you are displaying many numbers containing thousands, it might be helpful to include a comma after the leading number – so 1,507. If you do this, make sure you do it consistently for all affected numbers throughout the document.
Real	A real is a number with a decimal part – for example the numbers 2.5, 18.979 or 6,397.49795. You should make sure that you choose a display that is appropriate in terms of the level of detail you need to show.
Date	There are a number of date formats for you to use in the preparation of a spreadsheet. One aspect you should always remember, however, is that not all countries display day, month and year in the same order as in the UK. For example, in the US and parts of Europe, the month precedes the day.

Format choice	Description
Date *Cont.*	There are many different formats for dates – here are some examples: 08/04/1960 1960-04-08 08 April 1960 08/04/60 8-Apr-60
Currency	Currencies are usually preceded with a symbol that indicates what the currency is. For example a £ sign precedes values to denote UK currency – £14.99. Dollars (American for example) will be preceded by $, although there are a number of other countries in the world that have adopted the dollar as their currency. The symbol for the euro € is beginning to appear on many European keyboards, and can either be inserted through selecting a symbol in Microsoft Excel® or through the Alt Gr + 4 key.
Text	Text can be manipulated in many ways, some of which follow in the next section, but the choice of the font is also an important decision. **Serif** fonts are described as **having embellishments** and flourishes. These can be additional lines or curves. **Sans Serif** fonts are those **without embellishments**. Text set in **proportional fonts** allows each character to occupy a different amount of space, depending on which character it is. For example Bristol – the character 'i' uses less space than the remaining letters. W and M tend usually take up most space. Using **non-proportional** fonts (often also referred to as fixed fonts) will ensure that each character will be allowed to occupy the same amount of space. Let's compare the two: **Wiltshire** `Wiltshire` The former is proportional, the latter non-proportional or fixed.

Formatting to ensure fitness for purpose, e.g. bold, italics, borders, shading, column alignment, consistency

Additional formatting options are available to further enhance the presentation of a spreadsheet. These should be used carefully as the application of too many formats simultaneously can detract from the overall intention of the spreadsheet, which is to impart information.

Format choice	Description
Bold	**This text has been emboldened. This means it has been thickened to make it stand out.**
Italics	*Italicised text usually leans to the right. This draws the reader's attention to particular words or phrases.*
Borders	Borders can be used around specific cells to make them stand out. 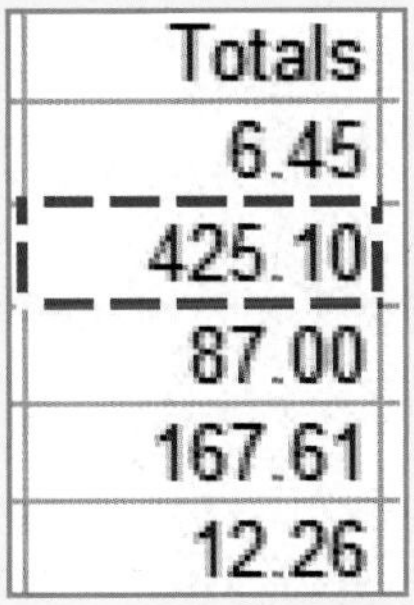 Figure 6.34 Borders
Shading	Shading can similarly make individual cells stand out – in this instance the shading has been applied to a cell containing a heading. 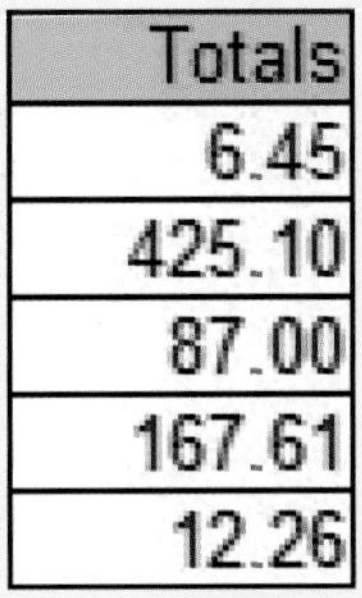 Figure 6.35 Shading
Column alignment	All data in a single column should be carefully aligned to make sure it appears to be tidy. This text is left aligned This text is right aligned This text is centred The same options can be applied to tables of numbers, although traditionally these will be right aligned – in fact if you enter numbers into a cell in Microsoft Excel® the system automatically aligns the numbers to the right by default.

Format choice	Description
Consistency	Whichever formats you choose to apply when developing your spreadsheet, you should ensure that they are applied consistently across the column, the row and ultimately the spreadsheet. Which looks better?

Totals		Totals
6.4525		6.45
425.1		425.10
87		87.00
167.61		167.61
12.258		12.26

Figure 6.36 Non-aligned   **Figure 6.37** Aligned

You will agree that Figure 6.37 is presented in a more appealing way.

To meet the needs of a particular user and context

As the range of possible user needs and potential contexts will be extensive, it is clearly difficult to define here. What would be most appropriate would be for you to look at examples of spreadsheets and decide how effective you think they are for the audience for which they are intended. Different approaches and ways of looking at these issues have already been covered in depth in **Unit 1**.

Unit Link

For more on adapting documentation and presentation style to suit a range of audiences see **Unit 1 – Communication and Employability Skills in IT**, which can be found in the companion **Core Text**, pages 1 to 44.

2.4 Alternative formats

Converting spreadsheet files to other formats to enable exporting

For the occasions when you might want to export an entire spreadsheet file, Microsoft Excel® offers you the opportunity to save the files in different formats.

To save in a different format, you merely need to choose a different file type when going through the save process.

A range of possible formats is now explored here:

Format choice	Description
xls	An eXceL Spreadsheet . This is the default format applied when you save a spreadsheet in Microsoft Excel®.
csv	This stands for Comma-Separated Value. If you save a spreadsheet in this format, the cells are separated by commas, and a new line denotes the beginning of a new line in the spreadsheet. Here is the spreadsheet that was used to make the graph in Figure 6.30:

Ice Cream Sales for 2007			
			Percentage of total
Month	£000s		sales
January	1597		7
February	1438		6
March	1499		7
April	1957		9
May	1586		7
June	2417		11
July	2683		12
August	2751		12
September	2100		9
October	1414		6
November	1563		7
December	1866		8
Total	22871		100

Figure 6.38 .xls format

The file has now been saved as a .csv file and imported into Microsoft Word®. This is how the file now looks:

```
Ice Cream Sales for 2007,,,

Month,£000s,,Percentage of total sales
January,1597,,7
February,1438,,6
March,1499,,7
April,1957,,9
May,1586,,7
June,2417,,11
July,2683,,12
August,2751,,12
September,2100,,9
October,1414,,6
November,1563,,7
December,1866,,8

Total,22871,,100
```

Figure 6.39 .csv format

Format choice	Description
txt	This format is a simple text file. The same ice cream sales graph has now been saved in this format and the new file imported into Microsoft Word®. This is how the content of the file looks now: ``` Ice Cream Sales for 2007 Month £000s Percentage of total sales January 1597 7 February 1438 6 March 1499 7 April 1957 9 May 1586 7 June 2417 11 July 2683 12 August 2751 12 September 2100 9 October 1414 6 November 1563 7 December 1866 8 Total 22871 100 ``` In this instance, the commas are missing and an attempt has been made by the software to align the information using default tabs. **Figure 6.40** .txt format
html	The HyperText Markup Language format option prepares the data to be used in the creation of web pages.

Remember that each of the formats will present the file in the file management system with a different icon, as shown in Figure 6.41.

What you should notice is that while the file extensions are different for each format, the file name can actually remain the same!

Ice Cream sales.csv   Ice Cream sales.txt   Ice Cream sales.xls

Figure 6.41 Different file type icons

3 Use functions and formulae to solve complex problems

3.1 Features and functions

Use of named ranges to identify areas of a spreadsheet

As suggested earlier in this unit, most spreadsheet software also has limited database capabilities. This can be extremely useful if you need to automatically insert values based on other input values.

Let's look at an example from Lee Office Supplies.

	A	B	C
1			
2	Product Code	Description	Resale Price
3	AB101	Ring Binder A4	2.79
4	AB102	Ring Binder Foolscap	3.01
5	AB306	Ring Binder A5 Landscape	3.74
6	BF397	Fine Line Pen Mixed (Box)	6.50
7	BF440	Fine Line Pen Blue (Box)	6.70
8	BF441	Fine Line Pen Black (Box)	6.70
9	BF449	Fine Line Pen Red (Box)	6.70
10	MR738	A4 Paper White 80gms	3.80
11	MR821	A4 Paper White 100gms	4.36
12	MR910	A4 Paper Cream 100gms	5.12
13	ZR997	Stapeler	3.99
14	ZR999	Hole Punch	4.74

Figure 6.42 Data extract imported from Microsoft Access®

First, we need to imagine that they are using a standard Microsoft Access® database to record stock information and stock transactions. Some or all of the data could be exported into a spreadsheet to provide information that can then be searched and further information extracted. In the data sample shown in Figure 6.42, 12 records have been copied and pasted into the spreadsheet, with their Product Code, Description and Resale Price visible. The detail has been pasted into Sheet 2 of a workbook, starting at cell A2.

The area of the spreadsheet that contains this data can be referred to in two ways:

A2:C14   cell reference for the range
StockInfo   name that applies to the whole area

What is the main advantage of naming the range? Simply that keying in row numbers and column identifiers each time you need a formula or function in the spreadsheet to refer to the designated area is prone to keying errors. In the event that the incorrect name is keyed in, nothing will happen because the name, incorrectly spelt, would not exist in its own right.

So how do you name a range? First, highlight the area that includes the cells you want as part of the range.

Then click on **Insert** as shown in Figure 6.43.

Now click on **Define**.

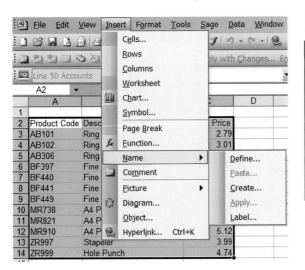

Figure 6.44 Defining the range

Figure 6.43 Naming the range

You will notice that the system has inserted a suggested name for the range – in this case **Product_Code** which is taken from the content of the cell in the upper left corner of the range. You will also notice that the area you highlighted has been displayed in the bottom of the dialogue box.

To input your own name for the range, simply delete the words Product_Code and insert StockInfo. Click on **OK**. The area has now been named.

If you now move to other sheets, you will see the named range appear as one of the available options in the **Name Box** in any of the spreadsheets in the same workbook, although you should be aware that the option will not be available via this method in other workbooks. When this is visible, clicking on it will automatically take you to the range in the appropriate sheet.

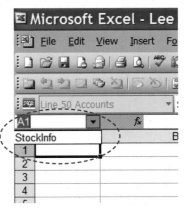

Figure 6.45 Name Box display containing the newly created named range

Now, in Sheet 1 we will set up the items part of an invoice with a table containing the Product Code, Description of the item, the Quantity purchased, the Price of the item and the Total.

We now want the Description of the item and the Price to be automatically inserted based on the Product Code as input by the user.

To do this we use the VLOOKUP (vertical look up) function. It works like this:

VLOOKUP(cell, range, column)

or

Look up the contents of the **cell** in the identified **range** and input the data for the **column** listed.

To insert the description once the Product Code has been inserted would be achieved with the following:

= VLOOKUP(A2,StockInfo,2)

When executed the system would perform a vertical lookup (looking down the first column of values in the named range, comparing the value on each line in the first column to the value in the designated cell, then extracting the relevant value in column 2.

	A	B	C	D	E
1	Product Code	Description	Quantity	Price	Total
2		=VLOOKUP(A2,StockInfo,2)		=VLOOKUP(A2,StockInfo,3)	=C2*D2
3		=VLOOKUP(A3,StockInfo,2)		=VLOOKUP(A3,StockInfo,3)	=C3*D3
4		=VLOOKUP(A4,StockInfo,2)		=VLOOKUP(A4,StockInfo,3)	=C4*D4
5		=VLOOKUP(A5,StockInfo,2)		=VLOOKUP(A5,StockInfo,3)	=C5*D5
6		=VLOOKUP(A6,StockInfo,2)		=VLOOKUP(A6,StockInfo,3)	=C6*D6
7		=VLOOKUP(A7,StockInfo,2)		=VLOOKUP(A7,StockInfo,3)	=C7*D7
8		=VLOOKUP(A8,StockInfo,2)		=VLOOKUP(A8,StockInfo,3)	=C8*D8
9		=VLOOKUP(A9,StockInfo,2)		=VLOOKUP(A9,StockInfo,3)	=C9*D9
10		=VLOOKUP(A10,StockInfo,2)		=VLOOKUP(A10,StockInfo,3)	=C10*D10
11		=VLOOKUP(A11,StockInfo,2)		=VLOOKUP(A11,StockInfo,3)	=C11*D11
12		=VLOOKUP(A12,StockInfo,2)		=VLOOKUP(A12,StockInfo,3)	=C12*D12
13		=VLOOKUP(A13,StockInfo,2)		=VLOOKUP(A13,StockInfo,3)	=C13*D13
14		=VLOOKUP(A14,StockInfo,2)		=VLOOKUP(A14,StockInfo,3)	=C14*D14
15		=VLOOKUP(A15,StockInfo,2)		=VLOOKUP(A15,StockInfo,3)	=C15*D15
16		=VLOOKUP(A16,StockInfo,2)		=VLOOKUP(A16,StockInfo,3)	=C16*D16
17		=VLOOKUP(A17,StockInfo,2)		=VLOOKUP(A17,StockInfo,3)	=C17*D17
18		=VLOOKUP(A18,StockInfo,2)		=VLOOKUP(A18,StockInfo,3)	=C18*D18
19		=VLOOKUP(A19,StockInfo,2)		=VLOOKUP(A19,StockInfo,3)	=C19*D19
20		=VLOOKUP(A20,StockInfo,2)		=VLOOKUP(A20,StockInfo,3)	=C20*D20
21		=VLOOKUP(A21,StockInfo,2)		=VLOOKUP(A21,StockInfo,3)	=C21*D21

Figure 6.46 Automated lookup in a named range

A similar formula is added to the Price column; the Total formula is simply the quantity multiplied by the price as looked up in column D.

When using this spreadsheet the user will simply need to insert the Product Code and the Quantity.

However, when you switch back from the formula view to normal view, you will notice that because there are no values in either the Product Code and Quantity columns, the formulae have returned the error message #N/A (see Figure 6.47). If you were to print this now, you would have #N/As visible on the print.

	A	B	C	D	E
1	Product Code	Description	Quantity	Price	Total
2		#N/A		#N/A	#N/A
3		#N/A		#N/A	#N/A
4		#N/A		#N/A	#N/A
5		#N/A		#N/A	#N/A
6		#N/A		#N/A	#N/A
7		#N/A		#N/A	#N/A
8		#N/A		#N/A	#N/A
9		#N/A		#N/A	#N/A
10		#N/A		#N/A	#N/A
11		#N/A		#N/A	#N/A
12		#N/A		#N/A	#N/A
13		#N/A		#N/A	#N/A
14		#N/A		#N/A	#N/A
15		#N/A		#N/A	#N/A
16		#N/A		#N/A	#N/A
17		#N/A		#N/A	#N/A
18		#N/A		#N/A	#N/A
19		#N/A		#N/A	#N/A
20		#N/A		#N/A	#N/A
21		#N/A		#N/A	#N/A

Figure 6.47 Normal view showing error messages due to absence of data in column A

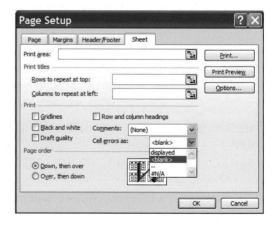

Figure 6.48 Supressing the error messages

Clearly, seeing these is useful when you are working with the spreadsheet, but you would not want them visible on any print that could be seen by a customer.

While the error messages cannot be suppressed in the normal view, they can be suppressed when printing. To do this, click on **File** then on **Page Setup** then click on the **Sheet** tab.

The default choice is to **display** the cell errors. From the drop-down list, select <**blank**>.

Now, through adding borders and shading to the original spreadsheet and pressing **Print Preview** you can see that error message are not visible.

Note. In order for the lookup function to work as intended, the data in the first column of the named range must be stored in alphabetical and/or numeric order. Also, you should be aware that if the user keys in a value that does not exist in the range, the previous good value will be used instead. Referring again to Figure 6.42, if the user were to key in a Product Code of AB201, the system would return the values for AB102 as the last known correct value in the list. For this reason, numbering products sequentially without any gaps would be essential.

Product Code	Description	Quantity	Price	Total
BF441	Fine Line Pen Black (Box)	7	6.70	46.90
ZR999	Hole Punch	2	4.74	9.48
MR738	A4 Paper White 80gms	5	3.80	19.00

Figure 6.49 Print preview showing error messages have been suppressed

Sharing files and data between users and tracking changes

If you need to share spreadsheet files and data with other users it is essential that changes are tracked.

Figure 6.50 Enabling the Share Workbook facility

In order to share a particular workbook you will need to enable sharing activity as this is usually locked by default. To enable sharing you need to have the spreadsheet file open, then click on **Tools** and then on **Share Workbook** (see Figure 6.50).

You will then need to check the Allow changes by more than one user at the same time option.

The second tab labelled Advanced on this dialogue box allows you to select a range of tracking and updating options, such as whether changes are recorded for tracking purposes, for how many days these records should be retained, and importantly whose changes should take priority in the event that there is a conflict between users (see Figure 6.51).

If appropriate you can also share files through a shared workspace, using the **Tools**, **Shared Workspace** options on the menu.

Figure 6.51 Tracking changes to the file

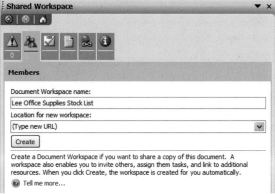

Figure 6.52 Sharing your workspace

Security issues

Ensuring that the data in a spreadsheet is secure can be achieved through two main ways:

◆ applying a password to a particular sheet or to the whole workbook, as shown in Figure 6.53;
◆ being selective about those to whom you give access and making sure that if they leave the organisation, their permissions are revoked.

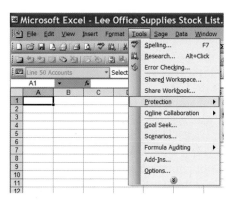

Figure 6.53 Protecting and setting up file sharing

Configuring the user interface

As with most software, the user interface can be configured to personalise the user's workspace.

◆ buttons or options can be added to particular menus or toolbars;
◆ new menus can be created containing all the commands the user needs most regularly.

Creating new menus is relatively straightforward:

Clicking on **Tools** then on **Customize**, click on the **Commands** tab and scroll down the **Categories** list until you come to New Menu (see Figure 6.54).

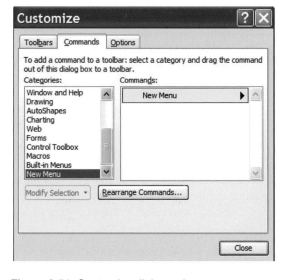

Figure 6.54 Customize dialogue box

With **New Menu** clicked and holding down the left mouse button, drag **New Menu** onto the menu bar (see Figure 6.55).

Once placed, right clicking the **New Menu** option will allow you to rename the menu (see Figure 6.56).

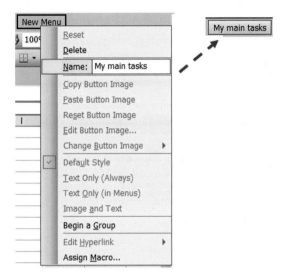

Figure 6.56 Renaming the new menu

Figure 6.55 Placing the New Menu

As with the process for creating a new menu, toolbars can also be created that hold a selection of icons that are specific to a user.

To remove a menu, click on **Tools** then on **Customize**. It is then simply a case of clicking and dragging the menu option back onto the **Customize dialogue box** to remove it from the options visible.

Use of add-ins

Figure 6.57 Adding in functionality

A range of add-ins for less popular functionality is also available. These features are not usually installed during a standard installation but can be added in at any time. To access this functionality, click on **Tools** then on **Add-ins** (as shown in Figure 6.57).

When you choose to run the required add-in and click on **OK**, if the functionality is not installed an error message will appear as shown in Figure 6.58.

Figure 6.58 Error

You will now be offered the opportunity to add the functionality, so click on **Yes**. Be aware, however, that you will probably be asked to reinsert the installation disks as shown in Figure 6.59.

If the disks are not available, you will not be able to install the features.

Figure 6.59 Prompt to reinsert the installation disks

Use a range of in-built functions, e.g. cell functions, lookup functions, text functions or statistical functions

A range of in-built functions is provided in most spreadsheet software that is accessed through the **Insert** menu, **Function** option.

These functions are readily available and can be used at any time. The list of functions, however, is numerous, and to begin to explain the individual categories and the functions themselves would take up an entire book in its own right. As a rule of thumb, if you need to use a function, check first whether it is available within the software before you begin to develop your own formula.

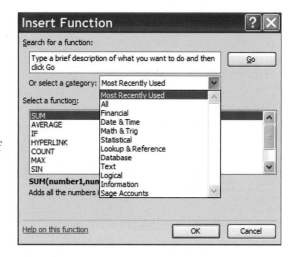

Figure 6.60 Using in-built functions

3.2 Formulae

Use relative and absolute cell references

When formulae are created they are developed with either relative or absolute cell referencing. What does this actually mean?

In order to understand this we need to appreciate what happens to formulae when they are **copied** and **pasted** into other cells or locations.

Here is an extract from a small spreadsheet:

	A	B	C	Formulae in column C
1	19	3	16	=A1 – B1
2	17	6	11	=A2 – B2
3	42	26	16	=A3 – B3
4	106	33	73	=A4 – B4

What we did (having keyed data into cells A1 to B4), was to input the following formula into cell **C1.**

= A1 – B1

We then **copied** and **pasted** the cells **down** as far as cell C4.

As we did so the formulae **adjusted themselves** dynamically and automatically to **accommodate** the **changing row numbers**:

Formulae in column C	
=A1 – B1	A1 to
=A2 – B2	A2 to
=A3 – B3	A3 to
=A4 – B4	A4

This is known as **relative** referencing because, as each cell is pasted into the next position, the software automatically changes all parts of the formula **relative** to the **last cell position**.

There are times, however, when **we do not want** the formula to change like this.

Look at the following example:

	A	B	C
1	7	6	42
2	22		132
3	5		30
4	18		108

Formulae in column C
= A1 * **B1**
= A2 * **B1**
= A3 * **B1**
= A4 * **B1**

Here cell **B1** contains a value that needs to be used (known as referencing) in **every calculation**. Without applying **absolute cell referencing**, as we **copy** and **paste** the cells **down** column C, B1 will become B2, then B3, then B4 (just as shown in the first example).

Using the **$** (**dollar**) symbol as part of the cell reference means that, even when copied and pasted, that particular value **will not change**.

Why would we choose to use absolute cell referencing rather than merely keying the value 6 into the formula? Because if each of the formula had contained the number, and the number had subsequently changed, we would have had to change four formulae, rather than just the contents of cell B1.

The types of data often declared as absolutes are things like interest rates, VAT rates or maybe a price. Choosing the absolute referencing option here will ensure that only a single value needs to be changed and thus all other formulae that rely on this particular data would be automatically updated through a single action.

Use logical functions, e.g. IF, AND, OR, NOT, SUMIF

Logical functions are different from mainstream formulae and functions because the latter are always executed whereas logical functions may or may not, depending on whether a criterion, or set of criteria, are met or not.

IF

IF functions (commonly known as IF statements) are designed to allow the user to carry out different actions dependant on testing a condition. These conditions can also be **nested** to test multiple conditions. In the following example, we are considering calculating whether an individual would qualify for a child, adult or concession ticket for entry into an art gallery:

> IF (the person's age is less than 18)
>> They will be classified as a child
> Else
>> Check again and IF (the person's age is greater or equal to 18 and is less than or equal to 60)
>>> They will be classified as an adult
>> Else
>>> They will be classified as a concession

This translates as:

> Check the persons age
>> Less than 18 is a child
>> Between 18 and 60 (inclusive) is an adult
>> If neither of the other two, they must be a concession

All IF statements have the same structure:

> IF (**condition**)
>> Do **this** if **true**
> Else
>> Do **that** if **false**

Here is a spreadsheet example:

	A	B	C
1	66	5	=IF(A1>50, A1 + B1, 0)

which means in full:

> if (A1 > 50)
>> the cell containing this logic statement will take the result of adding A1 and B1
> else
>> the cell containing this logic statement will take the result of 0

Looking at the data, what will the above function **return**?

Is A1 greater than 50?

> Yes – so add 66 and 5 together, which will give 71 in C1.

	A	B	C
1	66	5	=IF(A1>50, A1 + B1, 0)

Unit Link

For more on developing IF statements and logic statements see **Unit 18 – Principles of Software Design and Development**, which can be found in the companion **Core Text** on pages 247 to 290.

With the OR operator, the user can test multiple conditions but in a way that will allow the TRUE action to be undertaken in the event that any one of the conditions is evaluated to be true.

The structure is:

> IF (condition A is true) **OR** (condition B is true)
>> Do this because one of them is True
> Else
>> Do this because they are **both False**

Look at the following example – what will the result be?

	A	B	C
1	66	5	=IF(OR(A1<50,B1>4,A1+B1,0)

Here A1 is false because the value in that cell is greater than 50. However when the second part of the condition is tested you will find that B1 is indeed greater than 4 (so this will be true). The value 71 will be returned in C1.

On the other hand had the value of A1 been 66 and the value of B1 had been 2, both of the conditions would have been false and the value 0 would have been returned in C1.

AND

The **AND** operator again allows the user to check multiple cells, but unlike the **OR** operator where either part of the condition can be true for the condition to return the value of **True**, with the **AND** operator **BOTH** parts of the condition must be **True** for the **True** part of the statement to be executed.

The structure is:

> IF (condition A is true) AND (condition B is true)
>> **Do this because both of them are True**
> Else
>> Do this because they are both False

Look at the following example – what will the result be?

	A	B	C
1	46	5	=IF(AND(A1<50,B1>4,A1+B1,0)

Is A1 less than 50? Yes. Is B1 greater than 4? Yes. Therefore both conditions are indeed met and the result placed in C1 will be 51. If either of the conditions had not been met, the result would have been 0.

NOT

Trying to understand NOT can be quite challenging because you are effectively working with reversed logic.

Let's look at the following:

> =NOT(3+3=6)

Will this evaluate to true or false?

It will evaluate to **false**! Why? Because 3 + 3 is 6, you would expect it to be true, but the NOT reverses the logic.

=**NOT**(3+3=8) would evaluate to true, because 3 + 3 is indeed NOT 8.

SUMIF

The SUMIF function works slightly differently in that here all the values in a range are checked and any greater than or equal to the specified number (in this case 50), are added into the total, and the others are ignored.

	A	B
1	January	75
2	February	41
3	March	52
4	April	16
5	May	24
6	June	67
7	July	91
8		=SUMIF(B1:B7,">=50")

The total here would be 285.

To prove this is accurate, let's identify the relevant values and place in column C before adding and check the result.

	A	B	C
1	January	75	75
2	February	41	
3	March	52	52
4	April	16	
5	May	24	
6	June	67	67
7	July	91	91
8		=SUMIF(B1:B7,">=50")	=SUM(C1:C7)

Totals would be 285 and 285.

As with other parts of a developed spreadsheet, the results of all **logical** functions must be carefully tested and checked as part of the spreadsheet testing strategy because it is very easy to make a mistake.

Finally, you should have a basic understanding of **relational operator** symbols:

>   Greater than

<   Less than

=   Equal to

>= Greater than or equal to

<= Less than or equal to

Braincheck – Logical operators

Work out the answers to these complex expressions, given values for A, B and C. In each case specify the outcome.

   A = 100 B = 50 C = 12

1 =IF(A<75,A+B,A+C)

2 =IF(AND(A>75,B>30,C>9),A+B+C,0)

3 =IF(AND(A<50,B>30),A+B,0)

4 =IF(OR(A<50,B>30),A-B,0)

5 =SUMIF(A:C,"<=50")

6 =IF(A+B=150,"true","false")

7 =IF(OR(B=50,C<9),A,0)

8 =NOT(7+4=11)

How well did you do? See page 442 for answers.

4 Create efficient automated and customisable spreadsheets that enable easy analysis and interpretation

4.1 Sorting and summarising data

Use of sub-totals and facilities, e.g. pivot tables

A pivot table is a tool that can be used to summarise a data set and allow the data users to see the data from different perspectives.

Using the data in Figure 6.61, we will use the pivot table facility to provide subtotals and different views of the data.

Activity

This activity will walk you through creating a pivot table.

1 To begin you will need to open a new spreadsheet and key in the data as shown below.

Purchase Records for September 2007

Date	Supplier Name	Quantity	Description	Price	Total
01/09/2007	Kavana Shirts	100	T-shirts Blue XL	4.52	452.00
01/09/2007	Ramises	30	T-shirts Red L	3.44	103.20
04/09/2007	Maximum Ideas	45	Assorted Band logos	0.60	27.00
06/09/2007	Kavana Shirts	200	T-shirts Black L	4.70	940.00
07/09/2007	Kavana Shirts	150	T-shirts Black XL	4.60	690.00
10/09/2007	Addisons Imports	190	T-shirts Blue L Long-sleeved	5.60	1064.00
15/09/2007	Kavana Shirts	60	T-shirts Blue XL	4.52	271.20
21/09/2007	Maximum Ideas	15	Assorted Band logos	0.60	9.00
22/09/2007	Ramises	40	T-shirts Blue L Long-sleeved	5.30	212.00
22/09/2007	Kavana Shirts	55	T-shirts Red L	3.70	203.50
22/09/2007	Lataski Logos	50	Assorted Band logos	0.70	35.00
25/09/2007	Kavana Shirts	140	T-shirts Blue S	4.12	576.80
27/09/2007	Ramises	10	T-shirts Red XL Long-sleeved	5.10	51.00
28/09/2007	Kavana Shirts	15	Assorted Band logos	0.80	12.00
30/09/2007	Ramises	25	T-shirts Blue XL	4.60	115.00

Figure 6.61 Purchase data sorted by date only

2 To analyse the data we will now use the pivot table functionality. To access this we click on **Data**, then on **PivotTable and PivotChart Report** (see Figure 6.62).

Clicking this option will then activate the PivotTable Wizard (as shown in Figure 6.63).

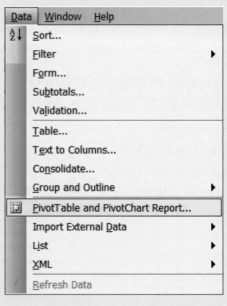

Figure 6.62 Accessing the functionality

Figure 6.63 PivotTable Wizard

In this instance we will be using the detail in the spreadsheet, although you can see that there are other options, for example using data gained from an external source.

Figure 6.64 Identifying the data area

The area holding the data to be used can either be keyed in as shown in Figure 6.64, or it can be defined as a named range and referenced in that way (see earlier in this unit chapter). Now click on Next.

Click on Finish to create the table. This will now place a template in a new worksheet (see Figure 6.66).

Figure 6.65 Locating the pivot table

We now need to drag and drop the items we would like in our pivot table from the field list and onto either the column, row or data sections shown.

In this instance we will choose to drop Supplier Name onto the **column fields**, Description onto the **row fields** and Total onto the **data items**.

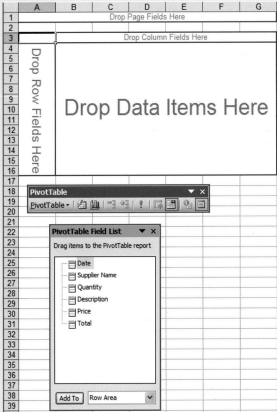

Figure 6.66 Pivot table template

Once this has been done, and the data area has been formatted to two decimal places, the view will look like that shown in Figure 6.67.

	A	B	C	D	E	F	G
1							
2							
3	Sum of Total	Supplier Name ▼					
4	Description ▼	Addisons Imports	Kavana Shirts	Lataski Logos	Maximum Ideas	Ramises	Grand Total
5	Assorted Band logos		12.00	35.00	36.00		83.00
6	T-shirts Black L		940.00				940.00
7	T-shirts Black XL		690.00				690.00
8	T-shirts Blue L Long-sleeved	1064.00				212.00	1276.00
9	T-shirts Blue S		576.80				576.80
10	T-shirts Blue XL		723.20			115.00	838.20
11	T-shirts Red L		203.50			103.20	306.70
12	T-shirts Red XL Long-sleeved					51.00	51.00
13	Grand Total	1064.00	3145.50	35.00	36.00	481.20	4761.70

Figure 6.67 Pivot table

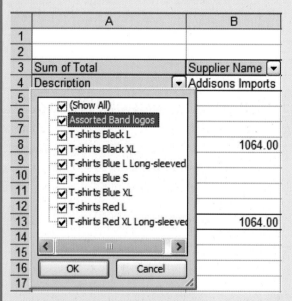

Figure 6.68 Description drop-down box

The function has placed totals for both the rows (to show how much was spent buying each product) and at the base of each column to show the spend with each supplier.

You will also notice that the **Supplier Name** and **Description** headings have also been replaced by drop-down boxes.

When you choose to view the list you will notice that all of the items are shown. You can now manipulate which items are shown and, similarly, through choosing specific Suppliers you can also change which data is visible. Filtering in this way will also adjust any relevant totals as can be seen in the filtered table in Figure 6.69.

	A	B	C
1			
2			
3	Sum of Total	Supplier Name ▼	
4	Description ▼	Kavana Shirts	Grand Total
5	T-shirts Black L	940.00	940.00
6	T-shirts Black XL	690.00	690.00
7	T-shirts Blue S	576.80	576.80
8	T-shirts Blue XL	723.20	723.20
9	T-shirts Red L	203.50	203.50
10	Grand Total	3133.50	3133.50

Figure 6.69 Filtered pivot table

Sorting data on multiple fields

The key issue with sorting data is ensuring that you select all the data across the rows and columns to be included when the records are moved. Failure to do this could result in data becoming mixed up and effectively useless.

In Figure 6.61 the data had been sorted in date order. We will now use the same data and sort it on multiple fields.

Activity

This activity will walk you through sorting data on multiple fields.

1 Using the same data created for the previous activity, highlight the area to be sorted (this is all the data excluding the headings).

	A	B	C	D	E	F
1						
2						
3	Purchase Records for September 2007					
4						
5	Date	Supplier Name	Quantity	Description	Price	Total
6	01/09/2007	Kavana Shirts	100	T-shirts Blue XL	4.52	452.00
7	01/09/2007	Ramises	30	T-shirts Red L	3.44	103.20
8	04/09/2007	Maximum Ideas	45	Assorted Band logos	0.60	27.00
9	06/09/2007	Kavana Shirts	200	T-shirts Black L	4.70	940.00
10	07/09/2007	Kavana Shirts	150	T-shirts Black XL	4.60	690.00
11	10/09/2007	Addisons Imports	190	T-shirts Blue L Long-sleeved	5.60	1064.00
12	15/09/2007	Kavana Shirts	60	T-shirts Blue XL	4.52	271.20
13	21/09/2007	Maximum Ideas	15	Assorted Band logos	0.60	9.00
14	22/09/2007	Ramises	40	T-shirts Blue L Long-sleeved	5.30	212.00
15	22/09/2007	Kavana Shirts	55	T-shirts Red L	3.70	203.50
16	22/09/2007	Lataski Logos	50	Assorted Band logos	0.70	35.00
17	25/09/2007	Kavana Shirts	140	T-shirts Blue S	4.12	576.80
18	27/09/2007	Ramises	10	T-shirts Red XL Long-sleeved	5.10	51.00
19	28/09/2007	Kavana Shirts	15	Assorted Band logos	0.80	12.00
20	30/09/2007	Ramises	25	T-shirts Blue XL	4.60	115.00

Figure 6.70 Data area

2 We will now sort by Supplier and then Description. To do this we activate both options simultaneously. Click on **Data** then on **Sort** and the sorting dialogue box appears as shown in Figure 6.71.

Figure 6.71 Sort interface

From the drop-down list first choose to **Sort by**, **Supplier name**, second choose **Then by**, **Description**.

Once you have clicked on **OK** you will see the sorted list as shown in Figure 6.72.

	A	B	C	D	E	F
1						
2						
3	Purchase Records for September 2007					
4						
5	Date	Supplier Name	Quantity	Description	Price	Total
6	10/09/2007	Addisons Imports	190	T-shirts Blue L Long-sleeved	5.60	1064.00
7	28/09/2007	Kavana Shirts	15	Assorted Band logos	0.80	12.00
8	06/09/2007	Kavana Shirts	200	T-shirts Black L	4.70	940.00
9	07/09/2007	Kavana Shirts	150	T-shirts Black XL	4.60	690.00
10	25/09/2007	Kavana Shirts	140	T-shirts Blue S	4.12	576.80
11	01/09/2007	Kavana Shirts	100	T-shirts Blue XL	4.52	452.00
12	15/09/2007	Kavana Shirts	60	T-shirts Blue XL	4.52	271.20
13	22/09/2007	Kavana Shirts	55	T-shirts Red L	3.70	203.50
14	22/09/2007	Lataski Logos	50	Assorted Band logos	0.70	35.00
15	04/09/2007	Maximum Ideas	45	Assorted Band logos	0.60	27.00
16	21/09/2007	Maximum Ideas	15	Assorted Band logos	0.60	9.00
17	22/09/2007	Ramises	40	T-shirts Blue L Long-sleeved	5.30	212.00
18	30/09/2007	Ramises	25	T-shirts Blue XL	4.60	115.00

Figure 6.72 The sorted list

Filtering data sets to extract information to meet a specific user need

With sorted or unsorted data there is also an AutoFilter function. Click on **Data, Filter** then on **AutoFilter** and the column headings will automatically become drop-down boxes. Selecting the drop-down menu beside **Description** for example, will allow the user to choose which item to display and it will extract only those records from the list that match the chosen description.

Date ▼	Supplier Name ▼	Quant ▼	Description ▼	Pri ▼	To ▼
01/09/2007	Kavana Shirts	100	Sort Ascending	4.52	452.00
01/09/2007	Ramises	30	Sort Descending	3.44	103.20
04/09/2007	Maximum Ideas	45	(All)	0.60	27.00
06/09/2007	Kavana Shirts	200	(Top 10...)	4.70	940.00
07/09/2007	Kavana Shirts	150	(Custom...)	4.60	690.00
10/09/2007	Addisons Imports	190	Assorted Band logos / T-shirts Black L	5.60	1064.00
15/09/2007	Kavana Shirts	60	T-shirts Black XL	4.52	271.20
21/09/2007	Maximum Ideas	15	T-shirts Blue L Long-sleeved	0.60	9.00
22/09/2007	Kavana Shirts	55	T-shirts Blue S / T-shirts Blue XL	3.70	203.50
22/09/2007	Lataski Logos	50	T-shirts Red L	0.70	35.00
22/09/2007	Ramises	40	T-shirts Red XL Long-sleeved	5.30	212.00
25/09/2007	Kavana Shirts	140	(Blanks) / (NonBlanks)	4.12	576.80
27/09/2007	Ramises	10	T-shirts Red XL Long-sleeved	5.10	51.00
28/09/2007	Kavana Shirts	15	Assorted Band logos	0.80	12.00
30/09/2007	Ramises	25	T-shirts Blue XL	4.60	115.00

Figure 6.73 Using AutoFilter to filter data

Similarly, you could choose to filter all the records for one particular supplier or for goods purchased on a single date. Usefully, the AutoFilter function can be switched on or off on demand.

Using these features and facilities will enable you to produce professional spreadsheets that meet user needs. If in doubt about what is required on a spreadsheet, or how the audience requires the data presented – ASK!

4.2 Interpretation methods

Comparisons of totals

Using data replicated over weeks, months, periods, quarters, bi-annually (twice a year) or annually, will enable you to identify any unusual occurrences that can be further investigated through the use of the functions as described in earlier sections.

An additional functional aspect of a spreadsheet package is located on the **Tools** menu under the **Compare and Merge Workbooks**. Using this functionality will certainly enable users to compare like files for different years where the files have essentially been used as templates.

Use of trend analysis to predict future events

Trend analysis is a useful management tool to help predict what will occur in the future. The more data you have available when undertaking a trend analysis, particularly from other years and comparable operational periods, will mean that your predictions are more likely to be accurate – although this is not always the case.

4.3 Charts and graphs

Use application facilities to create a range of charts and graphs with appropriate titles, labels and other features, e.g. axis scales, colours and annotation.

Being able to create charts and graphs is an important skill for anyone working with data through spreadsheets.

Using another pivot table, prepared to show the items purchased and the quantities as totals only, we now create a column chart.

When you use the data in a pivot table to create the chart or graph, once the wizard has been used to create the base chart (in the first instance a column chart), the interface is slightly different as it offers you the pivot table choices as menus and buttons, which means you can easily change, what pieces of data are used to make up the chart or graph (see Figure 6.74).

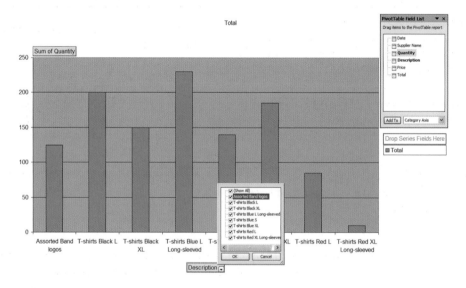

Figure 6.74 Chart made from a pivot table

As always, the title will need to be added, labels will need to be included or removed as required, the X axis (horizontal) will require a title (in this case **Description**), and the Y axis (vertical) will require a title, which in this instance could be **Sum of Quantity** or simply **Totals**.

Similarly, as with all charts, an appropriate general title would be required.

In all charts created in Microsoft Excel® the **chart area** can be formatted and the background colours changed. Similarly, annotation can be added.

Select appropriate chart type for data type, e.g. line, bar, column, pie or xy (scatter)

A range of chart types exist – some of which will now be explored:

◆ **Pie charts** are generally used where you want to visually represent data as part of a whole. Had we chosen a pie chart instead of a column chart in Figure 6.74, each column would have been represented by a slice of the pie. The larger the slice, the more it represents of the whole.

The pie chart you will see most often when working with computer systems is in the properties of a destination drive (such as your hard disk or a flash memory device; see Figure 6.75).

◆ **Column charts** (as shown in Figure 6.74) contain vertical bars (upright). This is probably the most commonly used chart type and is usually offered as the default or (first choice) by the Wizard. Column charts are useful for allowing users to visually compare columns of data.

◆ **Bar charts** – with horizontal bars (flat), bar charts are often used for comparing distances, for example. Many individuals, however, consider bar charts and column charts completely interchangeable in the way they represent data.

◆ **Line graphs** – these are good for comparing trends, as with the spreadsheet included at the beginning of this chapter.

When using any chart or graph, users must check and make certain that the chart will actually mean something to the data user. Consider the following pie chart. What is it telling you?

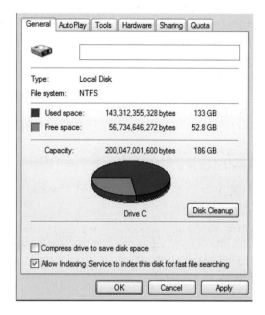

Figure 6.75 Pie chart used to display free and used disk space

Figure 6.76 Pie chart without annotation

In fact, this pie chart is not very useful. As it has no **no title** and **no key** or **legend,** the user is unlikely to understand what it is actually intended to present. This is a very common error made by users when creating such charts.

Justify choices

When creating charts and graphs, be prepared to explain your choices to users or managers. To avoid errors in this respect, always make sure you fully understand what you are trying to achieve in using this medium to present information.

4.4 Presenting

Using combined information to support an argument, e.g. table of data and chart

Professionally presented information is usually a combination of tables of data or information, charts or graphs and textual commentary that explains the images. In some cases, the images are used to provide a better understanding of the text.

Using combined information to support arguments will become easier with experience. As a general rule, always try to provide evidence to support both sides of an argument before drawing a conclusion.

Use of paste link to maintain currency of data, e.g. between worksheets, workbooks, packages

This topic has already been covered in section 2.1 earlier in this unit.

You should just remember that any links established between worksheets, workbooks, or files, are dynamic – and changing the source value will automatically lead to all those values reliant on the source value being updated. Remember that when re-opening a file that creates a dynamic link, you will be asked whether you wish to update the file when it is opened, or not.

4.5 Customisation

Methods of restricting data entry, e.g. hiding and protecting

Hiding columns and rows of data in a spreadsheet to prevent access by particular users is a simple procedure.

Simply select the columns you wish to hide, then click on **Format**, **Column** then **Hide** (this can be seen in Figure 6.77). The same technique is used for hiding rows.

This will not prevent the user accessing them if they choose to widen the columns. Hiding parts of the spreadsheet more thoroughly can be seen in the dialogue box shown in Figure 6.80.

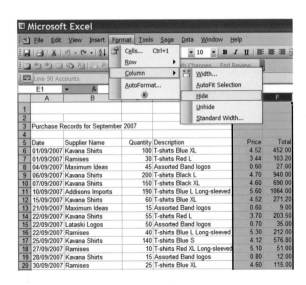

Figure 6.77 Hiding columns

Protecting the contents of rows or columns requires slightly reversed thinking! When protecting a whole sheet the developer will simply click on **Tools**, then **Protection** and then **Protect Sheet** (see Figure 6.78).

This action can be password protected, locking the whole worksheet so users will be unable to change any values.

The developer might, on the other hand, wish to protect the important parts of the spreadsheet, such as headings and totals, and only enable (or leave accessible) those areas that are safe for a novice user to use.

To do this the developer will need to unlock (make accessible) those areas that the user is free to access, prior to protecting the worksheet.

In Figure 6.79 the area that the user will be able to key into has been highlighted.

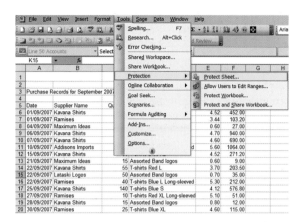

Figure 6.78 Protecting the worksheet

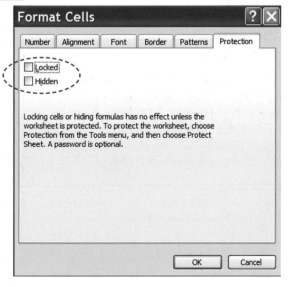

Now, selecting **Format**, **Cells** and the **Protection** tab will enable the dialogue box shown in Figure 6.80.

Figure 6.79 Highlighting the user access area

The **Locked** box needs to be unchecked, and **OK** selected. You will also notice that cells to be **Hidden** can be identified in the same way.

Modifying toolbars and menus to restrict user actions

In section 3.1 earlier in this unit, you were introduced to the concepts of creating custom menus. Clearly, if you were choosing to hide particular aspects of your data, or whole worksheets, you might also wish to limit the functionality that a user has access to by removing buttons or menus using the same interface as shown in Figure 6.55.

Figure 6.80 Unlocking cells

Data validation routines to ensure accuracy of input, e.g. data validation, range checking, presence of data such as not NULL

As with databases, one way to improve the accuracy of input in a spreadsheet is to create drop-down lists from which the user will be able to choose.

In addition, modern spreadsheet software includes **Validation** functionality on the **Data** menu, where having highlighted a particular cell or range of cells, a developer can simply set up a validation routine to be applied for any data that is input. In the example shown in Figure 6.81, the developer has chosen that only a whole number between 17 and 21 can be input into the range of highlighted cells.

Using the **Input Message** tab, the developer can add a message to alert the user to the acceptable values or format, which is activated when the user accesses any of the validated cells.

Alternatively, the user can simply use the **Error Alert** to highlight the problem once the user has attempted to move out of the cell having input data (see Figure 6.82).

4.6 Automation

Creation of workbook and global macros, e.g. for printing or formatting

The final topic for this unit is automation and you need to understand that macros can be created that will be local to a particular workbook (and can only be activated and applied within the open workbook), or they can be made global, so that they can be activated and used with any open workbook.

Recording a macro is a very straightforward process. You simply need to select **Tools**, then **Macro** and **Record New Macro** (as shown in Figure 6.83).

As soon as **Record New Macro** has been selected, the dialogue box shown in Figure 6.84 will appear. Here you will have to give the

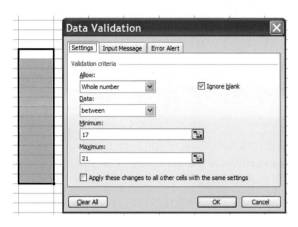

Figure 6.81 Implementing data validation

Figure 6.82 A customised error message alerting incorrect input!

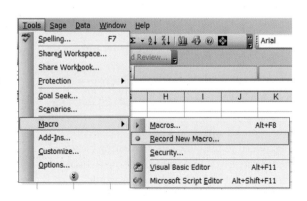

Figure 6.83 Recording a macro

Figure 6.84 Scoping the macro

macro a name, and you will select whether the macro will be visible to the workbook open at the time it was created, a new workbook not yet created, or whether it should be placed in a Personal Macro Workbook, which is what effectively makes the macro global because the Personal Macro Workbook is visible to all spreadsheets.

Once you click on **OK**, the macro will begin recording and every action you undertake will be logged, until you click on the **Stop Recording** button shown in Figure 6.85, which appears as soon as recording begins.

Figure 6.85 Stop recording button (on left)

Once the recording has been stopped, you can then add a button to an existing or user-defined menu (as shown earlier in this unit chapter). Then as shown in Figure 6.86 by selecting **Tools**, **Customize**, **Commands** and then selecting the **Macros** category, you will be able to drag and drop a button onto a toolbar, to which you can then assign the macro you have created.

Figure 6.86 Adding a custom button

Once added to the toolbar, the toolbar will look something like that shown in Figure 6.87.

Figure 6.87 A customised menu

Now it is simply a case of assigning the relevant macro to the button. To do this, left click on the menu button and select the macro you wish to assign from the list provided.

Macros you might like to record to enhance your spreadsheet could include:

◆ a print macro to always print a specific number of copies of a whole spreadsheet;
◆ a macro to select a specific area in a spreadsheet for printing;
◆ a macro that ensures that all columns are of the correct width to accommodate the data;

- a macro that ensures that all numeric columns have two decimal places.

The list of options is extensive. What you must ensure, however, is that you choose a macro that is going to be useful to the user, rather than just creating one to prove you can.

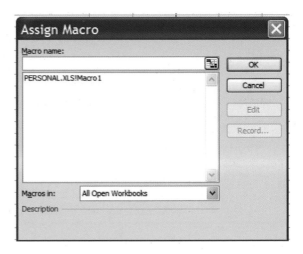

Figure 6.88 Selecting a macro to assign

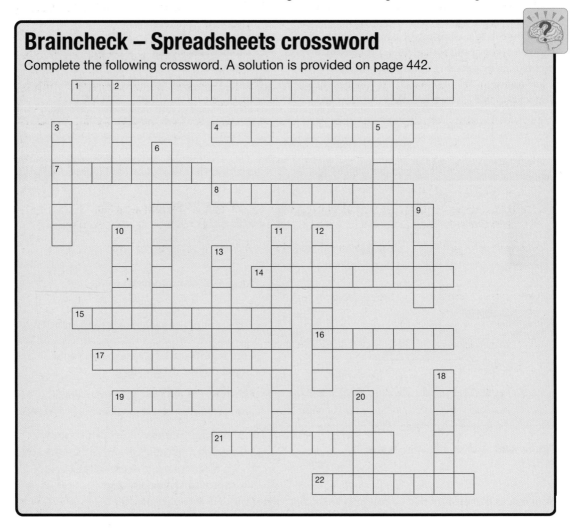

Braincheck – Spreadsheets crossword

Complete the following crossword. A solution is provided on page 442.

ACROSS

1 CSV
4 Filtering tool that just happens
7 _____ referencing, refering to a particular cell even if copied and pasted elsewhere
8 Making a spreadsheet, or parts of a spreadsheet, inaccessible
14 Drilling into existing data to explain unusual events at ever lower levels
15 Where a single data value is used elsewhere dynamically
16 Whole number
17 Sub-total and data set summarising functionality
19 A sum of money given to individuals or groups to be used for a particular purpose
21 Positioning – could be left, right or central
22 An illustration of data that finds itself in slices?

DOWN

2 Automated action recorded and placed on a button
3 Changing values to see what the outcome will be
5 Thicken text or numbers to make them stand out
6 Making an interface suitable for the individual
9 The type of analysis that compares period data to find unusual events
10 Extra functionality not usually installed at installation that can be included later?
11 The functionality designed to find a contributing value in a calculation
12 Keeping a record of how a file has been changed by users
13 Estimating the future
18 Use criteria to extract information from a data set
20 Selection of continuous cells that can be named?

 ## Achieving success

In order to achieve each unit you will complete a series of coursework activities. Each time you hand in work, your tutor will return this to you with a record of your achievement.

This particular unit has 11 criteria to meet: 6 Pass, 3 Merit and 2 Distinction.

For a **Pass**:

You must achieve **all** 6 Pass criteria.

For a **Merit**:

You must achieve **all** 6 Pass and **all** 3 Merit criteria.

For a **Distinction**:

You must achieve **all** 6 Pass, **all** 3 Merit and both Distinction criteria.

So that you can monitor your own progress and achievement in each unit, a recording grid has been provided (see below). The full version of this grid is also included on the companion CD.

Assignment	Assignments in this unit			
	U6.01	U6.02	U6.03	U6.04
Referral				
Pass				
1				
2				
3				
4				
5				
6				
Merit				
1				
2				
3				
Distinction				
1				
2				

Help with assessment

The content of this unit is heavily focused on advanced spreadsheet techniques, with a particular emphasis on complexity. It will not be sufficient to develop a simple spreadsheet, but requires one that has multiple pages, uses complex formulae and functions, and which makes use of sorting techniques, functionality such as pivot tables, and the ability to produce well-presented charts and graphs. This is the basic requirement to meet the **Pass** criteria.

For a **Merit**, evidence that you have gained additional skills through using advanced techniques are also required, along with evidence that your spreadsheet is accurate and uses a wide range of the features of spreadsheet software.

Distinction requires you to evaluate your spreadsheet and requires you to be able to fully justify your choices.

Online resources on the CD

Key fact sheets

Further reading

Day, A., 2005, *Mastering Financial Mathematics with Excel*, Financial Times Prentice Hall, ISBN 0764597809.

Hart-Davis, G., 2003, *How to Do Everything with Microsoft Office Excel 2003*, McGraw-Hill Education, ISBN 0072230711.

Harvey, G., 2003, *Excel 2003 All-in-one Desk Reference for Dummies*, Hungry Minds Inc. US, ISBN 076453758X.

Heathcote, R., 2004, *Further Excel 2000–2003,* Payne-Gallway Publishers, ISBN 1904467768.

Koneman, P., 2000, *Advanced Projects for Microsoft Excel 2000*, Prentice Hall, ISBN 0130885444.

Schmuller, J., 2005, *Statistical Analysis with Excel for Dummies*, Hungry Minds Inc. US, ISBN 0764575945.

Simonn, J., 2005, *Excel Data Analysis*, *2nd Edition*, Hungry Minds Inc. US, ISBN 0764597809.

Zapawa, T., 2005, *Excel Advanced Report Development*, Hungry Minds Inc. US, ISBN 0764588117.

Unit 10

Client-side Customisation of Web Pages

Capsule view

This unit is best studied after Unit 21 – Website Production and Management. A 60-hour unit, it is designed to extend the learner's knowledge of client-side scripting that was first experienced in that unit. If you have not read that unit yet, please do so and then return here.

As discussed before, websites have undergone a dramatic change in functionality over the last five years or so. Part of these changes can be attributed to the underlying complexity of their construction. Client-side scripting such as Netscape's JavaScript and Microsoft VBScript® have enabled sophisticated automation to occur, expanding the levels of interaction possible with the visitor. The use of cascading style sheets (CSS) has also encouraged the creation of stylish and site-wide formatting that can be individually tailored by the visitor with very little effort.

Although both JavaScript and VBScript are industry-relevant scripting languages we have decided to focus on the former as it is generally more popular in terms of website development. Electronic copies of all scripts can be found on the companion CD.

Learning aims

1 Understand the fundamentals of CSS.
2 Understand the fundamentals of a chosen scripting language.
3 Be able to control layout of a web page using CSS.
4 Be able to create an interactive web page.
5 Be able to test and review a web page which uses CSS and JavaScript.

1. Understand the fundamentals of CSS

1.1 Characteristics of CSS

Why use CSS?

Good question! The simple fact is that CSS will help in:

◆ keeping web page content **separate** from its formatting (makes editing easier);

◆ **saving time** by allowing multiple web pages to share the same formatting instructions;

◆ ensuring web pages are **consistently formatted**, e.g. corporate colours in a company's public website;

◆ making it easy to set **appropriate formatting** for different **output devices**, e.g. screen vs. printed;

◆ having quicker file downloads as formatting instructions are not duplicated in every HTML file.

Implementation styles

CSS works by (typically) storing formatting instructions in a **separate external file** (i.e. different from the .html document it is formatting).

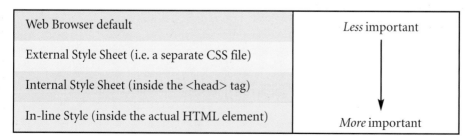

This external style sheet typically has a **.css** extension. Apart from that it is a normal **text file** and can be opened and edited in any basic **text editor** (such as Microsoft's **Notepad®**).

However, styles have a preferential pecking order for formatting:

Web Browser default	*Less* important
External Style Sheet (i.e. a separate CSS file)	
Internal Style Sheet (inside the \<head> tag)	
In-line Style (inside the actual HTML element)	*More* important

Style formatting cascades (unless over-ridden) – in other words a web page's general appearance (e.g. body text) is set initially by the web browser, although this may be in part over-ridden by settings in the CSS – which in turn may be partly over-ridden by formatting in the HTML document.

CSS example

Examine the following **HTML** (Test page.html):

```
<html>
<head>
<title>Test page</title>
</head>
<body>
<center>
<p>
<font face="arial" color="red">
This is a test
</font>
</p>
</center>
</body>
</html>
```

This is old-style HTML with both content **and** formatting.

When opened in **Mozilla Firefox** it will appear as Figure 10.1.

Figure 10.1 Test Page.html (notice the %20 in the filename, hexadecimal for 32 – the ASCII code for space)

You should be able to see that the text is surrounded by three **formatting criteria**:

This includes the **font** to use, the **colour** to use and an instruction to **centre** the text).

It should also be noted that the <**font**> tag (though still regularly used by many web designers) was actually **deprecated** in HTML 4.01 – encouraging the use of Styles instead.

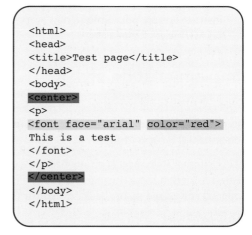

```
<html>
<head>
<title>Test page</title>
</head>
<body>
<center>
<p>
<font face="arial" color="red">
This is a test
</font>
</p>
</center>
</body>
</html>
```

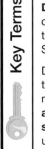

Key Terms

Deprecation is a common term in software development, especially in web-related technologies such as HTML, CSS and Sun's Java.

Deprecation occurs when older coding techniques **become outdated** as newer methods and techniques **become available**. Although the older methods will **still** work, they are not recommended for use.

Altering this formatting will require editing around the actual html content, which is a little messy.

External implementation of CSS

An alternative would be to store the formatting in a **separate** .css file. This technique is shown here. Here's the **revised** HTML file:

```
<html>
<head>
<title>Test page</title>
<link rel="stylesheet" type="text/css" href="Test page.css" />
</head>
<body>
<p>
This is a test
</p>
</body>
</html>
```

And the **new external** CSS file (Test page.css):

The link to the CSS file is placed with the HTML document's **head** section (highlighted in green). The 'p' specifies the HTML element being affected is the <p> tag.

However, as you can see in Figure 10.2, the output should be **identical**.

```
p
{
text-align: center;
color: red;
font-family: arial;
}
```

What is important is that we have now successfully **separated** the content from the formatting.

Internal (or Header) implementation of CSS

Figure 10.2 Test Page.html, now formatted with CSS

It is also possible to use an internal implementation of CSS, where the <**style**> tag is used within the HTML document's header.

Here is the same Test page.html file **rewritten** using this technique…

```
<html>
<head>
<title>Test page</title>
<style type="text/css">
p
{
text-align: center;
color: red;
font-family: arial
}
/style>
</head>
<body>
<p>
This is a test
</p>
</body>
</html>
```

In-line implementation of CSS

And finally, an in-line implementation of CSS is possible. As noted earlier, in-line CSS has the **highest priority** of any CSS formatting so will **over-ride** any previous CSS instructions.

Here's the same HTML rewritten with internal CSS style implementation.

```
<html>
<head>
<title>Test page</title>
</head>
<body>
<p style="text-align: center; color: red; font-family: arial;">
This is a test
</p>
</body>
</html>
```

It is absolutely vital to observe the use of **quotation marks** in the in-line implementation.

CSS box model

A web page can be thought of as a **document tree**, consisting of a number of different elements.

In order to **render** HTML document trees onto a monitor, a web browser must be able to understand and use a **visual formatting model**. This model can consist of zero or more **boxes**.

Every box has a **content area** (whether it contains text or images) and optional areas which **surround** it. These areas are called **padding**, **border** and **margin**.

The following diagram shows the relationship between these areas:

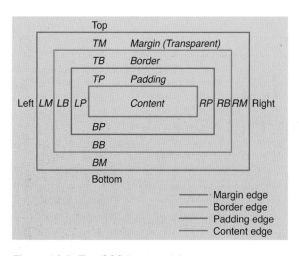

Each optional area can be split up into left, right, top and bottom segments. In Figure 10.3 these are annotated as RM for right margin, TB for top border, LP for left padding etc.

Each area has a perimeter and this is officially called an 'edge', therefore each area has four edges:

- content edge
- padding edge
- border edge
- margin edge or outer edge.

As with each area, every edge may be split up into left, right, top and bottom edges.

Figure 10.3 The CSS box model

It is also possible to change the **background style** of the various box areas. The following internal CSS example (Box model.html) highlights many of these features. **Indentation** (see section 4.4) has been added to improve **readability**.

```
<html>
  <head>
    <title>Formatting a box model with CSS</title>
    <style type="text/css">
      ul
      {
      background: lime;                  // Background is lime
      margin: 10px 10px 10px 10px;
      padding: 5px 5px 5px 5px;
      }                                  // No borders set
      li
      {
        color: blue;                     // text color is blue
        background: aqua;                // Content, padding is aqua
        margin: 10px 10px 10px 10px;
        padding: 15px 0px 10px 20px;     // Note 0px padding right
        list-style: circle               // A circular bullet
                                         // No borders set
      }
      li.withborder
      {
        border-style: dotted;
        border-width: medium;            // sets border width on all sides
        border-color: black;
      }
    </style>
  </head>
  <body>
    <ul>
      <li> first item in the list
      <li class="withborder">Second item in the list
    </ul>
  </body>
</html>
```

Figure 10.4 shows Box model.html's on-screen rendering.

Figure 10.4 Box model rendering

More on the Box Model

A more detailed exploration of the box model can be found on the W3C's website at:

http://www.w3.org/TR/REC-CSS2/box.html#box-dimensions

Selectors (basic CSS syntax)

CSS syntax has the following generalised form:

```
selector {property: value}
```

Let's examine these aspects separately:

◆ The **selector** is the **HTML tag/element** that requires formatting (e.g. <p>).
◆ The **property** is the attribute you want to format (e.g. its colour).
◆ The **value** is what you want to change the attribute to (e.g. red).

Therefore formatting the contents of a paragraph red would require:

```
p {color: red}
```

Note: only 16 standard colours are supported (by name) in the W3C CSS standards. These are (for reference): aqua, black, blue, fuchsia, gray, green, lime, maroon, navy, olive, purple, red, silver, teal, white and yellow.

All other colours should be referenced using the RGB (Red, Green, Blue) hexadecimal colour values (see section 1.2 for more information on this).

You may have noticed that some CSS lines use a semi-colon (;) and some don't. Generally they tend to be used when **multiple lines** of CSS are written for **one** HTML element/selector; in these cases, the semi-colon is used to **separate** the different properties being set.

More advanced CSS

As we have seen, it is possible to format more than one property per HTML element at the same time. This is achieved using a semi-colon (;) to separate the different properties:

```
body
{
text-align: center;
color: black;
font-family: "sans serif"
}
```

```
body
{
text-align: center;
color: black;
/* Font needs to be sans serif for best appearance */
font-family: "sans serif"
}
```

Also note that if a value is **more** than one word (e.g. Sans Serif) it should be placed in **quotation marks**. C# style **comments** may also be used in the CSS to document your formatting like so.

CSS classes

Clearly there may be occasions when there is a need to format a particular HTML element **differently** throughout a **single** page.

This can be achieved by using a CSS **class** and is illustrated by the following Heading example:

The HTML file (Test page2.html)…

```
<html>
<head>
<title>Test page</title>
<link rel="stylesheet" type="text/css" href="Test page2.css" />
</head>
<body>
<h1 class="blueov">New</h1>
<h1 class="blackul">Test</h1>
</body>
</html>
```

The accompanying CSS file (Test page2.css)…

```
H1.blueov
{
color: blue;
text-decoration: overline
}
H1.blackul
{
text-align: center;
color: black;
text-decoration: underline
}
```

This would display the following:

Figure 10.5 HTML headings with two different CSS formatting classes

CSS ID selector

The **most delicate** level of control is to target formatting to **one particular HTML element/tag.** This is achieved using **IDs.** An example is shown here:

```
p#intro
{
text-align: center;
color: blue
}
```

In this example, the ID is 'intro'.

Only a **paragraph element using the 'intro' ID** will be formatted using this defined style though other paragraphs (and other 'intro' ID formatting) may exist for other HTML elements.

Using the example CSS with the following **HTML** example:

```
<html>
<head>
<title>Test page</title>
<link rel="stylesheet" type="text/css" href="Test page3.css" />
</head>
<body>
<p id="intro">Welcome to my example!</p>
<p>This should not be affected and will have default browser
style.</p>
</body>
</html>
```

Here's how the resulting output would look:

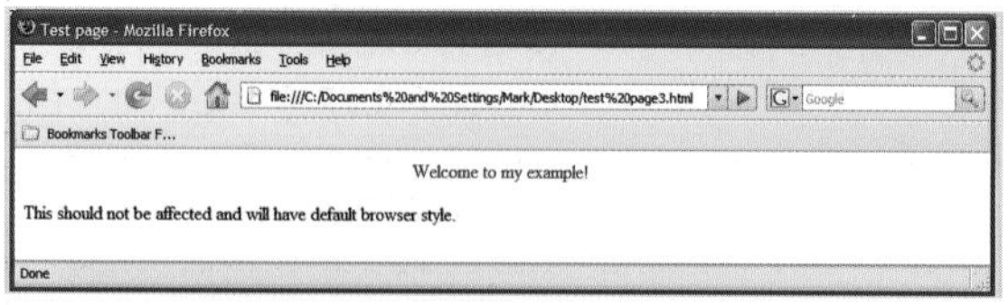

Figure 10.6 Two HTML paragraphs, but only the first one is formatted by CSS

Hiding CSS from older browsers

Although **modern** versions of all **major** web browsers (e.g. Mozilla Firefox, Microsoft Internet Explorer®, Opera, Safari etc.) should support CSS, there is always the possibility of some **older** software being used.

In order to prevent CSS **instructions** from being accidentally displayed, a number of **different methods** can be tried (success varies between browsers):

http://w3development.de/css/hide_css_from_browsers/

1.2 Uses of CSS

Common examples of CSS formatting include:

Background colour

The following internal CSS extract sets different background colours for different elements in the web page.

As you can see it is possible to specify an element's background colour using either one of the 16 W3C standard colour names (e.g. yellow) or by using the appropriate RGB colour code (whether this is specified in **hexadecimal pair** format (e.g. #00FF00) or by using the **denary based rgb function**.

Here is a table of comparison for common colours:

```
<html>
<head>
<style type="text/css">
body {background-color: teal;}
h1 {background-color: #00ffff;}
p {background-color: rgb(250,0,255);}
</style>
</head>
<body>
<h1>This is a test heading</h1>
<p>This is a test paragraph</p>
</body>
</html>
```

Colour	Colour name	Color HEX	Color RGB
	Black	#000000	rgb(0,0,0)
	Red	#FF0000	rgb(255,0,0)
	Green	#00FF00	rgb(0,255,0)
	Blue	#0000FF	rgb(0,0,255)
	Yellow	#FFFF00	rgb(255,255,0)
	Aqua	#00FFFF	rgb(0,255,255)
	Fuchsia	#FF00FF	rgb(255,0,255)
	Gray (note American spelling)	#C0C0C0	rgb(192,192,192)
	White	#FFFFFF	rgb(255,255,255)

Web safe colours

Some years ago the W3C created a palette of **216 web safe colours**, guaranteed to render the same on all computers running a 256-colour palette. The full list can be found here:

http://www.w3schools.com/html/html_colors.asp

Figure 10.7 shows how the background colour formatting has been applied.

Background images

Although they need to be used **carefully** (to prevent foreground text from being obscured), the use of background images is still reasonably popular with website designers.

Figure 10.7 Background formatting using CSS

In practice, a background can be added to many **different** HTML elements.

Here are some examples:

```
<html>
<head>
<style type="text/css">
body {background-image: url('blue and purples.jpg')}
td{background-image: url('blue.jpg')}
</style>
</head>
<body>
<table>
<tr><td>This is cell 1<td>This is cell 4
<tr><td>This is cell 2<td>Cell is cell 5
<tr><td>This is cell 3<td>Cell is cell 6
</table>
</body>
</html>
```

Figure 10.8 shows how different background colour formatting has been applied to both the body background and the table cells.

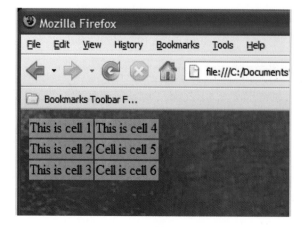

Figure 10.8 Background image formatting using CSS

Formatting text

Apart from changing the font colour CSS provides a **rich set** of formatting options for applying **style effects** to text. Although it is outside the remit of this text to cover all possibilities, the **most common** CSS text formatting options are covered in the following example:

```
<html>
<head>
<title>Text test page</title>
<link rel="stylesheet" type="text/css" href="Text.css" />
</head>
<body>
<h2>Demonstration of text formatting</h2>
<h3>Lots of different effects</h3>
<p id="oddformat">Welcome to my example!</p>
<p>I wonder why that's been underlined?</p>
</body>
</html>
```

```
h2
{
font-variant: small-caps;
}
h3
{
font-family: Verdana, Arial, Helvetica, sans-serif;
}
p
{
font-size: 30pt;
font-style: italic;
}
p#oddformat
{
text-align: center;
text-decoration: underline;
letter-spacing: 15px;
}
```

Figure 10.9 shows how these different CSS formatting options have affected the HTML content.

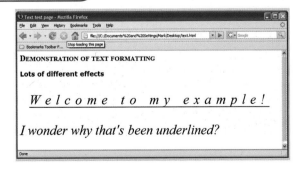

Figure 10.9 Demonstration of text formatting

This example includes:

```
h2 {font-variant: small-caps; }
h3 {font-family: Verdana, Arial, Helvetica, sans-serif;}
p
{
font-size: 30pt;
font-style: italic;
}
p#oddformat
{
text-align: center;
text-decoration: underline;
letter-spacing: 15px;
}
```

Capitalisation (with **text-transform** there are additional choices of uppercase, lowercase, capitalisation or none)

Typeface control (including a list of alternatives fonts to try if the first one isn't available)

Font size (expressed in points – pt – but see below)

Font style (with choices of italic, oblique or normal)

Text alignment (with choices of left, right, center (note spelling) or justify (for straight right-hand margins)

Text decoration (with choices of underline, overline, linethrough and blink)

Letter spacing (expressed in pixels – px – but again, see below)

CSS supports a number of different ways to **measure** elements, these include:

Name	How to write in CSS	Example
Points (1pt=1/72in)	pt	14pt
Pixels	px	12px
Ems (0.75ems = 12px)	em	0.5em
Inches (1in=2.54cm)	in	0.5in
Centimetres	cm	3cm
Millimetres	mm	20mm
Picas (about 1/6th in)	pc	12pc

We can put this together to build a simple HTML example with internal CSS demonstrating the different measurement units:

```
<html>
<head>
<title>Units test page</title>
</head>
<body>
<h1>Demonstration of text formatting using lots of
different units</h1>
<p>
 <span style="font-size: 14pt;">Hello!</span><br>
 <span style="font-size: 12px;">Hello!</span><br>
 <span style="font-size: 0.5em;">Hello!</span><br>
 <span style="font-size: 0.5in;">Hello!</span><br>
 <span style="font-size: 3cm;">Hello!</span><br>
 <span style="font-size: 20mm;">Hello!</span><br>
 <span style="font-size: 12pc;">Hello!</span><br>
</p>
</body>
</html>
```

The output from this combination of HTML and CSS can be seen in Figure 10.10.

Applying borders and padding

See the **Box Model** for more information.

Heading styles

Headings are important for a web page because their content (particularly <h1>) is often used by search engines to index the keywords for your page. Therefore it's a good idea to choose the wording carefully and ensure headings are used to control the flow of information on the page appropriately (it aids user navigation). See section 3.2 for more information.

Positioning elements

See the **Box Model** for more information.

Figure 10.10 Demonstration of different units affecting text size.

Creating columns

The use of the **<table>** tag in HTML is fairly common although it is often blamed for complex and long HTML files.

As an alternative, CSS and the **<div>** (**division**) **tag** can be used to split web page content into a number of different **columns** without the need to resort to the <table> tag. This is quite a **popular** technique for **modern** web page design where the **columnar format** is very often seen.

The following example demonstrates how it works:

```
<html>
<head>
<title>
Columns example
</title>
<style>
#div1
{
float:left;
width:40%;
color:green;
}
#div2
{
margin-left:40%;
color:blue;
width:60%;
}
</style>
<body>
<h1>Columns example</h1>
<div id="div1">
Lorem ipsum dolor sit amet, consectetuer adipiscing elit.
Quisque vulputate metus et odio. Fusce in diam quis arcu
condimentum imperdiet. Quisque ante sem, ultricies id, cursus
ac, fringilla eu, libero. Aenean pretium iaculis mauris. Donec
sodales vestibulum dolor.
</div>
<div id="div2">
Lorem ipsum dolor sit amet, consectetuer adipiscing elit.
Quisque vulputate metus et odio. Fusce in diam quis arcu
condimentum imperdiet. Quisque ante sem, ultricies id, cursus
ac, fringilla eu, libero. Aenean pretium iaculis mauris. Donec
sodales vestibulum dolor.
</div>
</body>
</html>
```

This creates a **40/60 per cent split** of the available Browser document **width** (see Figure 10.11):

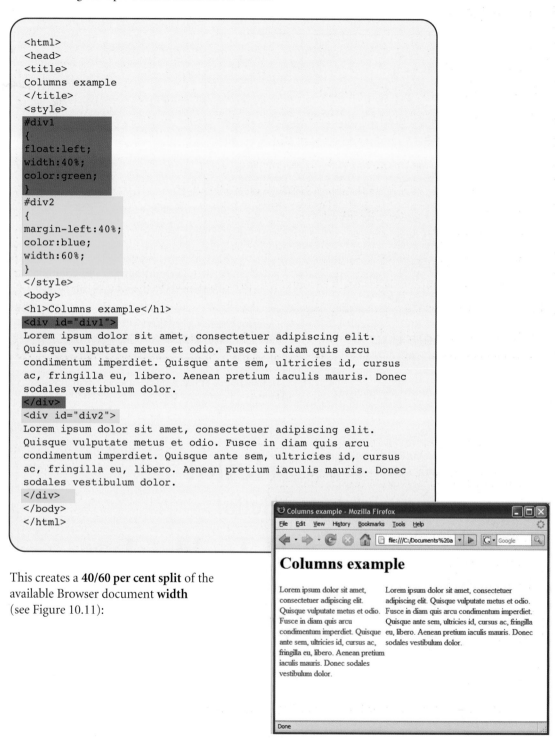

Figure 10.11 Columnar format without tables

Braincheck

Answer the following questions:

1 What is CSS?

2 Give three advantages of using CSS.

3 Which word is used to describe older HTML tags such as <font>?

4 What is the highest preference style for CSS?

5 Which term is used to represent the HTML tag in CSS?

6 Which symbol is used to separate different lines of CSS?

7 How many web safe colours are there?

8 Name three types of font style.

9 Name three types of text decoration.

10 Give three different units that can be used for measurement in CSS.

11 Name a common use of the <div> tag.

How well did you do? See page 443 for the answers.

Activity – Reproduce the following web page using CSS

Examine the following web page and try to **reconstruct it** using the CSS learnt so far.

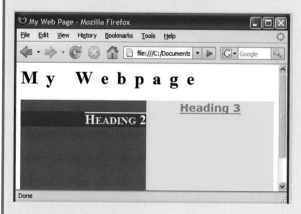

Figure 10.12 Web page CSS challenge

Note that this example does **not** use the HTML <table> tag.

2 Understand the fundamentals of a chosen scripting language

2.1 Characteristics of scripting languages

Netscape's **JavaScript**, created back in 1995, is by far the most **popularly used** scripting language when it comes to **client-side** customisation of web pages.

Despite what some people may say, **JavaScript** and **Java** are **not** the same thing! Although the name is **similar**, JavaScript is only distantly related to Sun's full object-oriented programming language. Scripting languages tend to have **looser rules** for dealing with **data**.

JavaScript is Netscape Communications' name for its own **ECMAscript dialect** and is in fact widely considered to be **object based** rather than being fully **object oriented**. In addition it has many similarities to event-driven programming (EDP) languages in that it can respond to both **user-generated** and **system-generated events**.

Unit Links

For further information on object-oriented programming refer to **Unit 25 – Object-Oriented Programming**, pages 378 to 428 and for event-driven programming please refer to **Unit 20 – Event-Driven Programming** in the **Core Text**, pages 291 to 346.

JavaScript's primary purpose is to provide **automation** and **interactivity** for existing **web pages**. Because of this, JavaScript is often included within the **HTML** page itself, although it is possible to store it **separately** in files (much like we have already seen with CSS, although these text files would have a **.JS extension**).

Another point to remember is that JavaScript is **case sensitive**. Please ensure that any examples keyed in are copied **carefully**.

JavaScript support

Although all of the major web browsers support JavaScript, their execution of such scripts can be **enabled** or **disabled** with various **security settings**. The following example demonstrates a simple test to see if JavaScript is enabled on a browser:

In this example, the JavaScript code **alert("Hello")** has been keyed directly into the **URL bar**.

This is acceptable but it isn't the usual way to use JavaScript.

JavaScript is normally placed **inside** HTML documents and as such can be read by the end user by simply asking their web browser to 'view page source'. JavaScript is primarily recognised by being enclosed in **<script> ... </script> HTML** tags. Optionally, the **version** of JavaScript can be specified (at the time of writing, 1.7 is the most recent), e.g.:

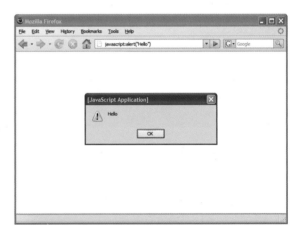

Figure 10.13 JavaScript enabled and working in Mozilla Firefox

```
<script language = "JavaScript 1.7">
:
: JavaScript code goes in here
:
</script>
```

Or more simply:

```
<script>
:
: JavaScript code goes in here
:
</script>
```

We can repeat the **alert** example using a standard **embedded** script like so:

```
<html>
<head>
<title>my first JavaScript</title>
</head>
<body>
<script>
alert("hello")
</script>
</body>
</html>
```

Hiding scripts from older browsers

As with CSS, some older browsers may **not** support JavaScript. In order to hide the JavaScript code and prevent it from being displayed on the web page, the following technique can be used:

```
<script language="JavaScript 1.7">
<!--
JavaScript code goes in here.
//-->
</script>
```

In this example, the web browser will treat the JavaScript code as **HTML comments** and **not** display it.

JavaScript objects

If you're already familiar with object-oriented design you will remember that objects are simply parcels of **properties** (data) and **methods** (functions). Where objects already exist, they represent **convenient** and **reusable** components for the would-be website designer.

The majority of JavaScript objects are those comprising the **visible** parts of HTML: the HTML document, a frame, a window, a form – even down to an individual text area. These all form part of the W3C's Document Object Model (**DOM**).

Some other objects are **abstract** – you can't really see them – but they do provide a useful facility. Included in this list are the **Math** object, the **Date** object, the **Array** object and the **String** object.

Another aspect of the object is the **event handler**.

Here's an example of the integration of HTML and JavaScript, demonstrating the use of an **event handler** and **in-built objects**:

```
<html>
<head>
<title>my first interactive javascript</title>
<script>
function showdate()
{
  today = new Date();
  document.writeln("Today is " + today);
}
</script>
</head>
<body>
<form>
<input type = "button" value = "show date" onClick =
"showdate()">
</form>
</body>
</html>
```

When the web page is loaded into a JavaScript-enabled browser (the example in Figure 10.14 is using Microsoft Internet Explorer®) a **clickable button** appears.

When the button is clicked this triggers the **onClick event handler** and will invoke the "**showdate**" **function**.

When the function executes, a new **Date()** **object** called 'today' is created, taking information from the client PC's **RTC** (Real Time Clock). This information is then sent to the web page via the **document.writeln** method, which adds text to the DOM. The output is shown in Figure 10.15.

Other objects, methods, triggers and event handlers will be discussed later in this learning outcome.

Figure 10.14 JavaScript awaiting a click event

Figure 10.15 JavaScript responding to the click event by invoking the "showdate" function

What JavaScript can do

In outline, a client-side scripting language such as JavaScript is capable of:

◆ controlling a document's **content**
◆ controlling a document's **appearance**
◆ controlling the web browser's **actions**
◆ controlling the web browser's **appearance**
◆ manipulating **images** on a web page
◆ interacting with **Java applets**

- interacting with **document content**
- interacting with the **user**
- reading and writing '**cookies**' (see section 2.2).

Most of these applications of JavaScript are covered in this unit. However, there are also some aspects of JavaScript that require more careful consideration, particularly those related to security. We'll take a look at those now.

Security issues

Client-side JavaScript is both **stored** and **executed** on the user's computer system. This is an important point to remember. Consequently, there are some **security issues** that need to be examined.

Aspects to examine here include:

Reading/writing client files (i.e. data files on the user's computer system)

The designers of JavaScript ensured that possible **malicious damage** to the user's **local computer system** whatever the actual hardware platform (e.g. PC, Apple Mac etc.) and operating system (e.g. Microsoft Windows®, Mac OS or Linux etc.) was **limited**.

The simple answer appears to be that use of standard HTML and JavaScript **will not allow** you to **access** the **local file system** to **read** or **write** files on a client computer system.

However, there are some fairly **inventive** ways around this, but they usually either involve **Java** or **server-side requests** so are outside the scope of this unit.

Opening/closing user windows

This can be achieved reasonably easily using a combination of JavaScript and HTML and makes use of the DOM **open**() method. All the website designer has to do is to name the file or URL to open.

How to open a new window:

```html
<html>
<head>
<title>
Open new pop-up window
</title>
<script>
function openNewWindow()
{
  window.open("KAM.html");
}
</script>
</head>
<body>
<h1>Open a pop-up window</h1>
<br>
<a href="javascript: openNewWindow()">Click here to open a new pop-up window.</a>
</body>
</html>
```

And here's the on-screen outcome:

This technique is often used by websites to place **pop-up adverts** on the web browser's screen, often to the **annoyance** of the user. Some pop-ups may have **pornographic**, **phishing** or (most commonly) **advertising** content. To combat this, many modern web browsers have **pop-up blockers**.

Closing a window can also be achieved using a similar technique, however it's important to remember to **name** the new window in order to identify which one to close.

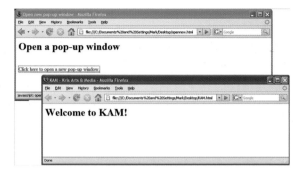

Figure 10.16 JavaScript opening a new pop-up window

Here's the same HTML and JavaScript, slightly modified, with buttons to both open **and** close a new 'child' window. The new code sections are highlighted in blue:

```
<html>
<head>
<title>
Open new pop-up window
</title>
<script>
function openNewWindow()
{
  child = window.open("KAM.html");
}
</script>
</head>
<body>
<h1>Open a pop-up window</h1>
<br>
<a href="javascript: openNewWindow()">Click here to open a new pop-up window.</a>
<br>
<a href="javascript: child.close()">Click here to close the new pop-up window.</a>
</body>
</html>
```

Opening new windows

There are many options for customising new web browser windows although some may be **over-ridden** by settings inside the web browser itself (e.g. opening new windows in a **tabbed pane** rather than a separate window).

Common options include **hiding** the **title bar** or web browser **toolbar**. Setting the new window's **dimensions** (its height and width, typically expressed in pixels) is also common.

More information can be found here:

http://www.w3schools.com/htmldom/met_win_open.asp

Again, as a result of JavaScript's security model, the script language is unable to access data from another window as this would be a clear **risk**.

It can, however, be made to send data from one window to another via several different workarounds. These are complex though and beyond the scope of this text.

Use of 'Cookies'

This is examined in **section 2.2**.

Placing scripts inside HTML

You've already seen the use of the <**script**> **tag** to place JavaScript code **within** your HTML.

However, sometimes you might want to use the **same JavaScript** on a number of **different** web pages. Rather than copying and pasting this code to **each** web page (which is rather time consuming and error prone) it is possible to use a link to an **external JavaScript** file.

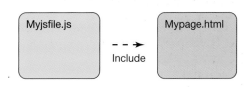

This is pretty much the same technique as that used with the CSS, the only real difference being that external JavaScript files use a '.JS' extension.

We can link to the external script like this:

```
<html>
<head>
<title>my linked JavaScript</title>
</head>
<body>
<script src="myjsfile.js"></script>
</body>
</html>
```

You must remember **not** to include the <script> tag again in the .JS file!

2.2 Use of a scripting language

Apart from displaying user alerts (see section 2.1), JavaScript is used for a number of common applications on a website.

Common uses
Prompting the user

A simple way of **interacting** with the user is to use the JavaScript '**prompt**' **method.**

The following code illustrates a simple example of this JavaScript technique.

```
<html>
<head>
<title>
Frankoni T-Shirts
</title>
<script>
function myPrompt()
{
var name = prompt("What is your name?", "Visitor");
var response = alert("Welcome, " + name + "!");
}
</script>
</head>
<body>
<h1>Frankoni T-Shirts</h1>
<h2>Welcome to Frankoni T-Shirts!</h2>
<form name="myform">
<input type="button" name="button" value="Introduce yourself!"
onclick="myPrompt()" />
</form>
</body>
</html>
```

The prompt method is **similar** to an alert, but offers a **text box** in which the user can enter a value. This value can then be stored in a variable and used in other JavaScript code.

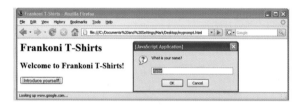

Figure 10.17 JavaScript opening a new prompt pop-up

Entering a name (e.g. 'Josie') into the textbox will then result in a follow-up alert:

Figure 10.18 JavaScript opening up a follow-up alert

Confirming choices

Another simple use of JavaScript is to process **confirmations**; these occur when a user is asked a question and has to respond with a 'yes' or a 'no'.

Here is a simple example you can try:

```html
<html>
<head>
<title>
Frankoni T-Shirts
</title>
<script>
function confirmLoading()
{
  var reply = confirm ("Click OK to continue loading, or CANCEL for Google site.")
  if (!answer)
    window.location="www.google.com"
}
</script>
</head>
<body onload="confirmLoading()">
<h1>Frankoni T-Shirts</h1>
<h2>Welcome to Frankoni T-Shirts!</h2>
Lorem ipsum dolor sit amet, consectetuer adipiscing elit.
</body>
</html>
```

And in the web browser:

Figure 10.19 JavaScript demonstrating a confirmation 'pop-up'

Another example of redirection is shown later in this chapter.

Browser detection

Although all web browsers are expected to follow set rules for rendering HTML, CSS, JavaScript etc., there are **discernable differences** between them that can sometimes make **portable** web page development quite difficult.

In order to ensure that a website **accommodates** the most popular web browsers **correctly**, it is possible to alter the web page content based on **identification** of the web browser **type** and **version**.

As a guide here is some recorded browser usage on a website in November 2007:

(Adapted from: http://www.w3schools.com/browsers/browsers_stats.asp)

The JavaScript code for this (in its most basic form) is pretty straightforward:

Microsoft Internet Explorer® (various)	56%
Firefox	36%
Opera	2%
Safari	2%
Mozilla (including Gecko, Netscape)	1%
Others (various)	3%

```html
<html>
<body>
<script>
function idBrowser()
{
 var browser=navigator.appName;
 var b_version=navigator.appVersion;
 var version=parseFloat(b_version);

 var message = "Browser name: "+ browser;
 message = message + "\nBrowser version: "+ version;
 alert(message);
}
</script>
<body>
<h1>Browser Identification</h1>
<br>
Click button to identify the Web Browser being used.
<form name="myform">
<input type="button" name="button" value="Identify Browser" onClick="idBrowser()">
</form>
</body>
</html>
```

The script uses two public **properties** of the built-in **navigator object**: **appName** and **appVersion**.

The application name of the web browser, e.g. **Microsoft Internet Explorer®**, should be returned by **appName**, and **appVersion** should return the application version of the web browser, e.g. **version 7.**

In this sample web page, a button is used to invoke a function called "idbrowser()". This then accesses the public properties, builds a suitable message and then outputs this via an alert.

Let's test this with Microsoft Internet Explorer®, version 7. As you can see from Figure 10.20, the script has identified the browser's **name correctly**, but **not** the version! This is actually **Microsoft's fault** rather than the script's (they identify their

Figure 10.20 JavaScript detects the web browser

own browser incorrectly). Fortunately Internet Explorer's JavaScript support differs little from version 4 (identified here) to version 7 (the browser actually being used) so there is no major consequence.

Redirecting the user

It is quite common to see one web page **automatically** redirect a user to **another** web page. This can be done for a number of reasons, e.g. to use a web page specific for a particular country that matches the user's location and language preference.

The following JavaScript uses the **onLoad** event handler to initiate a **three-second** (3000 milliseconds) **delayed** redirection to a new web page using the **DOM window object** and **location property**. The redirection is performed by the **"delayRedirect()" function**:

```html
<html>
<head>
<title>
This page will redirect after 3 seconds...
</title>
<script>
function delayRedirect()
{
  window.location = "newfile.html"
}
</script>
</head>
<body onLoad="setTimeout('delayRedirect()', 3000)">
<h3>You are about to be redirected...</h3>
<p>The page you requested has moved. Please update your bookmarks/favourites.</p>
</body>
</html>
```

Creating image rollovers

You have undoubtedly seen a rollover before. Reacting to whether the mouse **cursor** is **hovering over** an **image**, the browser **swaps** it to another image. Its most obvious use on the World Wide Web is for creating web page **navigation** (e.g. **highlighting buttons**).

The following JavaScript code makes use of **two button images** (button1.jpg and button2.jpg) to create a simple rollover effect that acts as an HTML image link to another website:

```html
<html>
<head>
<title>
 Creating rollovers using JavaScript
</title>
<script>
 rollover = new Array()
 rollover[0]= new Image(184,55)
 rollover[0].src = "button1.jpg"
 rollover[1] = new Image(184,55)
 rollover[1].src = "button2.jpg"
```

```
  function changeImage()
  {
  document.button.src = rollover[1].src;
  return true;
  }
  function revertImage()
  {
  document.button.src = rollover[0].src;
  return true;
  }
</script>
</head>
<body>
<h2>JavaScript rollover example</h2>
<a href="http://www.krisartsandmedia.co.uk" onmouseover="changeImage()"
onmouseout="revertImage()">
<img src="button1.jpg" name="button" width=184 height=55 border=0>
</body>
</html>
```

Let's test this web page and then examine its workings…

Figure 10.21 Rollover with default button1.jpg image

When the mouse cursor **hovers** over the image the **onmouseover event handler** is **triggered**.

As you can see from Figure 10.22, the image has been **replaced** with button2.jpg by the JavaScript **changeImage() function**.

When the mouse cursor moves **away** from the button image, the **onmouseout event handler** is **triggered**.

The JavaScript **revertImage()** function dutifully changes the image source **back** to the **original** button1.jpg file.

The core element of this JavaScript solution is the use of the 'rollover' array to store **both** the image **filename** and **dimensions** of **each** button. Depending on which event handler is triggered, the image source of the button element (highlighted in **yellow**) is **changed** in the JavaScript using the **Document.button.src** reference.

This is another example of accessing the DOM.

Figure 10.22 Rollover with replacement button2.jpg image

Figure 10.23 Rollover with original button1.jpg image again

Checking/validating form input (handling forms)

JavaScript is often used to check **form input**, especially the content of textboxes where a user has to **manually** enter their name, postcode or email address.

Often these entries are left **blank** (so are **null**) or have **incorrect data** entered (e.g. **invalid email addresses**).

The following JavaScript example demonstrates a **validation** of the user's email address:

```
<html>
<head>
<script>
function checkEmail(email)
{
atpos=email.value.indexOf("@");
dotpos=email.value.lastIndexOf(".");
if (atpos <1 || (dotpos-atpos)<2 )
{
alert("Please enter a valid email address");
return false;
}
else
{
return true;
}
}
function validateForm(thisform)
{
if (checkEmail(thisform.useremail)==false)
{
thisform.useremail.focus();
return false;
}
}
</script>
</head>
<body>
<h1>Frankoni T-Shirts</h1>
<h2>Keep informed on new tees via email!</h2>
<form action="acknowledge.html" onsubmit="return validateForm(this);"
method="post">
Your email
<input type="text" name="useremail" size="25">
<input type="submit" value="submit">
</form>
</body>
</html>
```

In this example, JavaScript is used to prevent the posting of the user's email if the email address they enter does not meet the validation requirements.

Their requirements are: should **have** an '@' (at symbol); should **have** a '.' (dot); and the dot has to be **at least two** characters **after** the @ symbol.

If these criteria are not met, the email address is deemed to be invalid and the form is not submitted, returning the browser's **focus** to the email textbox for another attempt.

Figure 10.24 shows the web page loaded into a web browser.

This JavaScript example relies on two different functions:

Figure 10.24 Invalid email address alert

◆ **checkEmail()**

This function locates the character position of both the '@' and '.' symbol in the entered email address. If the **either** (or **both**) conditions **fail** (they **aren't true**), an **error message** is displayed via an **alert** and the function returns a '**false**' value. If **either** condition is true, the function returns a '**true**' value.

◆ **validateForm()**

This function, called by the form's **onsubmit** event handler, uses the **checkEmail()** function. If the email it sends fails the check above, the **posting** of the **form's data** to the next web page (acknowledge.html) **is aborted** and the **focus** returns back to the email text box.

It is possible to use JavaScript to perform many different types of form-based validations (see section 4.3 for more examples).

Maintaining cookies

Cookies

The **HTTP protocol** which controls the transfer of web pages from the web server to the web client is said to be '**stateless**'. This essentially means that it doesn't really take into account the fact that this may be your 1st, 3rd or 122nd visit to a particular website.

Clearly there is often a need to **remember** things about you: **your preferences** on the website and **your browsing history** with the website. This gives your browsing experience a sense of **continuity** and **familiarity**.

This data is stored on **your computer system** in small **text files** called '**cookies**'.

Each cookie has basic data, stored as a long piece of text that contains:

◆ a **name-content** pair containing the actual data being stored;
◆ an **expiry date** (for when it's no longer valid);
◆ the **domain and path** of the server to which it should be sent.

Clearly there's a balance here between **user-friendliness/website customisation** and the user's **privacy**.

Fortunately most modern web browsers have **cookie management** facilities that let you **see** the cookies and, if necessary, **delete** them (see Figure 10.25).

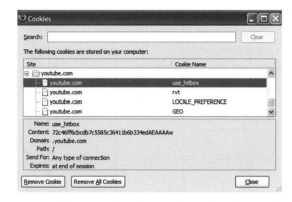

Figure 10.25 Cookie management in Mozilla Firefox showing YouTube cookies stored

It is also common to have the ability to **prevent** cookies from being stored (accepted from the visited web server) although this can thwart some websites from **operating properly** (and you may be asked to re-enable them before continuing). Mozilla Firefox's cookie options are shown in Figure 10.26.

Working with cookies in JavaScript is fairly straightforward.

Figure 10.26 Controlling cookie settings in Mozilla Firefox.

Creating a cookie

```
function createCookie(name,content,expiry)
{
if (expiry)
{
var date = new Date();
date.setTime(date.getTime()+(expiry*24*60*60*1000));
var expires = "; expires="+date.toGMTString();
alert("Cookie successfully created :)");
}
else
var expires = "";
document.cookie = name + "=" + content + expires + ";path=/";
}
```

This section of code, accepts three parameters (the cookie **name**, its **content** and **expiry date**).

It then creates a new date object ("date") and adds onto it the number of days indicated by the expiry parameter (converted to milliseconds). This is then converted to a Greenwich Mean Time (GMT) format string.

If no expiry is set, the expiry value is left **blank**. The cookie's value is then set as its name, followed by its content, the expiry date and a path.

Using a cookie

This is perhaps the most complex aspect of cookie processing as it has to access the **correct cookie** and **extract** the different parts of the cookie's information from one long piece of text.

The code itself uses a number of **array** and **string processing functions** to find the correct cookie (by name) out of all those currently existing on a system.

Once located it displays the **cookie's name** and **content** via an **alert**.

```
function useCookie(name)
{
 var cname = name + "=";
 var cookielist = document.cookie.split(';');
 for(var i=0;i < cookielist.length;i++)
 {
 var each = cookielist[i];
 while (each.charAt(0)==' ')
 each = each.substring(1,each.length);
 if (each.indexOf(cname) == 0)
 alert("Cookie name:
"+name+"\n"+"Content:"+each.substring(cname.length,each.length)
);
 }
 return null;
}
```

JavaScript syntax

The JavaScript code for the **useCookie() function** is quite complex.
For support on the syntax, please refer to section 2.3 in this unit where elements such as **loops** and **decision making** are covered in more detail.

Removing a cookie

By far the **easiest** function to write! This function simply creates a new cookie with the same name, no content and an expiry of −1 days. The '−1' expiry value (**yesterday**) will cause the cookie to be **immediately** removed from the client's computer system by the web browser.

```
function removeCookie(name)
{
 createCookie(name,"",-1);
}
```

We can put this all together with a little HTML to create a full cookie-driven experience:

```
<html>
<head>
<title>
Cookie tester
</title>
<script>
function createCookie(name,content,expiry)
{
  if (expiry)
  {
    var date = new Date();

    date.setTime(date.getTime()+(expiry*24*60*60*1000));
    var expires = "; expires="+date.toGMTString();
    alert("Cookie successfully created :)");
  }
  else
      var expires = "";
  document.cookie = name + "=" + content + expires + ";path=/";
}

function useCookie(name)
{
  var cname = name + "=";
  var cookielist = document.cookie.split(';');
  for(var i=0;i < cookielist.length;i++)
  {
    var each = cookielist[i];
    while (each.charAt(0)==' ')
      each = each.substring(1,each.length);
    if (each.indexOf(cname) == 0)
      alert("Cookie name:
"+name+"\n"+"Content:"+each.substring(cname.length,each.length));
  }
    return null;
}

function removeCookie(name)
{
  createCookie(name,"",-1);
}

</script>
</head>
<body>
<h1>Cookie Tester</h1>
<br>
<form name="myform">
Cookie name?
<input type="text" name="cookie" value="" size="20">
Cookie content?
<input type="text" name="cookiecontent" value="" size="10">
Cookie expiry? (in days)
<input type="text" name="cookieexpire" value="" size="3">
```

```
<br><br>
<input type="button" name="button1" value="Create Cookie"
onClick="createCookie(cookie.value,cookiecontent.value, cookieexpire.value)">
<input type="button" name="button2" value="Display Cookie"
onClick="useCookie(cookie.value)">
<input type="button" name="button3" value="Remove Cookie"
onClick="removeCookie(cookie.value)">
</form>
</body>
</html>
```

When the web page is loaded it will look like the image in Figure 10.27.

Figure 10.27 Cookie Tester in Mozilla Firefox

This webpage has three text boxes for input ('cookie', 'cookiecontent' and 'cookieexpire').

It also has three buttons that generate click events handled by their JavaScript **onClick event handlers**.

Let's key in some sample cookie values:

Figure 10.28 Cookie Tester in Mozilla Firefox with values keyed in

Clicking on the **'Create Cookie' button** will pass **all three** inputs ('username', 'Matthew' and '28') **into** the **createCookie() function**.

Once the createCookie function has processed this data, an **alert** is used to confirm that the cookie has been **created**.

Figure 10.29 Cookie Tester confirms creation of the cookie

Figure 10.30 Cookie Tester displays the new cookie and its content

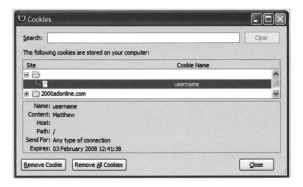

Figure 10.31 Cookie management in Mozilla Firefox showing our new cookie

We can then use the **'Display Cookie' button** to pass just the cookie **name** ('username') to the **useCookie() function**. This should **access** the cookie stored on the user's local system and display its **name** and content in an alert.

It should of course be possible to check the web browser's cookie management facility to see this value (see Figure 10.31).

We can then use the **'Remove Cookie' button** to pass just the cookie **name** ('username') to the **removeCookie() function**. This will effectively force the existing cookie to expire and be automatically deleted by the web browser.

Clearly this example is artificial – the management of cookies is usually **hidden** from the visitor (unless their web browser security settings are high).

However, now that you know how to **create**, **use** and **delete** a cookie it should be possible to remember values specific to an individual user and use them to make their **next visit** just a bit more personalised, even if it's just to welcome them back by their name (e.g. 'Hello Matthew!').

2.3 Scripting language constructs

The JavaScript language is large and cannot be completely covered by this text (that would be a book in itself – see **Further Reading** at the end of this unit for some recommendations).

It is possible however to cover the basic **syntax** elements that comprise the JavaScript language:

◆ variables and values
◆ operators
◆ assignment statement and its operators
◆ dot operator, objects and methods
◆ decision making (if...else, switch statement)
◆ loops (for, do...while and while)
◆ functions (calling, parameter passing)
◆ common event handlers
◆ common methods
◆ common properties.

Each of these elements is accompanied by some sample code.

Variables and values

Variables

A variable is a form of **identifier**; a 'name' which **represents** a **value**.

In JavaScript a variable is used to **store** and **retrieve data** from the computer's RAM. Every variable should have a **unique** (and **meaningful**) name. Since JavaScript is **case sensitive**, a variable called 'name' would **not** be the same as one called 'NAME'.

So, if we want to store our user's age in a variable:

```
var age = 20;
```
or just
```
age = 20
```

As you may notice, the '**var**' keyword is **optional** in JavaScript.

This is essentially a combination of a declaration and an assignment.

A better practice would have been to add a single-line comment, so:

```
var age = 20; // Will store the user's age
```

In JavaScript variable names must either start with a **letter** (A to Z or a to z) or an **underscore**.

Unlike other more formalised programming languages (e.g. C#, Java etc.), JavaScript **doesn't** require the developer to specify a **data type** (e.g. integer, string etc.). This often leads to accusations of it being '**poorly typed**' – a **major detraction** for many professional website developers.

Variable lifetime

Variables declared **within** a function are said to be '**local**' to that function and so can **only** be used **inside** that function. When the function ends, the variable is **deleted**. It is quite possible to **reuse** the **same** local variable names in a number of **different** functions.

However, if a variable is declared **within** the <script> **tag** but **before** a list of functions, **all the functions** can access it. We call this a '**global**' variable. Global variables have a **longer lifetime** than local variables; they 'die' when the browser **closes** the page.

Operators

JavaScript supports a fairly rich set of operators, almost identical to those in C++, Java and C#:

Arithmetic operators

These are the basic building blocks for forming **arithmetic expressions** (calculations involving numbers).

Here is a list of JavaScript arithmetic operators:

Arithmetic operation	JavaScript symbol	Code example	Result
Add	+	X = 8; Y = 2; Z = X + Y;	Z = 10
Subtract	–	X = 8; Y = 2; Z = X - Y;	Z = 6
Multiply	* (asterisk)	X = 8; Y = 2; Z = X * Y;	Z = 16
Divide	/ (forward slash)	X = 7; Y = 2; Z = X / Y;	Z = 3.5
Modulus (obtains the remainder)	% (percentage)	X = 8; Y = 2; Z = X % Y;	Z = 0
Increment (increase by 1)	++	X = 8; X++;	X = 9
Decrement (decrease by 1)	--	Y = 8; Y--;	Y = 7

In addition, **parentheses** (brackets) may be used to alter the natural order of operations (division, multiplication, addition and subtraction). For example:

average = num1 + num2 + num3 / 3

isn't the same as:

average = (num1 + num2 + num3) / 3

The **second** version (forcing all the **addition** to be **performed first**) is the **correct one** and requires the use of parentheses.

Activity

Convert the following arithmetic calculations to JavaScript expressions:

The numbers of centimetres in an inch is 2.54. Write JavaScript to calculate how many centimetres in 6.5 inches.

Degrees Celsius can be found by first subtracting 32 and then multiplying by 5/9. Write JavaScript to calculate what 98°F is in degrees C.

How well did you do? See page 443 for the answers.

Logical operators

The following table lists the most common logical operations and their JavaScript implementations:

Logical operation	JavaScript implementation
AND	&&
OR	||
NOT	!

Relational operators

This is a set of operators that make **direct comparisons between values**. The **result** of this type of comparison can **only** be **true** or **false**.

The following table lists these relational operations and their JavaScript implementations:

Relational operator	JavaScript implementation
==	Equal to (test for equality in values)
===	Equal to (test for equality in values and data types)
!=	Not equal to (test for inequality)
>	Greater than
<	Less than
>=	Greater than *or* equal to
<=	Less than *or* equal to

Help with relational operators

Can't remember which symbol is '**Less than**'?

Remember, it's just a **squashed** 'L':

$<$ess than

Braincheck

Work out whether these expressions **evaluate** to **TRUE** or **FALSE**:

10 > 5
6 == 6
2 != 3
6 === "6"
FALSE == FALSE
10 > 3 AND 12>=12
–3 < 2 OR 90 < 17
"MATTHEW" == "Matthew"
(12–2) >= (36/4)

How well did you do?
See page 443 for the answers.

Assignment statement and its operators

In JavaScript, an assignment statement is used to **give** a variable a value.

When an assignment is successfully performed, the **previous value** stored in the variable is **overwritten**. The assignment statement makes use of the basic **assignment operator** ('='):

```
age = 14; // set user's age

name = "Smith"; // set user's surname

gradeavq = 56.5; // set user's grade
                 average
```

If the variable is being assigned for the **first time** we call this process 'initialisation'. Some programming languages **do not** initialise new variables to **sensible** starting values (e.g. 0). Where this does not happen automatically, initialisation must occur to ensure that the variables are ready for use.

JavaScript also has a number of specific **assignment operators** (often called 'compound' assignments) which perform more complex assignments:

Assignment operator	Code example	Result
=	X = 2; Y = 4; X = Y;	X = 4
+=	X = 3; Y = 4; X += Y;	X = 7
-=	X = 9; Y = 4; X -= Y;	X = 5
*=	X = 2; Y = 4; X *= Y;	X = 8
/=	X = 12; Y = 4; X /= Y;	X = 3
%=	X = 7; Y = 2; X %= Y;	X = 1

Dot operator, objects and methods

As previously mentioned, JavaScript is seen by most website developers to be an **object-based language**. As a result it has a number of **in-built objects**, with each object having a number of documented **properties** and **methods**.

The **dot operator** ('.') is used to **separate** objects names **from** their methods and properties.

Here is a simple example that illustrates this point:

```html
<html>
<head>
<title>
KAM Visitor sign-up
</title>
<script>
function myName()
{
 var name = document.myform.username.value;
 var length = name.length;
 if (length > 10)
 alert ("Please try again.\nNo more than 10 letters.");
 else
 alert ("Welcome to KAM, " + name.toLowerCase());
}
</script>
</head>
<body>
<h1>KAM Visitor sign-up</h1>
<h2>Welcome to Kris Arts and Media! (KAM)</h2>
Please enter a nickname for yourself (max 10 letters)...
<br>
<br>
<form name="myform">
<input type="text" name="username" value = "" size = "10">
<input type="button" name="button" value="Introduce yourself!"
onclick="myName()">
</form>
</body>
</html>
```

In this example, JavaScript is being used to **validate the length** of the nickname entered by the user into the 'username' text box on the web page.

It does this by accessing the 'value' property of the 'username' text box and then finds its size in characters by accessing the 'length' property. Both of these properties are shown in green.

Likewise, the user's nickname is displayed in lower case by the accessing the 'toLowerCase()' string method (shown in yellow).

It is important to note that the **tell-tale difference** between properties and methods is that a method will typically have **brackets after** the method name.

See **common methods** and **common properties** for more.

Figure 10.32 Nickname is validated with the length property and formatted with the toLowerCase method

More string object methods and properties

There are far too many string object methods and properties to list here. A complete reference for these can be found at:

http://www.w3schools.com/jsref/jsref_obj_string.asp

Decision making (if...else, switch statement)

Although programs can be built from a **simple sequence** (one event following another), these only provide limited solutions:

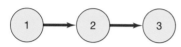

Here, as you can see, the solution follows steps **1**, **2** and **3**. **No step is missed, no step is repeated**.

More complex solutions require the ability to **make choices**.

e.g.

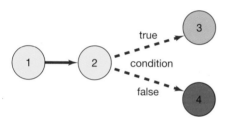

In this example, a condition is made **after** step 2.

If the condition is **true**, step **3** is performed.

If the condition is **false**, step **4** is performed **instead**.

It **isn't** possible to perform **both** steps 3 and 4 – the script has a **choice** to make.

If...else statement

Most programming and scripting languages perform these types of decision using an **if...else statement**; JavaScript is no exception.

If...else statements take the general format:

Things to remember:

◆ The 'else' part of the **if...else statement** is **optional**. If you don't have any action for the 'false' part, **don't have** an 'else'.

◆ Braces '{' and '}' are used to form blocks around code that is intended to be **kept together**. If only one line of code is required for either the true or false part, the braces are optional.

```
if (condition)
{
  code to be performed if condition is true
}
else
{
  code to be executed if condition is false
}
```

Here is a simple example of an if…else statement in JavaScript:

```
<html>
<head>
<title>
Lee Office Supplies
</title>
<script>
function showGreeting()
{
  var date = new Date();
  var hour = date.getHours();
  if (hour < 12)
  {
    alert("Good morning!");
  }
  else
  {
    alert("Good afternoon!");
  }
}
</script>
</head>
<body onload = "showGreeting()">
<h1>Lee Office Supplies</h1>
<h2>Welcome to Lee Office Supplies</h2>
<p>
Lorem ipsum dolor sit amet, consectetuer adipiscing elit. Vivamus ut dolor sit
amet arcu eleifend commodo. In eget dui et diam dapibus porttitor. Morbi quis
dui et massa
</p>
</body>
</html>
```

And a more complex example:

```
<html>
<head>
<title>
Maths Quiz
</title>
<script>

function makeRandom(n)
{
  var randnum = Math.floor(Math.random()*n+1);
  return randnum;
}
```

```
function loadRandom()
{
  document.myform.num1.value = makeRandom(10);
  document.myform.num2.value = makeRandom(10);
}

function checkResult()
{
  var result = 0;
  var num1 = parseInt(document.myform.num1.value);
  var num2 = parseInt(document.myform.num2.value);
  var guess = parseInt(document.myform.guess.value);
  result = num1 + num2;
  if (result == guess)
    alert("Well done!  You guessed correctly.");
  else
    alert("Unlucky! The correct answer is " + result);
}
</script>
</head>

<body onload = "loadRandom()">
<h1>Maths Quiz</h1>
<h2>Guess the sum of the two numbers and press the button!</h2>
<br>
<form name="myform">
<input type="text" name="num1" value = "" size = "3">
+
<input type="text" name="num2" value = "" size = "3">
=
<input type="text" name="guess" value = "" size = "3">
<input type="button" name="button" value="Am I right?" onclick="checkResult()">
</form>
</body>
</html>
```

In this example, the JavaScript loads two random values (between 1 and 10) into the form and asks the user to guess their sum.

In detail:

Each random number is created by the makeRandom() function which is called twice by the loadRandom() function that is run by the page's onload() event handler.

The user can then enter a guess at the sum of the number and press the button to see if they are correct.

The button's onclick() event handler calls the checkResult() function and this function performs the addition of the two random numbers and compares its sum to the user's guess using an if…else statement.

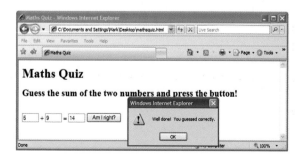

Figure 10.33 The user guesses correctly

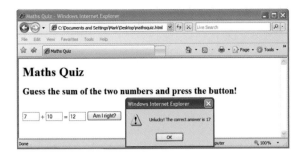

Figure 10.34 The user guesses incorrectly

If the numbers are the same (they are equal), a 'Well done' message is displayed via an alert.

If the numbers **aren't** the same (they are **not equal**), an 'Unlucky' message is displayed via an alert – along with the real answer.

Refreshing the web page with the **F5 key** (on Microsoft Explorer® or Mozilla Firefox) will generate new random numbers.

Switch statements

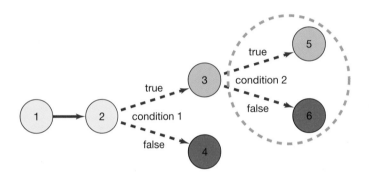

Sometimes the programmer wishes to check for **multiple possibilities**.

Two primary techniques are available, first the **'nested' if…else**.

As you can see from this diagram, the **second if…else** is **nested** into the **'true' part** of the **first if…else**.

Use of nested if…else statements is common but can lead to unnecessary over-complication.

Case (or switch) statements simplify things somewhat by being able to pick a single matching value from a list of possibilities.

The case statement works **more effectively** because it can make **individual comparisons** against **each possible matching value**. If the comparison is **true** (they match), the resulting action (3, 4 or 5) is performed.

Let's put this into a practical JavaScript example.

Imagine that we have stored the **day of the week** as an **integer variable** (e.g. 0 is Sunday, 1 is Monday, 2 is Tuesday etc.). What we'd like to do is examine the variable and be able to **output the correct day** of the week in text, i.e. 'It's Monday!'

Examine the following JavaScript example, which is coded using **nested if…else statements**.

```
<html>
<head>
<title>
Lee Office Supplies
</title>
<script>
function showGreeting()
{
  var date = new Date();
  var day = date.getDay();
  if (day == 0)
    alert("It's Sunday!");
  else
    if (day == 1)
      alert("It's Monday!");
    else
      if (day == 2)
        alert("It's Tuesday!");
      else
        if (day == 3)
          alert("It's Wednesday!");
        else
          if (day == 4)
            alert("It's Thursday!");
          else
            if (day == 5)
              alert("It's Friday!");
            else
              alert("It's Saturday!");
}
</script>
</head>
<body onload = "showGreeting()">
<h1>Lee Office Supplies</h1>
<h2>Welcome to Lee Office Supplies</h2>
<p>
Lorem ipsum dolor sit amet, consectetuer adipiscing elit.
Vivamus ut dolor sit amet arcu eleifend commodo. In eget
dui et diam dapibus porttitor. Morbi quis dui et massa porta
</p>
</body>
</html>
```

Figure 10.35 It's Tuesday!

Figure 10.35 shows typical output from the JavaScript code (assuming it's Tuesday).

As you can see, even though indentation has been used to show the underlying logic, this looks rather **untidy** and **inefficient**.

The **switch statement** version of this in JavaScript is more straightforward:

```
<html>
<head>
<title>
Lee Office Supplies
</title>
<script>
function showGreeting()
{
  var date = new Date();
  var day = date.getDay();
  switch(day)
  {
    case 0 : alert("It's Sunday!");
             break;
    case 1 : alert("It's Monday!");
             break;
    case 2 : alert("It's Tuesday!");
             break;
    case 3 : alert("It's Wednesday!");
             break;
    case 4 : alert("It's Thursday!");
             break;
    case 5 : alert("It's Friday!");
             break;
    case 6 : alert("It's Saturday!");
             break;
    default: alert("Invalid Day!");
  }
}
</script>
</head>
<body onload = "showGreeting()">
<h1>Lee Office Supplies</h1>
<h2>Welcome to Lee Office Supplies</h2>
<p>
Lorem ipsum dolor sit amet, consectetuer adipiscing elit.
Vivamus ut dolor sit amet arcu eleifend commodo. In eget
dui et diam dapibus porttitor. Morbi quis dui et massa porta
</p>
</body>
</html>
```

As you may have noticed, the **default option** is available to **catch** any **unexpected values**.

Switch statements can also handle **multiple matches**, for example if we want to **cheer** on the **weekend** a **minor modification** is needed:

```
case 6:
case 0: alert("It's the Weekend!");
        break;
}
```

Loops

Loops or **iterations** allow the scripter to make something happen **repeatedly**.

Normally loops will repeat **until** they are **told to stop**. This is achieved by using a **conditional statement**, e.g. **reply == 'Y'** will repeat the loop while a reply is 'Y' (for 'Yes').

Post-check conditioning occurs when the conditional statement is placed **after the actions**, e.g.:

Because of this, the actions in a post-check conditioned loop will **always** work **at least** once.

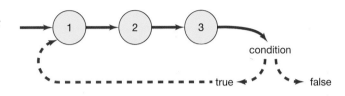

```
<script>
counter = 1;
do
{
    document.write("The number is " + counter + "<br>");
    counter++;
}
while ( counter <= 10;
</script>
```

In JavaScript a post-check loop can be created by using a '**do…while**' like so:

In this example, a post-check condition is used to repeat the loop **while** the **counter** is **less than or equal to 10**. Each **cycle** of the loop **outputs** the

counter's **current value** (starting from 1) and **increments** the counter. The loop **stops** when the condition is **no longer true**: i.e. when the counter gets to **11**.

The resulting screen output would be:

Pre-check conditioning occurs when the conditional statement is placed **before** the actions, e.g.:

Placing the condition at the start of the loop has an interesting effect; if the loop condition is found to be false to begin with, its actions will **never** be processed.

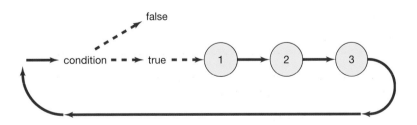

Figure 10.36 Output from post-check do…while loop

In JavaScript a pre-check loop can be created by using a 'while' loop:

```
<script>
counter = 1;
while (counter <= 10)
{
  document.write("The number is " + counter + "<br>");
  counter++;
}
</script>
```

The resulting screen output would be the same as Figure 10.36.

For loop

Another type of pre-conditioned loop is the **for** loop.

The **for** loop is used when the number of times the events are to be repeated is **known** at the **start**.

The following script will again generate the same output as Figure 10.36:

```
<script>
for (counter = 0; counter <= 10; counter++)
{
  document.write("The number is " + counter + "<br>");
}
</script>
```

For...In loop

Javascript's **for...in** loop is a more **specialist** version of its standard for loop. It is mainly used to automatically step through **elements** in a **document** or an **array**.

The following example demonstrates the use of the for...in loop to display the elements in an array:

```
<html>
<body>
<script>
var counter;
var sevendwarves = new Array();
sevendwarves [0] = "Sleepy";
sevendwarves [1] = "Grumpy";
sevendwarves [2] = "Dopey";
sevendwarves [3] = "Bashful";
sevendwarves [4] = "Happy";
sevendwarves [5] = "Sleepy";
sevendwarves [6] = "Sneezy";
for (counter in sevendwarves)
{

document.write(sevendwarves[counter]
+"<br>");
}
</script>
</body>
</html>
```

Figure 10.37 Output from for...in array example

And the resulting output in Figure 10.37:

Activity

Frankoni T-shirts Ltd requires an interactive web page (with client-side JavaScript) that will calculate the **production cost** and **projected sales price** of a designer T-shirt.

Frankoni buy blank shirts at the following rates: Small (£3 each), Medium (£4 each), Large (£6 each) and eXtra Large (£7 each).

It costs Frankoni £2.50 to print the customer's design on the T-shirt.

Frankoni aims to make a 30 per cent profit on each T-shirt sold.

Code a scripted web page that will calculate and output production costs, projected sales and the profit of selling a user-specified quantity of each type of T-shirt.

Braincheck

Answer the following questions…

1 What is a variable?
2 When does a global variable 'die'?
3 Name three different types of operator.
4 What does the modulus operator do?
5 What is the assignment statement used for?
6 Name two things that could follow the dot operator.
7 Name two ways of making a decision.
8 What is the alternative statement to a nested…if?
9 Name a post-conditioned loop in JavaScript.
10 A for…in loop can be used to cycle through…?

How well did you do? See page 443 for the answers.

Functions (calling, parameter passing)

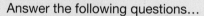

Key Terms

Functions

In JavaScript, a function is simply a **block of code** that will be executed automatically by an **event handler** or when the function is manually **called**.

Functions can be reusable, especially if they are in a separate '**.js**' file.

Many code samples in this unit use JavaScript functions.

Generally functions exist **between** the <script>...</script> tags in a HTML file. The name of the function should be **descriptive**.

The general format of a **simple** function is:

Sometimes a function may need **specific data** in order to work properly. Data values that are **passed into** it for processing are called **parameters**.

```
function yourFunctionName()
{
    function code goes here
}
```

Parameters are added into the **parentheses after** the function name. The **order** of the parameters **does not matter**, but when the function is called, the arguments supplied must be in the **same order**. More on this later!

Here is an example of a function with **two parameters**:

```
function yourFunctionName(variable1, variable2)
{
    function code goes here
}
```

The following JavaScript example performs the simple task of converting pound sterling into US dollars.

```
<html>
<head>
<title>
Currency Conversion
</title>
<script>
function poundsToDollars(p,r)
{
    var conv = 0;
    conv = parseFloat(p.value) * parseFloat(r.value);
    document.myform.dollars.value = conv;
}
</script>
</head>
<body>
<h1>Currency Conversion</h1>
<br>
<form name="myform">
Pounds
<input type="text" name = "pounds" value="0" size = "5">
X Exchange rate
<input type="text" name = "rate" value="0" size = "5">
=
<input type="text" name = "dollars" value = "0" size = "5">
Dollars
<input type="button" name = "button" value="Convert"
onclick="poundsToDollars(pounds,rate);">
</form>
</body>
</html>
```

The JavaScript **function 'poundsToDollars()'** is called when the '**Convert' button** is clicked.

This will pass in the values in the two text boxes ('**pounds**' and '**rate**'). In the function they are accepted as **parameters** 'p' and 'r'. Note the order is the **same**.

Inside the function a **new variable** is created ('**conv**') to store the converted value. The two values are **explicitly** converted to decimal numbers and multiplied, storing the result in the new '**conv**' variable.

The '**conv**' variables value is then sent back to the 'dollars' text box on the **form**.

Here is a sample test run of this JavaScript solution:

Figure 10.38 Output from currency conversion

Common events

Events are actions that are **detectable** by JavaScript; some events may be caused by the **user**, some may be caused by the **computer system** itself. All **HTML elements** (e.g. buttons, text boxes, checkboxes, windows etc.) have **associated** events. You have seen **many** of these event handlers used to launch JavaScript functions throughout this chapter.

Common JavaScript methods include, in alphabetical order:

Event name	This event occurs when...
onabort	The loading of an image is interrupted
onblur	An element on a web page loses focus
onchange	The user changes the content in a text field
onclick	When the user clicks the mouse on an object
ondblclick	When the user double-clicks the mouse on an object
onerror	When an error occurs while a document or an image is loading
onfocus	An element on a web page gets focus
onkeydown	Any key is pressed
onkeypress	Any key is pressed or held down by the user
onkeyup	A key that was held down is released
onload	A page or an image has finished loading
onmousedown	A mouse button is pressed
onmousemove	The mouse is moved by the user
onmouseout	The mouse is moved off an element
onmouseover	The mouse is moved over an element
onmouseup	A mouse button is released
onreset	The form's reset button is clicked by the user

Event name	This event occurs when...
onresize	A window or frame changes size, e.g. through user preference
onselect	Text is selected by the user
onsubmit	The form's submit button is clicked by the user
onunload	The user exits the current web page

The following example demonstrates the use of the **'onkeyup' event** to create a simple 'keypress' counter for a feedback form:

```
<html>
<head>
<title>Lee Office Supplies Feedback</title>
<script>
function checkMessage()
{
   var len = 0;
   var max = 150;
   var charsleft = 0;
   len = document.myform.message.value.length;
   charsleft = max - len;
   document.myform.remaining.value = charsleft;
}
</script>
</head>
<body>
<h1>Lee Office Supplies</h1>
<h2>Customer Feedback</h2>
<p>Please leave us some feedback on your order.</p>
<form name="myform">
<textarea rows="5" cols="30" name="message" onkeyup="checkMessage();">
</textarea>
Characters left
<input type="text" name = "remaining" value="0" size = "3" readonly>
</form>
</body>
</html>
```

Figure 10.39 shows the test run of this particular JavaScript:

Figure 10.39 Output from onkeyup event example

Common methods

Methods are functions that form **part** of an object.

Common JavaScript methods include:

Method name	Description
click()	click() can be used with any HTML element capable of generating an onclick() event. click() is used to **manually simulate** a mouse click on an HTML element.
open()	The more common usage of the open() method is to open a new window in the browser. It is possible to specify the source HTML page, the name of the window, whether it has scrollbars or a status line, and its width and height. e.g. `newWindow = window.open ('test.html', 'new window','scrollbars=no,status=yes,width=350,height=300');`

select()	The select() method is used to highlight text in a form's text box. It is often used in conjunction with the **focus() method** to direct a user's attention to a text entry that has to be **re-keyed**.
	
	e.g. if '**myform**' is the name of the form and '**username**' the text box:
	
	`document.myform.username.focus();`
	
	`document.myform.username.select();`

write()	Most commonly used in conjunction with the **document object** to print text directly to the web page. e.g. `document.write("Hello");` It can also be used to print variables: e.g. `document.write("Welcome, "+ username);`

Common properties

Properties are the attributes that form **part** of an object. Common JavaScript properties that relate to **HTML <form> elements** (e.g. Textbox) include:

Property name	Description
size	The number of characters in the textbox selected
maxLength	The maximum number of characters in the text box selected
value	The value in the textbox selected
type	The type of element
readOnly	Whether or not the textbox permits keyboard entry by user

Here is an example of these properties being accessed:

```html
<html>
<head>
<title>Properties check</title>
<script>
function displayProperties()
{
  var newtext;
  newtext="Size: "+ document.getElementById("user").size+"\n";
  newtext+="Type: " + document.getElementById("user").type+"\n";
  newtext+="Value: " + document.getElementById("user").value+"\n";
  newtext+="Max:"+document.getElementById("user").maxLength+"\n";
  newtext+= "Read only?"+document.getElementById("user").readOnly;
  document.getElementById("results").value = newtext;
}
</script>
</head>
<body>
<h1>Properties check</h1>
<form name="myform">
<p>Key text in box then click button.</p>
<input type="text" id = "user" value="" size = "5">
<input type="button" name ="mybutton" value="Find out!"
onClick="displayProperties();">
<p>Some properties of the textbox are:</p>
<textarea rows="5" cols="30" id="results">
</textarea>
</form>
</body>
```

The output from this script is shown in Figure 10.40.

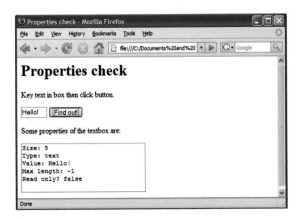

Figure 10.40 Output from textbox elements example

```
<html>
<head>
<title>
Tables
</title>
<style>
#div1
{
float:left;
width:50%;
color:white;
background-color:#6699CC;
}
#div2
{
margin-left:50%;
color:white;
background-color:6633FF;
width:50%;
display: table-cell;
vertical-align: middle;
}
textarea
{
display: block;
margin-left: auto;
margin-right: auto;
}
body
{
background-color:#6699CC;
}
</style>
<script>
function showTables(numtable,numtimes)
{
  if (numtimes>=1 && numtimes<=12)
  {
    var counter;
```

```
      var result;
      var output;
      output = "The "+ numtable + " times table\n";
      for(counter = 0;counter <= numtimes;counter++)
      {
        result = counter * numtable;
        output += counter+" x "+numtable+" = "+result+"\n";
      }
      document.getElementById("results").value = output;
    }
    else
    {
      alert("Sorry!\n The number of rows must between 1 and 12.");
    }
  }
</script>
</head>
<body>
<h2>Child's Times Tables</h2>
<div id="div1">
<p>Enter table required and number of rows. Click ok button to create table!</p>
<form name="myform">
<p>Which table?</p>
<input type="text" name="mytable" value="0" size="3">
<p>How many rows?</p>
<input type="text" name="myrows" value="12" size="4">
<input type="button" name="button1" value="ok"
onClick="showTables(mytable.value,myrows.value)">
</div>
<div id="div2">
<textarea rows="12" cols="25" id="results">
</textarea>
</div>
</form>
</body>
</html>
```

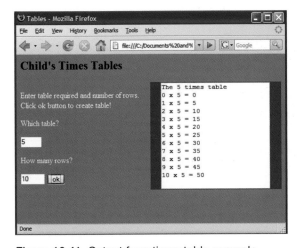

Figure 10.41 Output from times table example

The output from this script is shown in Figure 10.41.

3. Be able to control layout of a web page using CSS

This is primarily a practical learning outcome. As such, the best way to work through it is to examine some good CSS examples.

CSS has many uses; let's take a look at some of its more common applications…

3.1 Design

CSS does not have to be written 'by hand' – many applications are available that feature **WYSIWYG** ('**w**hat **y**ou **s**ee **i**s **w**hat **y**ou **g**et') CSS editors; these allow you to design a page **visually**, and this then **automatically generates** the required CSS.

Scorecard for CSS graphical tool

+ **Time-saving**; it's quicker than coding CSS manually
+ **Less error prone**; syntax errors unlikely to occur
+ **Ensures consistency**; all CSS coded to the same style
+ **Easy integration** with **HTML** and **JavaScript**
+ Helps web designer to **learn CSS**
− Usually **not free**, can be **expensive**
− **Web design applications** can be complicated to **learn**

Commercial examples of **WYSIWYG CSS** editors include:

◆ WestCiv's **Style Master** http://www.westciv.com/style_master/

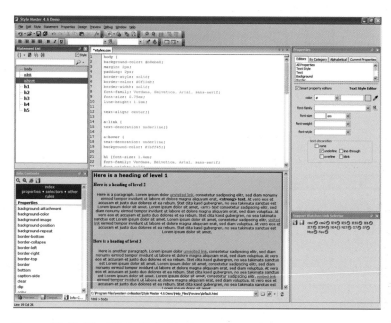

Figure 10.42 WestCiv's Style Master

◆ Blumental Software's Rapid CSS Editor **http://www.blumentals.net/rapidcss/**

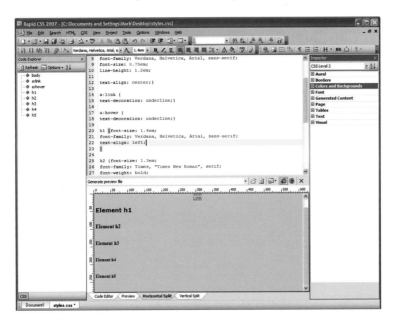

Figure 10.43 Blumental Software's Rapid CSS Editor

◆ Adobe's Dreamweaver CS3® **http://www.adobe.com/products/dreamweaver/**

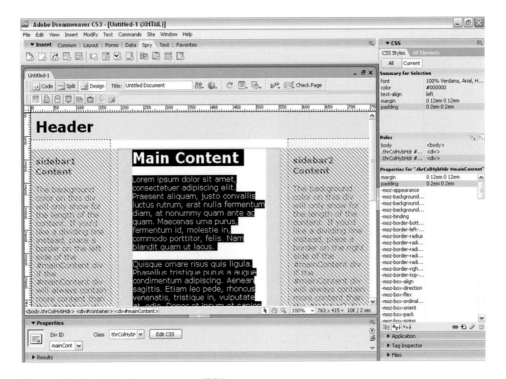

Figure 10.44 Adobe Dreamweaver CS3

3.2 Headings

Headings are an important element of an HTML page and can be fully **styled** through CSS.

The following example demonstrates:

Adding colour

Font size

Font weight

Background image or colour

```
h1
{
font-family: Verdana, Helvetica, Arial, sans-serif;
font-weight: bolder;
color: #ffffff;
background-image: url(bluetile.jpg);
font-size: 20pt;
font-style: normal;
}
h2
{
font-size: 18pt;
font-family: Verdana, Helvetica, Arial, sans-serif;
font-weight: bold;
text-align: left;
font-style: normal;
color: #6666ff;
background-color: #99ccff;
}
```

And some **test content** with these style settings for **<h1>** and **<h2>**:

Here is a heading of level 1

Here is a heading of level 2

Figure 10.45 Heading styling

For the record, the image file bluetile.jpg looks like this:

3.3 Lists

A common element found in web pages is the **unordered list, <ul>**.

Figure 10.46 bluetile.jpg (32 x 32 pixels)

Although lists can be used for simple **lists of items**, they are also used for more complex applications like **website navigation** (e.g. horizontal or vertical menus).

The following examples demonstrate CSS for **styling** list elements.

Here's how to build a simple unordered list, formatted with CSS:

```
<style>
#mylist
{
border: 2px solid #000;
margin: 2em;
width: 10em;
padding: 5px;
}
</style>
<div id="mylist">
<ul>
<li>Item 1</li>
<li>Item 2</li>
<li>Item 3</li>
<li>Item 4</li>
<li>Item 5</li>
</ul>
</div>
```

And on screen in Figure 10.47:

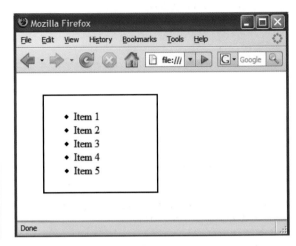

Figure 10.47 Styling the <ul> tag

The <**a**> and <**ul**> tags can be used to create a **menu** when appropriate CSS styling is applied.

Note. This code is specifically designed for Microsoft Internet Explorer®.

```
<style>
#buttons
{
width: 12em;
border-left: 3px #000000 solid;
padding: 0 0 1px 0;
margin-bottom: 1px;
font-family: Verdana, Lucida, Geneva, Helvetica, Arial, sans-serif;
background-color: #b9cade;
color: #4b225b;
}
#buttons ul
{
list-style: none;
margin: 0;
padding: 0;
border: none;
}

#buttons li
{
border-bottom: 1px solid #b9cade;
margin: 0;
}
```

▶

```
#buttons li a
{
display: block;
padding: 5px 5px 5px 0.5em;
border-left: 10px #a33db7 solid;
background-color: #6057bc;
color: #ffffff;
text-decoration: none;
width: 100%;
}
#buttons li a:hover
{
border-left: 10px solid #1c64d1;
background-color: #d2add7;
color: #ffffff;
}
</style>
<div id="buttons">
<ul>
<li><a href="customers.html">Customers</a></li>
<li><a href="orders.html">Orders</a></li>
<li><a href="feedback.html">Feedback</a></li>
<li><a href="questions.html">Questions</a></li>
<li><a href="about us">About us</a></li>
</ul>
</div>
```

This makes it a viable alternative to having a series of **JavaScript Rollovers** (see section 2.2). It also has the advantage of requiring only **minor** text changes to the .HTML file rather than having to recreate two **new** images for **every** rollover link. As a result, this technique offers **much quicker maintenance**.

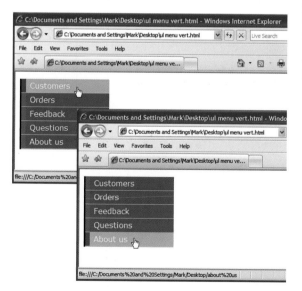

A **hover effect** is used to **highlight the hyperlink** when the **mouse cursor** is resting on it.

A time-lapsed sequence of the **vertical** menu system in use is shown in Figure 10.48.

Figure 10.48 CSS vertical menu navigation at work in Microsoft Internet Explorer®

Similar CSS formatting can be used to create a **horizontal** menu system as shown from the time-lapsed screen captures in Figure 10.49.

Note. This code is specifically designed for Mozilla Firefox.

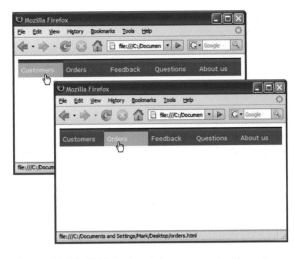

In the second example the same list is arranged **horizontally**, sitting within a **container** called '**menubox**'. Most of the CSS formatting is the same as that encountered in the vertical menu.

Figure 10.49 CSS horizontal menu navigation at work in Mozilla Firefox

```
<style>
#menubox
{
border-top: 2px #000000 solid;
border-bottom: 2px #000000 solid;
width: 100%;
margin: 0 auto;
padding: 0 0 0 0;
font-family: Verdana, Lucida, Geneva, Helvetica, Arial, sans-serif;
background-color: #b9cade;
color: #4b225b;
}
ul#menulist
{
list-style: none;
padding: 0;
margin: 0 auto;
width: 100%;
font-size: 0.8em;
}
ul#menulist li
{
display: block;
float: left;
width: 20%;
margin: 0;
padding: 0;
}
ul#menulist li a
{
display: block;
width: 100%;
padding: 0.5em;
border-top: 5px #a33db7 solid;
```

▶

```
      color: #ffffff;
      text-decoration: none;
      background: #f7f2ea;
}
#menubox>ul#menulist li a { width: auto; }
ul#menulist li#active a
{
background-color: #6057bc;
color: #ffffff;
}
ul#menulist li a:hover, ul#menulist li#active a:hover
{
color: #ffffff;
background-color: #d2add7;
border-top: 5px solid #1c64d1;
}
</style>
<div id="menubox">
<ul id="menulist">
<li id="active"><a href="customers.html" id="current">Customers</a></li>
<li id="active"><a href="orders.html">Orders</a></li>
<li id="active"><a href="feedback.html">Feedback</a></li>
<li id="active"><a href="questions.html">Questions</a></li>
<li id="active"><a href="about us">About us</a></li>
</ul>
</div>
```

3.4 Pseudoclasses and links

Pseudoclasses

Although we have seen that a **selector** representing the **HTML element** (e.g. 'a' for **anchor <a>**) can be used to specify formatting for **that** element, it is also possible to use **pseudoclasses**.

These give you even finer control over the element as they give you the ability to apply certain styles to specific **states** of an element.

Links

Example pseudoclasses for the <**a**> element include: **:link, :visited, :hover**, and **:active**.

We saw :hover used in section 3.3 to help create the horizontal and vertical menu systems. However, it's more commonly used as part of a group of CSS statements that simply control the way **links appear** on a web page (and, in particular, **removing** the default underline).

The following example **removes all underlines** (a possible **value** of the **text-decoration** property) from **all** link **states** and changes the **colour** of the **hover state only** to **red**:

```
<html>
<head>
<title>
Lee Office Supplies
</title>
<style>
a:link {text-decoration: none;}
a:visited {text-decoration: none;}
a:active {text-decoration: none;}
a:hover {text-decoration: none; color: red;}
</style>
</head>
<body>
<h1>Lee Office Supplies</h1>
<h2>Welcome to Lee Office Supplies</h2>
<p>
If you are querying a previous <a href="orders.html">order</a> or want
to change your <a href="user.html">user profile</a> please ensure you
are <a href="login.html">logged in</a> first.
</p>
</body>
</html>
```

The output from this HTML and CSS is shown in Figure 10.50.

Modifying the previous <**style**> section of the previous CSS example creates a **border** around **only** the '**hover**' link state:

```
<style>
a:link {text-decoration: none}
a:visited {text-decoration: none}
a:active {text-decoration: none}
a:hover
{
  border-top: medium solid blue;
  border-bottom: medium solid blue;
  border-left: medium solid blue;
  border-right: medium solid blue;
}
</style>
```

The output from this HTML and amended CSS is shown in Figure 10.51.

It is also possible to increase the **active area** of the link when the mouse hovers above it by changing the **font-size** and **font-weight** property values:

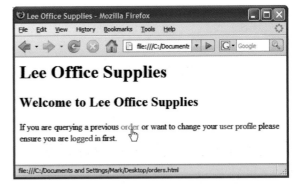

Figure 10.50 Red hover links, no underlines – an example of pseudoclasses

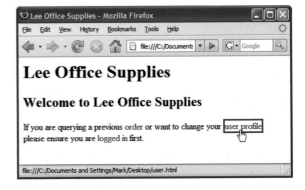

Figure 10.51 Blue links with border on hover state

```
<style type="text/css">
a:link {text-decoration: none}
a:visited {text-decoration: none}
a:active {text-decoration: none}
a:hover {font-size:24; font-weight:bold; color: green;}
</style>
```

The effect of this can be seen in Figure 10.52.

Figure 10.52 Green links in hover state with an increased active area to click

Links and background images

It is also possible to manipulate the links by adding a **background image**. The following example shown in Figure 10.53 demonstrates this effect:

Figure 10.53 Graphical backgrounds for each link

The HTML and CSS required is shown below:

```
<html>
<head>
<title>
Lee Office Supplies
</title>
<style>
ul
{
margin: 0;
padding: 0;
list-style: none;
}
ul li
{
margin: 2px 0 6px 0;
padding: 0;
font-weight: bold;
line-height: 64px; // height of image being used
background-repeat: no-repeat;
background-position: 0 50%;
}
ul li a
{
text-decoration: none;
padding-left: 96px; // width of image + extra space
}
#login { background-image: url(login.gif); }
#order{ background-image: url(order.gif); }
#profile { background-image: url(profile.gif); }
</style>
<body>
<h1>Lee Office Supplies</h1>
<h2>Welcome to Lee Office Supplies</h2>
<ul>
<li id="login"><a href="login.html">Login</a></li>
<li id="order"><a href="order.html">Query Orders</a></li>
<li id="profile"><a href="profile.html">Your profile</a></li>
</ul>
</body>
</html>
```

As you can see, the addition of simple icon images helps to convey the **purpose** of each link. In this example, **either** the icon **or** the text may be clicked to activate the link.

4. Create an interactive web page

4.1 Script requirements

The most basic elements of **script requirements** can be broken down into **three steps**:

Identifying the necessary **Inputs**	Typically represented by values entered into **HTML forms**. Inputs can be of the following types: ◆ text boxes (or text fields) ◆ radio buttons ◆ checkboxes ◆ text area ◆ drop-down box ◆ buttons ◆ JavaScript pop-up dialogues. When planning input into an interactive web page, the designer must decide **what type** of **input mechanism** is best. In general, **more data entry errors** occur through the use of **text boxes and text areas**, so **avoid these** if possible. Selection elements such as radio buttons, checkboxes and drop-down boxes are **much better** and often preferred by the user.
Work out the **Processing**	These are the **calculations** that are required in order to make the web page **interactive**. The processing requires the web page designer to use their **problem-solving skills** and it is perhaps this aspect that is **closest** to the role of a traditional programmer. Processing can be **modelled** through the use of **appropriate design tools** such as **flowcharts** or **pseudocode**. Processing can be broken down into taking the user's **input**, using these in **set calculations** and then **converting** them into the **required outputs**.
Produce the required **Outputs**	The output from an interactive web page can be **varied**. Specifically it is likely to consist of **HTML content**, **CSS formatting** and **values** calculated from set calculations. Other possible outputs include: ◆ images and animations ◆ sound effects ◆ music ◆ emails ◆ control of remote equipment, e.g. webcams ◆ customer orders ◆ search results including hyperlinks.

The design process of **storyboarding** is a useful tool for visually describing inputs and outputs expected from an interactive web page.

4.2 Design script

A number of **design tools** can be used to help **plan** the required script required for an interactive web page.

The two most common design tools are pseudo code and flowcharts.

Pseudo code

Pseudo code is a way in which we can write solutions using an ordinary **natural language**. The common convention is to use **English**, but other languages are equally valid.

The main thing to remember is **not** to use any specific **scripting terms**; try to keep the wording as simple as possible.

The following example shows some pseudo code for the child's **times table** web page processing in section 2.3.

```
Get table required from the html form
Get number of rows required from the html form
If number of rows is valid (between 1 and 12)
    For counter = 1 to number of rows
        result = counter x table required
        Append result line to output
    EndFor
    Send output to textarea on html form
Else
    Display an error message
Endif
```

Go back to section 2.3 and **compare** this pseudo code to the scripted solution.

Activity

Frankoni T-shirts Ltd requires an interactive web page (with client-side JavaScript) that will calculate the **production cost** and **projected sales price** of a designer T-shirt.

Frankoni buy blank shirts at the following rates: Small (£3 each), Medium (£4 each), Large (£6 each) and eXtra Large (£7 each).

It costs Frankoni £2.50 to print the customer's design on the T-shirt.

Frankoni aims to make a 30 per cent profit on each T-shirt sold.

Write **pseudo code** and a **flowchart** to produce the processing for a web page that will calculate and output production costs, projected sales and the profit of selling a user a specified quantity of each type of T-shirt.

Flowcharts

Flowcharts are a familiar **visual tool** for describing the **logical steps** needed to solve a problem. Many user manuals use them to explain complex sequences of instruction.

Flowcharts use a standard set of drawn symbols:

Terminator An oval symbol that is used to start or end the flowchart	**Decision** A diamond symbol used for making choices, e.g. if…else etc.
Process A rectangle that is used to show an action or calculation that must be performed	**Input or Output** A parallelogram can either be used to specify a user's input or the desired output
Connector A circle that is used to connect different sections of a flowchart together, particularly when drawing flow arrows would be difficult	**Flow Arrows** Arrowed lines used to indicate the flow of logic in the solution. Logic, by default, goes top-to-bottom, left-to-right

As with any design tool, the flowchart **should not contain any programming language**, only **natural language**, e.g. English should be used. A limited use of general symbols is acceptable.

The following example revisits the child's times table web page processing again. This time the processing is described using flowchart notation.

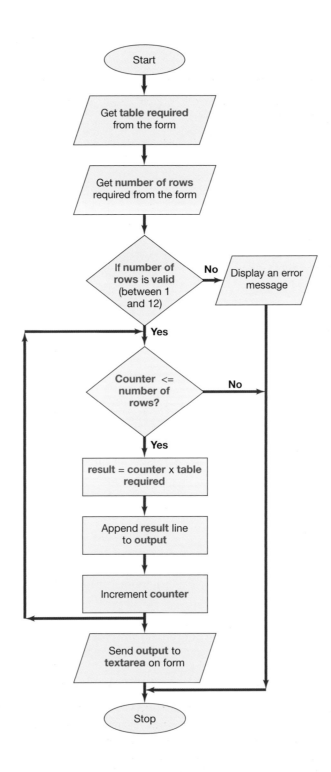

4.3 Implement script

Let's take a look at some common elements of interactive web pages that are created with JavaScript.

Rollovers are, of course, a very popular JavaScript example (see section 2.2 for a working example) as are **client-side processing of calculations** (see section 2.3).

Here are some of the other common JavaScript implementations.

Clocks

The computer system's **Real Time Clock** (**RTC**) can be used to generate a 'ticking' clock on a web page. This works by accessing the JavaScript **Date**() object and its associated **methods: getHours**(), **getMinutes**() and **getSeconds**().

```html
<html>
<head>
<title>
JavaScript clock
</title>
<script>
function updateTime()
{
  var newDate = new Date();

  document.myClock.now.value = ""
  + newDate.getHours() + ":" + newDate.getMinutes() + ":"
  + newDate.getSeconds();

  setTimeout("updateTime()", 1000);
}
function startTime()
{
  setTimeout("updateTime()", 500);
}
</script>
</head>
<body onload="startTime()">
<form name="myClock">
The time is:
<input name="now" type="text" size="8">
</form>
</body>
</html>
```

When the web page loads, the **onload**() **event handler** is used to call the **startTime**() function. This in turn executes the **updateTime**() method after 0.5 seconds. From here, updateTime() **calls itself** again **every second** after getting the RTC's time again and formatting it into the "**now**" **text box element** on the "**myClock**" **HTML form**. Functions calling functions is a little dangerous as it uses a programming concept called **recursion**. To keep things simple we have left out the clearTimeout() method for now.

JavaScript **timing events** are used by **DOM's Window** object's **setTimeout()** and **clearTimeout()** **methods**. These basically allow statement execution to be **delayed** a number of milliseconds (1000 = 1 second).

Figure 10.54 shows a series of **time-lapsed screen captures** demonstrating the JavaScript clock:

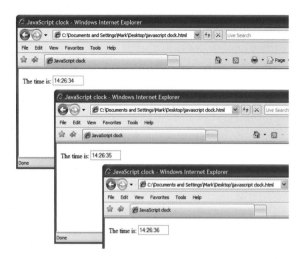

Figure 10.54 Output from the JavaScript clock example

Mouse movement followers

A common web page enhancement is to 'follow' the mouse cursor, either with text or a trail of images. This is particularly useful as it improves the **visibility** of the mouse cursor.

The following short example uses a combination of **CSS**, **JavaScript** and the **HTML DOM** to create a small green sphere follower for the cursor.

A time-lapsed image of the mouse movement follower can be seen in Figure 10.55.

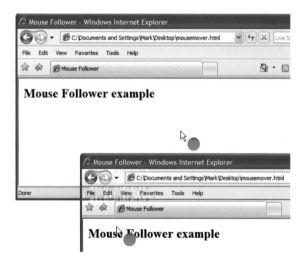

Figure 10.55 Output from the JavaScript mouse follower example

Here is the corresponding JavaScript code (Note. This code is designed to work in Microsoft Internet Explorer®):

```html
<html>
<head>
<title>
Mouse Follower
</title>
<div id="mousefollow" style="position:absolute"><img src="greenblob.gif"></div>
<script>
if (document.all)
{
  trailcontainer = document.all.mousefollow.style;
}
else
{
  if (document.getElementById)
  {
    trailcontainer = document.getElementById("mousefollow").style;
  }
  else
  {
    if (document.layers)
    {
      document.captureEvents(Event.MOUSEMOVE);
      trailcontainer = document.layers.mousefollow;
    }
  }
}

function followMouse(e)
{
  if (document.all)
  {
    trailcontainer.left = event.clientX + 8 +'px';
  }
  else
  {
    trailcontainer.left = e.x + 8+'px';
  }
  if (document.all)
  {
    trailcontainer.top = event.clientY + 8+'px';
  }
  else
  {
    trailcontainer.top = e.y + 8 + 'px';
  }
}

document.onmousemove=followMouse; // followMouse(event)implicit
</script>
</head>
<body>
<h2>Mouse Follower example</h2>
</body>
</html>
```

In this fairly complex example, the DOM's **Document Object's onmousemove event** is handled by the **followMouse()** function. This function moves the **container** ('**mousefollow**') of the image to down and right of the mouse's **current position**.

Due to differences in the way that the DOM's events are handled in Microsoft Internet Explorer® and Mozilla Firefox, just one version is presented here.

Calendar

Calendar examples can be **quite complex** as they have to handle different **years** (including leap years where, as you know, the number of days in February changes from 28 to 29 days) and be aware of the **number of days** in each **month**.

The following example displays a simple calendar using a combination of **inline CSS** (to format the calendar's output) and **JavaScript** to calculate the days for the month in question. A test run of the calendar JavaScript code is shown in Figure 10.56.

```html
<html>
<head>
<title>
Calendar
</title>
<script>
var months = ["January","February","March","April","May","June","July",
"August","September","October","November","December"];
var todaydate = new Date();

function drawCalendar(m, y)
{
  // days in each month except February
  var daysinmonth = [31,0,31,30,31,30,31,31,30,31,30,31];
  // calendar headings
  var weekinitials = "smtwtfs";
  var oD = new Date(y, m, 1);
  oD.od=oD.getDay()+1;

  if (y==todaydate.getFullYear() && (m+1)==todaydate.getMonth()+1)
  {
    scanfortoday=todaydate.getDate();
  }
  else
  {
    scanfortoday=0;
  }

  // Leap year check              daysinmonth[1]=(((oD.getFullYear()%100!=0)&&
(oD.getFullYear()%4==0))||(oD.getFullYear()%400==0))?29:28;

  var tmpstring = '<div style="width:200px;border:2px solid black;">';

  tmpstring += '<table style="width:200px;border:2px solid black;"
cols="7" cellpadding="1" border="1" cellspacing="0"><tr
align="center">';
  tmpstring += '<td colspan="7" align="center" style="background
-color:blue;font:bold 14px verdana;color:white;">'+months[m]+' - '+y;
```

▶

```
    tmpstring += '</td></tr><tr align="center">';
    for(s=0;s<7;s++)
    {
      tmpstring+='<td style="background-color:gray;font:bold 12px
      verdana;color:white;">'+weekinitials.substr(s,1)+'</td>';
    }
    tmpstring+='</tr><tr align="center">';
    for(i=1;i<=42;i++)          // assume 42 days (7 days x 6 weeks)
    {
      if ((i-oD.od>=0) && (i-oD.od<daysinmonth[m]))
      {
        x= i-oD.od+1;
      }

else
    {
      x= ' ';
    }
    if (x==scanfortoday)        // highlight current date
    {
      x='<span style="color: white;font-weight: bold;background
      -color:salmon;">'+x+'</span>';
    }
    tmpstring+='<td style="font-size:12px;font-
    family:verdana;color:black;background-color:lavender;
    padding:2px;">'+x+'</td>';

    if(((i)%7==0)&&(i<36))      // start a new row of table
    {
      tmpstring+='</tr><tr align="center">';
    }
  }
  tmpstring+='</tr></table></div>';   // end the table
  return tmpstring;
}
function makeCalendar(mymonth,myyear)
{
  var selmonth = months.indexOf(mymonth.value);
  document.write(drawCalendar(selmonth ,myyear.value));
}
</script>
</head>
<body>
<h2>Calendar</h2>
<form name="myCal">
Month
<input type ="text" name="month" value = "" size="15">
Year
<input type ="text" name="year" value = "" size="4">
<input type ="button" name ="button" value="Make Calendar"
onclick="makeCalendar(month,year);">
</form>
</body>
</html>
```

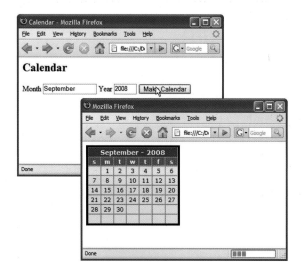

Figure 10.56 Calendar output

Form validation

The following JavaScript and HTML displays a simple **customer feedback form**.

It **validates** whether the user has entered any **comments** by checking the **length** of the inputted text. In addition, the user **cannot submit** the form if they have asked for details but **not yet** completed the email textbox.

```html
<html>
<head>
<title>Customer Feedback</title>
<script>
function validateComments()
{
  if(document.feedback.freetext.value.length<1)
  {
    alert ("Please add some comments.");
    document.feedback.freetext.focus();
    return false;
  }
}
function emailcheck()
{
 if(document.feedback.update[0].checked)
 {
   var emailstring=document.feedback.email.value;
   if (emailstring.indexOf("@")==-1
&&document.feedback.update[0].checked);
    {
    alert("Before you submit, please input\na valid email
address. Thanks.");
    document.feedback.email.focus();
    return false;
    }
 }
}
</script>
</head>
<body>
<h1>Lee Office Supplies
<h2>Customer Feedback</h2>
<form enctype="multipart/form-data" name = "feedback" action = "process.php"
method = "post" onsubmit="return emailcheck()">
```

```
Did you find our service:
<select name = "verdict">
<option = poor>poor
<option = good>good
<option = excel>excellent
</select><br>
Do you want e-mail notification when the site is updated?<br>
<input type="radio" name="update">yes, please.<br>
<input type="radio" name="update" checked>no, thanks.<br>
Your e-mail:
<input type="text" name="email" size = "30"><br>
<textarea name = "freetext" cols = "40" rows = "5" onblur="validateComments()">
</textarea>
<input type = "submit" name="send" value = "send">
</form>
<script>
document.feedback.verdict.focus();
</script>
</body>
</html>
```

4.4 Good practice

Website developers, much in line with programmers working in other languages, are **encouraged** to use good practices to assist the **documentation** of their work.

Client-side JavaScript is downloaded to the user's computer system when the HTML page it 'sits' within is received from the remote web server. From this perspective, any user can **View Page Source** in the web browser and examine the JavaScript code that makes the interactivity elements work.

The developer can decide to 'obfuscate' – making it **deliberately difficult** for the user to decipher how the JavaScript solution works – if they want to.

More likely the developer will take pride in their work and **document** the code for **future maintenance** and **ease of modification**. In fact, they may be under organisational orders to do so.

Common elements of good practice include:

Use of comments	Much like other programming and scripting languages, JavaScript can support commenting. There are two methods:
	Single line comments
	Uses the '//' to comment a single line…
	e.g.
	`var tax = 0.23; // Tax is 23%`
	… or to comment out a line of code which is not needed (was there for debugging only) or may be 'buggy' (i.e. not working).
	e.g.
	`// document.myform.usrname.focus();`

Use of comments *cont.*	**Multi-line comments**
	Uses the '/* */' pairing to span a number of lines. Often used to describe the purpose of a JavaScript function.
| | ```
/*
This function will calculate a random
number between 1 and 10 inclusive.
*/
``` |
Self-documenting variables	Where possible variables used in JavaScript should be meaningful and descriptive.
	What this means is that they should:
	◆ use a unique name that clearly describes their purpose; ◆ be memorable to the website designer; ◆ use lowercase and uppercase consistently; ◆ avoid names already used for HTML elements.
	Also recall that JavaScript is case sensitive; variables spelt the same but using different cases are considered to be different.
Indentation	Indentation is used to highlight the underlying structure of script code. This is particularly helpful when if…else statements and loops such as do…while, while and for are used.
	Nested code can be particularly difficult to decipher if indentation is not used. The resulting 'flat' code can be difficult to read.
	Please compare the following extracts:
	Flat code
| | ```
function checkEmail(email)
{
atpos=email.value.indexOf("@");
dotpos=email.value.lastIndexOf(".");
if (atpos <1 || (dotpos-atpos)<2 )
{
alert("Please enter a valid email address");
return false;
}
else
{
return true;
}
}
``` |

Indentation *cont.*	Indented for readability
| | ```
function checkEmail(email)
{
  atpos=email.value.indexOf("@");
  dotpos=email.value.lastIndexOf(".");
  if (atpos <1 || (dotpos-atpos)<2 )
  {
    alert("Please enter a valid email address");
    return false;
  }
  else
  {
    return true;
  }
}
``` |
| | From a glimpse, it should be possible to quickly work out the code that is dependent on the true/false choice made by the if…else statement. |

Older web pages may not have commenting or indentation in an effort to keep **file sizes** small. This was more important in the past where expensive dial-up connections had relatively **slow download speeds**, so large files with redundant comments and indentation were a luxury.

With modern, quick **broadband connections**, it is less of a concern.

5 Test and review a web page that uses CSS and JavaScript

5.1 Testing

Testing a web page (or larger website) relies on a number of different checks that should be performed before the product is deployed and/or released to the client.

These checks include:

Does the layout match the preferred design?

Ultimately this test relies on the comparison between the **client's original vision** for the website (what they wanted) and the website as **developed** by the designer.

Generally these comparisons should **not** be left to the last minute!

A good web designer will give their client **regular progress updates** and **screen captures** of the site as it is **being developed**.
```

Feedback from the client regarding the progress made **is vital**: if the design is considered to be veering from that originally requested it can quickly be brought back on track after **review**.

The use of CSS to **quickly alter** website presentation is therefore a boon.

Does the interactivity work as specified?

JavaScript code often can contain (non-fatal) **warnings** and (fatal) **errors** that **prevent** a web page's interactivity from working **as expected**.

JavaScript generally does **not** have a good reputation for debugging. To help website developers with JavaScript problems, modern web browser often have **built-in debug facilities** that can highlight the **cause** of the problem but **fall short** of providing the actual **remedy**.

In Mozilla Firefox, a **JavaScript error console** can be accessed from either the **Tools** menu or by typing '**javascript:**' into the URL address bar.

The console tells the website developer (for each error or warning):

◆ error message description;
◆ the file the error is in (as a clickable hyperlink);
◆ the line number that the error can be found (in the identified file).

The code can then be loaded into Firefox's own text file editor and the error **located** and **fixed**.

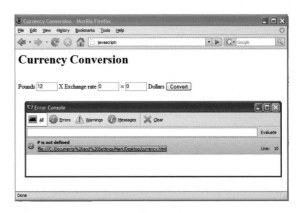

Figure 10.57 Mozilla Firefox's error console shows a scripting error

Figure 10.58 Mozilla Firefox shows the scripting error (the variable should be a lowercase 'p')

More help with script debugging – Mozilla

Undoubtedly a superior tool for debugging JavaScript on Mozilla Firefox is Venkman, a free JavaScript debugger plug-in.

Instructions for installing and using this can be found here:

https://addons.mozilla.org/en-US/firefox/addon/216

Microsoft's Internet Explorer® has similar basic debug facilities displaying a **warning icon**, bottom left, when a problem is encountered.

Figure 10.59 Microsoft Internet Explorer® has identified a problem…

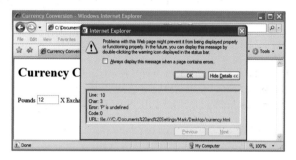

Double-clicking this **icon** will display a similar pop-up, typically identifying exactly the same error message as Mozilla Firefox.

Again, neither browser's built-in debug tool will help the author to **fix** the error, so the process can be exceptionally **time consuming**.

Figure 10.60 A pop-up will tell the developer what the error actually is

More help with script debugging – Microsoft®

Undoubtedly a superior tool for debugging JavaScript on Internet Explorer® is the **Microsoft Script Editor®**, a free component of Microsoft Office XP/2003®.

Instructions for installing and using this can be found here:

http://msdn.microsoft.com/library/default.asp?url=/library/en-us/dnfp2k2/html/odc_fpdebugscripts.asp

Various **third-party software** is available that will help debug JavaScript code:

◆ SplineTech's **JavaScript** HTML Debugger (www.javascript-debugger.com)
◆ Parakey's **Firebug** (http://www.getfirebug.com/js.html)
◆ **Drosera** JavaScript Debugger (http://webkit.org/blog/61/introducing-drosera/)
◆ IE Inspector's **AxScripter** (www.ieinspector.com/scriptdebugger).

Basic questions for testing functionality include:

◆ Does it provide the **desired functionality**?
◆ Does it work **efficiently**?

- Does it work **reliably?**
- Does it calculate **accurately?**

The only real method for checking this is **extensive testing**, using a suitable **test plan** (with real-world **test data**).

As with testing any type of program, **test data** should contain values that are **normal**, **extreme** (valid, but unlikely) and **erroneous**.

Does the website work as expected on different platforms?

This applies to **operating system**, e.g. Microsoft Windows®, Apple Mac OS and Linux, and **web browsers,** e.g. Microsoft Internet Explorer®, Mozilla Firefox, Opera and Safari.

This is, of course, a key question.

As we have seen, **functionality** (and **support** for JavaScript and CSS) can **vary** from web browser to web browser and even in different releases of the same browser.

The only way to find out is to physically **lab test** our website with **each** browser.

A **portability test grid** for **each web page** could be used to record the findings:

Test element for: Page1.HTML	Browsers tested			
	Mozilla Firefox (PC)	Mozilla Firefox (Linux)	MS IE (PC)	Safari (Apple Mac OS)
Search facility working?	✓	✓	✓	✗
'Calculate' button working?	✓	✓	✓	✓
'Submit' button working?	✗	✗	✗	✗
.CSS formatting acceptable?	✗	✓	✓	✓

These findings suggest a **complete script failure** for the **'Submit'** button and some **platform-specific issues** for the **.CSS** and the **Search Facility**.

How much time is dedicated to fixing these problems may depend on the **commercial value** placed on each platform (i.e. which ones are **more popular** and therefore **justify** the **extra time** and **effort** taken to fix their scripting/CSS issues).

Validation tools

CSS can be **validated** by the W3C at:

http://jigsaw.w3.org/css-validator/

Uploading or 'cut and pasting' the CSS code allows the validation tool to check to see if your code is **well formed** (similar tools also exist for most markup languages, e.g. HTML).

For example, examine the following (**deliberately poor**) CSS:

```
h2 {font-variant: small-caps; }
h3 {font-family: Verdana, Arial, Helvetica, sans-serif;}
p
{
font-size: 30;
font-style: italic;
}
p#oddformat
{
text-align: centre;
text-decoration: underline;
letter-spacing: 15px;
}
```

And the output from the validation tool in Figure 10.61:

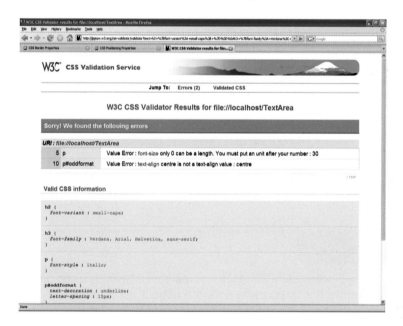

Figure 10.61 Correctly identified CSS problems

As you can see, the validation tool has correctly identified both CSS errors.

Activity

Visit the W3C validation tool and use it to validate some of your own CSS code.

Validate webpage via its URL:

http://jigsaw.w3.org/css-validator/#validate-by-uri

Validate uploaded file:

http://jigsaw.w3.org/css-validator/#validate-by-upload

Validate by inputted CSS:

http://jigsaw.w3.org/css-validator/#validate-by-input

Unit Links

Unit 19 – Web Server Scripting and **Unit 21 – Website Production and Management** are both complementary to this unit. Many of the concepts and practices covered here are reinforced there.

This unit, **Unit 10**, is a **Specialist Unit** on the following BTEC National Certificate and Diploma routes:

Networking

Software Development

Systems Support

As such it has links to a number of other units, principally:

Unit 4 – IT project

Unit 12 – Developing Computer Games

Unit 18 – Principles of Software Design and Development

Unit 19 – Web Server Scripting

Unit 20 – Event-Driven Programming

Unit 25 – Object-Oriented Programming

In addition this unit has identified direct links with:

Unit 7 – Systems Analysis and Design

Achieving success

In order to achieve each unit you will complete a series of coursework activities. Each time you hand in work, your tutor will return this to you with a record of your achievement.

This particular unit has 11 criteria to meet: 5 Pass, 3 Merit and 3 Distinction.

For a **Pass**:

    You must achieve **all** 5 Pass criteria

For a **Merit**:

    You must achieve **all** 5 Pass and **all** 3 Merit criteria

For a **Distinction**:

    You must achieve **all** 5 Pass, **all** 3 Merit **and** 3 Distinction criteria.

So that you can monitor your own progress and achievement in each unit, a recording grid has been provided (see below). The full version of this grid is also included on the companion CD.

Assignment	Assignments in this unit			
	U10.01	U10.02	U10.03	U10.04
Referral				
Pass				
1				
2				
3				
4				
5				
Merit				
1				
2				
3				
Distinction				
1				
2				
3				

Help with assessment

The key issues with this unit is to be **aware** of CSS and a selected client-side scripting language (likely to be JavaScript) and **correctly use them** to **control the layout** of a series of HTML web pages and **add interactivity** to them.

The **Merit criteria** focus on **your ability to make sensible comparisons**. Three forms of comparisons are required: **different ways of incorporating CSS**, the **difference in implementing two aspects of CSS** and how scripted web pages can be **implemented in varied ways** by two **different** web browsers.

For a **Distinction** you to need focus on the improvement and maintenance aspects of your web pages. In particular, you should be able to **alter the web page's layout by amending the CSS** (and **explain the impact this has** on maintenance time and overall difficulty). You should also be capable of **demonstrating possible extensions** to the web page's **interactivity** or **functionality** in order to **improve** the visitor's experience.

Online resources on the CD

Key fact sheets
Electronic slide show of key points
Sample scripts for JavaScript and CSS
Multiple choice self-test quizzes
Tutorials for JavaScript debugging

Further reading

Bartlett, K., 2006, *Sams Teach Yourself CSS in 24 Hours*, 2nd Edition, Sams, ISBN 0672329069.

Castro, E., 2002, *HTML for the World Wide Web with XHTML and CSS*, 5th Edition, Peachpit Press, ISBN 0321130073.

Cederholm, D., 2004, *Web Standards Solutions: The Markup and Style Handbook*, Apress US, ISBN 1590593812.

Meyer, E., 2004, *CSS Pocket Reference*, 2nd Edition, O'Reilly, ISBN 0596007779.

Negrino, T. and Smith, D., 2003, *JavaScript for the World Wide Web*, 5th Edition, Peachpit Press, ISBN 032119439X.

Pollock, J., 2004, *JavaScript: A Beginner's Guide*, 2nd Edition, McGraw-Hill Education, ISBN 0072227907.

Schmitt, C., 2004, *CSS Cookbook*, O'Reilly, ISBN 0596005768.

Shea, D. and Holzschlag, M., 2005, *The Zen of CSS Design: Visual Enlightenment for the Web*, Peachpit Press, ISBN 0321303474.

Weakley, R., 2005, *Sams Teach Yourself CSS in 10 Minutes*, Sams, ISBN 0672327457.

Web Server Scripting

Capsule view

This unit is best studied **after** Unit 21 – Website Production and Management. A 60-hour unit, it is designed to **complement** the learner's knowledge of client-side scripting that is the focus of Unit 10 – Client-side Customisation of Web Pages. If you have not read **either** of these units yet, please do so and then return here.

Although both PHP and ASP.NET are industry-relevant server-side scripting languages we have decided to focus on the former as it is generally more popular in terms of website development.

You may also find Unit 5 – Advanced Database Skills useful reinforcement for the database elements covered here.

Electronic copies of all scripts can be found on the companion CD.

Learning aims

1 Understand the purpose and use of web server scripting.
2 Be able to use web server scripting for server-side functionality.
3 Understand the security and ethical issues affecting web server scripting.

1 Understand the purpose and use of web server scripting

1.1 Server scripting languages: server-side versus client-side

'Scripting' (or 'script') languages are usually formed from **short**, **meaningful** instructions that are used to **automate processes** in a computer system. **Batch files** and Job Control Languages (**JCL**) are typical examples of scripting.

In terms of **web page design**, scripting may be either **client-side** (as seen in **Unit 10**) or **server-side**.

The following table demonstrates how these two types **differ**:

Factor	Server-side scripting	Client-side scripting
Executed on the client computer system	No	**Yes** – just like HTML, Java, Flash and ActiveX. This increases the strain on the user's system resources (e.g. RAM, processing time).
Executed on the web server	**Yes**, executed on the remote web server.	No
User can view the source code for the script (is it insecure?)	**No**; it never leaves the web server	**Yes**, it is part of the page downloaded by the browser.
Needs special browser plug-ins to make it work?	No	**Sometimes**, e.g. JavaScript needs a JavaScript **interpreter** built into the web browser
Is a threat to the client computer's security?	**No** – although some environment data may be available (see section 3.2).	**Possibly**; some client-side scripting can be malicious and, when downloaded and executed, can cause problems for the user.

Web server scripting languages

A number of different server-side scripting languages exist; here are the most common:

◆ PHP
◆ JSP
◆ ASP.NET

Although the practical aspects of this unit will focus on PHP, it is important to have an overview of alternative technologies as an active IT practitioner.

PHP

PHP (**PHP: H**ypertext **P**re-processor or **P**ersonal **H**ome **P**age) is a **server-side scripting** language that works on a number of different hardware platforms and operating systems (this makes it 'cross-platform').

PHP's job is to **create dynamic web page content**.

What this means is that the HTML sent to the client PC requesting the page is **written by a PHP script** rather than being coded **manually** by a person.

The generated HTML often comes from **live database queries** so the information sent to the client's web browser should be **up to date**.

The following diagram illustrates this point:

The steps in a typical PHP scenario are:

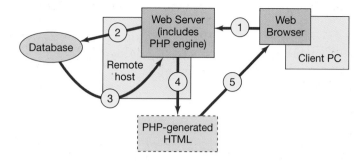

Figure 19.1 How server-side scripting works

1 The user's web browser makes a **request** for a particular piece of information; this request is sent **via the Internet** to a **remote host** running a **web server**.
2 The PHP script **queries** (usually with a **Data Manipulation Language** such as **SQL**) a linked **database** and a **results set** (of data) is created.
3 The **results set** is returned to the PHP engine (or module).
4 The PHP engine **converts** the data in the result set into **valid HTML**, adding **formatting** as necessary.
5 The web server '**serves**' the **dynamically created HTML** page **back** to the client PC's web browser.

A common use of such scripting is in **search engines**, particularly those used to check **stock** in an **online shop**. **Message boards** and **forums** can also use PHP extensively. Because the client PC only ever receives the generated HTML document, the end user **never gets to see** the PHP scripts involved.

Here is some sample PHP code:

```
<?php
  echo "<b>BTEC</b> National Diploma";
?>
```

Note the use of the '**<?php**' and '**?>**' **block tags** to indicate the **start** and **end** of the PHP script and the **semi-colon** marking the **end** of the PHP **statement**.

PHP Scorecard

+ Fast
+ Stable
+ Relatively easy to learn (similar to C, C++, JavaScript etc.)
+ Open source (free!)
+ Secure; it's kept up to date to prevent threats from hacking
+ PHP module available for many different web servers
+ It is cross-platform; available on many different hardware platforms and operating systems
+ Large library of pre-written routines are available
+ Very well documented with lots of examples

Many popular **enterprise-level** organisations use PHP. These include: Cisco, Vodafone, Motorola, Siemens, Sony Ericsson, CBS, Philips, Lufthansa and Deutsche Bank.

As of January 2008, the current PHP version is **PHP5**.

JSP

Java Server Pages (**JSP**) are HTML pages with Java code **embedded** into them. A special **JSP compiler** is used to generate a **Servlet** from the JSP page.

JSP files use a '**.JSP**' extension to distinguish themselves from standard HTML files.

Here is some sample JSP code:

```
<html>
<body>
The time is now <%= new java.util.Date() %>
</body>
</html>
```

You will notice that the technique shown in the JSP example lets us **switch** from HTML **to** JSP by using the '<%=' and '%>' tags. **Inside** these tags we are free to write JSP code. In this example, the **Date()** **object** is used to return the **current date** and **time**.

In order to use JSP the selected web server must be JSP-enabled. **Apache Tomcat** is one such application and can be found at: http://tomcat.apache.org/.

Microsoft ASP.NET®

ASP.NET ('dot net') is the follow-up to Microsoft's earlier Active Server Pages (**ASP**).

As with PHP it can be used to create **dynamic web page content. Unlike** PHP, which is available on a number of different computer platforms, ASP.NET is designed to run specifically on **Microsoft Windows®** operating systems.

ASP.NET is part of Microsoft's larger **.NET® platform** – a **framework** of software components that are built **onto** the Windows® operating system. The .NET framework provides a **large collection** of **reusable classes** that are ideal for creating **new Windows applications**.

ASP.NET prides itself on its **simple programming model** and has a number of **built-in controls** and services that enable **fast solutions** to **common web application problems**, often with little need for additional code.

ASP.NET is typically used with Microsoft **IIS®** (Internet Information Server) web server application. ASP.NET files typically use a '**.aspx**' extension to distinguish themselves from standard HTML files.

It is also worth noting that ASP.NET files are **compiled** rather than **interpreted** and, as a result, enjoy improved performance when executed.

Here is some sample ASP.NET code which creates a clickable button:

```
<script runat="server">
Sub submit(Source As Object, e As EventArgs)
 Button1.Text="You clicked it!"
End Sub
</script>

<html>
<body>
<form runat="server">
<asp:Button id="Button1" Text="Click it!" runat="server" onClick="submit"/>
</form>
</body>
</html>
```

ASP.NET also supports older **ASP render blocks** ('<%=' and '%>') for **compatibility**, allowing the developer to switch in and out of ASP syntax as they need to.

```
<% Dim I As Integer
For I = 0 to 7 %>
 <font size="<%=I%>"> This is ASP!</font> <br>
<% Next %>
```

Finally, ASP.NET is also language-independent. This means that you can develop a server-side web application using whichever Microsoft language (e.g. Visual Basic, Visual J# etc.) that fits the problem best.

1.2 Web server scripting advantages

Historically, web server-side processing was achieved with the use of **executable programs** created with traditional **languages** such as **C** and **scripting languages** such as **Perl**.

The **running** of these programs and **returning** the results were managed by a special **protocol** created by the **N**ational **C**enter for **S**upercomputing **A**pplications (**NCSA**) called **CGI** (**C**ommon **G**ateway **I**nterface) which sat **between** the **web browser** and the **executables**.

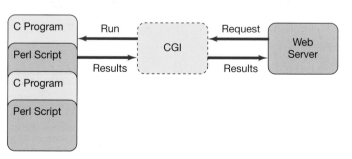

Here is an example of a **CGI processing request** from an **HTML Form**:

```
<html>
<head>
<title>
Kris Arts & Media (KAM) Ltd.
</title>
</head>
<body>
<form action="http://www.kamlimited.co.uk/cgi-bin/customer.pl" method="GET">
<p>For customer information, please enter your email</p>
<input type="test" name="email" size="20"/>
<p>
<input type="submit" value="Accept"/>
<input type="reset" value="Cancel"/>
</p>
</form>
</body>
</html>
```

This example would post the form data to the 'customer.pl' (**Perl script**) for processing. The Perl script would then generate an **HTML response**, which is sent **from** the web server **back** to the client.

Unfortunately, CGI has several **disadvantages**:

◆ The executables are **separate processes** (not directly controlled by the web server).
◆ The executables are **platform-dependent** (may not work on all hardware/operating systems).
◆ **Poorly written** executables can **crash** or **time-out**.

In comparison, newer web server scripting techniques offer a number of **advantages**:

+ Scripts are **interpreted** (decoded line-by-line into machine instructions) so generally run with a **low processing overhead** on the web server.
+ The web designer does not need to **know** the complexities of the web server interface; these are **hidden** within economical **APIs** (**A**pplication **P**rogramming **I**nterfaces).
+ The script module (engine) is directly integrated into the web server application.
+ Scripts can be **executed directly** by the web server's script module, reducing the need for operating system calls to external executable programs. This is much **quicker**!
+ Scripts are run on the web server; no script source is sent to the client's web browser; the code is therefore very **secure**.
+ Content is based on **live data**, e.g. dynamic information generated from a **database**.
+ Because processing is server-side, **web browser software can be basic** – perfect for **mobile client devices** such as PDAs and Smartphones where **CPU processing** may be **limited** due to power constraints.

The following diagram shows how modern server-side scripting solutions such as PHP work:

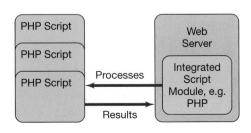

1.3 Web server scripting disadvantages

Although server-side scripting offers many advantages whether CGI or newer server-side methods are used, there are some negative points:

– **Debugging tools** may be scarce.
– Server-side scripting has **no direct control** over the **user interface** (e.g. the **appearance** of the web browser).
– Server-side scripting can be **more difficult** to develop.
– In order to **test** server-side scripting, both a host running a web server **and** a client computer system running a web browser is required. This is **more complicated** than testing client-side scripting, which just requires a web browser.

Note. It is possible to set a computer up to run client/server and take on **both roles**; we'll look at this in more detail in section 2.1.

2 Use web server scripting for server-side functionality

2.1 Programming

PHP can be used for a number of different server-side solutions.

The most common types of functionality include:

◆ **accessing databases**, including techniques such as:
  ◆ **appending** new records
  ◆ **deleting** existing records
  ◆ **amending** existing records
  ◆ **performing** a user query
◆ uploading files to the server
◆ security such as login systems
◆ environmental data.

The following section will examine these functions by providing **sample PHP solutions** which are **tested**, **commented** and **fully explained**.

Getting started

From a practical perspective it is worthwhile covering the downloading, installation and testing of a suitable PHP test platform.

In order to proceed we need to identify the necessary **hardware** and **software components**. These typically include:

◆ PC
◆ Windows or Linux operating system
◆ PHP
◆ web server (usually Apache HTTPD)
◆ MySQL (a relational database system).

WAMP or LAMP?

Although these items can be downloaded and assembled **separately**, many **pre-packaged solutions** exist for Windows and Linux.

WAMP stands for **W**indows **A**pache **M**ySQL **P**HP
LAMP stands for **L**inux **A**pache **M**ySQL **P**HP

Example **WAMP packages** include:

WAMPServer http://www.wampserver.com/en/
Xampp http://www.apachefriends.org/en/xampp-windows.html
Server2Go http://www.server2go-web.de/

Example **LAMP packages** include:

Xampp http://www.apachefriends.org/en/xampp-linux.html
LAMPStack http://bitnami.org/stack/lampstack

The following section demonstrates the installation of **WAMPServer** in 11 easy steps!

These steps can be followed whether you are installing onto a server or a client (for client/server support).

1 **Download** the WAMPServer package:

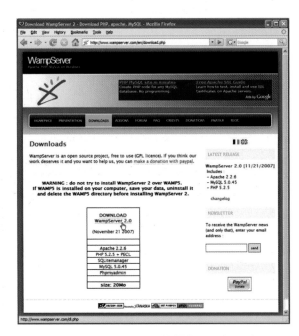

Figure 19.2 Downloading WAMPServer from the website

2 **Install** the WAMPServer package. **Double click** on the icon to **start** the installation process.

Figure 19.3 Welcome screen for WAMPServer installation

3 Read and accept the License Agreement:

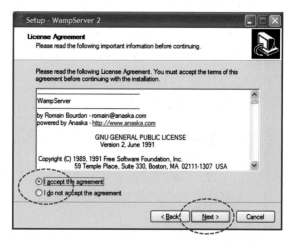

Figure 19.4 WAMPServer License Agreement

4 Select an appropriate **installation folder**. **Note.** Choose this folder **carefully** as we will be returning to it later!

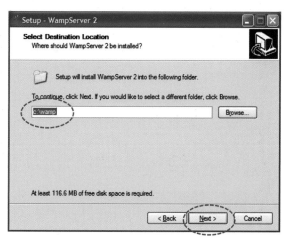

Figure 19.5 WAMPServer installation folder

5 Choose to create both a **Quick Launch icon** and a **desktop shortcut**.

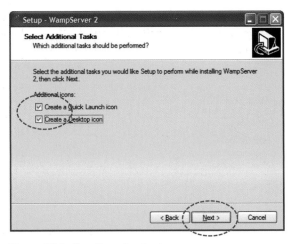

Figure 19.6 Creating shortcuts

6 One **final check** before you press the **Install** button.

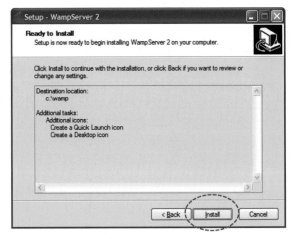

Figure 19.7 Confirmation of the installation details; you can go back and change them

7 Sit back and **wait** for the installation to complete.
A **progress bar** should keep you informed of the progress.

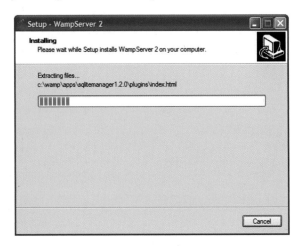

Figure 19.8 Progress bar for WAMPServer installation

8 WAMPServer may detect your favourite web browser; select it as the **default browser** if you wish.

Figure 19.9 Web browser detected!

9 WAMPServer will ask if you'd like to install its **homepage**. Click **Yes**.

Figure 19.10 WAMPServer homepage

10 The next few dialogues will ask you to enter configuration information for WAMPServer. Don't panic! If you get these wrong you can always change them later.
For now, **accept** the **default entries** unless instructed to key in something different.

Hopefully WAMPServer has now **successfully installed** and has offered you the opportunity to **launch** it **immediately**.

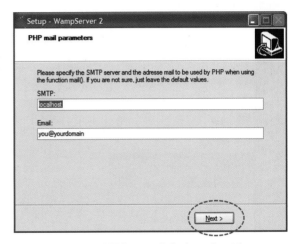

Figure 19.11 WAMPServer default mail settings

11 **Leave** the check box **ticked** and click the **Finish** button.

Now WAMPServer is **installed** and **running** we can give it a **test**.

Figure 19.12 WAMPServer ready to launch!

Using WAMPServer

The Windows **system tray** (bottom right of your desktop usually) should have a new WAMPServer icon.

Figure 19.13 WAMPServer icon in the system tray

Starting Apache web server

The first step is to test the **Apache web server**.

This is done by **left clicking** on the system tray **WAMPServer icon**:

Figure 19.14 WAMPServer pop-up menu

Select the '**Start All Services**' option from the menu. This will start **Apache**, the PHP engine and the MySQL database. It is now possible to **test** the installation. Let's start by testing **Apache**.

About Client/Server

WAMPServer turns your PC into both a client **and** a server. This means that when the **web browser client** (e.g. Mozilla Firefox or Microsoft Internet Explorer®) requests a page from '**Localhost**' (your PC's default name), it is actually asking the **server part** of your PC to supply it. This is exactly the same process that occurs when accessing a **remote** web server!

This is **totally different** to opening a web page as a **local file**. If .PHP files are opened as local files they **will not process correctly**. Be careful.

Another point to remember is that your PC is now **vulnerable** to **external** web page requests. Use '**Stop All Services**' when you have **finished** your testing. All Server processes (Apache, PHP and MySQL) will then **halt**.

To test the Apache web server, enter '**Localhost**' into the web browser's **address bar**.

Figure 19.15 Accessing 'Localhost'

If this works properly, the Apache web server should respond to the **Localhost** URL by displaying its **default web page** (usually **index.php** or **index.html**):

If this appears, your Apache web server is working fine.

If this **doesn't** appear retrace your steps to see if you have **missed something** or **keyed** 'Localhost' **incorrectly**.

The **'root' folder** of the web server is '**<root folder>\WWW**' where <root folder> is the folder selected at **stage 4** of the installation. This is usually '**C:\WAMP**'.

Find this folder and inspect it: You should see 'index.php' there.

Figure 19.16 Apache's default web page – 'index.php'

Accessing databases

Use **MySQL** to create the following database table for **Lee Office Supplies' stock control**.

| Database: leeoffsup |||||
| Table: StockItems |||||
ItemCode	ItemDesc	ItemStockQty	ItemUnitPrice	ItemCategory
LOS001	A4 Paper x 500 sheets (white)	100	3.50	Paper
LOS002	A4 Paper x 500 sheets (blue)	205	3.70	Paper
LOS003	A4 Paper x 500 sheets (yellow)	300	3.70	Paper
LOS004	Ballpoint pen x 40 (red ink)	30	10.00	Pens
LOS005	Ballpoint pen x 40 (blue ink)	40	10.00	Pens
LOS006	Ballpoint pen x 40 (green ink)	20	10.00	Pens
LOS007	Pencil eraser x 50	10	10.00	Erasers

Creating the database and table in MySQL

Most students are familiar with **Microsoft's Access®** – a **r**elational **d**atabase **m**anagement **s**ystem (**RDMS**) which is part of the **Microsoft Office®** suite of business applications.

Access isn't the only RDMS – many others exist in the commercial sector.

MySQL is one such alternative. It is **powerful**, **flexible**, **integrates** well with PHP and is **free**.

In order for the server-side PHP script to generate dynamic web page content it is necessary for it to be able to access a database and its tables.

This unit chapter assumes you understand the **fundamental concepts** of databases.

Unit Link

For further information on Databases or just a refresher on the subject, please refer to **Unit Chapter 5 – Advanced Database Skills**, pages 47 to 100.

MySQL – command line interface v. graphical user interface?

MySQL can be used via the command line or via a graphical user interface. Both methods have their advantages and disadvantages.

In order to present a more realistic scenario for learners and to help practitioners reacquaint themselves with these environments, this tutorial follows the command line interface as best practice.

Step 1: Start the WAMPServer MySQL service

Click the WAMPServer icon on the system tray.

Then select the menu options: **MySQL** -> **Service** -> **Start/Resume Service** (as shown in Figure 19.17).

Figure 19.17 Starting MySQL service

Step 2: Access the MySQL console

To access the MySQL command line interface (also known as the 'MySQL console'), select the menu options: **MySQL -> MySQL console**. This is shown in Figure 19.18.

You should then be presented with a **DOS-style command box**, prompting for a password.

There shouldn't be a **password**, so just press the **Enter/Return key**. If asked, the **default username** is usually '**root**'.

Figure 19.18 Launching the MySQL console

You will then be presented with a welcome message, as shown in Figure 19.19.

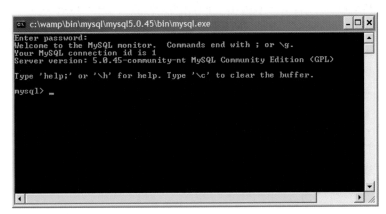

Figure 19.19 MySQL console

Step 3: Set up the database

The next step is to set up the **database** we are going to use for Lee Office Supplies. We'll abbreviate this to 'leeoffsup'.

Type:

```
create database leeoffsup;
```

and press the **Enter/Return** key.

Notice the use of the **semi-colon** to mark the end of the statement; this is called '**committing**'.

Figure 19.20 Successful creation of the database

The next step is to make this database **active**. We do this by typing:

> use leeoffsup;

and press the **Enter/Return** key.

This is an important step as the database will be used as the **container** for the **tables** we will create for the web server scripting examples that follow.

Step 4: Create the StockItems table

To create the StockItems table it is necessary to provide the **definition** (or **structure**) of the table. This is achieved by specifying the **field names**, **field types** and **sizes** (in characters, where appropriate).

We can also identify whether fields can be **null** (have no contents) and which field is to be treated as the **primary key** (making a row **unique**).

Simple data types are used: '**varchar**' is for strings of characters, '**int**' for integers (whole numbers) and '**decimal**' for real numbers (with decimal places).

MySQL – Data types

More MySQL data types (for version 5.0) can be found here:

http://dev.mysql.com/doc/refman/5.0/en/data-types.html

Here is the suggested definition for the StockItems table:

Field Name	Field type	Field Size	Can be Null?	Primary Key
ItemCode	Varchar	6	No	Yes
ItemDesc	Varchar	40	Yes	
ItemStockQty	Int	11	No	
ItemUnitPrice	Decimal	7 digits including 2 decimal places	No	
ItemCategory	Varchar	20	No	

To create the table, type the following **very carefully**:

```
CREATE TABLE StockItems (ItemCode varchar(6) NOT NULL, ItemDesc varchar(40) NULL,
ItemStockQty int NOT NULL, ItemUnitPrice decimal(7,2) NOT NULL, ItemCategory
varchar(20) NOT NULL, PRIMARY KEY(ItemCode));
```

Figure 19.21 shows this happening in the MySQL console:

```
c:\wamp\bin\mysql\mysql5.0.45\bin\mysql.exe                    _ □ ✕
Enter password:
Welcome to the MySQL monitor.  Commands end with ; or \g.
Your MySQL connection id is 2
Server version: 5.0.45-community-nt MySQL Community Edition (GPL)

Type 'help;' or '\h' for help. Type '\c' to clear the buffer.

mysql> use leeoffsup
Database changed
mysql> CREATE TABLE StockItems (ItemCode varchar(6) NOT NULL, ItemDesc varchar(4
0) NULL, ItemStockQty int NOT NULL, ItemUnitPrice decimal(7,2) NOT NULL, ItemCat
egory varchar(20) NOT NULL, PRIMARY KEY(ItemCode));
Query OK, 0 rows affected (0.23 sec)

mysql>
```

Figure 19.21 Successful creation of the StockItems table

As you may have guessed, it is quite common for developers to make **keying errors** at this point. MySQL will respond with an **error**. Previous MySQL commands are accessible via a **command history**. Simply use the **up** and **down cursor keys** to access the offending command, edit it and press **Enter** again.

Step 5: Checking the StockItems table

It is possible to list the **tables** in the **leeoffsup database**.

Type:

```
show tables;
```

and press the **Enter** key.

Any tables held in the leeoffsup database will be listed (see Figure 19.22):

```
mysql> show tables;
+--------------------+
| Tables_in_leeoffsup |
+--------------------+
| stockitems         |
+--------------------+
1 row in set (0.00 sec)

mysql>
```

Figure 19.22 Tables in the leeoffsup database

In addition, it is possible to **describe** the **table's definition**.

Type:

```
describe stockitems;
```

and press the **Enter** key.

```
mysql> describe stockitems;
+--------------+-------------+------+-----+---------+-------+
| Field        | Type        | Null | Key | Default | Extra |
+--------------+-------------+------+-----+---------+-------+
| ItemCode     | varchar(6)  | NO   | PRI |         |       |
| ItemDesc     | varchar(40) | YES  |     | NULL    |       |
| ItemStockQty | int(11)     | NO   |     |         |       |
| ItemUnitPrice| decimal(7,2)| NO   |     |         |       |
| ItemCategory | varchar(20) | NO   |     |         |       |
+--------------+-------------+------+-----+---------+-------+
5 rows in set (0.01 sec)

mysql>
```

Figure 19.23 Confirming the definition of the stockitems table

It appears that our table has been successfully defined. Let's now turn our attention to placing data into the table. This is called '**populating**'.

Step 6: Populating the StockItems table

Populating the StockItems table can be achieved in a number of ways. Perhaps the simplest technique is to use **MySQL Insert** statements.

This is shown in the following example.

Type:

```
INSERT INTO stockitems VALUES ("LOS001", "A4 Paper x 500 sheets
(white)", 100, 3.50, "Paper");
```

and press the **Enter** key.

MySQL should respond with a confirmation message as shown in Figure 19.24:

```
mysql> INSERT INTO stockitems VALUES ("LOS001", "A4 Paper x 500 sheets (white)", 100, 3.50, "Paper");
Query OK, 1 row affected (0.00 sec)

mysql>
```

Figure 19.24 Insert MySQL statement

Step 7: Performing a simple query

The MySQL **Select statement** is one of those **most frequently** used. It is used to **interrogate** the database and produce a **results set**. This results set is then processed and returned to the client.

Let's use a simple Select statement to show the data we have just inserted into the **StockItems** table.

Type:

```
select * from stockitems;
```

and press the **Enter** key.

This statement will select **all rows** and **all fields** (specified with the '*' asterisk wildcard symbol) in the table.

The results of this command are shown in Figure 19.25:

```
mysql> select * from stockitems;
+----------+------------------------------+--------------+--------------+--------------+
| ItemCode | ItemDesc                     | ItemStockQty | ItemUnitPrice | ItemCategory |
+----------+------------------------------+--------------+--------------+--------------+
| LOS001   | A4 Paper x 500 sheets (white) |          100 |          3.50 | Paper        |
+----------+------------------------------+--------------+--------------+--------------+
1 row in set (0.00 sec)

mysql>
```

Figure 19.25 Performing a simple query

Step 8: Completing the population of the StockItems table

Repeat the instructions in **step 6** for the **other stock items** that need to be inserted into the table.

When you have added them **all**, **repeat** the **Select query** to achieve the results as shown in Figure 19.26.

```
mysql> select * from stockitems;
+----------+-------------------------------+--------------+--------------+--------------+
| ItemCode | ItemDesc                      | ItemStockQty | ItemUnitPrice | ItemCategory |
+----------+-------------------------------+--------------+--------------+--------------+
| LOS001   | A4 Paper x 500 sheets (white) |          100 |          3.50 | Paper        |
| LOS002   | A4 Paper x 500 sheets (blue)  |          205 |          3.70 | Paper        |
| LOS003   | A4 Paper x 500 sheets (yellow)|          300 |          3.70 | Paper        |
| LOS004   | Ballpoint pen x 40 (red ink)  |           30 |         10.00 | Pens         |
| LOS005   | Ballpoint pen x 40 (blue ink) |           40 |         10.00 | Pens         |
| LOS006   | Ballpoint pen x 40 (green ink)|           20 |         10.00 | Pens         |
| LOS007   | Pencil Eraser x 50            |           10 |         10.00 | Erasers      |
+----------+-------------------------------+--------------+--------------+--------------+
7 rows in set (0.00 sec)
```

Figure 19.26 StockItems table is now fully populated

Step 9: Creating the HTML web-based interface

The following example demonstrates how we will use PHP to access the MySQL database in order to generate live results. It performs a basic 'all data' query, much like the manually issued MySQL statement as shown in step 8. **Formatting** has mostly been **removed** to keep the code short.

```php
<?php
mysql_connect(localhost,"root","");
mysql_select_db("leeoffsup") or die("Unable to select database");
$query="SELECT * FROM StockItems";
$result=mysql_query($query);
$num=mysql_num_rows($result);
mysql_close();
echo "<b><center>Lee Office Supplies - Stock Items</b>";
$i=0;
echo "<table border=1><tr><td>Item Code</td><td>Item Desc</td>";
echo "<td>Item Stock Qty</td>";
echo "<td>Item Unit Price</td><td>Item Category</td></tr>";
while ($i < $num)
{
  $ItemCode = mysql_result($result,$i,"ItemCode");
  $ItemDesc = mysql_result($result,$i,"ItemDesc");
  $ItemStockQty = mysql_result($result,$i,"ItemStockQty");
  $ItemUnitPrice = mysql_result($result,$i,"ItemUnitPrice");
  $ItemCategory = mysql_result($result,$i,"ItemCategory");

  echo "<tr><td>$ItemCode</td><td>$ItemDesc</td><td align=right>";
  echo "$ItemStockQty</td>";
  echo "<td align=right>$ItemUnitPrice</td>";
  echo "<td>$ItemCategory</td></tr>";
  $i++;
}
echo "</table><center>";
echo "$num Stock items found.";
?>
```

Figure 19.27 Start All Services from the WAMPServer's system tray icon

This code should be keyed into a suitable **text editor** (such as Microsoft Notepad®) or a bespoke **PHP editor**. The file should be saved as 'display.php' in the **default folder** representing the web server's **virtual root** – this is usually '**C:\wamp\www**'.

You can test this PHP once all WAMP services (not just MySQL) have been started (see Figure 19.27):

Step 10: Testing the PHP

Load a **web browser** (it should not matter which one you use).

Then, enter the following into the web browser's **address bar**:

and press **Enter**.

The web server's linked PHP engine should process the script, use SQL to interrogate the MySQL database 'leeoffsup' and its 'StockItems' table, generating dynamic web page content for us.

The results are shown in Figure 19.28.

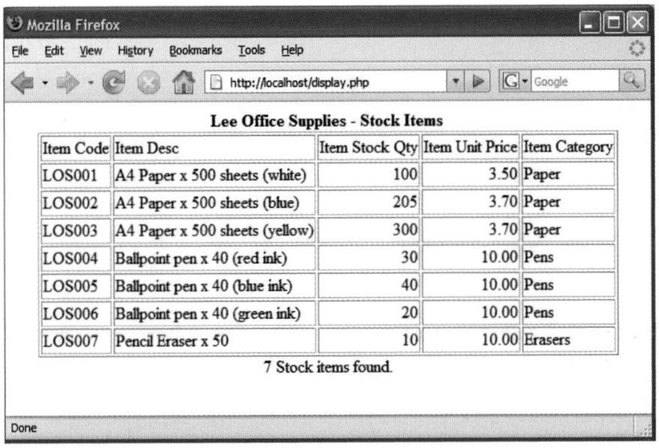

Lee Office Supplies - Stock Items

Item Code	Item Desc	Item Stock Qty	Item Unit Price	Item Category
LOS001	A4 Paper x 500 sheets (white)	100	3.50	Paper
LOS002	A4 Paper x 500 sheets (blue)	205	3.70	Paper
LOS003	A4 Paper x 500 sheets (yellow)	300	3.70	Paper
LOS004	Ballpoint pen x 40 (red ink)	30	10.00	Pens
LOS005	Ballpoint pen x 40 (blue ink)	40	10.00	Pens
LOS006	Ballpoint pen x 40 (green ink)	20	10.00	Pens
LOS007	Pencil Eraser x 50	10	10.00	Erasers

7 Stock items found.

Figure 19.28 Dynamically created web page content, courtesy of Apache, MySQL and PHP

Peeking at the HTML source doesn't help!

Unlike client-side scripting, its server-side relative, as powered by PHP, does **not** reveal its processing secrets because no PHP is actually sent to the client. To prove this, let's take a look at the HTML source code for this web page:

```
<b><center>Lee Office Supplies - Stock Items</b><table border=1><tr><td>Item
Code</td><td>Item Desc</td><td>Item Stock Qty</td><td>Item Unit Price</td><td>Item
Category </td></tr><tr><td>LOS001</td><td>A4 Paper x 500 sheets (white)</td><td
align=right>100</td><td
align=right>3.50</td><td>Paper</td></tr><tr><td>LOS002</td><td>A4 Paper x 500
sheets (blue)</td><td align=right>205</td><td
align=right>3.70</td><td>Paper</td></tr><tr><td>LOS003</td><td>A4 Paper x 500
sheets (yellow)</td><td align=right>300</td><td
align=right>3.70</td><td>Paper</td></tr><tr><td>LOS004</td><td>Ballpoint pen x 40
(red ink)</td><td align=right>30</td><td
align=right>10.00</td><td>Pens</td></tr><tr><td>LOS005</td><td>Ballpoint pen x 40
(blue ink)</td><td align=right>40</td><td
align=right>10.00</td><td>Pens</td></tr><tr><td>LOS006</td><td>Ballpoint pen x 40
(green ink)</td><td align=right>20</td><td
align=right>10.00</td><td>Pens</td></tr><tr><td>LOS007</td><td>Pencil Eraser x
50</td><td align=right>10</td><td
align=right>10.00</td><td>Erasers</td></tr></table><center>7 Stock items found.
```

As you can imagine, protecting the inner workings of a website is invaluable in such security-conscious applications as e-commerce.

Step 11: PHP code review

Before we progress, let's **review** that PHP code and **colour code** the various sections for easier explanation.

```php
<?php
mysql_connect(localhost,"root","");
mysql_select_db("leeoffsup") or die("Unable to select database");
$query="SELECT * FROM StockItems";
$result=mysql_query($query);
$num=mysql_num_rows($result);
mysql_close();
echo "<b><center>Lee Office Supplies - Stock Items</b>";
$i=0;
echo "<table border=1><tr><td>Item Code</td><td>Item Desc</td>";
echo "<td>Item Stock Qty</td>";
echo "<td>Item Unit Price</td><td>Item Category</td></tr>";
while ($i < $num)
{
  $ItemCode = mysql_result($result,$i,"ItemCode");
  $ItemDesc = mysql_result($result,$i,"ItemDesc");
  $ItemStockQty = mysql_result($result,$i,"ItemStockQty");
  $ItemUnitPrice = mysql_result($result,$i,"ItemUnitPrice");
  $ItemCategory = mysql_result($result,$i,"ItemCategory");

  echo "<tr><td>$ItemCode</td><td>$ItemDesc</td><td align=right>";
  echo "$ItemStockQty</td>";
  echo "<td align=right>$ItemUnitPrice</td>";
  echo "<td>$ItemCategory</td></tr>";
  $i++;
}
echo "</table><center>";
echo "$num Stock items found.";
?>
```

And the PHP code analysis:

	These lines start and end the PHP script.
	This section connects to the MySQL server running on the localhost. It uses 'root' as a username and no password. Once connected it attempts to open a database called 'leeoffsup'. An error message is displayed if it fails. It then creates an SQL SELECT query and uses this to generate a matching results set. The number of rows in the results set is then stored and the MySQL connection is closed.
	This section displays the web page heading, creates an HTML table and its column headings. It also creates a variable called 'i' (for 'index'), setting it to 0.
	This section creates a pre-conditioned while loop. It will continue to work, looping through each row of the results set until the 'i' variable reaches the same value as the total number of rows.
	This section copies the values of each table field in the current row into a variable. The variables are then placed into the cells of an HTML table row. Importantly, this section also increments the value of 'i'; this moves it onto the next row of the results set.
	This section occurs after all rows of the results set have been processed and the while loop is finished. It simply ends the HTML table and then outputs confirmation of the number of rows in the record set.

Appending new records

Now we have introduced the basic concepts, let's move onto some meaningful processing.

Appending new records is a fairly straightforward process.

First we need to create a **basic HTML form** that will **submit** a **new Stock record**.

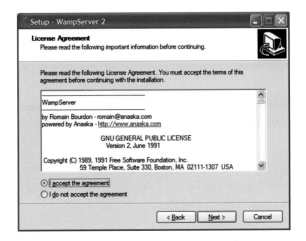

Once the **submit button** is **clicked**, the **data** is **posted** to the PHP script, which does the processing. This uses an SQL INSERT statement to **append the record** to the database's **StockItems table**.

The user is then greeted with a **pop-up message** to confirm that the data has been successfully added.

Step 1: Creating NewStock.html

This form should use basic **HTML** and **CSS** to create a simple input form that reflects the data needs for the StockItems data.

You can add **client-side validation** if you wish.

Here is sample HTML, CSS and JavaScript for the New Stock form:

Unit Link

For further information on **CSS formatting** and **client-side validation** of input forms using **JavaScript**, please refer to **Unit 10 – Client-side Customisation of Web Pages**, sections 1.2 (pages 153 to 160) and 2.2 (pages 173 to 185).

```html
<html>
<head>
<title>
Lee Office Supplies - Add New Stock
</title>
<script>
function validateForm(thisform)
{
  if (thisform.ItemCode.value.length<6)
  {
    thisform.ItemCode.focus();
    alert("Stock Code must be 6 letters\neg. LOS123");
    return false;
```

```
    }
}
</script>
<style>
#div1
{
float:left;
color:black;
width:200px;
line-height:150%;
margin-bottom:10px;
}
#div2
{
width:150px;
background-color:cyan;
margin:0;
padding:0;
border:0;
}
select,input
{
background-color:powderblue;
}
#div3
{
width=480px;
text-align:center;
}
body
{
font-family: Verdana, Arial, Helvetica, sans-serif;
background-color:cyan;
}
</style>
</head>
<body>
<div id="div3">
<h1>Lee Office Supplies</h1>
<h2>Add New Stock</h2>
</div>
<form name="newstock" action="update.php" onsubmit="return validateForm(this);"
method="post">
<div id="div1">
Item Code<br>
Item Description<br>
Item Stock Qty<br>
<input type="text" name="ItemCode" size="6">
<input type="text" name="ItemDesc" size="40">
<input type="text" name="ItemStockQty" size="11">
<input type="text" name="ItemUnitPrice" size="9">
<select size="1" name="ItemCategory">
    <option selected value="Paper">Paper</OPTION>
    <option value="Pens">Pens</OPTION>
    <option value="Erasers">Erasers</OPTION>
    <option value="Files">Files</OPTION>
    <option value="Adhesives">Adhesives</OPTION>
```

> This line of code is important as it links this .html document with the .php file that will do the processing.
>
> This line will post the form inputs to the second file (as long as the validation is successful).

> These lines of code are highlighted in yellow because they specify the form element names for each input.
>
> We'll need to know these to grab the posted data in update.php.

```
</select></div>
<div id="div3">
<input type="submit" value="Submit">
</div>
</form>
</body>
</html>
```

Figure 19.29 shows its **rendered appearance** in a typical web browser (in this case, Microsoft Internet Explorer®):

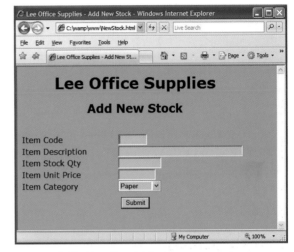

Figure 19.29 NewStock.html

In an effort to avoid using tables, **DIVs** have been used to organise the page. In addition, **JavaScript validation** has been added to the **ItemCode textbox**. This **prevents** the Submit button from working until a six-digit code has been entered (see Figure 19.30).

The opportunity for further input errors has been **reduced** by creating a **drop-down selection** for **ItemCategory**. This will also ensure **data consistency** for entries to this field, which will help **queries** later on.

Figure 19.30 Validation alert

Step 2: Creating Update.php

Update PHP code is pretty straightforward, fortunately. It works by making similar connections to the database but instead of running a **SELECT** query, it executes an **INSERT** command.

The key to this process is the '**harvesting**' of the **posted form values**. This is shown in the block of code highlighted in yellow. Each form element's contents are **copied** into **local PHP variables**.

These variables are then **shoe-horned** back into the **INSERT command** in the **correct order**. This is shown in the block of code highlighted in green. If you're wondering why some variables have **quotes** and some **do not** – well, it's simply a question of whether the field is **text** or **numeric** (numeric fields **do not** need them).

A simple **JavaScript alert** is used to flash a confirmation to the user that the new data has been successfully added.

```php
<?php
mysql_connect(localhost,"root","");
mysql_select_db("leeoffsup") or die("Unable to select database");
$ItemCode = $_POST['ItemCode'];
$ItemDesc = $_POST['ItemDesc'];
$ItemStockQty = $_POST['ItemStockQty'];
$ItemUnitPrice = $_POST['ItemUnitPrice'];
$ItemCategory = $_POST['ItemCategory'];
$query = "INSERT INTO StockItems VALUES
('$ItemCode','$ItemDesc',$ItemStockQty,$ItemUnitPrice,'$ItemCategory')";
mysql_query($query);
mysql_close();
?>
<script>
alert ("New Stock Item has been successfully added.");
</script>
```

Step 3: Testing

With the web server running, it's time to test the solution.

Figure 19.31 shows a **new stock item** being entered into the **NewStock.html** form…

Looks good; now **click** the **Submit button**.

Figure 19.31 New stock item's data being keyed in

A confirmation should then appear:

Figure 19.32 Confirmation alert

The soundest way to make sure that the **backend database** (**leeoffsup**) has been updated is to inspect the **StockItems table** in the MySQL console (see Figure 19.33).

```
mysql> select * from stockitems;
+----------+-----------------------------------+--------------+--------------+--------------+
| ItemCode | ItemDesc                          | ItemStockQty | ItemUnitPrice| ItemCategory |
+----------+-----------------------------------+--------------+--------------+--------------+
| LOS001   | A4 Paper x 500 sheets (white)     |          100 |         3.50 | Paper        |
| LOS002   | A4 Paper x 500 sheets (blue)      |          205 |         3.70 | Paper        |
| LOS003   | A4 Paper x 500 sheets (yellow)    |          300 |         3.70 | Paper        |
| LOS004   | Ballpoint pen x 40 (red ink)      |           30 |        10.00 | Pens         |
| LOS005   | Ballpoint pen x 40 (blue ink)     |           40 |        10.00 | Pens         |
| LOS006   | Ballpoint pen x 40 (green ink)    |           20 |        10.00 | Pens         |
| LOS007   | Pencil Eraser x 50                |           10 |        10.00 | Erasers      |
| LOS008   | A4 Lever Arch folders (blue x 10) |           60 |        10.00 | Files        |
+----------+-----------------------------------+--------------+--------------+--------------+
8 rows in set (0.00 sec)
```

Figure 19.33 MySQL view of the new StockItems record

This looks very encouraging; the data for the new stock item has been successfully appended into our StockItems table.

Of course, we could always **re-run** our very own **display.php** to test it.

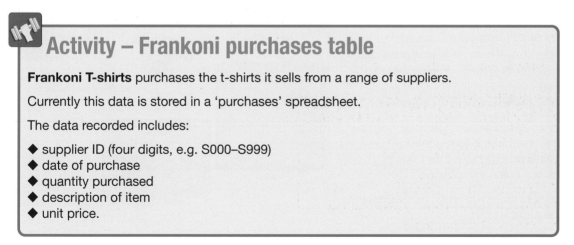

Figure 19.34 Display.php's view of the new StockItems record

And again we can see that the new record (**Stock Item LOS008**) has been **successfully** added.

Activity – Frankoni purchases table

Frankoni T-shirts purchases the t-shirts it sells from a range of suppliers.

Currently this data is stored in a 'purchases' spreadsheet.

The data recorded includes:

◆ supplier ID (four digits, e.g. S000–S999)
◆ date of purchase
◆ quantity purchased
◆ description of item
◆ unit price.

Here is the sample data:

Date	Supplier ID	Quantity	Description	Price
01/09/2007	S101	100	T-shirts Blue XL	4.52
01/09/2007	S102	30	T-shirts Red L	3.44
04/09/2007	S103	45	Assorted Band logos	0.60
06/09/2007	S101	200	T-shirts Black L	4.70
07/09/2007	S101	150	T-shirts Black XL	4.60
10/09/2007	S104	190	T-shirts Blue L Long-sleeved	5.60
15/09/2007	S101	60	T-shirts Blue XL	4.52
21/09/2007	S103	15	Assorted Band logos	0.60
22/09/2007	S101	55	T-shirts Red L	3.70
22/09/2007	S105	50	Assorted Band logos	0.70
22/09/2007	S102	40	T-shirts Blue L Long-sleeved	5.30
25/09/2007	S101	140	T-shirts Blue S	4.12
27/09/2007	S102	10	T-shirts Red XL Long-sleeved	5.10
28/09/2007	S101	15	Assorted Band logos	0.80
30/09/2007	S102	25	T-shirts Blue XL	4.60

Tasks:

1 Create a backend MySQL database table to store these purchases instead.

2 Populate the table with the sample data provided (above).

3 Create a 'display.php'-style script to display this data on a web page. Test it.

4 Create a 'newpurchase.html' form and 'update.php' script to add new purchase data into the table. Test it.

5 Review your solution. Does it perform as expected?

Performing a user query

It is quite common for a user to want to search a commercial online database for specific information, e.g. 'all games for the Microsoft Xbox360®', 'all CD albums by My Chemical Romance'.

In order to achieve this, we need to create a **query form** (**Query.html**) and suitable PHP script (**Query.php**) that will **interrogate** the MySQL database using a **refined** SELECT statement.

For our StockItems table, it is likely that we could search on a number of **different criteria** (e.g. by price, by category, by description).

Our example will search by the **primary key**, ItemCode.

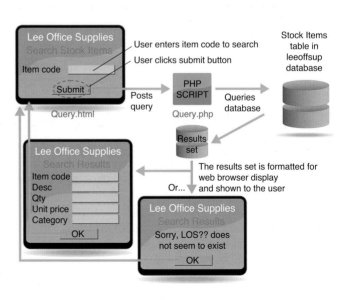

Step 1: Creating Query.html

This form should use basic **HTML** and **CSS** to create a simple query form that allows the user to key in an item code that they wish to search for.

You can add **client-side validation** if you wish, such as validating the Item Code input by the user.

Here is sample HTML, CSS and JavaScript for the Query form:

```html
<html>
<head>
<title>
Lee Office Supplies - Search Stock Items
</title>
<script>
function validateForm(thisform)
{
   if (thisform.ItemCode.value.length<6)
   {
      thisform.ItemCode.focus();
      alert("Stock Code must be 6 letters\neg. LOS123");
      return false;
   }
}
</script>
<style>
select,input
{
background-color:powderblue;
margin: 5px 0 0 0;
}
body
{
font-family: Verdana, Arial, Helvetica, sans-serif;
background-color:cyan;
text-align:center;
}
</style>
</head>
<body>
<h1>Lee Office Supplies</h1>
<h2>Search Stock Items</h2>
<form name="QueryStock" action="Query.php" onsubmit="return validateForm(this);"
method="post">
Item Code <input type="text" name="ItemCode" size="6"><br>
<input type="submit" value="Submit">
</form>
</body>
</html>
```

Figure 19.35 shows its **rendered appearance** in a typical web browser (in this case, Mozilla Firefox):

Figure 19.35 Query.html

Step 2: Creating Query.php

Again, this script is fairly straightforward.

It works by making similar connections to the database as the original 'display.php' script. However, rather than displaying **all** rows of the tables, it needs to **limit** the results set to **just** the record matching the Item Code **specified by the user** on the Query form.

The trick to this process is to '**harvest**' the **posted form value (itemcode)** and insert it into a slightly modified **SELECT** statement.

MySQL – More on the SELECT statement

The MySQL SELECT statement is **very** versatile.

In addition to display all fields for all rows, it is possible to limit both the fields displayed and the records selected.

E.g. limiting fields:

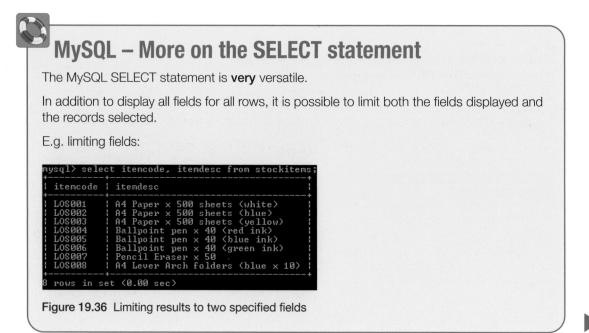

Figure 19.36 Limiting results to two specified fields

E.g. limiting rows:

```
mysql> select * from stockitems where itemcode = "LOS007";
+----------+------------------+--------------+---------------+--------------+
| ItemCode | ItemDesc         | ItemStockQty | ItemUnitPrice | ItemCategory |
+----------+------------------+--------------+---------------+--------------+
| LOS007   | Pencil Eraser x 50 |         10 |         10.00 | Erasers      |
+----------+------------------+--------------+---------------+--------------+
1 row in set (0.03 sec)
```

Figure 19.37 Limiting results to one particular row using a 'where' clause

It is also possible to **combine** these operations, specifying limited fields for a particular row:

```
mysql> select itemcode, itemdesc from stockitems where itemstockqty >= 100;
+----------+--------------------------------+
| itemcode | itemdesc                       |
+----------+--------------------------------+
| LOS001   | A4 Paper x 500 sheets (white)  |
| LOS002   | A4 Paper x 500 sheets (blue)   |
| LOS003   | A4 Paper x 500 sheets (yellow) |
+----------+--------------------------------+
3 rows in set (0.00 sec)
```

Figure 19.38 Codes and descriptions for items with 100 or more in stock

For more on MySQL SELECT statement (for version 5.0):

http://dev.mysql.com/doc/refman/5.0/en/select.html

In order to perform this operation we need to insert the **posted form value** into the 'where' clause of the SELECT statement. In the following PHP solution, harvesting the posted form value is shown in **yellow**, the insertion of this value into the SELECT statement is shown in cyan.

Here's the full PHP script for this process:

```php
<?php
mysql_connect(localhost,"root","");
mysql_select_db("leeoffsup") or die("Unable to select database");
$ItemCode = $_POST['ItemCode'];
$query = "select * from StockItems where itemcode='$ItemCode';";
$result=mysql_query($query);
$num=mysql_num_rows($result);
mysql_close();
?>
<html>
<head>
<title>
Lee Office Supplies - Search Results
</title>
<style>
table
{
background-color:powderblue;
width:70%;
```

> Unlike previous examples, this PHP script **switches** in and out of 'plain' HTML.
>
> The **<?php** and **?>** tags (highlighted **green**) show when PHP is **active**. Outside these tags, the code is **normal HTML**.
>
> This '**mix and match**' approach is very popular.

```
margin-left:15%;
margin-right:15%;
}
th
{
text-decoration:bold;
}
body, p
{
font-family: Verdana, Arial, Helvetica, sans-serif;
background-color:cyan;
text-align:center;
}
</style>
</head>
<body>
<h1>Lee Office Supplies</h1>
<h2>Search Results</h2>
<?php
if ($num>0)
{
   echo "<table border=1><tr><th>Item Code</th><th>Item Desc</th>";
   echo "<th>Item Stock Qty</th>";
   echo "<th>Item Unit Price</th><th>Item Category</th></tr>";
   $ItemCode = mysql_result($result,$i,"ItemCode");
   $ItemDesc = mysql_result($result,$i,"ItemDesc");
   $ItemStockQty = mysql_result($result,$i,"ItemStockQty");
   $ItemUnitPrice = mysql_result($result,$i,"ItemUnitPrice");
   $ItemCategory = mysql_result($result,$i,"ItemCategory");

   echo "<tr><td>$ItemCode</td><td>$ItemDesc</td><td align=right>";
   echo "$ItemStockQty</td>";
   echo "<td align=right>$ItemUnitPrice</td>";
   echo "<td>$ItemCategory</td></tr>";
   echo "</table><center>";
}
else
{
   echo "<p>Sorry, $ItemCode does not seem to exist!<p>";
}
?>
<form>
<input type="button" value="OK" onclick="history.back();">
</form>
</body>
</html>
```

> The number of rows retrieved (should be 1) is used to detect whether a match has been made. **Unsuccessful searches** display a 'Not found' message in the 'else' part of the **pink-highlighted** if statement, bypassing the results processing.

> A simple **JavaScript 'onClick' handler** is used to instruct the browser to return to the **previous page** in its **history**. This will of course take the user back to the search page for another attempt. This is shown in grey.

With the web server running, it's time to test the query solution we have created.

Figure 19.39 shows a **valid item code** being entered into the **query.html** form...

Figure 19.39 Query.html with a search value

Now click on the **Submit** button and:

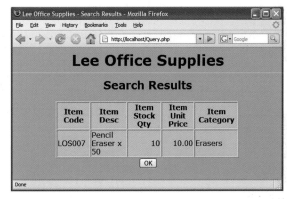

Figure 19.40 Query.php generates a successful outcome

However, if we'd searched for an item that **doesn't exist** (e.g. LOS*234*):

Figure 19.41 An unsuccessful search

Activity – Frankoni search facility

Extend your **Frankoni T-shirts** solution by adding a facility to **search** the **purchases table** for goods bought from a **specific supplier**.

Tasks:

1 Create a 'Query.html'-style front-end for the user to key-in the supplier ID they wish to search on. Test it.

2 Create a 'Query.php' script to search for purchases from the supplier specified and output these in a tabular format. Ensure that **only** the 'date', 'description' and 'price' fields are displayed. As before, the user should be informed about unsuccessful searches. Test it.

3 Review your solution. Does it perform as expected?

Deleting existing records

In addition to searching for a specific row (or collection of rows), it is quite common for data to be **deleted from database tables** as part of regular **operations** and **maintenance**.

In order to achieve this, we can modify our **query form** (**Query.html**) and modify the PHP script (**Query.php**) in order to find the stock item that needs deleting. Once found, and if the user **confirms** the deletion is required, we will use a new script ('delete.php') to erase the selected stock item from the table.

Again we, search by the **primary key**, ItemCode.

MySQL – the DELETE statement

The MySQL DELETE statement is relatively **easy** to learn and operates in a fashion similar to the SELECT statement.

In order to delete rows from a table, it is necessary to specify (a) the **table name** and (b) **which rows** need to be deleted using the **'where' clause**.

The following example demonstrates a typical DELETE statement:

Figure 19.42
Deleting stock item LOS008; a second SELECT query proves it's been removed

For more on MySQL DELETE statement (for version 5.0):

http://dev.mysql.com/doc/refman/5.0/en/delete.html

The following diagram shows one possible approach to the deletion process:

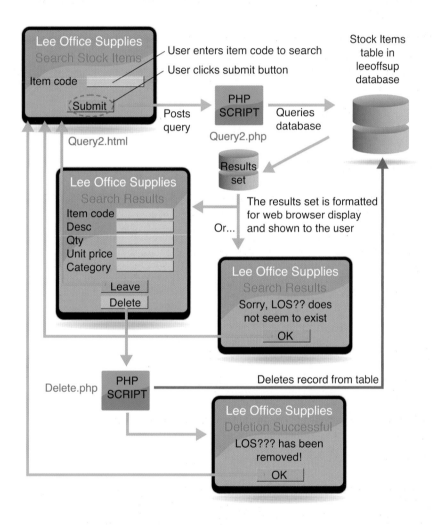

Step 1: Creating Query2.html

```html
<html>
<head>
<title>
Lee Office Supplies - Delete Stock Items
</title>
<script>
function validateForm(thisform)
{
  if (thisform.ItemCode.value.length<6)
  {
    thisform.ItemCode.focus();
    alert("Stock Code must be 6 letters\neg. LOS123");
    return false;
  }
}
</script>
<style>
select,input
{
background-color:powderblue;
margin: 5px 0 0 0;
}
body
{
font-family: Verdana, Arial, Helvetica, sans-serif;
background-color:cyan;
text-align:center;
}
</style>
</head>
<body>
<h1>Lee Office Supplies</h1>
<h2>Delete Stock Items</h2>
<form name="DeleteStock" action="Query2.php" onsubmit="return validateForm(this);"
method="post">
Item Code <input type="text" name="ItemCode" size="6"><br>
<input type="submit" value="Submit">
</form>
</body>
</html>
```

This file is **almost** identical to Query.html. The differences are highlighted in **green**.

The major alterations are the change of the page title, the web page heading and the linking of this html form to a different PHP script ('**Query2.php**').

Step 2: Creating Query2.php

Again, this script is fairly straightforward with only minor changes required from the original 'query.php' script. The modified code is highlighted in **green**.

```php
<?php
mysql_connect(localhost,"root","");
mysql_select_db("leeoffsup") or die("Unable to select database");
$ItemCode = $_POST['ItemCode'];
$query = "select * from StockItems where itemcode='$ItemCode';";
$result=mysql_query($query);
$num=mysql_num_rows($result);
mysql_close();
?>
<html>
<head>
<title>
Lee Office Supplies - Search Results
</title>

<style>
table
{
background-color:powderblue;
width:70%;
margin-left:15%;
margin-right:15%;
}
th
{
text-decoration:bold;
}
body, p
{
font-family: Verdana, Arial, Helvetica, sans-serif;
background-color:cyan;
text-align:center;
}
</style>
</head>
<body>
<h1>Lee Office Supplies</h1>
<h2>Search Results</h2>
<?php
if ($num>0)
{
  echo "<table border=1><tr><th>Item Code</th><th>Item Desc</th>";
  echo "<th>Item Stock Qty</th>";
  echo "<th>Item Unit Price</th><th>Item Category</th></tr>";
  $ItemCode = mysql_result($result,$i,"ItemCode");
  $ItemDesc = mysql_result($result,$i,"ItemDesc");
  $ItemStockQty = mysql_result($result,$i,"ItemStockQty");
  $ItemUnitPrice = mysql_result($result,$i,"ItemUnitPrice");
  $ItemCategory = mysql_result($result,$i,"ItemCategory");
  echo "<tr><td>$ItemCode</td><td>$ItemDesc</td><td align=right>";
  echo "$ItemStockQty</td>";
```

```
        echo "<td align=right>$ItemUnitPrice</td>";
        echo "<td>$ItemCategory</td></tr>";
        echo "</table><center>";
        echo "<form name='DeleteStock2' action='delete.php' method='post'>";
        echo "<input type='hidden' name='ItemCode' value='";
        echo $ItemCode;
        echo "'> <input type='button' value='Leave' onclick='history.back();'>";
        echo "<input type='submit' value='Delete!'>";
    }
    else
    {
        echo "<form name='DeleteStock2'>";
        echo "<p>Sorry, $ItemCode does not seem to exist!<p>";
        echo "<input type='button' value='Leave' onclick='history.back();'>";
    }
    ?>
    </form>
    </body>
    </html>
```

Perhaps the most important addition here is the use of a **hidden form field** to **forward** the itemcode entered in 'query2.html' to 'delete.php'. Because it is hidden it will **not be visible** to the user. Additional changes are also made to prevent the 'Delete!' button from being displayed if no matching record is found.

Step 3: Creating delete.php

```php
<?php
mysql_connect(localhost,"root","");
mysql_select_db("leeoffsup") or die("Unable to select database");
$ItemCode = $_POST['ItemCode'];
$query = "delete from StockItems where itemcode='$ItemCode';";
$result=mysql_query($query);
mysql_close();
?>
<html>
<head>
<title>
Lee Office Supplies - Deletion
</title>
<style>
body, p, h1, h2
{
font-family: Verdana, Arial, Helvetica, sans-serif;
background-color:cyan;
text-align:center;
}
</style>
</head>
<body>
<h1>Lee Office Supplies</h1>
<h2>Deletion Successful</h2>
<p><?php echo $ItemCode ?> has been removed!</p>
<form>
<input type="button" value="OK" onclick="history.go(-2);">
</form>
</body>
</html>
```

> In this PHP script, the **primary key** ('Itemcode') is used to identify the record to erase from the **StockItems** table.
>
> If you look closely, you can see how the **posted itemcode** value is inserted into the **DELETE statement** in the **appropriate** position.

Delete.php is the **key** script in the sequence, because it actually performs the required deletion from the **StockItems table**. As you will see, the code uses an adapted version of the **DELETE statement**.

The key lines of script are highlighted in **green**.

Step 4: Testing

Let's load the first web page and try to delete an item of stock ('LOS008'):

Figure 19.43 Query2.html with an Item Code to delete…

Figure 19.44 Query2.php displays the matched record with an option to delete it

Clicking the **Submit** button should load Query2.php as shown in Figure 19.44:

Clicking the **Delete!** button should **load** and **execute** Delete.php as shown in Figure 19.45:

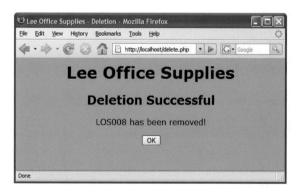

Figure 19.45 Delete.php confirms that the matched record has been deleted

A glimpse back in the MySQL database will confirm the deletion (see Figure 19.46):

```
| LOS008  | A4 Level Arch folders (blue x 10)  |                60 |   10.00 | Files |

6 rows in set (0.00 sec)

mysql> select * from stockitems;
+---------+-------------------------------+--------------+---------------+--------------+
| ItemCode | ItemDesc                      | ItemStockQty | ItemUnitPrice | ItemCategory |
+---------+-------------------------------+--------------+---------------+--------------+
| LOS001  | A4 Paper x 500 sheets (white)  |          100 |          3.50 | Paper        |
| LOS002  | A4 Paper x 500 sheets (blue)   |          205 |          3.70 | Paper        |
| LOS003  | A4 Paper x 500 sheets (yellow) |          300 |          3.70 | Paper        |
| LOS004  | Ballpoint pen x 40 (red ink)   |           30 |         10.00 | Pens         |
| LOS005  | Ballpoint pen x 40 (blue ink)  |           40 |         10.00 | Pens         |
| LOS006  | Ballpoint pen x 40 (green ink) |           20 |         10.00 | Pens         |
| LOS007  | Pencil Eraser x 50             |           10 |         10.00 | Erasers      |
+---------+-------------------------------+--------------+---------------+--------------+
7 rows in set (0.00 sec)
```

Figure 19.46 The record ('LOS008') has vanished from the StockItems table

Of course, the PHP script also accommodates for the user trying to delete a stock item that **doesn't exist** or trying to delete the same stock item twice.

Figure 19.47 Trying to delete an invalid stock item

In each case, the **Delete!** button is **removed** as it's not needed. This just gives the user the option of leaving the deletion process.

Amending existing records

The last file processing operation to tackle is the 'amend'. Amendment of a record occurs when some of its data is **changed** by the user. This could be performed to **correct an error** (e.g. a bad stock item description) or to change a specific detail as part of normal usage, e.g. increasing the level of stock present when a new delivery is received from the supplier.

The following example demonstrates how a **stock issue** (e.g. a **customer purchase**) would **reduce** the number available for a particular stock item.

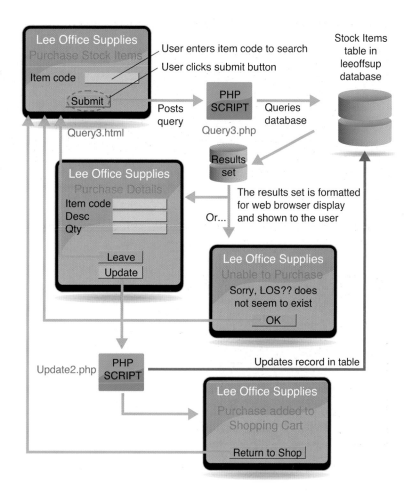

Step 1: Creating Query3.html

This file is **almost** identical to Query.html and Query2.html. As before, the differences are highlighted in **green**.

```
<html>
<head>
<title>
Lee Office Supplies - Purchase Stock Items
</title>
<script>
function validateForm(thisform)
{
  if (thisform.ItemCode.value.length<6)
  {
    thisform.ItemCode.focus();
    alert("Stock Code must be 6 letters\neg. LOS123");
    return false;
```

```
    }
}
</script>
<style>
select,input
{
background-color:powderblue;
margin: 5px 0 0 0;
}
body
{
font-family: Verdana, Arial, Helvetica, sans-serif;
background-color:cyan;
text-align:center;
}
</style>
</head>
<body>
<h1>Lee Office Supplies</h1>
<h2>Purchase Stock Items</h2>
<form name="PurchaseStock" action="Query3.php" onsubmit="return
validateForm(this);" method="post">
Item Code <input type="text" name="ItemCode" size="6"><br>
<input type="submit" value="Submit">
</form>
</body>
</html>
```

The major alterations are the change of the page title, the web page heading and the linking of this html form to a different PHP script ('**Query3.php**').

Step 2: Creating Query3.php

Similar modifications are made with this script. The modified code is highlighted in **green**.

```
<?php
mysql_connect(localhost,"root","");
mysql_select_db("leeoffsup") or die("Unable to select database");
$ItemCode = $_POST['ItemCode'];
$query = "select itemcode, itemdesc from StockItems where itemcode='$ItemCode';";
$result=mysql_query($query);
$num=mysql_num_rows($result);
mysql_close();
?>
<html>
<head>
<title>
Lee Office Supplies - Purchase Results
</title>
<style>
table
{
background-color:powderblue;
width:70%;
```

> In this PHP script, the **SELECT statement** is modified to **only** return those fields of the table that are **really** needed, e.g. stock item's code and its description.

```
margin-left:15%;
margin-right:15%;
}
th
{
text-decoration:bold;
}
body, p
{
font-family: Verdana, Arial, Helvetica, sans-serif;
background-color:cyan;
text-align:center;
}
</style>
</head>
<body>
<h1>Lee Office Supplies</h1>
<?php
if ($num>0)
{
  echo "<h2>Purchase Results</h2>";
  echo "<form name='PurchaseStock2' action='update2.php' method='post'>";
  echo "<table border=1><tr><th>Item Code</th><th>Item Desc</th>";
  echo "<th>Item Stock Qty</th></tr><tr><td>";
  $ItemCode = mysql_result($result,$i,"ItemCode");
  $ItemDesc = mysql_result($result,$i,"ItemDesc");
  echo "<input name='ItemCode' value='$ItemCode' type='text' size = '6'
readonly>";
  echo "</td><td>$ItemDesc</td><td align=left>";
  echo "<input name='PurchaseQty' type='text' width='6' value='0'></td></tr>";
  echo "</table>";
  echo "<input type='button' value='Leave' onclick='history.back();'>";
  echo "<input type='submit' value='Purchase'>";
}
else
{
  echo "<h2>Unable to Purchase</h2>";
  echo "<form name='PurchaseStock2'>";
  echo "<p>Sorry, $ItemCode does not seem to exist!<p>";
  echo "<input type='button' value='Leave' onclick='history.back();'>";
}
?>
</form>
</body>
</html>
```

> The form is moved to enclose the complete table. In addition, the ItemStockQty field is **replaced** by an editable text box. It is **this** quantity that will be used to **update** the ItemStockQty field in the table. The ItemCode is added to the form as a read-only text box.

Step 3: Creating Update2.php

As you may expect, Update2.php is the **key** script in the sequence, because it actually performs the required update of the **ItemStockQty field** in the **StockItems table**. As you will see, the code uses an adapted version of the **UPDATE statement**.

MySQL – the UPDATE statement

The MySQL UPDATE statement is relatively **easy** to learn and operates in a fashion similar to the SELECT and DELETE statements.

In order to update values in a row in a table, it is necessary to specify (a) the **table name** and (b) **which field** needs to be updated by using 'set' and optionally (c) in which rows using the **'where' clause**.

The following example demonstrates a typical UPDATE statement:

```
| LOS003  | A4 Paper x 500 sheets (yellow) |          300 |         3.70 | Paper    |
| LOS004  | Ballpoint pen x 40 (red ink)  |           30 |        10.00 | Pens     |
| LOS005  | Ballpoint pen x 40 (blue ink) |           40 |        10.00 | Pens     |
| LOS006  | Ballpoint pen x 40 (green ink)|           20 |        10.00 | Pens     |
| LOS007  | Pencil Eraser x 50            |           10 |        10.00 | Erasers  |
+---------+-------------------------------+--------------+--------------+----------+
7 rows in set (0.00 sec)

mysql> update stockitems set itemstockqty = itemstockqty-10 where itemcode="LOS004";
Query OK, 1 row affected (0.00 sec)
Rows matched: 1  Changed: 1  Warnings: 0

mysql> select * from stockitems;
+---------+-------------------------------+--------------+--------------+-------------+
| ItemCode | ItemDesc                     | ItemStockQty | ItemUnitPrice | ItemCategory |
+---------+-------------------------------+--------------+--------------+-------------+
| LOS001  | A4 Paper x 500 sheets (white) |          100 |         3.50 | Paper       |
| LOS002  | A4 Paper x 500 sheets (blue)  |          205 |         3.70 | Paper       |
| LOS003  | A4 Paper x 500 sheets (yellow)|          300 |         3.70 | Paper       |
| LOS004  | Ballpoint pen x 40 (red ink)  |           20 |        10.00 | Pens        |
| LOS005  | Ballpoint pen x 40 (blue ink) |           40 |        10.00 | Pens        |
| LOS006  | Ballpoint pen x 40 (green ink)|           20 |        10.00 | Pens        |
| LOS007  | Pencil Eraser x 50            |           10 |        10.00 | Erasers     |
+---------+-------------------------------+--------------+--------------+-------------+
7 rows in set (0.00 sec)
```

Figure 19.48 Updating stock item LOS004; a second SELECT query proves it has been adjusted

For more on MySQL UPDATE statement (for version 5.0):

http://dev.mysql.com/doc/refman/5.0/en/update.html

The major alterations to this script are highlighted in **green**.

Perhaps the most significant change is the use of **two posted values**: ItemCode and **PurchaseQty**. The latter representing the number of items required by the user and therefore the value to **decrease** the **ItemStockQty** field by.

Both these posted values are converted into **PHP variables** and are then inserted into a **modified UPDATE statement**.

```php
<?php
mysql_connect(localhost,"root","");
mysql_select_db("leeoffsup") or die("Unable to select database");
$ItemCode = $_POST['ItemCode'];
$PurchaseQty =$_POST['PurchaseQty'];
$query = "update stockitems set itemstockqty = itemstockqty -$PurchaseQty where itemcode='$ItemCode';";
$result=mysql_query($query);
mysql_close();
?>
<html>
<head>
<title>
Lee Office Supplies - Purchase Stock
</title>
<style>
body, p, h1, h3
{
font-family: Verdana, Arial, Helvetica, sans-serif;
background-color:cyan;
text-align:center;
}
</style>
</head>
<body>
<h1>Lee Office Supplies</h1>
<?php
echo "<h3>$PurchaseQty x $ItemCode added to Shopping Cart</h3>";
?>
<form>
<input type="button" value="Return to Shop" onclick="history.go(-2);">
</form>
</body>
</html>
```

Step 4: Testing

Let's load the first web page ('**Query3.html**') and try to purchase **four units** of item 'LOS004':

Figure 19.49 First, search for the item we want to purchase

Once the item has been found, let's order **four units**:

Figure 19.50 The user has found the item and enters desired quantity

Unless the user chooses to abort the purchase by clicking the 'Leave' button, the final script ('Update2.php') will execute once 'Purchase' is clicked. This should process the required update operation and display a confirmation message:

Figure 19.51 Confirmation message of a successful purchase

If we examine the backend MySQL database, it should confirm the adjusted stock quantity available (see Figure 19.52):

```
 LOS003  | A4 Paper x 500 sheets (yellow) |           300 |     3.70 | Paper
 LOS004  | Ballpoint pen x 40 (red ink)   |            30 |    10.00 | Pens
 LOS005  | Ballpoint pen x 40 (blue ink)  |            40 |    10.00 | Pens
 LOS006  | Ballpoint pen x 40 (green ink) |            20 |    10.00 | Pens
 LOS007  | Pencil Eraser x 50             |            10 |    10.00 | Erasers
+--------+--------------------------------+---------------+----------+---------+
7 rows in set (0.00 sec)

mysql> select * from stockitems;
+----------+--------------------------------+--------------+---------------+--------------+
| ItemCode | ItemDesc                       | ItemStockQty | ItemUnitPrice | ItemCategory |
+----------+--------------------------------+--------------+---------------+--------------+
| LOS001   | A4 Paper x 500 sheets (white)  |          100 |          3.50 | Paper        |
| LOS002   | A4 Paper x 500 sheets (blue)   |          205 |          3.70 | Paper        |
| LOS003   | A4 Paper x 500 sheets (yellow) |          300 |          3.70 | Paper        |
| LOS004   | Ballpoint pen x 40 (red ink)   |           26 |         10.00 | Pens         |
| LOS005   | Ballpoint pen x 40 (blue ink)  |           40 |         10.00 | Pens         |
| LOS006   | Ballpoint pen x 40 (green ink) |           20 |         10.00 | Pens         |
| LOS007   | Pencil Eraser x 50             |           10 |         10.00 | Erasers      |
+----------+--------------------------------+--------------+---------------+--------------+
7 rows in set (0.00 sec)
```

Figure 19.52 Reduction of four units for ItemCode LOS004

Activity – Frankoni search facility

Extend your **Frankoni T-shirts** solution by adding the following facilities:

1 The facility to delete a purchase from a specified supplier.
2 The facility to alter the quantity of a particular supplier order.
3 Review your solutions. Do they perform as expected?

Uploading files to the server

A common web application is the **uploading of files** from a **local client system** to a **remote server**. This is the core functionality of a number of different online systems including web-based email, message boards, online galleries for videos (e.g. YouTube) and social networking sites such as Facebook, Bebo and MySpace.

There are many different ways that this process can be performed.

The heart of the operation is a basic file transfer. The user selects a file via their operating system's File Open dialogue (the appearance of this will vary from OS to OS). This is then transferred to a target directory on the web server.

For **security reasons** the **file type** may be checked before being accepted (executables or script files may be banned). In addition, **file management** may disallow files over a certain **size**.

The following example demonstrates a basic PHP server-side script solution.

Figure 19.53 Sample file upload from www.2shared.com

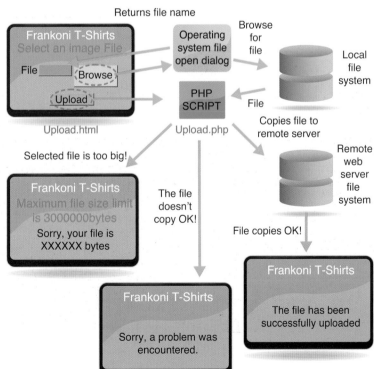

Here is the code for **'Upload.html'**:

```html
<html>
<head>
<title>
Frankoni T-shirts Image Upload
</title>
</head>
<body>
<h1>Frankoni T-Shirts</h1>
<form enctype="multipart/form-data" action="upload.php" method="post">
Please select an image file for your T-Shirt:
<input name="filename" type="file">
<br>
<input type="submit" value="Upload">
</form>
</body>
</html>
```

Upload.html is a short file whose most important feature is the use of the 'file' HTML form element. This will generate an OS-specific File Open dialogue. The name of this form element is 'filename' – this will become important when we examine 'Upload.php'.

Importantly, the 'multipart/form-data' encoding clause is used when a form needs to post binary data (like our data file). Here is the companion code for 'Upload.php':

```php
<html>
<head>
<title>
Frankoni T-shirts Image Upload
</title>
</head>
<body>
<h1>Frankoni T-Shirts</h1>
<?php
$targetfolder = "./images/";
$targetfolder = $targetfolder.basename($_FILES['filename']['name']);
$filesize = basename($_FILES['filename']['size']);
if ($filesize > 300000)
{
 echo "Maxiumum file size limit is 300000 bytes.<br>";
 echo "Sorry, your file is $filesize bytes!";
}
else
{
  if(move_uploaded_file($_FILES['filename']['tmp_name'],$targetfolder))
  {
    echo "The file ";
    echo basename($_FILES['filename']['name']);
    echo " has been successfully uploaded";
  }
  else
```

▶

```
    {
        echo "Sorry, a problem was encountered.";
    }
}
?>
</body>
</html>
```

In green:

This code is reasonably easy to work through. First, the target folder is identified ('./images/'). This is relative to the virtual 'root' of the web server (e.g. 'C:\wamp\www').

The name of the posted filename (from Upload.html) is appended to the target folder.

The file size of the identified file is obtained by examining the 'size' property.

In yellow:

This code performs a simple if…else statement to see if the file's size is above the specified limit (300,000 bytes). If it is too large, an error message is output. Otherwise, processing continues.

In cyan:

This section of code performs the **file copy** from a **temporary folder** to the **specified target folder**. If this transfer performs **satisfactorily**, a confirmation is displayed. If an error occurs, an apology is shown instead.

Let's test this PHP upload script.

The file we are going to upload is 'mysmiley.bmp'; it's a small bitmap file located on the user's desktop. It is 62.9 KB (**64,454 bytes**) in size.

Let's load the first web page from the server ('**upload.html**'):

Figure 19.54 mysmiley.bmp

Figure 19.55 Upload.html

Click the **Browse** button and a **File upload dialogue** should appear:

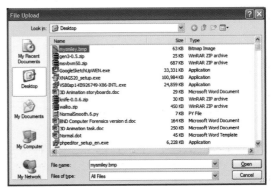

Figure 19.56 File upload dialogue

We select the 'mysmiley.bmp' file and click 'Open'.

The selected filename (its full **logical pathname**) will appear in the text box.

Figure 19.57 The file is selected

Pressing the **Upload** button will load and execute the '**Upload.php**' script:

Figure 19.58 Confirmation that the file upload has been successful

Hopefully, the confirmation message should be on-screen. This can be checked by browsing the web server's '**images**' folder for the uploaded file.

And here it is (see Figure 19.59):

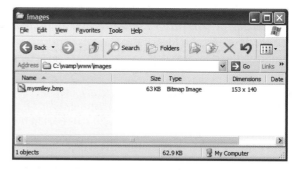

Figure 19.59 mysmiley.bmp safely uploaded to the server

Once on the web server, the file can be processed by other PHP scripts, e.g. to form an **online gallery**, to provide a **visual image** for a stock item, to provide an **avatar image** for a messageboard user.

Security (e.g. login systems)

Providing websites with login systems requiring **usernames** and **passwords** is a popular application of server-side scripting.

We can create a PHP login system using a few components.

Step 1: Creating a user table

The starting point for this project is to create a simple MySQL table that can store user details.

We'll add this table into the **Lee Office Supplies** database, calling the table '**users**'.

Here is some **sample** data:

Database: leeoffsup Table: users					
UserID	**FirstName**	**SecondName**	**Username**	**Password**	**Email**
UID001	Helen	Troy	HelenT	Planet10	HT@somewhere.com
UID002	Shekhar	Chopra	ShekharC	123Water	SC@myplace.co.uk
UID003	Mark	Beach	MBeach	MB9999	Mark@Beachy.com

Creating the database and table in MySQL

Here is the suggested definition for the StockItems table:

Field Name	Field type	Field Size	Can be Null?	Primary Key
UserID	Varchar	6	No	Yes
FirstName	Varchar	20	Yes	
SecondName	Varchar	20	Yes	
Username	Varchar	10	No	
Password	Varchar	10	No	
Email	Varchar	20	No	

To create the table, type the following **very carefully** into an open **MySQL console** session:

```
CREATE TABLE Users (UserID varchar(6) NOT NULL, FirstName varchar(20), SecondName
varchar(20), Username varchar(10) NOT NULL, Password varchar(10) NOT NULL, Email
varchar(20) NOT NULL, PRIMARY KEY(UserID));
```

Figure 19.60 shows the table's description in MySQL:

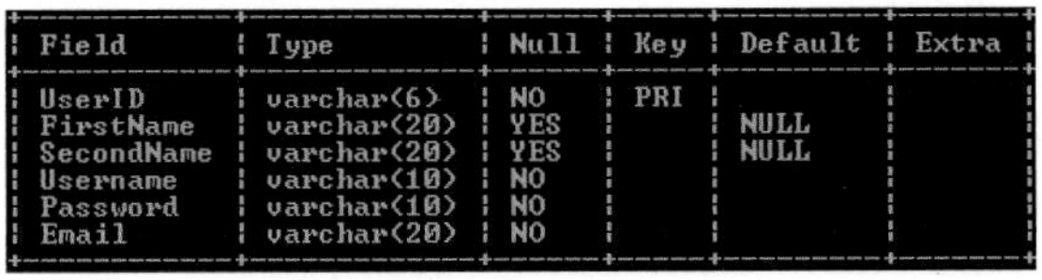

Field	Type	Null	Key	Default	Extra
UserID	varchar(6)	NO	PRI		
FirstName	varchar(20)	YES		NULL	
SecondName	varchar(20)	YES		NULL	
Username	varchar(10)	NO			
Password	varchar(10)	NO			
Email	varchar(20)	NO			

Figure 19.60 User table description

Once the table has been defined, it is possible to **populate** it with new data:

```
Insert into users values ("UID001", "Helen", "Troy", "HelenT", "Planet10",
"HT@somewhere.com");

Insert into users values ("UID002", "Shekhar", "Chopra", "ShekharC", "123Water",
"SC@myplace.co.uk");

Insert into users values ("UID003", "Mark", "Beach", "MBeach", "MB9999",
"Mark@Beachy.com");
```

A quick SELECT query will display the data now safely stored in the table, see Figure 19.61:

```
mysql> select * from users;
+--------+-----------+------------+----------+----------+--------------------+
| UserID | FirstName | SecondName | Username | Password | Email              |
+--------+-----------+------------+----------+----------+--------------------+
| UID001 | Helen     | Troy       | HelenT   | Planet10 | HT@somewhere.com   |
| UID002 | Shekhar   | Chopra     | ShekharC | 123Water | SC@myplace.co.uk   |
| UID003 | Mark      | Beach      | MBeach   | MB9999   | Mark@Beachy.com    |
+--------+-----------+------------+----------+----------+--------------------+
3 rows in set (0.00 sec)
```

Figure 19.61 User table populated with data

Step 2: Understanding the login process

The login process works by presenting the user with a simple HTML form ('**login.html**') that asks them to enter their **username** and **password**.

The password uses a **special input type** (called, unsurprisingly, '**password**') which **replaces** typed characters with **asterisks** (the '*' symbol) for added security.

When the user clicks the 'Login' button, a PHP script ('**LoginCheck.php**') is used to query the database table 'Users' for an entry that matches the **inputted combination** of username and password. It is worth noting at this point that **MySQL SELECT** queries are **not case sensitive** by default (**see 'LoginCheck.php'** for a solution).

If no records are found, a 'Sorry, wrong password' message is displayed along with the option to try again.

If a record is found, a second script is called ('**LoginWelcome.php**') that welcomes the user (by **name**, extracted from the table as part of the query) to the website.

The system relies on PHP's ability to use **session global variables** – **values** that are effectively 'hidden' but can be accessed while the **web browser session** is **active** (or the session is terminated by the user logging out). If any subsequent web page loads and fails to find a session variable for the username, it can force the user back to the login. Session variables are stored in a **default folder** as **session text files**.

Unlike **cookies** (**Unit 10 – Client-side Customisation of Web Pages see section 2.2**), session variables are **not** stored on the client system; they **remain** on the server for improved security.

Here is a diagram giving a **visual overview** of the login process:

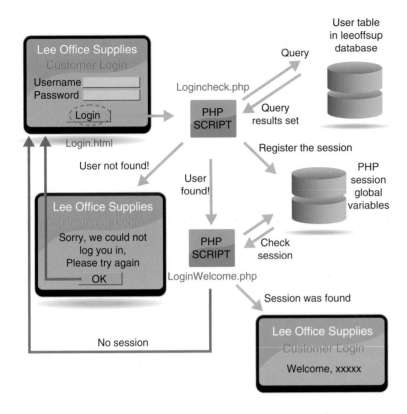

Step 3: Writing Login.html

The following section of code, contains the HTML for 'Login.HTML'.

You will notice that the **<form> tag** has been highlighted in green and that the two form elements that store the inputted username and password are highlighted in cyan. Otherwise, the rest of this script is fairly unremarkable and should be pretty easy to follow.

```
<html>
<head>
<title>
Lee Office Supplies - Customer Login
</title>
<style>
table
{
background-color:powderblue;
width:30%;
margin:auto;
}
body
```

```
{
font-family: Verdana, Arial, Helvetica, sans-serif;
background-color:cyan;
text-align:center;
}
</style>
<body>
<h1>Lee Office Supplies</h1>
<h2>Customer Login</h2>
<form name="mylogin" method="post" action="LoginCheck.php">
<table border="0" align="center">
<tr><td>Username</td>
<td><input name="username" type="text"></td></tr>
<tr><td>Password</td>
<td><input name="password" type="password"></td></tr>
</table>
<input name="submit" type="submit" value="Login"></td></table>
</form>
</body>
</html>
```

Figure 19.62 shows the on-screen appearance of Login.html. **Note the asterisks in the password text box.**

Figure 19.62 Login.html with sample input

Step 4: Writing LoginCheck.php

This script is the main workhorse of the login system. It is this script's **responsibility** to harvest the **posted username** and **password** and attempt to **find a matching user** in the Lee Office Supplies **'Users' table**.

As mentioned earlier, it is also responsible for **creating** the **global session variables**.

Here is the recommended PHP:

```php
<?php

mysql_connect(localhost,"root","");
mysql_select_db("leeoffsup") or die("Unable to select database");
$username=$_POST['username'];
$password=$_POST['password'];
$query="select * from Users where Username='$username' and binary
Password='$password'";
$result=mysql_query($query);
$num=mysql_num_rows($result);
mysql_close();
if($num==1)
{
  $firstname = mysql_result($result,$i,"FirstName");
  session_start();
  $_SESSION["firstname"] =$firstname;
  $_SESSION["username"] =$username;
  $_SESSION["password"] =$password;
  header("location:LoginWelcome.php");
}
else
{
  echo "<style>body, h1, h2 {font-family: Verdana, Arial, Helvetica, sans-serif;";
  echo "background-color:cyan;";
  echo "text-align:center;}";
  echo "</style>";
  echo "<h1>Lee Office Supplies</h1>";
  echo "<h2>Customer Login</h2>";
  echo "Sorry, we could not log you in.<br>";
  echo "Please try again.";
  echo "<form><input type='button' value='OK' onclick='history.back();'></form>";
}
?>
```

In this section, the **yellow** code is harvesting the posted username and password. The **green** code is performing the SELECT query on the Users table. It is trying to find a record with matching username and password. Prefixing the 'Password' field with 'binary' will force a case-sensitive check.

If a match is found (at least one row is present in the results set), the FirstName field is extracted and stored. Then a session is started and three session variables are created ('firstname', 'username' and 'password') for future use. This code is highlighted in **cyan**.

The **pink** line code then performs a redirect to 'LoginWelcome.php'.

If **no match** is found, an **error message** is displayed, along with a **clickable button** that will return the user to the previous page to try the password again.

Step 5: Writing LoginWelcome.php

The purpose of LoginWelcome.php is to demonstrate how session variables can be checked and different outcomes can be performed depending on whether they **do** or **do not** exist on the web server.

Here is the recommended PHP:

```php
<?php
session_start();
if(!session_is_registered(username))
{
 header("location:Login.html");
}
?>
<html>
<head>
<title>
Lee Office Supplies - Customer Login
</title>
<style>
table
{
background-color:powderblue;
width:30%;
margin:auto;
}
body
{
font-family: Verdana, Arial, Helvetica, sans-serif;
background-color:cyan;
text-align:center;
}
</style>
<body>
<h1>Lee Office Supplies</h1>
<h2>Customer Login</h2>
<p>Welcome back, <?php echo $_SESSION["firstname"]; ?>!</p>
</body>
</html>
```

This script is far more straightforward. Initially a section of PHP (highlighted in **yellow**) is used to see whether a username session variable has been stored. Of course, this can only exist if the user had successfully entered a correct username and (case-sensitive) password.

If the session variable does not exist, the user is redirected to the login page ('Login.html'). This effectively prevents users who haven't logged in from accessing the rest of the page.

The remainder of the page is (by now) familiar CSS and HTML. A short PHP extract (highlighted in **green**) is used to display the user's **first name** as part of a friendly greeting. It does this by accessing the **stored session variable** 'firstname'.

The next step is to perform a full test.

Step 6: Testing

First, an **unsuccessful test** using a **valid** user but **incorrect** password:

Figure 19.63 Login.html with incorrect password

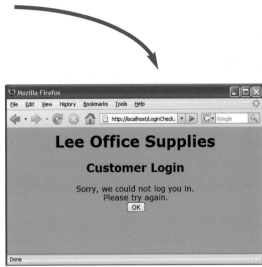

Figure 19.64 LoginCheck.php can't validate the user

Let's try that **again**, this time with the **correct** password!

Figure 19.65 Login.html with correct password

Figure 19.66 LoginWelcome.php

This time the password is accepted and **LoginCheck.php** redirects to **LoginWelcome.php** and greets the user by their first name:

Finally, we can **remove all session variables** using **session_unset()** and **end the active session** using **session_destroy()**.

Environmental data

PHP is capable of finding environmental data about itself (i.e. PHP, the web server, its hardware and operating system) and the connected web client.

Although this information can be extracted separately, a handy function called 'phpinfo()' can be used to produce neatly categorised tables of environmental data.

Figure 19.67 shows an extract of the information supplied by using the phpinfo() function:

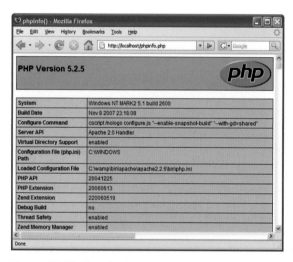

Figure 19.67 Results from phpinfo()

The next example will demonstrate PHP's ability to find out things **individually** about the connected web client. This is achieved using the **getenv() function**:

```php
<?php
 $ipaddr = getenv("REMOTE_ADDR");
 echo "Your IP address is $ipaddr";

 $agent = getenv("HTTP_USER_AGENT");
 echo "<br>Your client software is $agent";
?>
```

REMOTE_ADDR is the **IP** (Internet Protocol) address of the web client (**127.0.0.1** is known as the 'loopback address' for computers acting as **both** client and server).

HTTP_USER_AGENT is the web browser software the user is using.

The general format for the information is: **software/version library/version**

Figure 19.68 shows the web browser output:

Environmental data can be used in PHP to adjust the performance of a script or more closely tailor its output to the configuration of the web server or the user's system.

Figure 19.68 Web client environment data

PHP – More on getenv()

For more on the getenv() function, please refer to:

http://uk.php.net/manual/en/function.getenv.php

and

http://hoohoo.ncsa.uiuc.edu/cgi/env.html

Braincheck!

Answer the following questions…

1 What is the difference between a WAMP and a LAMP?
2 What is the loopback address and when would it be used?
3 What is MySQL?
4 What are SELECT, INSERT, UPDATE and DELETE?
5 What is the advantage of a session variable over a cookie?
6 What does the PHP function getenv() provide?
7 Which type of HTML form element displays asterisks rather than typed text?
8 Sending form data from one HTML page to another is called………?
9 Name two attributes on which we could prevent a file from being uploaded.
10 What are the default MySQL names for the host, user and password?

How well did you do? See page 444 for the answers.

2.2 Documentation

Requirements specification

For a server-side scripted solution, all components should be considered. The following diagram maps these elements to the different components connected to a server-side scripted solution:

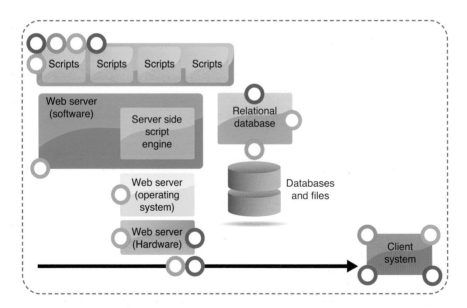

Functionality is the **key consideration** as meeting the needs of the stakeholder is typically the **measurement for success** for any software development project. Functionality should consider **user inputs**, **processes**, **outputs** and **data storage**. All of these have a direct bearing on the scripts written and executed by the server and the backend databases and tables created to support them.

Before server-side scripting can begin, the developer should have a sound idea of all of the requirements.

Internally documented code

Just as with any client-side scripting, server-side developers are **strongly encouraged** to use good practices to assist the **documentation** of their work.

The developer, usually taking pride in their work (or following organisational standards), will **document** the code for **future maintenance** and **ease of modification**. This is particularly important due to the complexities often found in more advanced PHP scripts.

Common elements of good practice include:

Use of comments	Much like other programming and scripting languages, PHP can support commenting. There are two methods:
	Single-line comments
	Uses the '//' to comment a single line…
	e.g.

	``
	<?php
	echo "Hello World!"; //output Hello World
	?>
	``

	… or to comment-out a line of code that is not needed (was there for debugging only) or may be 'buggy' (i.e. not working).
	e.g.
	``` // $ipaddr = getenv("REMOTE_ADDR"); ```
	Multi-line comments
	Uses the '/*' and '*/' pairing to span a number of lines. This is often used immediately before a complex section of PHP code to describe its purpose:
	``` /* This section of PHP will connect to the database and query the sales table for all January 2008 orders */ ```
Self-documenting variables	Where possible variables used in PHP should be **meaningful** and **descriptive**.
	What this basically means is that they should:
	1 start with a dollar sign ($); they won't work if they don't;
	2 use a unique name that clearly describes their purpose;
	3 be memorable to the website designer;
	4 use lowercase and uppercase consistently;
	5 avoid names already used for html elements.
	Also recall that PHP is case sensitive; variables spelt the same but using different cases are considered to be different.

Indentation	Indentation is used to highlight the **underlying structure** of script code. This is particularly helpful when if…else statements and loops such as do…while, while and for are used.

Nested code can be particularly difficult to decipher if indentation is not used. The resulting 'flat' code can be difficult to read:

Compare the following extracts:

Flat code:

```
if ($num == 0){echo "Sorry, no matches have been found.";} else
{echo "$num matches have been found";}
```

Indented for readability:

```
if ($num == 0)
{
    echo "Sorry, no matches have been found.";
}
else
{
    echo "$num matches have been found";
}
```

From a glimpse, it should be possible to quickly work out the code that is dependent on the true/false choice made by the if…else statement. |

2.3 Testing and debugging

As you have seen throughout section 2.1, **live testing** is a **vital aspect** of any server-side scripted solution.

However, it is important to **plan** and **document** any test fully.

Each test should contain such information as:

◆ test data selected – **normal**, **extreme** (valid, but unlikely) and **erroneous**
◆ date of test
◆ results that are expected
◆ results that actually occur when the scripts are executed.

Dealing with errors

Testing should help reveal **obvious problems** (from **error messages** that occur in the client's web browser) or those that are stored in the **PHP error log** (typically a text document in the **'logs' folder**).

It is possible to **enable** or **disable** either type of error reporting using PHP settings.

Errors encountered in PHP scripts often give **three** important pieces of information:

◆ the **name** of the **php script file** in which the error was encountered;
◆ the **line number** in the php script file where the error was encountered;
◆ a **description of the type of error** encountered.

Corrective action can be applied by **identifying** the error, **modifying** the PHP source code, **re-saving** the file and then trying to **execute** the code once more.

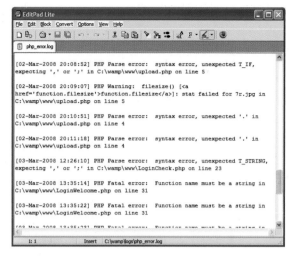

Figure 19.69 Extract of the PHP error log

Severity of errors

PHP is **interpreted** (it is executed **line-by-line**); what this means is that it will work **until** an error is encountered. The PHP problems can be categorised based on their **severity**:

Notice	A polite reminder of a silly oversight, e.g. using a PHP variable before declaring it. It's trivial but you should try to be **tidy**!	Minor issue
Strict notice	More serious – advice from the interpreter that some of your code may be deprecated (i.e. you are using outdated techniques or functions). Ideally you should **update** your code.	
Warning	Something's odd – but it's not serious enough to stop the PHP interpreter from running! You **should** really fix this.	
Parse error	You've got the PHP syntax wrong and the script stops. This is usually missing punctuation, e.g. semi-colons, quotation marks etc. You **have** to fix this.	
Fatal error	A severe problem has been encountered forcing your script to stop. You **have** to fix this.	Severe problem!

Some third-party tools are available that assist the debugging process because they are PHP aware.

Examples of third-party tools include:

Adobe Dreamweaver   http://www.adobe.com/products/dreamweaver/

NuSphere PhpED and PhpExpress http://www.nusphere.com/products/index.htm

Zend Zend Studio   http://www.zend.com/products/studio/

ActiveState Komodo Edit   http://www.activestate.com/Products/komodo_ide/

Common tools include:

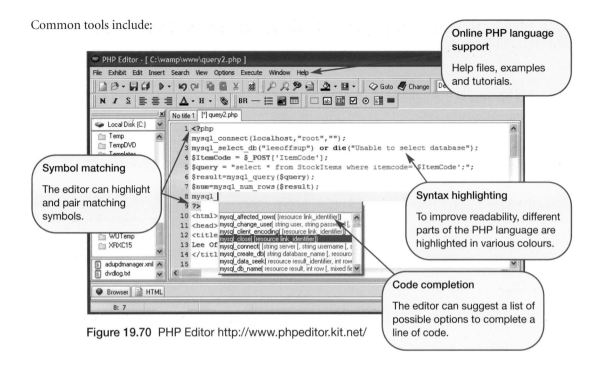

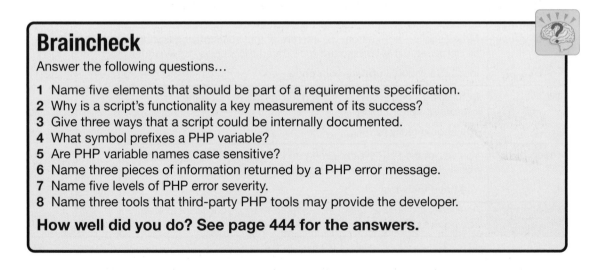

Figure 19.70 PHP Editor http://www.phpeditor.kit.net/

Other common techniques including using 'echo' (or 'print') to **display the contents** of PHP variables while a script is running; many errors are caused by variables storing unexpected values.

Braincheck

Answer the following questions…

1 Name five elements that should be part of a requirements specification.
2 Why is a script's functionality a key measurement of its success?
3 Give three ways that a script could be internally documented.
4 What symbol prefixes a PHP variable?
5 Are PHP variable names case sensitive?
6 Name three pieces of information returned by a PHP error message.
7 Name five levels of PHP error severity.
8 Name three tools that third-party PHP tools may provide the developer.

How well did you do? See page 444 for the answers.

3 Understand the security and ethical issues affecting web server scripting

3.1 Security issues

Server-side scripting languages such as PHP are **vulnerable**, to a degree, from **malicious attacks**.

The most common problems stem from:

◆ **coding vulnerabilities**, e.g. not validating strings that have been posted from a web page;
◆ **password liabilities**, e.g. using plain-text passwords that are not encrypted on sensitive systems;
◆ **poor configuration**, e.g. leaving developmental settings 'open';
◆ **SQL injection**, e.g. malicious code being inserted into SQL queries, compromising SQL databases;
◆ **poor session management**, i.e. not keeping sensitive session data in a secure location;
◆ **buffer overflow** – vulnerability caused when a script tries to store too much data in temporary storage;
◆ **visibility of errors** – PHP's habit of displaying interpretation errors on the client system.

Generally, the best rule is to research common server-side scripting techniques and aim for 'best practice' using recognised (and recommended) standards.

More guidance on security issues

For industry perspectives of common security issues, please refer to:

Open Web Application Security Project (OWASP)

http://www.owasp.org/index.php/Main_Page

National Institute of Science and Technology (NIST)

http://csrc.nist.gov/

3.2 Ethical issues

Ethics – A definition

'The branch of philosophy concerned with evaluating human action. Some distinguish ethics, what is right or wrong based on reason, from morals, what is considered right or wrong behaviour based on social custom.'

Source: www.thenagain.info/Webchron/Glossary/Glossary.html

As we have seen, server-side scripting languages such as PHP can **interrogate** a client-side system via **environmental settings** and **find out things about it**, e.g. the web browser being used, the operating system being used, the Internet Protocol address of the client system (and from that, their country of residence and Internet Service Provider if we wish).

For some people, this can be seen as an **infringement** of their **privacy**: they want to browse the World Wide Web **anonymously**. However, just like walking through a city littered with strategically placed closed-circuit cameras, being invisible is not easy!

The question is: **where is the privacy line drawn?**

The website developer therefore has a **responsibility** to use the technology at their disposal in a **conscientious** and **accountable fashion**. Moreover, in the UK any data stored **about** the user should be held in **accordance** with the **Data Protection Act (1998)**. The problem of course is that not all web servers (and online organisations) are based in the UK.

Statistics are a critical reflection of web page activity. Perhaps the most important statistic is the measurement of accesses (or '**hits**') a website has enjoyed.

PHP counters are relatively easy to create:

```php
<?php
 $file = fopen('counter.txt',r);
 $hits = fread($file, filesize('counter.txt'));
 $hits++;
 echo $hits;
 fclose($file);
 $file = fopen('counter.txt',w);
 fwrite($file,$hits);
 fclose($file);
?>
```

This script opens the text file for reading. It then increments the value read from the file and echoes this to the web page. The file is then reopened for writing and the incremented hit counter overwrites the previous value. The file is then closed once more.

This script file would be named '**counter.php**'.

A website would **access** the '**counter.php**' script like so:

```php
<body>
Visits :
<?php
 include "counter.php";
?>
</body>
```

All that would be needed is to create a **text file** called '**counter.txt**' in the **same folder** as **both scripts**. The webmaster would then key in the **starting number** for the **counter** (usually 0) and save the file.

However…

…given the importance of **high hit counters** on a website to **attract lucrative advertising deals**, it could be suggested that some webmasters may '**adjust**' the figures to make the site seem **more popular** – and therefore more of a prospect for online advertisers.

This of course would be **unethical**.

But it **wouldn't** be difficult: just editing and increasing the number in the text file.

Such are the ethical issues that you must consider.

Unit Links

Unit 10 (Client-side Customisation of Web Pages) and **Unit 21** (Website Production and Management) are both complementary to this unit. Many of the concepts and practices covered here are reinforced there.

This unit, **Unit 19**, is a **Specialist Unit** on the following BTEC National Diploma routes:

Networking

It is also a **Specialist Unit** on the following BTEC National Certificate and Diploma routes:

Software Development

Systems Support

As such it has links to a number of other units, principally:

Unit 4 – IT project

Unit 10 – Client-side Customisation of Web Pages

Unit 18 – Principles of Software Design and Development

Unit 20 – Event-Driven Programming

Unit 21 – Website Production and Management

Unit 25 – Object-Oriented Programming

In addition this unit has identified direct links with:

Unit 5 – Advanced Database Skills

Achieving success

In order to achieve each unit you will complete a series of coursework activities. Each time you hand in work, your tutor will return this to you with a record of your achievement.

This particular unit has 13 criteria to meet: 6 Pass, 4 Merit and 3 Distinction.

For a **Pass**:

　You must achieve **all** 6 Pass criteria.

For a **Merit**:

　You must achieve **all** 6 Pass and **all** 4 Merit criteria.

For a **Distinction**:

　You must achieve **all** 6 Pass, **all** 4 Merit **and** 3 Distinction criteria.

So that you can monitor your own progress and achievement in each unit, a recording grid has been provided (see below). The full version of this grid is also included on the companion CD.

Assignment	Assignments in this Unit			
	U19.01	U19.02	U19.03	U19.04
Referral				
Pass				
1				
2				
3				
4				
5				
6				
Merit				
1				
2				
3				
4				
Distinction				
1				
2				
3				

Help with assessment

The **Pass criteria** for this unit are unusually complex for the BTEC National Diploma scheme, forming a combination of documentary tasks and challenging practical activities for you to complete. You will need to be aware of three applications of web server scripting and be able to practically demonstrate these by creating and editing a text file and by creating a simple login system. In addition you will be asked to work with error logs and be able to identify and describe security and ethical issues linked with this technology.

To achieve a **Merit** you will need to be able to compare client-side and server-side scripting technologies, using the latter to create website statistics, a multi-user login system and a database query system.

The first **Distinction** criterion involves the real-world evaluation of using client- and server-side scripting solutions in tandem. You are also required to investigate client-side environmental data by accessing the web browser's size and display resolution. The final criterion involves evaluation of the real-life security and ethical issues associated with server-side scripting.

Online resources on the CD

Key fact sheets
Electronic slide show of key points
Sample PHP scripts
Multiple choice self-test quizzes

Further Reading

Duthie, A. and MacDonald, M., 2003, *ASP.NET in a Nutshell*, O'Reilly, ISBN 0596005202.

Hudson, P., 2005, *PHP in a Nutshell*, O'Reilly, ISBN 0596100671.

Seven, D., Gaster, B., Kent, D., Sabbadin, E., Conway, R., Basiura, R., Lakshminarayanan, S. and Sivakumar, S., *ASP.NET Security*, Wrox Press Ltd, ISBN 1861006209.

Shiflett, C., 2005, *Essential PHP Security*, O'Reilly, ISBN 059600656X.

Unit 23

Installing and Upgrading Software

Capsule view

This 60-hour unit focuses on an often neglected aspect of computer systems – the software.

While much focus is placed on professional practice when it comes to selecting, repairing and installing new hardware components, software complexities are mostly overlooked.

The correct and reliable installation of software is often a core factor in computer systems performance, reliability and end-user satisfaction.

This unit attempts to explain the planning and procedures that organisations (and their IT professionals) need to adopt when installing (or upgrading) a new software component. This includes aspects of planning, practical skills and the recognition that strict record keeping and user acceptance testing (UAT) are vital.

Learning aims

1 Understand why software needs installing or upgrading.
2 Understand how to prepare for a software installation or upgrade.
3 Be able to install or upgrade software.
4 Understand the completion and handover process.

Software is a collective term used to describe the **programs** (instructions) that **control** a computer system's **hardware**. Software **can't** be **touched** in the physical sense. Software is generally loaded from a backing storage device (e.g. a hard disk) into RAM (random access memory) for execution as needed.

Hardware is a term used to categorise any **physical elements** of a computer system that are **tangible** (i.e. **can** be **touched**). This includes the monitor, keyboard, mouse, case, power supply unit, motherboard, central processing unit etc.

Firmware is a term that usually describes a program that is stored on a chip, such as a read-only memory (**ROM**) chip, rather than being loaded from a backing storage device (e.g. hard disk) temporarily into a computer's system **RAM** for processing.

For example, a computer's **BIOS** (**B**asic **I**nput **O**utput **S**ystem) chip is responsible for basic control of the system until the larger, more complex operating system is loaded; this is a form of firmware. Many household devices such as MP3 players, games consoles (e.g. Sony PlayStation 3 and Xbox360) and mobile telephones have firmware that can be updated ('flashed') to expand their functionality or improve their reliability.

1 Understand why software needs installing or upgrading

Without software a computer system cannot really do anything; this is a very clear argument for installation! However, **why** do we perform upgrades?

Installation is the process of **loading software** from an **external media** (e.g. DVD, CD etc.) to a local computer system's **backing storage** (i.e. hard disk) so that it can be used.

Upgrade is the process of **replacing** an **outdated** piece of **software** (or hardware) with a **more recent** version or a **better alternative**. If this is simply a case of modifying **some** of the program code, it can be referred to as an **update**.

Note. When upgrades **fail** (as they sometimes do), a practitioner may be forced to revert to an **older** version of the software (or hardware). This is called **downgrading**.

1.1 Prompts for change

So **why** install or upgrade software? There are a few possible **drivers for change**.

Changes to the computer system

Changes to a computer system have a **knock-on effect**.

When hardware is changed, **compatibility issues** between the software and hardware may occur.

In order to resolve this it may be necessary to **upgrade** the existing software to a newer version which has **better compatibility**.

For example, changing a computer system's graphics card may make it difficult to run specialist graphic manipulation software.

Changes to other elements of a computer system can also have an effect, e.g. **upgrading to a new operating system** (such as Windows Vista®) may cause **incompatibilities** with older software **applications**.

Fix the bugs

Although the majority of software is subjected to a thorough **q**uality **a**ssurance (**QA**) process to test for 'bugs' and unexpected problems before commercial release, many products are bought that contain errors which cause the software to **crash** (stop working), **lock-up** (stop responding) or **behave unreliably**.

When these mistakes are discovered, it is likely that the software developer (or publisher, if different) will release an **updated version** or a 'patch' which can **fix the problems** with the software's code.

In the most **severe cases** (e.g. **security flaws**), users are directed to perform these upgrades **as soon as possible**. This is a common feature of upgrades for operating systems, web browsers and server software.

Newer version

Software is sometimes upgraded simply because a new version is released.

Newer versions typically:

◆ work faster and more efficiently;
◆ offer new features and functionality;
◆ have better compatibility;
◆ resolves issues reported by users of the previous version.

Most modern software is **Internet aware**: this means that it is possible for the software to connect to a remote server to check to see if a newer version is available.

Figure 23.1 Grisoft's warning that AVG7.5 is being upgraded to version 8

If an update **is** available, the user is typically given the opportunity to download it.

Figure 23.2 Hewlett-Packard software searches online for an update

Of course, it is up to the user to decide if they want to perform (some or all) of the updates found.

It is always worth remembering that some updates can introduce system problems that didn't exist before (see section 1.3).

Needs have changed

Software is purchased for a reason: it **fills a need** identified by a user or an organisation. It is quite common for a user's needs to **change or grow** beyond the capabilities of the software they currently use.

For example, a website development team may be happy to use a **basic HTML editor** to create **simple websites**. However, as customer demands become **more complex** they consider purchasing a more sophisticated website design application that offers a **fuller set of features** in order to produce a **better product**.

Wanting **additional functionality** is perhaps the **most common** reason to upgrade or install new software.

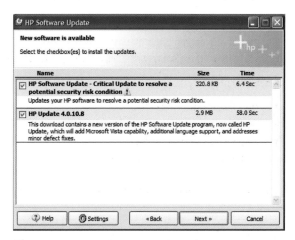

Figure 23.3 Two updates are found; one is considered to be critical

Users who have **officially registered** their software can often upgrade on a regular basis for **reduced rates**. See section 4.2 for more details

Company policy

Many organisations often have **policies** that control **which** particular piece of software is used for common business applications such as word-processing, spreadsheets, email, web browsing, databases etc. Doing so ensures that any **documents** (or data) created can be **easily shared** between their employees **without** compatibility issues.

They will also have a company-wide program of **installation** and **upgrade**, designed to roll out changes to their employees' computer systems in a planned, controlled and systematic manner.

Perhaps two of the most common company-wide changes that are made are updates to office productivity suites (e.g. Microsoft Office®) and the operating system itself (e.g. upgrading to a new release of Microsoft Windows® or Mac OS).

1.2 Justification for change

In order to justify a change it is necessary to present an argument that describes the trade-off between the cost of purchasing new software and the benefits which are likely to be gained.

In most organisations, this is known as a **business case**.

Key questions to answer in any business case

1 What is the software **called**?
2 **What function** does the software serve?
3 **Why** is the software **needed**?
4 How much does the software **cost**?
5 Will **extra training** be required for employees to use it? If so, **how much**?
6 How will the employees' work **improve**?
7 Are there any **risks?** (See section 1.3.)

Typical benefits of using new software include:

◆ increased **productivity**;
◆ improved **efficiency**;
◆ extra functionality may **automate** existing tasks;
◆ improved **customer service**;
◆ extra functionality may open up **new lines of customer business** or services;
◆ improved **data sharing** and **communication** within the organisation.

It is of course quite possible that management may decide that the potential costs (and risks) **far outweigh** the potential benefits; in this case, the software installation (or upgrade) is **not** sanctioned.

1.3 Risks

It is almost inevitable that from time-to-time the installation or upgrade of software **will** go wrong.

The results of this can have a **profound effect** on the user of the computer system and a wider impact on their organisation.

Possible impacts include:

◆ potential **loss of service** (for users, i.e. employees and customers);
◆ **loss of income** while services are incapacitated;
◆ introduction of **incompatibility issues**;
◆ new version of software may be **unstable**;
◆ users and customers may **not like it**; preferring the previous version.

Risk reduction measures

A number of different techniques can be employed to **reduce the risk** of software upgrades and updates.

These include:

◆ performing a limited **pilot deployment** of the new version;
◆ **creating backups** (of data and software);
◆ creating a '**bookmark**' **position** for the operating system so that settings can be **rolled back**. This is often called a '**system recovery point**' (see section 4.4 for more details);
◆ installing the upgrade (or update) at a **low-risk time** (e.g. at the weekend so that it can be tested).

It is a sobering thought perhaps that most software developers advise users to **upgrade 'at their own risk**'. This is typically because the computer systems market uses such an **incredibly diverse** mix of hardware and software that it is **almost impossible** to **test** a new piece of software with **every** possible **permutation**.

Braincheck

Answer the following questions.

1 What is the difference between software and hardware?
2 What is the difference between software and firmware?
3 What is the difference between an upgrade and an update?
4 Give three reasons for updating/upgrading software.
5 Which process provide justification for an update/upgrade?
6 Give three risks associated with updating/upgrading software.
7 Give three techniques that can be used to reduce upgrade risk.

How well did you do? See page 445 for the answers.

Online resources on the CD

Business case template for new software
Technician's installation checklist
Key fact sheets
Electronic slide show of key points
Multiple Choice self-test quiz
You may use these while preparing for assessments.

2 Understand how to prepare for a software installation or upgrade

As with many tasks that face the IT practitioner, preparation is key. A simple truth is perhaps, 'fail to plan, plan to fail!'.

We can view the process of software installation and upgrade as a cyclical process, initiated (usually) by the point at which the **user's needs change** as shown in Figure 23.4 (although, as we've seen in section 1.1, there may be other drivers).

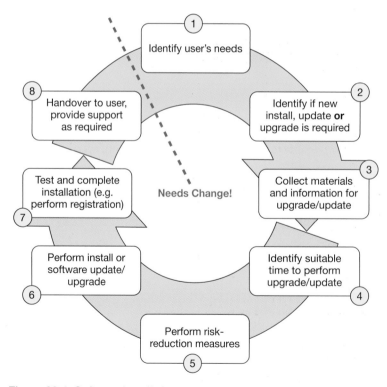

Figure 23.4 Software installation process

In this section we are concerned with phases **1 to 4** of the cycle.

2.1 Installations and upgrades

At some point it is necessary to decide **whether** a **new installation** is required (i.e. new software for a computer system) or if it is simply a case of **upgrading an existing piece** of software.

Sometimes a software application starts to **misbehave**; this can be because its **installation** has become **damaged** and, as a result, it is **not functioning reliably**.

In these instances it is advisable to **uninstall the current copy** and install a **fresh copy**. Such drastic measures aren't always necessary however.

The flowchart in Figure 23.5 suggests a possible approach for deciding which route to take.

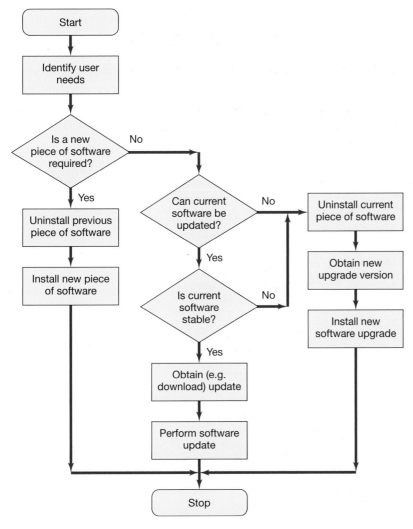

Figure 23.5 Deciding on new install, full upgrade or simple update

2.2 Planning

As indicated, **planning** is the vital component in good preparation.

In terms of software installations and upgrades, several aspects should be considered:

◆ **Materials**

It is important to gather together any materials needed for installation (or upgrade) – see section 2.4 for more details.

◆ **Requirements**

New software has certain requirements in order to work correctly, e.g. will **new hardware** be needed or will a **different operating system** be necessary?

Requirements are often categorised as:

  ◆ **minimum** (just enough to get the software running)

  ◆ **recommended** (to get the best results from the software), e.g. **Microsoft Vista®** (**Home Basic edition**) **requirements**

Minimum requirements
800 MHz processor and 512 MB of system memory
20 GB hard drive with at least 15 GB of available space
Support for Super VGA graphics
CD-ROM drive

Recommended requirements
1 GHz 32-bit (x86) or 64-bit (x64) processor
512 MB of system memory
20 GB hard drive with at least 15 GB of available space
Support for DirectX 9 graphics and 32 MB of graphics memory
DVD-ROM drive
Audio output
Internet access

(adapted from: http://www.microsoft.com/windows/products/windowsvista/editions/systemrequirements.mspx)

◆ **Timing**

The timing for installation and upgrade has to be carefully selected so as to provide a **minimum level of disruption**. Installations at **low-risk times** such as **holidays**, **weekends** or **evenings** are common.

◆ **Communication**

Ongoing communication between the IT practitioner and all interested parties is vital. Interested parties may include:

  ◆ **end user** – to discuss **progress** and their needs (e.g. **future training needs**);

  ◆ **IT practitioner's manager** – for guidance and technical advice;

  ◆ **software publisher** – to discuss technical issues requiring expert support and customer service.

◆ **Gaining permissions and access**

It is common for organisations to make their user workstations **secure**, effectively limiting what software and features a user can access.

In order to perform installations and upgrades on a computer system, **special privileges** are often required (e.g. an **Administrator's account**).

In addition, it may be necessary to be aware of **user names** and **passwords.**

◆ **Backout procedures**

A backout procedure is simply the ability to reverse changes if they cause system disruptions (i.e. risk reduction).

This may include activities such as:

◆ uninstallation

◆ data backup and recovery

◆ use of system recovery points.

◆ **Personal factors**

A key aspect of successful planning is ensuring that the IT practitioner has:

◆ **skills** and **experience necessary** to perform the task;

◆ **enough time** to do the job **thoroughly.**

2.3 Guidance

As an IT practitioner part of your role will be to provide **advice** and **guidance** on installation procedures if you are **unable** to perform the task **yourself** (e.g. you may have to provide directions to a **colleague** over the telephone or by email).

You may also have to give the user a **basic understanding** of the new software being installed **prior** to recommending **further training** (if needed). This may include:

◆ how to **start** the software;

◆ how to perform **basic operations**;

◆ how to **safely quit** the software;

◆ how the software may **differ** to previous versions or other products the user may have used.

Guidance will also be required in the event that **escalation** is required.

Key Terms

Although most installations and upgrades proceed smoothly and without incident, occasionally things **do** go wrong.

When an IT practitioner feels events are moving **beyond** their level of experience it is usually recommended that they transfer the task to a **more senior** (and **knowledgeable**) **colleague**, e.g. their line manager, for resolution.

This process is commonly known as 'escalation'.

2.4 Material

An important part of planning is obtaining the required materials.

Materials checklist

You will need the following:

◆ **Computer system** (with hardware suitably upgraded, if it was required)
◆ **Software package** to install or upgrade
   This may be any **physical media** (e.g. a floppy disk, CD or DVD), an **archived 'zip' file** or an **internet link** for download.
   You must make sure that **any** installation files are **thoroughly checked** for **viruses** before they are used.

Figure 23.6 Installation materials

◆ **Installation/upgrade instructions**
   This may be a **printed document**, **electronic document** (e.g. Adobe .pdf file) or short **'readme.txt'** text file.
◆ **Proof of license arrangements**
◆ **Activation information**
   Typically a selected **user name**, **serial number** or **product key**.
   Product keys are often printed on manuals or on CDs. For software purchased online they may be e-mailed to the customer.
   Additionally, if the activation is online (via website or email) a live Internet connection will be required. Telephone activation is also commonly used as is (to a lesser degree these days with the rise of electronic communication) postal activation. See section 4.2 for more.
◆ **Additional utilities**
   You may need these (e.g. archive software such as WinZip) in order to complete the task.

3 Install or upgrade software

This section, concerned with phases **5 to 6** of the cycle, reflects the practical skills necessary to install or upgrade new software. In order to explain this effectively a typical installation has been followed.

Case Study

KAM (Kris Arts and Media) have decided to branch into **3D designs** for advertising and promotions. As part of a business case, KAM's management have identified an excellently featured **freeware 3D modelling application** called **Blender** which will give their artists some experience with the media before they decide to invest in a more expensive commercial alternative.

Blender can be downloaded for **free** from:

Figure 23.7 Blender splash screen

http://www.blender.org/download/get-blender/

It is available for **Microsoft Windows®**, **Linux** and **Apple Mac OS X**.

3.1 Installation/upgrade processes

Following the flowchart in section 2.1, it is clear that this is a **new software product** (KAM **doesn't** already **have** another 3D modelling application installed).

The first step is to check to see if the computer systems (PCs running Microsoft Vista®) have a **hardware specification suitable** for running Blender (see requirements, section 2.2).

The technician performs a hardware inspection of all KAM PCs and checks against Blender's requirements.

KAM PC specifications	Blender minimum requirements	Blender recommended requirements
Microsoft Vista® (64-bit)	Windows 98, ME, 2000, XP or Vista	Windows 98, ME, 2000, XP or Vista
2.2 Ghz AMD Quad Core Phenom	300 MHz CPU	2 Ghz dual CPU
4 GB Ram	128 MB Ram	2 GB Ram
465 GB free hard disk space	20 MB free hard disk space	20 MB free hard disk space
1600 x 1200 pixel display with 32-bit colour	1024 x 768 pixel display with 16-bit colour	1920 x 1200 pixel display with 24-bit colour
3 button mouse	3 button mouse	3 button mouse
Open GL graphics card with 512 MB RAM	Open GL graphics card with 16 MB RAM	Open GL graphics card with 128 or 256 MB RAM

Blender requirements were found at: http://www.blender.org/features-gallery/requirements/.

A simple check reveals a slight deficiency in the display specifications but everything else meets (or exceeds) **recommended requirements**. This would indicate that the software **can** be supported by the hardware present at KAM.

In order to continue we need to download the correct version – a version for Windows Vista®.

We have the choice of either downloading an **Installer** or just an **archive** (.**zip file**) which would need **manual** installation.

It is probably **more advisable** to choose the **full installer package** – click the appropriate link.

Figure 23.8 Obtaining the correct downloadable package

Figure 23.9 File is ready for download

Clicking **Save** will **start** the download process. The download speed at KAM is around 8 Megabits per second (a generous bandwidth) which will mean a quick download for the Blender Installer.

The file will download to a **destination folder** on the client system PC at KAM. The actual folder will vary depending on the web browser's (Mozilla Firefox) settings.

The KAM PC has the **Windows Desktop** as the **default directory** (see Figure 23.9).

At this point it is advisable to ensure all sensitive **user data** is **backed up** and that a **system restore point** has been created. Please refer to section 4.3 for more on these important processes.

Once we have **confirmed** with the end user that all their important data and settings have been backed up, we are free to proceed. Remember, **ongoing communication** with the end user is **vital**.

It is advisable to perform the installation process as an Administrator.

Clicking the **Open** link as shown in Figure 23.10 will **start** the installation process.

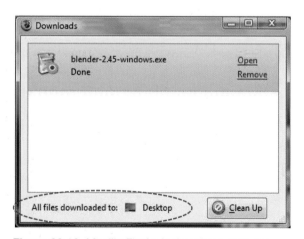

Figure 23.10 Mozilla Firefox's download dialogue

Figure 23.11 Windows' warning dialogue

Vista, as XP before, will display a warning dialogue (see Figure 23.11). Click **OK** to proceed – the KAM PC has **active anti-virus** and **spyware detection** and the Blender Installer has **not** caused a problem for either.

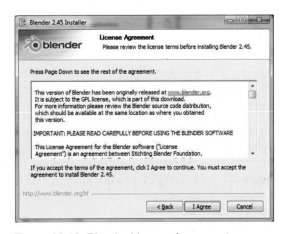

Vista should respond with **Blender's Installer Welcome Dialogue** (see Figure 23.12).

Click **Next** to continue. You will be presented with Blender's **License Agreement** (see Figure 23.13).

Figure 23.12 Blender welcome dialogue

Read through the Blender License Agreement noting any **contractual issues** that may need to be reviewed by KAM's management before you continue. Remember – it's not **too late** to back out; you can still click the **Cancel** button.

If you are satisfied (and it is likely that these terms and conditions will have already been checked by your line manager), click '**I Agree**' to continue.

Figure 23.13 Blender License Agreement

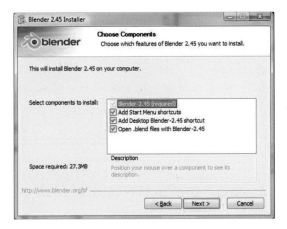

Figure 23.14 Blender components dialogue

Most software applications are installed in **component form**. Generally, a '**typical' installation** will select the **most commonly used** components. Blender has the option to customise the application by selecting and deselecting the required components.

This dialogue (see Figure 23.14) creates the necessary **menu** and **desktop shortcuts** (which are wanted by the KAM end user) and also adds a **file association** in Microsoft Vista Explorer® between '**.blend**' files and **Blender** (this means that **double-clicking** a 3D Blender model file will open it automatically in Blender).

Click **Next** to continue.

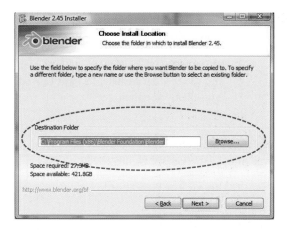

Figure 23.15 Install location dialogue

The next step lets the technician **confirm** the **installation target folder**; it is likely to default to the common 'Program Files' folder. Unless there is an **organisational need** to alter this it should be left **unchanged**. This is shown in Figure 23.15.

Click **Next** to continue.

Figure 23.16 shows the installation progress dialogue, complete with common **progress bar** which gives feedback to the technician about the **status** of the install.

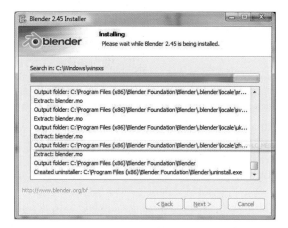

Figure 23.16 Installation progress dialogue

Once the installation process has fully completed, a completion dialogue should appear (see Figure 23.17). Typically it will give the technician the option of launching the application immediately. It is normally advised to **resist** doing so and just click the **Finish** button.

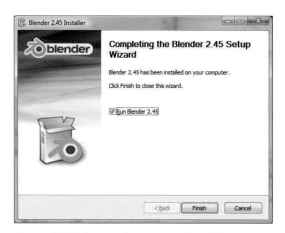

Figure 23.17 Installation completion dialogue

You should now check that the required **menu** and **desktop shortcuts** have been created as shown in Figures 23.18 and 23.19.

Figure 23.18 Check menu item created   **Figure 23.19** Check desktop shortcut created

Tidying up steps should include:

◆ moving the Blender installer executable **from** the desktop onto a removable device;
◆ **logging out** and allowing the user to log back in;
◆ **testing** that blender launches **properly** via **both** shortcuts;
◆ **register** the software (if/as required by organisation policy, if possible).

The next crucial step is **testing**.

Testing

Testing, phase 7 of our cycle, is one of the **most important** and **overlooked** stages of installation.

It is not uncommon for an installation to proceed very smoothly only to have the program **behave unexpectedly** by **crashing** or **freezing** when asked to perform the most simple of tasks.

Unfortunately technicians often **forget** to check this part of the process and find themselves **called back** and confronted by **upset** and **confused** end users; obviously it's **better** to avoid this happening.

Testing contributes to the overall **quality of service** that the end user is receiving and will assist the **handover process** (see section 4.2).

How to test – technician

This depends greatly on the software being installed and it is quite common for the technician to have problems when performing the testing as they may not have the **specialist IT user skills** necessary for the application in question.

Generally though, a technician **is** capable of testing some **basic software functionality** such as:

◆ starting the software application;
◆ creating a basic file (e.g. a 3D model);
◆ saving a basic file to the local file system;
◆ loading the basic file back into memory again;
◆ quitting the program safely.

This may be performed as part of a technician's **installation checklist**.

How to test – user

User **a**cceptance **t**esting (**UAT**) ensures that the user has an opportunity to test the installed software themselves **before** signing off the technician's installation job as complete.

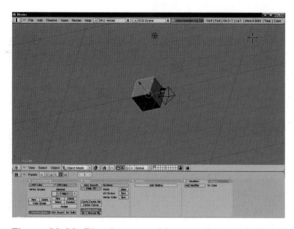

It is very likely that the end user will have the **specialist skills** necessary to give the installed software a **thorough** test, using more of the software application's functionality. Perhaps, **most importantly**, the user should check that the new software does indeed **meet the needs originally identified!**

Figure 23.20 Blender at work!

3.2 Loading facilities

Loading facilities are **critical** but often choices depend on the **availability** of the software itself. Although most commercial software is available on **CD** or (increasingly) **DVD format** a vast amount of software is installed through **Internet download** from website-based **HTTP transfers** or **FTP sites**.

A number of options exist for loading facilities.

Media	Notes and scorecard
Floppy disk	Perhaps the **oldest** media still in use; the rise of USB (Universal Serial Bus) pen drives have made these **almost obsolete**. + Useful for **very small** utilities + Usually virus checked − **Minimal storage** (only 1.44 megabytes) − **Slow** reading speed − Easy to **damage**; **corruption** likely − Many new computer systems **don't have** floppy disk drives!
Hard disk	Hard disks are **relatively fast**, using either PATA (Parallel Advance Technology Attachment) or newer SATA (Serial ATA) devices. + Speed + Hard disks are very inexpensive (gigabyte/£) + Reliable + Less likely to corrupt data + Access can be secured + Usually virus checked − Data has to get onto the hard drive − Not portable
Compact Disc (CD)/ Digital Versatile Disc (DVD)	As software became **more complex** the sheer practicality of issuing it on **multiple** floppy disks **reduced** (some software used to come on 20+ floppy disks); the optical disc emerged as the natural alternative. CDs in the mid 1990s and DVDs in the early 2000s became the **de facto distribution** media for new software. + **Speed** (faster than floppy, slower than hard disk) + **Capacity** (CD = 650 Megabytes, DVD = 17 Gigabytes max) + Relatively **inexpensive** to produce and duplicate + **Comprehensive error correction** and **detection** algorithms **reduce** likelihood of data corruption + User familiarity (from audio CDs) + DVDs have enough capacity to handle most software − Prone to **piracy, illegal copies** − Can be **infected** with viruses (but are usually identified) − Not all systems have DVD-ROM drives for reading DVDs
Internet download	Internet distribution of software is on the **increase**. Many software packages can be downloaded after valid serial keys are purchased online. + **Reduced prices** (no media, no shipping charges) + **Latest version** guaranteed − Installation file usually has to be transferred to disk before it can be executed − Download rates vary on available Internet connection's **bandwidth** − **No physical media** (for backup) until written to removable disk

4 Understand the completion and handover process

4.1 Handover

An IT practitioner's role as technician is **not complete** even though **initial testing** of the new software has worked well.

There are a number of other **activities** that the technician has to perform before they can consider the installation/upgrade to be satisfactorily completed.

These include:

◆ **Configuring the software to meet customer needs**
It is not uncommon for a user to request that their software is configured in a particular way. This could include, for example:
   ◆ setting software defaults (e.g. author initials in a word-processing program, fonts, colours);
   ◆ setting auto-save timings;
   ◆ whether the installed software starts automatically when the operating system loads;
   ◆ creating menu or desktop shortcuts;
   ◆ configuring menus and toolbars;
   ◆ conversion of previous data files to work with the new software;
   ◆ deleting any temporary files used during installation that are no longer needed;
   ◆ replacing any customisations (e.g. macros) that existed on the previous version.

◆ **Formal handover to the customer**
The technician would supply:
   ◆ **instructions** for using the software – this may be **verbal** or **printed** (e.g. a manual or user guide) or **electronic** ('readme.txt' text files or a .pdf file);
   ◆ information on where to access **further training** if required;
   ◆ **contact information if problems occur** while the software is being used.

◆ **Reaching customer acceptance**
This is the point when the end user is happy with the installed software, has tested it to their satisfaction (see **UAT**) and effectively signs off the job as complete. It is not uncommon for the technician to ask the end user to sign a **release form** confirming customer acceptance has taken place. Once acceptance has taken place, the technician can formally log the job as **closed**, complete their **records** and take the **installation media** (e.g. CDs/DVDs) and **registration information** back to the organisation's IT services department for safe keeping.

If things don't go well during testing, it is likely that the technician will need to **back out**, restoring the original system to the point before the new software was installed.

This typically involves:

1 **uninstalling** the new software;
2 **reinstalling** the previous version/product;
3 recovering **data files**;
4 recovering **computer system settings**.

For more on this see section 4.3 on data integrity.

4.2 Product registration

Information collected at registration

A typical installation program may request the following information through registration:

◆ personal name
◆ company name (if applicable)
◆ gender (male, female)
◆ date of birth/age
◆ how many employees in your organisation (if applicable)
◆ postal address (including country)
◆ contact telephone number
◆ email address
◆ how and where you purchased the software
◆ what software you used previously (if this is an upgrade from a competitor)
◆ a username/password to log in to the publisher's website

If you are entering this information on behalf of a company, it is likely that a standard set of responses has been agreed (e.g. official company name, a single contact name and telephone contact number etc.).

In addition, it is possible that it can **harvest information** about your **computer system** and its Internet **connection** (including the **IP address** and the **ISP** – Internet Service Provider – being used).

Figure 23.21 RealPlayer's registration dialogue

What do publishers do with this information?

Most publishers will have a **privacy policy** or **statement** which is made freely available to its customers. It simply details (although very often in complex language) what the organisation **will** and **will not do** with any data you have supplied.

A **sample** privacy policy (for Realnetworks Inc. RealPlayer) can be seen in Figure 23.22.

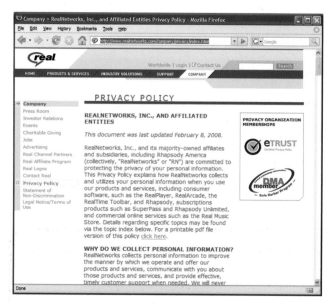

Figure 23.22 Realnetworks Inc. RealPlayer privacy policy

(**http://www.realnetworks.com/company/privacy/index .html**)

Purpose of registration

Registration has many purposes:

◆ identifies your copy as being **valid** (i.e. legal and not pirated);
◆ provides the publisher with **information** about the people (and organisations) buying its products;
◆ provides the publisher with a **way of communicating directly** with its customers (usually via email);
◆ collects information about how you **discovered** the software (helps their marketing and advertising);
◆ helps publishers to **personalise** your software;
◆ helps publishers to understand **how** their software is being used by its customers;
◆ users can opt into **a 'bug reporting' scheme** to help '**live test**' their product and improve its reliability.

Registration scorecard

There are **pros** and **cons** to registering a software package.

After registering the software publisher may:

+ keep you informed of any new upgrades to the package;
+ offer reduced prices on new products or services;
+ provide new bonus downloads;
+ send via email a lost serial number if re-installation is required;
+ provide limited technical support;
+ enter your name in a competition prize draw;
+ offer an extended warranty;
− pass your personal information (e.g. name and email address) onto other interested third parties, usually for marketing purposes;
− know you are using their software (can be seen as an infringement of privacy).

Licensing

Key Terms

A **software license** is a legal agreement between the publisher of the software and the user of the software.

Typically a license has to be (a) **read** and (b) **accepted** before installation will continue.

A particularly common form of software license is the **EULA – E**nd **U**ser **L**icense **A**greement.

This is essentially the same as a software license, giving the user **permission** to use the software. It also specifies the **conditions** that the user is expected to agree to, the most common being the agreement not to **illegally share the software** with others or **attempt to modify it** (by attempting to 'reverse engineer' the program code).

It may also have a **disclaimer** protecting the publisher from any **data loss, loss of service** or **damage to hardware** experienced while using their software. This places the **responsibility** of ensuring good data integrity **firmly** on the user.

Broadly speaking, **two different types** of license exist:

◆ open source/free software license
◆ commercial or proprietary license.

Open source is made (as the name suggests) **freely available** to the **public domain** with its **source code**. This lets other developers **modify** and **improve upon** the product; in return **they** release their modification into the public domain as well. Open source software therefore becomes public **intellectual property** (**IP**). Most **Linux software** is distributed under this license.

Commercial software is typically **restricted** in **use** and **duplication** with the **legal ownership** and **copyright** of the program **remaining** with the publisher. Microsoft® operating systems and application software (e.g. Microsoft Word®) use this form of license.

Dongles and other protection schemes

Many publishers use various **protection methods** to legally reinforce their commercial software licenses and reduce instances of **software piracy**.

A common technique in industries such as **C**omputer **A**ided **D**esign/**C**omputer **A**ided **M**anufacture (**CAD/CAM**) is the use of the **dongle**.

A **dongle** is a **small electronic device** that connects into a computer system and is used by a program to **authenticate itself**; if **no** dongle is found, the program will **refuse** to work.

Other protection methods include:

◆ **copy protection** on discs (i.e. CDs and DVDs)
◆ username and **serial number**
◆ **Internet**-based **product activation**
◆ **telephone**-based **product activation**
◆ **d**igital **r**ights **m**anagement (**DRM**) for audio and video files.

Figure 23.23 Wibu Systems' Wibu key

Activity – Licensing confusion

Research the following terms:

◆ freeware

◆ shareware

◆ abandonware.

Why might an organisation decide to use **only** commercial software?

Answer: Commercial software usually guarantees customer support.

4.3 Data integrity

Software that is **poorly written** or **incompatible** can cause an operating system to **malfunction** and, as a consequence, cause **data loss** or **data corruption**.

Clearly it is therefore a recommended practice to protect the **computer system** and **its data** by performing timely **back-up procedures**.

Operating system specifics

The BTEC National Diploma scheme entry for Unit 23's learning content 4.3 seems to be slightly biased in its suggestions towards Microsoft® operating systems, i.e. Microsoft XP® and Microsoft Vista®.

Although terms like 'system recovery point' and 'registry' can be used generically it is far more likely that these are specific references to the concepts used in Microsoft's family of operating systems. This may be seen as an earnest attempt to cater to the software families you are most likely to encounter at home, work, school or college.

Key Terms

In **earlier** versions of Microsoft Windows®, **separate '.ini' (initialisation files)** were used to specify **user preferences** for **separate** programs.

More **recent** versions of Windows® use a **structured database of information** to store details of the computer system **setup**, its **users' preferences, installed software, hardware configuration** and **drivers** – this is called the **Registry**.

Figure 23.24 Windows® Registry (unexpanded tree-view)

The Registry is constantly being **read** and **written to** while Windows® is being **used**. If the Registry becomes **corrupted** by malfunctioning (or poorly installed/upgraded software) it is possible that the operating system will **not function correctly** (or, in extreme cases, even **boot**).

In Windows®, the Registry is broken down into several '**hives**' (a bit like a folder) which are used to collect together **related settings**, e.g. all the settings about the **current user** (HKEY_CURRENT_USER), the **computer system** (HKEY_LOCAL_MACHINE).

These hives are stored as **physical files** (e.g. ntuser.dat is HKEY_CURRENT_USER) on the computer system's hard disk, although their **location** varies between different versions of Windows®.

The website '**Registry Guide for Windows**' is a useful resource:

http://www.pctools.com/guides/registry/

Activity – Exploring the Registry

Caution: Changes to the Registry are **immediate** and you could **corrupt** or **disable** your computer system. Please explore the registration only **under suitable supervision**!

To explore the Registry:

1 Click **Start**.

2 Click **Run**.

3 Type '**Regedit**' (short for 'Registry Editor') into the Run dialogue.

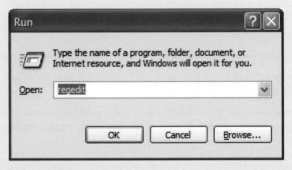

Figure 23.25 Starting Regedit

4 Click **OK.**

5 Regedit will typically display **top level Hive names** (although you may see a different view if the Registry has been previously explored – Regedit remembers the last settings that have been viewed).

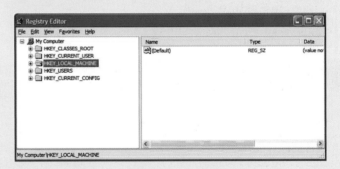

Figure 23.26 Typical Regedit appearance

6 You can navigate the Registry in the same way that you move around different folders in Windows Explorer, **expanding** and **collapsing** different hives by using the '+' and '-' symbols.

7 Try to find:

Settings for installed software

hint: **\HKEY_LOCAL_MACHINE\SOFTWARE**

Settings for your computer system's user and organisation information

hint: **\HKEY_CURRENT_USER\Software\Microsoft\MS Setup (ACME)**

8 Use **File**, then **Exit** to quit when finished.

Recovery points

A **recovery point** (as it is known in Microsoft Windows®), **bookmark** or **snapshot** are terms used to described an electronic 'image' that contains the **core settings** of the computer's **operating system**. If badly behaved software causes the operating system to **malfunction**, a **previously saved recovery point** can be used to **reverse** the damage.

The following activities describe how to **create** a recovery point and then use it to **restore** an operating system (in this case, Windows XP®).

Activity – Setting a system recovery point in Microsoft Windows XP®

To manually set a system recovery point:

1 Click **Start**.

2 Select **All Programs**.

3 Select **Accessories**.

4 Select **System Tools**.

5 Select **System Restore**.

You should now see a 'Welcome' page (see Figure 23.27).

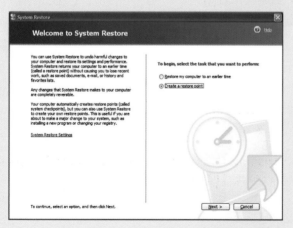

Figure 23.27 Windows XP® System Restore dialogue

6 Select '**Create a restore point**' and then click **Next**.

▶

7 Enter a **short description** for this **new** restore point (e.g. 'just before I installed application XXXXXXXX') as shown in Figure 23.28.

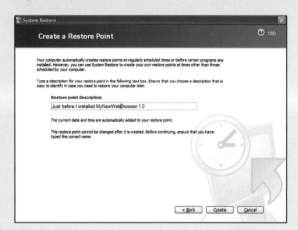

Figure 23.28 Entering a description for the system restore point

8 Select **Create**.

Windows XP should respond (after a short period writing to hard disk) with confirmation that the new restore point has been created.

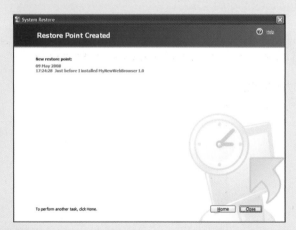

Figure 23.29 Confirmation of a new system restore point

It should now be possible to reverse damage to the operating system's Registry by using this restore point.

Activity – Restoring a system recovery point in Microsoft Windows XP®

Once a restore point has been created it is fairly straightforward to use:

1 Click **Start**.

2 Select **All Programs.**

3 Select **Accessories.**

4 Select **System Tools.**

5 Select **System Restore.**

You should now see the same **'Welcome' page** from Figure 23.27.

6 This time, choose 'Restore my computer to an earlier time' as in Figure 23.30.

> **To begin, select the task that you want to perform:**
>
> ⦿ Restore my computer to an earlier time
>
> ○ Create a restore point

Figure 23.30 Choosing to restore

7 You will then be presented with a calendar showing a number of possible restore points. Most of these are likely to be routine checkpoints created by the operating system.

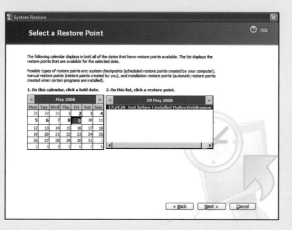

Figure 23.31 Selecting a restore point

8 Navigate to the restore point you wish to use; it is entirely possible that **multiple restore points** may exist for the **same day** – if this happens, the **short descriptions** should help you determine which to use.

9 Click **Next**.

10 You will then be presented with a **confirmation screen** as seen in Figure 23.32.

Figure 23.32 Confirming the restore point

This screen reminds you of some vital points:

◆ You will **not** lose any data or documents created after the restore point.

◆ You need to **close down** all active applications **before** continuing.

◆ The computer system will automatically restart once the process finishes.

11 When the computer system reboots it will be using system settings from the earlier restore point.

Backing up

As far as data loss goes, **prevention** is **far better** than cure!

Copy of Registry data

Data stored in Windows' Registry can be copied in a number of ways.

◆ **copying the entire file** containing the **relevant hive** (e.g. **ntuser.dat** for HKEY_CURRENT_USER) to another drive, CD etc.;

◆ copying all the Registry hives in **one go** (usually from C:\windows\system32\config) to another drive, CD etc.;

◆ **exporting specific Registry keys** in **particular hives** that are required to separate '**.reg' files**. This can be performed in **Regedit** using **File**, then **Export** menu options. A '.reg' file can be double-clicked to **reinsert** its entries into the Registry, overwriting any incorrect values.

Note. Options 1 and 2 are generally only possible when the registry files are **not** in use, i.e. accessing these disk files via another operating system (e.g. a separate bootable operating system disk).

Copy of user data

In a Windows® operating system, it is common for data to be stored in the '**My Documents**' folder, with software applications creating **specific application sub-folders** for saving user data.

The location of this folder is:

    <Drive>\Documents and Settings\<Username>\My Documents

where <Drive> is typically C: and <Username> is the logged on username, e.g.

    C:\Documents and Settings\Mark\My Documents

Files may be copied manually to another drive, CD etc.

Problems typically occur when data files are **not** written to the 'My Documents' location: files may be **scattered** in a number of places on a hard disk and it may be difficult to find them all.

Activity – Locating user data

Technician's usually have administrative control of a computer system when performing data backup.

As a result they can browse all users' data.

On a Windows operating system, browse to:

    C:\Documents and Settings\

And discover how many users have '**My Documents**' folders.

Backup utilities

Many **utility software products** exist that help the technician to backup **user** (and **registry**) **data**. Windows XP Professional that has its own (often maligned) **Backup utility** ('**ntbackup.exe**') which performs this function (the utility is also available on the Windows XP Home® installation CD). Windows Vista® uses a similar tool called Windows Backup but it uses a different file format.

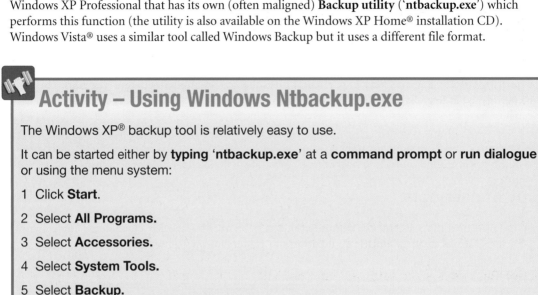

Activity – Using Windows Ntbackup.exe

The Windows XP® backup tool is relatively easy to use.

It can be started either by **typing '**ntbackup.exe**'** at a **command prompt** or **run dialogue** or using the menu system:

1 Click **Start**.

2 Select **All Programs.**

3 Select **Accessories.**

4 Select **System Tools.**

5 Select **Backup.**

As you will see, Backup is a **wizard-driven process**.

Let's work through a typical example.

Figure 23.33 Backup Wizard

6 Click **Next**.

7 The following options will appear (see Figure 23.34).

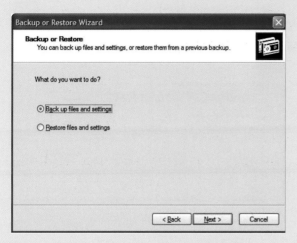

Figure 23.34 Choosing to back up or restore

Select 'Back up files and settings' and click **Next**.

8 The following dialogue (see Figure 23.35) determines what will be backed up. The options are:

◆ all documents and settings for the logged-in user;

◆ all documents and settings for all users;

◆ all data on the computer system.

In addition, the technician can choose to **manually select** the folders to backup.

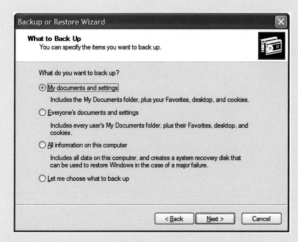

Figure 23.35 Choosing what will be backed up

Let's select the current user's documents and settings.

9 The next step is to identify the **media** to use for backup. Typically this is another **fixed media drive** (i.e. **second hard disk**).

Click the **Browse** button to **select** the drive you want to use, ensuring that the destination drive selected has **enough free space**.

The name of the backup file created will reflect the entry in the 'Type a name for this backup' text box, so name it **sensibly** and **meaningfully**.

Click **Next** to continue.

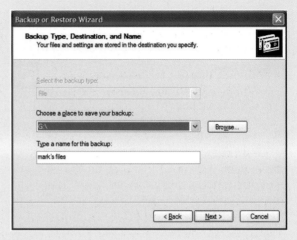

Figure 23.36 Choosing a place to save your backup

10 The next dialogue (see Figure 23.37) gives you the option of clicking an **Advanced** button to specify **additional settings**.

Figure 23.37 Option to choose advanced backup settings

Additional settings, for advanced users only, include the options to:

◆ perform **full** or **incremental** backups;

◆ **schedule automatic** backups;

◆ use **compression**;

♦ **verify** the backup written (**compare** it to the **original data** to check the copy's **accuracy**).

You may **experiment** with these settings as an **additional activity**; for now, we will use the **default settings**.

Click **Finish** to continue.

11 The backup procedure will commence. The time taken will vary depending on the **volume of data** being copied, the **speed of the devices used** and whether **compression** has been selected. A new dialogue informs the user of the **backup progress** (see Figure 23.38).

The **same wizard** can be used to **restore** a **previously created** backup file.

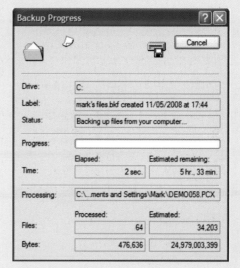

Figure 23.38 Backup progress

Imaging the hard drive

Although the **Windows XP® Ntbackup.exe utility** can be used to copy all data on a drive, it is often criticised (mostly because of its speed) and many alternative products may be used instead.

One technique is to create an **electronic 'image'** of the **entire hard disk** before the new software is installed. This requires specific **disk-imaging software**.

Commercial examples	Website URL
Symantec Norton Ghost	http://www.symantec.com/norton/products/overview.jsp?pcid=br&pvid=ghost14
Acronis True Image	http://www.acronis.com/homecomputing/products/trueimage/index.html
Paragon Drive Backup	http://www.drive-backup.com/home/personal/
Freeware alternatives	Website URL
Miray HDClone	http://www.miray.de/products/sat.hdclone.html
Ranish Partition Manager	http://www.ranish.com/part/
Excelcia SelfImage	http://selfimage.excelcia.org/

CD and **DVD burning software** may also be used to back up data from a hard disk but, given the comparative volumes of data, a **large number** of CD and DVD discs will be needed (a typical CD stores approximately 650 Megabytes, the largest DVD stores 16 Gigabytes).

Figure 23.39 shows a typical Backup Wizard from Nero.

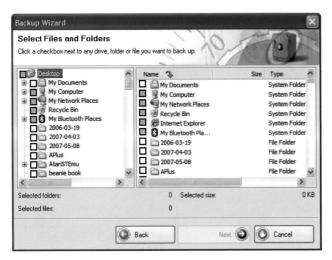

Figure 23.39 Nero Backup Wizard

Braincheck

Answer the following questions:

1 Name four elements of planning.
2 Name the eight phases of installation.
3 What is the difference between minimum and recommended requirements?
4 Name three interested parties a technician should communicate with.
5 What is a 'backout' procedure?
6 What is UAT?
7 Give four pieces of information that may be collected during registration.
8 Name four reasons why publishers find registration useful.
9 Give three reasons to register a software product.
10 What is a EULA?
11 What is a dongle?
12 What is a system recovery point?
13 What is the Registry?
14 What is a hive?
15 In a modern Windows® operating system, where is user data normally stored?

How well did you do? See page 445 for the answers.

Unit links

Unit 23 is a Specialist Unit on the BTEC National Award and the BTEC National Certificate.

It is also a Specialist Unit on the following BTEC National Certificate and Diploma routes:

IT and Business

Networking

Software Development

Systems Support

As such it has links to a number of other units, principally:

Unit 2 – Computer Systems

Unit 4 – IT Project

Unit 16 – Maintaining Computer Systems

Unit 28 – IT Technical Support

Unit 29 – IT Troubleshooting and Repair

Unit 35 – Impact of the Use of IT on Business Systems.

Achieving success

In order to achieve each unit you will complete a series of coursework activities. Each time you hand in work, your tutor will return this to you with a record of your achievement.

This particular unit has 12 criteria to meet: 6 Pass, 4 Merit and 2 Distinction.

For a **Pass**:

You must achieve **all** 6 Pass criteria

For a **Merit**:

You must achieve **all** 6 Pass and **all** 4 Merit criteria

For a **Distinction**:

You must achieve **all** 6 Pass, **all** 4 Merit **and** both Distinction criteria.

So that you can monitor your own progress and achievement in each unit, a recording grid has been provided (see below). The full version of this grid is also included on the companion CD.

Assignment	Assignments in this Unit			
	U23.01	U23.02	U23.03	U23.04
Referral				
Pass				
1				
2				
3				
4				
5				
6				
Merit				
1				
2				
3				
4				
Distinction				
1				
2				

Help with assessment

The **Pass criteria** for this unit are a mixture of planning, practical and documentation tasks. On the planning side you need to be able to describe the motivations for software installation/upgrade and the risks of performing them; this may be achieved as part of planning an actual installation and upgrade. From a practical viewpoint you will be asked to then physically perform an installation and an upgrade. Finally you will need to produce suitable documentary evidence to explain the registration process.

The **Merit criteria**, requiring deeper thought, ask you to explain the advantages and disadvantages of installing new software or performing an upgrade. In addition you need to be able to describe in detail the requirements of preparing an upgrade or fresh install. Finally, you will be asked to design a procedure to ensure data integrity and potential backout; you'll also have to implement the former.

The **Distinction criteria** revolve around justification; you will need to be able to justify a particular installation and upgrade, and evaluate the risks involved by explaining how they could be reduced.

Online resources on the CD

Technician checklist
Key fact sheets
Business case template
Electronic slide show of key points
Multiple choice self-test quiz

Further Reading

Shaw, N., 2000, *Strategies for Managing Computer Software Upgrades*, Idea Group US, ISBN 1930708041.

Honeycutt, J., 2005, *Microsoft Windows Registry Guide, Second Edition*, Microsoft Press, ISBN 0735622183.

Honeycutt, J., *Sams Teach Yourself Windows Registry in 24 Hours*, Sams, ISBN 0672315521.

Websites

Microsoft	www.microsoft.com
Apple	www.apple.com
Linux	distrowatch.com

Unit 24

Digital Graphics and Computers

Capsule view

This is a 60-hour unit which is designed to support learners in working with digital graphics.

During this unit you will be introduced to the basic production considerations involved when creating an image. You will also learn about the various file formats that exist and when each should be used to obtain the most appropriate image.

Although the IT Practitioners qualification does not have the same focus and scope as the BTEC National Diploma in Media Production, you will be encouraged to explore graphics manipulation programs and develop a competency in performing basic operations to alter and enhance your own images.

It is possible to explore many aspects of this unit using basic accessories such as Microsoft Paint®, however the availability of open source and freeware alternatives such as The Gimp mean that near-professional outcomes are no longer out of reach even when funds are limited.

Other technical issues such as image compression and colour depth are also explored, rounded off by an overview of the importance of review and crucial copyright issues.

This unit should therefore be seen as a primer for working in digital graphics.

Learning aims

1 Know the hardware and software required to work with graphic images.
2 Understand types of graphic images and graphical file formats.
3 Be able to use editing tools to edit and manipulate technically complex images.
4 Be able to create and modify graphic images to meet user requirements.

1 Know the hardware and software required to work with graphic images

1.1 Hardware

Let's start by defining some important key terms.

> **Key Terms**
>
> **Hardware** is a term used to categorise any **physical elements** of a computer system that are **tangible** (i.e. those that can be **touched**).
>
> Although dedicated graphics manipulation **software** is a vital component, the initial **acquisition** of images is performed by computer hardware.
>
> Hardware is also responsible for an **image's processing**, **storage** (temporary and permanent) and its final **output**.
>
> This section examines the different types of hardware you need to be familiar with to complete your studies in this unit.

Image processing can be best described by the diagram shown in Figure 24.1.

It is possible to explore each hardware device in minute detail but this is the role of other units in the IT Practitioner scheme; our goal here is to provide a simple overview of each and describe how it fits into the learner's workflow when working with digital graphics.

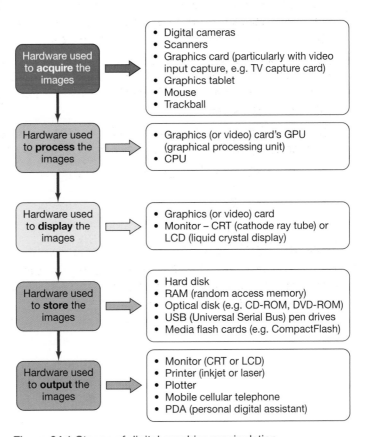

Hardware used to acquire the images
- Digital cameras
- Scanners
- Graphics card (particularly with video input capture, e.g. TV capture card)
- Graphics tablet
- Mouse
- Trackball

Hardware used to process the images
- Graphics (or video) card's GPU (graphical processing unit)
- CPU

Hardware used to display the images
- Graphics (or video) card
- Monitor – CRT (cathode ray tube) or LCD (liquid crystal display)

Hardware used to store the images
- Hard disk
- RAM (random access memory)
- Optical disk (e.g. CD-ROM, DVD-ROM)
- USB (Universal Serial Bus) pen drives
- Media flash cards (e.g. CompactFlash)

Hardware used to output the images
- Monitor (CRT or LCD)
- Printer (inkjet or laser)
- Plotter
- Mobile cellular telephone
- PDA (personal digital assistant)

Figure 24.1 Stages of digital graphics manipulation

Process and display

A graphics card or video card is a **specialist** component of computer hardware that is used to **convert binary data** into **graphical images** for display on an output device. The term **video card** is often used **interchangeably**.

Graphics cards are capable of **manipulating** the image in certain ways, relieving the processing 'load' on the computer system's CPU and thus **speeding up** the overall computer system's performance.

Figure 24.2 Modern graphics card

On more inexpensive computer systems the **GPU** may be **integrated** into the motherboard (normally the **northbridge** chip). Integrated GPU's (often called an **IGP – integrated graphics processor**) tend to have the reputation of being **technically inferior** to separate graphics cards (which can be expensive and offer specialist features).

An integrated GPU is typically **disabled** when an external graphics card is inserted into the motherboard.

Common video card connections include (oldest first):

◆ **p**eripheral **c**omponent **i**nterconnect (**PCI**)
◆ **a**dvanced **g**raphics **p**ort (**AGP**)
◆ PCI Express (**PCIe**).

Graphics cards are controlled by the computer system through a special **program** called a **driver**. In order to work correctly, the driver must be **compatible** with the **hardware** and the **operating system** being used.

For example, a graphics card's driver for Windows Vista® **will not work** for Linux.

Figure 24.3 Graphics card in motherboard's PCIe slot

Key components inside a graphics card include:

◆ **GPU** – processes 2D and 3D images and video
◆ **VRAM** (**v**ideo **r**andom **a**ccess **m**emory) – stores the images, see section 3.2
◆ **video connections** – sends video signals from graphics card to output device (e.g. monitor).

Data capture devices

Data capture devices are used to **acquire images**, converting them into **binary data** so that the computer system (and its user) can **manipulate** them.

Common data capture devices include:

Digital cameras

These handy devices are the most popular way of **capturing photographic images** in a **digital format** (i.e. stored in a **computer-friendly** file format, usually .jpg). Although only popularly in use since the mid-1990s they now outsell their traditional film-based rivals.

Digital camera technology has improved greatly since its introduction with current models having **light-sensitive sensor** grids capable of capturing over **10,036,224 pixels** (picture cells) of data; this is often referred to as **10 Megapixels**. In simple terms, the **higher** this number, the **better the resolution** of the **image** taken.

Many mobile cellular telephones also incorporate digital camera components, which have helped to **popularise** the technology (although their sensor resolution is often considerably below the standards found in dedicated cameras made by companies such as Canon, Nikon and Olympus).

Figure 24.4 Digital camera

Digital cameras can **transfer** their data to a computer system via **USB cable** or by removing their **media flash card** (many modern computer systems have **external** or **internal card reader** devices). Some cameras require a specific driver in order for communication with the computer system.

Digital camera scorecard

+ Easy to use (just point and click)
+ No consumables (film); memory cards are reusable
+ Anyone can 'process' the photographs (i.e. copy, print etc.)
+ Only produce prints for wanted images (so no waste)
+ Encourages experimentation (no wasted film)
+ No need to scan photographs (already in digital format)
+ Some digital images can be edited in-camera
– People often don't print the photographs!
– Needs operating system-specific driver for communication.

Scanner

Not all images are photographic in nature; very often images that need to be manipulated in a computer system have already been printed **traditionally** (i.e. onto paper) in the form of **diagrams**, **illustrations**, **cartoons** etc.

In these instances it is necessary to use an input device called a **scanner**.

Flatbed scanners (the most common type) use a light-sensor bar (containing a charged-coupled device (**CCD**)) that sweeps across an image which has been placed face-down onto a glass plate. The

Figure 24.5 Flatbed scanner

CCD registers variations in reflected colour and rebuilds the original image line-by-line as a digital file that it then uploads to the computer system for editing, saving or printing.

Almost all modern scanners are connected to their computer system via USB cable (from which some also draw their electrical power).

Scanning resolutions are measured in **DPI** (**d**ots **p**er **i**nch).

DPI to pixel conversion

The formula for converting from dpi to pixels is:

Pixels = Inches × DPI

For example, a **photograph (8 inches wide × 6 inches high) scanned** at **150 DPI** would be:

X Pixels = 8 × 150 = **1200**

Y Pixels = 6 × 150 = **900**

The resulting image would be 1200 × 900 pixels (a total of 1,080,000 pixels).

Like a digital camera, scanners require operating system-specific drivers in order to communicate with the computer system correctly.

TWAIN (no real acronym) is an open-source protocol used by developers of graphics manipulation software to incorporate direct support for scanner hardware.

Well-known scanner manufacturers include Canon, Epson and Hewlett-Packard.

Graphics tablet

Although a mouse can be used to good effect when creating images manually, most professional graphic artists prefer a **graphics tablet** and a **pen**. They are also sometimes called a **digitizer** or **drawing tablet**.

A graphics tablet lets the artist interact with graphic manipulation and creation software as they would with a **normal pen**. This gives the artist an incredible level of **control** and **precision** over the various tools they are using.

Again most modern graphics tablets connect to a computer system (such as a PC or Apple Mac) using USB (although some do support wireless or Bluetooth connectivity). The price for these varies due to their accuracy and physical size.

Figure 24.6 Graphics tablet

Wacom (www.wacom.com) is perhaps the most well-known manufacturer with a variety of different models to suit all practical uses.

File storage

After an image has been **captured** it has to be saved in a particular **file format** (see section 2) onto a particular form of **file storage**.

File storage can either be **temporary** or **permanent**.

Devices such as internal **hard disks** tend to be used for **temporary storage** (while the image is being manipulated). **External hard disks** (often connected by USB) may offer another alternative.

More **permanent storage** can be found in **optical media** such as **recordable CD** (**c**ompact **d**isc) and **DVD** (**d**igital **v**ersatile **d**isc).

Flash pen drives

Also known as 'flash drives', 'thumbdrives' etc., they were introduced in the late 1990s as a replacement to floppy disks.

Pen drives are an increasingly popular form of backing storage due to their **portability**, **ease of use** and **value for money**. Based on NAND-flash architecture developed by Toshiba in the late 1980s, a pen drive consists of a male **USB** connector, a **PCB** (**p**rinted **c**ircuit **b**oard) containing **flash memory** and a **clock crystal** (for synchronisation).

These components are typically housed in **toughened plastic packaging** which includes a **removable** (or swivel) **cap** to protect the sensitive contents from **e**lectro**s**tatic **d**ischarge (**ESD**).

Figure 24.7 Inside a USB pen drive

Some pen drives might also have **light-emitting diodes** (LEDs) to indicate read/write status, a **write-protect switch** and a hoop for connecting a **keychain** or **lanyard**.

Pen drives are compatible with the majority of modern operating systems including Microsoft Windows® (2000 onwards), Mac OS (9.x onwards) and various Linux distributions.

Media flash cards

There are many different formats of flash memory cards currently available and in use inside digital cameras, mobile cellular telephones and portable game consoles. Most flash cards use the same NAND-flash architecture as pen drives but come in a number of different **form factors**. Common varieties include:

◆ **CompactFlash** (**CF**) created by SanDisk in 1994
◆ **MultiMediaCard** (**MMC**) created by SanDisk and Siemens AG in 1997
◆ **Memory Stick** (**MS**) created by Sony in 1998, varieties include Pro, Duo and micro.
◆ **Secure Digital** (**SD**) created by Panasonic, Toshiba and SanDisk in 1999
◆ **xD-Picture Card** (**xD**) created by Olympus and Fujifilm in 2002.

Figure 24.8 Various flash memory cards and flash card reader

It is becoming increasingly common for computer systems (especially PCs) to have **front bezels** that contain **multi-format card reading slots**. External card readers are also available and relatively inexpensive, connecting to the system via a standard USB port.

1.2 Output medium

For images to be of any practical use they must be output.

The type of output device used is a direct reflection of the media and usage required by the client.

The most common types of output are as follows.

Printer

Modern computer systems use two types of printer: **laser** and **inkjet** with drivers available for most mainstream operating systems. Most printers deal with **A4 paper** (210 x 297 mm) although smaller sizes (e.g. A5, envelopes) are compatible.

Figure 24.9 Laser printer

Figure 24.10 Inkjet printer

Printers vary greatly in quality of print with some performing better with **text** and others being superior with **images**. In addition laser and inkjet printers may be **monochrome** (black only) or **colour**. It should not be a surprise to read that colour printing technologies are much more costly.

The general concensus appears to be that although **laser printing** is **more expensive** in terms of **initial outlay** (i.e. the printer hardware and the toner (for laser) or ink (for inkjet) cartridges), the **overall cost of printing** each page is **lower**.

The biggest considerations for a printer are therefore:

◆ **quality** of output (measured in dpi and number of colours used in the printing process)
◆ **speed** of output (measured in ppm – pages per minute)
◆ **cost** of consumables (replacement toner or ink cartridges)
◆ **size of paper** supported (e.g. A4, A3 etc.)
◆ **type of paper** supported (e.g. matt, glossy, photographic etc.).

Popular manufacturers for printers include HP (Hewlett-Packard), Canon, Brother, Samsung and Xerox.

Plotter

A plotter is a specialised form of printing device that is often used to draw **vector-style images** using a computer-controlled pen. Plotters are typically used in **CAD** (**c**omputer-**a**ided **d**esign) applications for drawing **plans** and **schematics** onto page sizes up to **A1** (594 x 841 mm).

Older plotters may be **drum** or, more commonly, **flatbed based**. Figure 24.11 shows a modern plotter from Hewlett-Packard that uses a combination of drum and printer technology.

Figure 24.11 HP Designjet T1100

Computer monitor

The monitor (sometimes called a **VDU** or **v**isual **d**isplay **u**nit – although this is an outdated term now) is used to display **output** from the computer's graphics (or video) card and as such **cannot** provide a permanent image.

In terms of computer graphics, the monitor can be used to showcase computer art, web page design elements or animations.

There are two basic types of monitor that you are likely to encounter:

◆ **CRT** (**c**athode **r**ay **t**ube)-based;
◆ **TFT** (thin-film-transistor)-based, which form most **LCD** (**l**iquid **c**rystal **d**isplay) screens.

Both types of monitor work by combining **RGB** (**r**ed, **g**reen and **b**lue) **pixels** to form full-colour images.

The biggest considerations for a monitor are:

◆ **VIS** (viewable image size) – a diagonal measurement in inches of the useable viewing area;
◆ **dot pitch** – a measurement of distance between pixels of the same colour; a smaller number means a sharper image is possible (e.g. 0.23mm is better than 0.24mm);
◆ **response time** – time taken for a pixel to change between black and white and back again; this is measured in milliseconds (thousandths of a second) with smaller again being better;
◆ **refresh rate** – the number of times per second that a display is refreshed; this is measured in hertz, with higher refresh rates proving less tiring and irritating to the viewer;
◆ **maximum resolution** – the highest resolution in pixels (vertical and horizontal) that can be shown.

Due to their **smaller** desk 'footprint' and **lower emission levels** in heat and radiation, TFTs have quickly become the most popular form of display device, although purists may still prefer the **crispness** of a CRT image, mainly due to their **responsiveness**.

Other devices such as **mobile cellular telephones** and **PDAs** also use LCD technology to display graphical images. These obviously have a lower maximum resolution and VIS, although for improved portability their power consumption is usually more modest to extend the battery life.

1.3 Software

Application software for processing images comes in many different forms.

Dedicated vector graphics software

As discussed in section 2.3, these applications support the **S**calable **V**ector **G**raphics (**SVG**) image file format as **standardised** by the **W3C** (**World Wide Web Consortium**).

Well-known, industry-recognised products include:

◆ Corel CorelDRAW®
  www.corel.com
◆ **InkScape** (open source)
  www.inkscape.org
◆ Adobe Illustrator®
  www.adobe.com
◆ Xara Xtreme
  www.xara.com

Figure 24.12 Inkscape

Dedicated bitmap software

Perhaps the most common images are bitmap formats which represent images as a **grid of pixels** (see section 2.3 for more information).

Common applications that support this format include:

◆ Microsoft Paint®
◆ Corel Paintshop Pro®
  www.corel.com
◆ The GIMP (**G**NU **I**mage **M**anipulation **P**rogram)
  www.gimp.org
◆ Adobe Fireworks®
  www.adobe.com

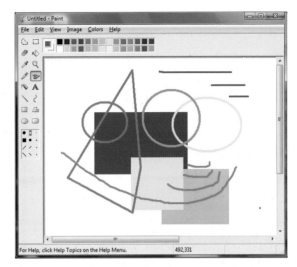

Figure 24.13 Microsoft Paint® in Windows Vista®

Dedicated photo-manipulation software

Photo-manipulation software often support standard tools for enhancing and editing photographs.

These tools include:

◆ resizing
◆ rotating
◆ cropping
◆ flash 'red eye' reduction
◆ adjusting colour balance
◆ adjusting light levels
◆ healing rips and abrasions
◆ retouching.

The world's best known photo-manipulation software is undoubtedly **Photoshop**, part of Adobe's Creative Suite (**CS**):

◆ Adobe Photoshop®
◆ Adobe Photoshop Elements
  www.adobe.com

There is also an **online version** of Adobe Photoshop that lets registered users manipulate photographs using a range of tools (though not as extensively as either full offline package), create a gallery and share it with others:

◆ Adobe Photoshop Express
  https://www.photoshop.com/
  express/landing.html

Figure 24.14 Adobe Photoshop Express

Note. Images that have been retouched are often described as being 'photoshopped'; it's not an adjective that its developers apparently approve of as it often is used in a negative way.

Graphics facilities embedded in other applications

Many other types of application (e.g. office productivity suites) also let the user **insert** and **manipulate** images.

Microsoft Word® has basic editing facilities consisting of a **Drawing** and **Picture toolbar**. These let the user create basic images and manipulate them. They can also insert images from other files.

Although these editing facilities are basic, they prove to be a **convenient alternative** to using a more fully featured graphics application.

Other tools

There are many other tools that you may want to use in addition to graphic and photo manipulation applications.

These include:

◆ image viewers
◆ photo galleries
◆ file conversion software.

Most operating systems have their own tools for **previewing images** (as **thumbnails**) and as **galleries**.

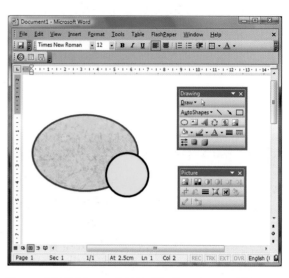

Figure 24.15 Microsoft Word®'s Drawing and Picture toolbars

Figure 24.16 Windows Vista® Photo Gallery

In addition a wide range of third-party tools are available:

◆ ACD Systems **ACDSee www.acdsee.com**
◆ Google **Picasa picasa.google.com**
◆ VOWSoft PicaLoader **www.vowsoft.com**

Figure 24.17 Google Picasa running on Windows Vista®

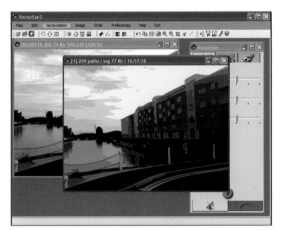

Figure 24.18 Siame's VectorEye creates a vector from a bitmap

Although most graphics and photo-manipulation applications are capable of saving images in a number of compatible formats, some conversions may require **specific tools**, e.g.

◆ Siame's VectorEye converts **bitmap images** to **vector images**
  www.siame.com
◆ **Zamzar** offers **free online conversion** between a number of different graphical formats
  www.zamzar.com

2 Understand types of graphic images and graphical file formats

2.1 File handling

Graphic manipulation software can store images in a number of different **file formats**. Unfortunately for graphics work you need to be aware of a bewildering array of different file formats.

As noted in section 1.2, the most common graphic file formats are either **bitmap (rasterised)** images or **vector-based**.

A more detailed overview and comparison of these can be found in section 2.2.

Key Terms

A **file format** describes the way that the data in the file is **organised** and **structured**. Different file formats are used for different types of data, e.g. images are stored very differently to sounds. An application must recognise a particular file format before it can correctly read its data.

It is common for most files to have a **file extension** that tells both the **user** and the **computer system** what **type of format** the data is stored in.

Converting files

Most modern graphics manipulation software can convert images between many different file formats.

For example, the GIMP has support for many popular formats (e.g. GIF, JPG, PCX, TGA etc.) but also has its own proprietary GIMP format.

Caution – Converting files

Some file conversions are **one-way processes**; once the file has been converted it may be **impossible** to convert the image **back** to its original format.

This usually occurs when a target file format uses a **lower** colour depth.

As a result, colour information stored in the original image will be lost as the conversion occurs – the computer will **reduce** the number of colours by **approximating** the original colours to their **nearest equivalents** in the smaller palette.

For example, converting a 24-bit colour bitmap (JPG) file to a GIF file will reduce it to a 256 (8-bit) colour palette.

Figure 24.19a Man and cat (.JPG)

Figure 24.19b Man and cat (.GIF)

Once the detailed levels of **colour graduation** have been lost it is **almost impossible** to get them back. This is particularly noticeable when the images are of **naturalistic** images (especially people). The recommendation is to therefore keep the original copy of file **safe**.

File sizes

The size of an image file depends on a number of different factors, these include:

- ◆ **physical size** of the image – e.g. measuring in pixels X by Y
- ◆ **colour depth** of the image
- ◆ **file format** – whether there is any **compression**
- ◆ number of **frames** – the image may contain a number of different frames for animation (e.g. animated GIF)
- ◆ number of **layers** – the image may contain a number of unmerged layers (see section 3.2).

Some file formats store the image efficiently by **compressing** the graphical information; sometimes this causes **data to be lost** – we call this a 'lossy' format.

File formats that **don't** lose any graphical information are called 'lossless'. For an accurate representation of the original image this is the **best type** of format to use.

File formats

As noted, there are many different file formats. The following table lists the **most common** and **noteworthy** formats you are likely to encounter during your studies. It also notes whether they are **compressed**.

Name of image format	Bitmap	Vector	Proprietary	What is it?	Compressed?
.BMP	✓	✗	✗	Microsoft Windows Bitmap file. See section 2.3 for more details	Optional
.GIF	✓	✗	✗	Compuserve Graphics Interchange Format file. See section 2.3 for more details	Yes
.JPG .JPEG	✓	✗	✗	Joint Photographic Experts Group file. See section 2.3 for more details	Yes
.PCX	✓	✗	✗	Older Microsoft Windows Bitmap file, developed by ZSoft Corporation	Optional
.PNG	✓	✗	✗	Portable Network Graphics file. See section 2.3 for more details	Yes
.PSD	✗	✗	✓	Adobe PhotoShop Data image format. Native to Photoshop but many other applications can read it	Optional
.PSP	✗	✗	✓	Paintshop Pro image format	Optional
.SVG	✗	✓	✗	W3C Scalable Vector Graphics. See section 2.3 for more details	No
.TGA	✓	✗	✗	Truevision Targa file format	Optional
.TIFF	✓	✓	✗	Aldus Tagged Image File Format now maintained by Adobe	Optional
.WMF	✓	✓	✗	Microsoft Windows Metafile	No

2.2 File management

File management is a vital skill for any IT practitioner, particularly those keeping a **media library** well **organised**.

Here is a short list of advisable **precautions** and **practices** to follow.

Naming files

File names should be **meaningful**, **describing** the **content** of the image.

Digital cameras often use **generic numbering** e.g. DSC00001, DSC00002 etc. when they name pictures; this isn't particularly descriptive but it is at least usually **chronological** (time-based).

In this example, the **DSC** prefix is short for **D**igital **S**till **C**amera, a naming convention used by **Sony** digital cameras and **Sony-Ericsson** mobile telephones. Many other prefixes are used by different manufacturers, e.g. Nikon use **DSCN**, Canon use **IMG** etc.

Digital camera file systems usually follow the **D**esign rule for **C**amera **F**ile system (**DCF**), which specifies a **DCIM** (**D**igital **C**amera **I**mage **M**anagement) **folder** to store its images (see Figure 24.20 for an example).

Figure 24.20 DCIM folder containing images of Gloucestershire Flood 2007

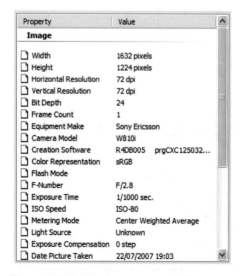

Figure 24.21 Windows accesses the image's EXIF information

Details such as the **date taken**, **size** and **colour depth** are **not** required in the filename as these can be gleaned by the operating system in the form of an advanced **file summary** (for .JPG pictures that contain **EXIF** (Exchangeable Image File) **information**, see Figure 24.21 for an example).

Useful resources for more information on DCF and EXIF

JEITA (Japan Electronic and Information Technology Association) website (English):

http://www.jeita.or.jp/english/

EXIF Reader (Image Data File Analysis) application:

http://www.takenet.or.jp/~ryuuji/minisoft/exifread/english/

Unofficial EXIF website:

http://www.exif.org/

Standard images (i.e. those scanned or drawn by the artist) also have **file properties** that reduce the need for **cluttering** the filename (see Figure 24.22) with **unnecessary** details.

This information stores the **dimensions** of the image (in **pixels**), the **dpi**, **colour depth** (see section 3.2) and the **number of frames** in the image.

Naming files is therefore a **personal preference** unless you have to comply with **organisational policy** (or perhaps file names given by your tutor at school or college).

Property	Value
Image	
Width	420 pixels
Height	434 pixels
Horizontal Resolution	96 dpi
Vertical Resolution	96 dpi
Bit Depth	8
Frame Count	1

Figure 24.22 Summary information for a GIF File

Folder structures

Good organisation of image files is **vital**. It is common to **divide** disk storage into a number of folders (or **sub-directories**) that **group together** images for the **same project**.

Each folder should have a **sensible name** that **accurately describes** the images stored inside.

Although most operating systems provide **thumbnail facilities** for folders containing image files (see Figure 24.23), the use of **third-party image** cataloguing software is very popular (see section 1.3, 'other tools' for more information).

Figure 24.23 Folders showing thumbnails of their contents

Working with files

All operating systems have support for basic file operations.

Typical file operations include:

◆ rename
◆ copy (usually performed through a copy and paste facility)
◆ delete
◆ move (usually performed through drag-and-drop mouse movement).

You will need to demonstrate competency in performing these operations for this unit.

Using compression

As you will see in section 2.3, many image file formats contain **compression algorithms** that **reduce the size of the data.**

Compression tools can also be **manually used** to compress and **parcel up** image files that are deemed to be too large into a single **archive** file. This is useful for **transport** (e.g. between different computers) using either **removable media** (such as USB pen drives or flash media cards) or **email attachments**.

Although modern operating systems such as Windows Vista® have compression facilities built in, it is still possible to purchase popular third-party **commercial compression products** such as:

◆ **WinZip®** (**www.winzip.com**) for Microsoft Windows®
◆ **Winrar** (**www.rarlab.com**) for Microsoft Windows® (shown in Figure 24.24)
◆ **StuffIt** (**SmithMicro.com/StuffIt**) for Apple Mac OS X or Microsoft Windows®.

Freeware alternatives also exist such as:

◆ **7-zip** (**www.7-zip.org**).

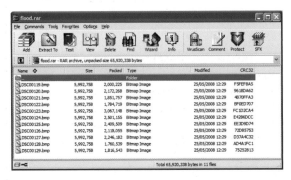

Figure 24.24 Winrar archive storing compressed lossless bitmap images

2.3 Graphic images

This section focuses on the **most popular** types of image formats, discussing their **features** and making comparisons of their respective **strengths** and **weaknesses**.

Type of image	Essential facts	Scorecard
Bitmap (.BMP)	The BMP **bitmap** file format was created by Microsoft® and is extensively used in the Windows® operating system. A bitmap file consists of **many smaller dots** or **pixels**; this is also known as a **'raster'** image. If the image is zoomed the separate pixels become very **'blocky'** (commonly referred to as being **'pixellated'**) and the image loses **quality**. Classic bitmap graphics are **not efficient** as **every pixel** must be physically stored. The **lack of compression** means that they require significant **RAM** (when being edited) and **hard disk space** (when being stored). **Various** bitmap formats exist, with some using a form of basic compression called **Run Length Encoding** (**RLE**) which reduces file size somewhat by representing **repeating patterns** of colour codes as type (length), e.g. 1,1,1,1,2,2,2,2,2 becomes 1(4), 2(5). A common term to describe this format is **'lossless'**. The standard extension for a bitmap file is **'.bmp'** although, as we will see, **other bitmap formats** exist.	+ Lossless format + Can store images up to 32-bit colour depth; this makes it ideal for realistic images such as photographs + Very well-known (and established) file format compatible with most graphic packages – Very large image size; not ideal for downloading as part of a website – Image will lose detail when magnified, becoming blocky and unattractive requiring a process called 'anti-aliasing' to graduate the edges of shapes from foreground to background colour to create a smoother transition: Figure 24.25 Bitmap pixels and anti-aliasing – Bitmaps have to be a **rectangular shape**
Vector (.SVG)	Vector images are built from **combinations** of different basic **geometrical shapes** such as **points**, **lines**, **curves** and **polygons**. Because they are **mathematically 'described'**, they require very little memory. In addition, they do **not** lose any detail or become blocky when they are **scaled** or **rotated**. Common vector graphics packages include: ♦ CorelDRAW ♦ Adobe Photoshop ♦ Adobe Illustrator ♦ Inkscape.	+ Suffer **no loss of detail** when scaled + Image is **not limited** to being a rectangular shape as they have no background; they can therefore appear in front of other images, which is useful for innovative webpage design + Can be converted to a standard bitmap image through a process called 'rasterising'

Type of image	Essential facts	Scorecard
Vector (.SVG) *cont*.	The most common vector format (and extension) is the Scalable Vector Graphics (SVG) as **standardised** by the **W3C**. For more on SVG: **www.w3.org/Graphics/SVG/** An interesting web-based SVG drawing application can be found at: **www.amaltas.org/svgapp/**	– Images are generally not **100 per cent photorealistic** as they are limited to combinations of basic geometric shapes, although they **can** be used very creatively to create stunning illustrations: Figure 24.26
Bitmap (.JPG)	Developed as an alternative to GIF images, this is another type of bitmap format created by the **Joint Photographic Experts Group**. Unlike BMP files, JPEG files use a complex algorithm that **compresses** similarly coloured blocks in an image. Because of this JPEGs are generally considered to be **'lossy'** and can become **blocky** when the compression rate is set too **high**. The standard extensions for a jpeg file are **'.jpg'** or **'.jpeg'**. For more on **JPG**: **www.jpeg.org**	+ Have an **efficient** image size + **Very web friendly** as they are ideal for compressing photographic images + Works best on images with more than 256 (8-bit) colours – Is a **lossy format** so data (and therefore **image quality**) is removed during compression

Type of image	Essential facts	Scorecard
Bitmap (.GIF)	A **Graphics Interchange Format** file (correctly pronounced as 'jif'). GIFs are **compressed** using an algorithm called Lempel-Ziv-Welch (**LZW**, after its inventors) which is **lossless**. GIFs are the preferred file format for **line-based artwork** and **cartoons**; typically because a single image is limited to a maximum palette of **256 colours**, which also makes them a **poor choice** for **photographs**. The original format is called **GIF87A**, reflecting the year that they were introduced by internet service provider **Compuserve**. A further revision called **GIF89A**, adds support for **multiple frames** of **animation**; these are commonly known as 'animated GIFs'. **Disputes** over the use of the LZW compression algorithm led to the development of the **PNG format** as a **natural successor**.	+ Have an **efficient** image size + **Very web friendly** as they are ideal for compressing **line art** with sharp edges + **GIF89a** supports **animation** – this is a technique **widely used** on the internet. It also adds the ability to have **transparent backgrounds**, giving GIFs a **non-rectangular appearance** if desired + **Animated GIFs** can be created **online** (for free) at sites such as **Gickr**: **gickr.com/upload_files** – Maximum of **256-colour palette** makes them **unsuitable** for photographs but ideal for line art (e.g. cartoons) – A process called **'dithering'** is used to place two limited shades **together** to **fool the eye** into seeing a **blended** colour instead – **Modern** web pages tend to use .PNG images **instead**
Bitmap (.PNG)	The **Portable Network Graphics** file format was created by the **W3C** (World Wide Web Consortium) as a replacement for the GIF format, mainly as a result of the disputes over the LZW compression algorithm. PNG files are **lossless**, compressed bitmaps. Created in 1995, the PNG format is slowly becoming more popular for web images as it offers **similar features** to both GIF and JPG.	+ Have an **efficient** image size + Is a **lossless format** so no data (and therefore **image quality**) is removed during compression + Can store images up to 24-bit colour depth; this makes it an alternative to .JPG for **realistic images** such as photographs + Deals with sharp edges generally better than JPGs + PNGs can have **transparent** backgrounds – PNGs **don't** support animation – Software support for PNG can be patchy

Braincheck

Answer the following questions…

1 Name three bitmap file formats.
2 Name two forms of compression algorithm used in image formats.
3 Why was the Portable Network Graphics format created?
4 Name two advantages of a vector image.
5 What is the name of the most common vector graphics file format?
6 What is an animated GIF?
7 Give two disadvantages of a BMP file format.
8 Do PNG files support animation?
9 Vector images are converted to bitmap images through a process called…?
10 What is anti-aliasing?

How well did you do? See page 446 for the answers.

Activity

On a disk you own, create the following folder structure:

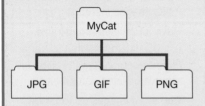

1 **Create** or **acquire** (see section 3.1) a simple picture of a **cat**.

2 **Save** the picture as **mycat.bmp** in the **MyCat folder.**

3 **Save** this picture in a number of different image formats (preferably JPG, GIF, PNG)

4 **Compare** the file sizes of each format. **Which** is more efficiently stored?

5 **Move** the files into their correct subfolder (e.g. mycat.jpg into the JPG subfolder).

6 **Rename** all graphic files from 'mycat' to 'yourcat', retaining the correct file extension in each case.

3 Use editing tools to edit and manipulate technically complex images

3.1 Graphic creation

When working with graphics, the verb '**acquire**' is used to describe the general act of **obtaining** a **digital** (i.e. computerised) **image** from another source (e.g. a photograph or printed image).

Common methods of acquiring images include:

◆ **screen capture.** Most operating systems (i.e. Microsoft Windows®, Apple Mac OS X, Linux distributions etc.) have the inbuilt facility to '**grab**' the current screen display and either copy to a **file** or the **memory-based clipboard facility** (for pasting into documents etc.).

In Windows:
  ◆ pressing the **Print Screen ('Prt Scr') key** will copy the entire screen display to the clipboard;
  ◆ pressing **Alt + Print Screen** key will copy the active window to the clipboard.

In Mac OS X:
  ◆ pressing **Command-Shift-3** will copy the entire screen display to a new image file;
  ◆ pressing **Command-Shift-4** will provide a cross-hair that allows the user to select which portions of the screen to copy to a new image file;
  ◆ pressing **Control-Command-Shift-3 (or 4)** is similar but sends the image to the clipboard.

In popular **Linux distributions** such as **Ubuntu** (www.ubuntu.com):
  ◆ pressing the **Print Screen ('Prt Scr') key** will copy the entire screen display to the clipboard;
  ◆ pressing **Alt + Print Screen** key will copy the active window to the clipboard;
  ◆ in Ubuntu's **GNOME** Windows Manager, use the **Applications → Accessories → Take Screenshot** menu option.

There are also many third-party utilities for providing more advanced screen capture facilities:
◆ **digital camera**
◆ **scanning**
◆ **downloading from the Internet** (but see section 4.3 regarding copyright concerns)
◆ **freehand drawing** using a mouse or graphics tablet and pen.

3.2 Tools and techniques

In order to complete your studies in this unit it is likely that you will be asked by your tutor to **demonstrate competence** in many different **tools** and **techniques** using a graphics manipulation package.

The following section demonstrates the **most common tools** and **techniques** in graphics manipulation using **The Gimp**.

Freehand draw

Freehand draw is often used to create new content, usually with either a **pencil** or **paintbrush tool**.

Common adjustments include: the width of the pencil, the shape of the brush and the foreground colour being used.

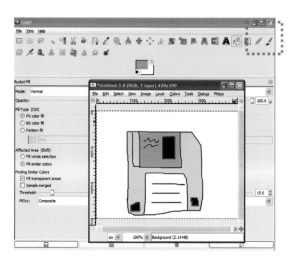

Figure 24.27 The Gimp's pencil and paintbrush tools are ringed

Rotate

Rotation will typically **transform** an image's orientation by either a **fixed** or **specified number of degrees clockwise** or **anti-clockwise**.

Rotation will alter the dimensions of the image (i.e. X becoming Y, Y becoming X).

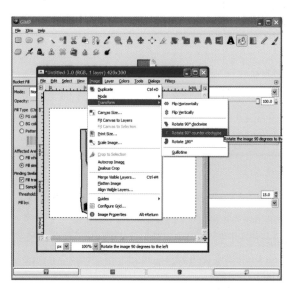

Figure 24.28 The Gimp's Transform menu, performing rotation

Flip

Another type of transformation is the **flip**.

Flip will invert the image either **horizontally** (mirroring) or **vertically** (inverting).

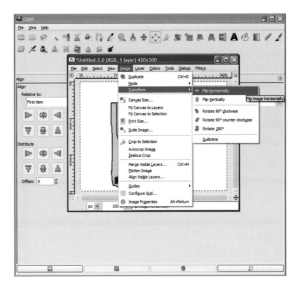

Figure 24.29 The Gimp's Transform menu, performing a flip

A **horizontal flip** is shown in Figure 24.30

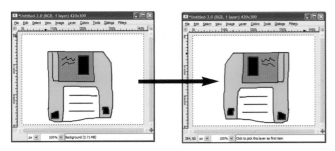

Figure 24.30 The Gimp performs a horizontal flip

A **vertical flip** is shown in Figure 24.31

A flip causes **no change** to the dimension of the image.

The flip can be **reversed** by either **undoing** the most recent transformation or simply **performing the same flip** again.

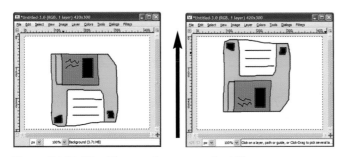

Figure 24.31 The Gimp performs a vertical flip

Crop

Cropping is the process of **trimming** (basically removing) **unwanted portions** of an image as required.

This is achieved by **altering** the **top, bottom, left** or **right borders** of the image, which also resizes the image.

If an original image is cropped and then **resaved**, the trimmed material is **lost** – be warned!

Some graphics manipulation tools have **specific crop tools**, others (such as The Gimp) **crop to the current selection** (often denoted by an **animated dotted line**).

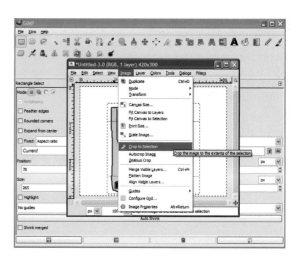

Figure 24.32 The Gimp's 'Crop to Selection' option

It is also common to find '**autocrop**' functions that remove **unwanted white space** from around the main image.

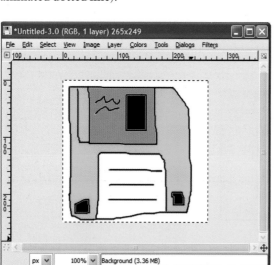

Figure 24.33 Disk image is cropped, removing unwanted white space

Resize

As the name suggests, resizing is the process of changing the **dimensions** of an image (its **height** and **width**).

The **mathematical relationship** between an image's height and width is called the '**aspect ratio**': usually it's **1:1**.

If an image is stretched horizontally **but not** vertically (or vice versa) the **aspect ratio changes** and the image becomes **distorted**.

Images are typically resized manually, by specifying **pixels/centimetres** or by using **percentages** (e.g. made '50% larger').

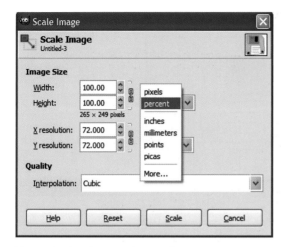

Figure 24.34 Resizing (scaling) options in The Gimp

This is also known as **scaling** an image.

Any change of image size will naturally affect the physical size of the file.

In the example shown in Figure 24.34, The Gimp has options for scaling the image by either adjusting the width and height or by adjusting the X and Y resolution.

The width and height can be **locked** (aspect ratio maintained) or **unlocked** (aspect ratio is not maintained and the image can be distorted). This is toggled on and off by the chain link icon.

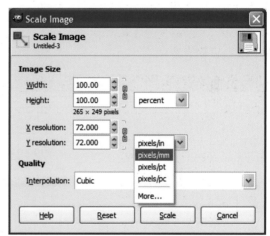

Figure 24.35 More resizing (scaling) options in The Gimp

Width and height can be altered using **pixels**, **percentage**, **inches**, **millimetres**, **points** and **picas**.

The X and Y resolution options can be similarly locked and have units measured in pixels per inch, pixels per millimetre, pixels per point and pixels per pica.

Inverting colour e.g. colour balance

The majority of graphics manipulation programs handle **colour** very well.

Common colour-based processes include:

◆ inverting colours (see Figure 24.36);

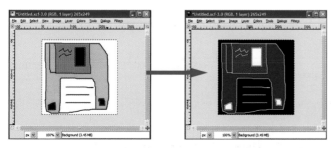

Figure 24.36 Inverting colours using The Gimp

- adjusting red, green and blue colour levels (see Figure 24.37);
- adjusting the brightness and contrast;
- posterising (reducing the number of colours in an image);
- desaturating (reducing colours to greyscales).

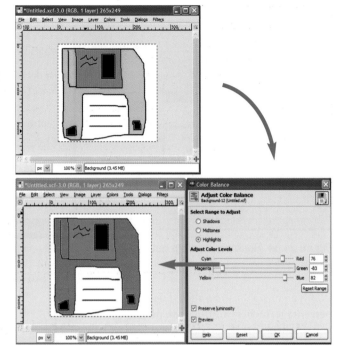

Figure 24.37 Adjusting the RGB colour balance

Key Terms

Colour depth is a term used to describe the **maximum number of colours** available for use in a computer image.

Colour depth works on a **binary** (base 2) principle.

For example **4-bit colour** would provide **16 different binary patterns** that each represent a different colour. An individual **pixel's** colour would be described by a **4-bit binary code**:

0000 0001 0010 0011 0100 0101 0110 0111

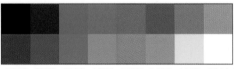

1000 1001 1010 1011 1100 1101 1110 1111 (white)

An image with **resolution** of **640 × 480 pixels** with **4-bit colour** would require **150** Kilobytes of storage.

So how is this worked out?

640 × 480 pixels = **307,200 pixels**
1 pixel = **4 bits**
307,200 × 4 = 1,228,800 bits
1,228,800 bits / **8** (bits per byte) = **153,600 bytes**
153,600 bytes / **1024** (bytes per Kilobyte) = **150 Kb**

Common colour depths include:

◆ **1-bit colour** (black and white, also known as 'monochrome')
◆ **8-bit colour** (256 colours)
◆ **16-bit colour** (65,536 colours, also known as 64K or **high colour**)
◆ **24-bit colour** (16,777,216 or 16.7 million colours, also known as **true colour**).

True colour is a combination of 24 bits (8 bits for **red**, 8 bits for **green** and 8 bits for **blue**) used to describe the **RGB** (**r**ed, **g**reen and **b**lue components) of any particular shade. Some file formats such as GIFs use 8 bits but the colours used are **not fixed**; they use their own 256-colour **palette**. This means different GIFs could potentially be using totally different 256-colour palettes!

Scientists believe that the **human eye** is only capable of distinguishing between approximately **10 million different shades**. In reality, this means that true colour displays are demonstrating ranges of colours that we can't discriminate between.

Many graphic manipulation programs let the artist change the colour depth **manually**. This can be particularly useful if images are required with **lower colour depths** (i.e. 256 colours) **without** altering the actual file format (e.g. converting from a 24-bit bitmap file to an 8-bit bitmap).

4 Create and modify graphic images to meet user requirements

4.1 User requirements

Your needs **as an artist** may be **completely different** to those of the client.

Key Terms

The **client** is best defined as the person or organisation who has requested your product and/or services. They may be paying or non-paying; your professional level of commitment to them should not alter.

The **target audience** is the specified **group** or **category** of persons who you want the product to **appeal** to. These may be known as the **users**.

The target audience might be based on geographic region, age, gender or economic status (this is known as the '**demographics**').

User needs

In order to create an image it is important to understand the **target audience's needs** as **communicated to you** by the client. This forms the **client brief**, e.g. a new letterhead for their printed communications or a new illustration on their website. In both cases, **their customers are the users**. User needs **may** be simple; e.g. the image should be **attractive**, **convey meaning** very **quickly** and be **immediately recognisable**.

Client requirements describe the **specific list of features** to which the image must conform:

◆ physical image size
◆ colour depth (how many colours used, see section 3.2)
◆ image resolution
◆ file size
◆ file format
◆ realistic, cartoon or impressionistic visual style
◆ colour schemes to use.

Constraints

While working on your brief you need to be aware of the **constraints** that are imposed upon you. These **limiting factors** often include:

◆ house style
◆ image size
◆ intended use (print, video, web page etc.)
◆ file size (especially for downloading)
◆ production costs – how time (and money) can be invested into completing the brief
◆ timescale – how quickly the brief must be completed
◆ output media (CD, paper, LCD, CRT etc.).

Case Study

Lee Office Supplies have asked **KAM (Kris Arts and Media)** to create a new **company logo** for them. Lee have been using the same logo for over ten years and have decided to relaunch their successful website with a **new corporate theme** (using mainly purple and gold).

Use a **graphics manipulation program** to **design a new logo** suitable for their website. You have been asked to ensure that the logo measures **no more** than **500 × 500 pixels** and is **below 80 Kilobytes** in **size**.

4.2 Reviewing

The **review process** is a vital stage of undertaking in any graphic design work.

Reviewing should **initially** be performed by the **designer**, ensuring that the image is thoroughly checked against the following criteria:

◆ If the image contains text has it been **proofread** for errors?
◆ Is the **physical size** of the image appropriate?
◆ Is the **file size** of the image appropriate (e.g. for **downloading**)?
◆ Is the **resolution** of the image appropriate?
◆ Is the **file format** as requested?
◆ Does the image **meet** the **user's requirements** and **client's expectations**?

Additionally the **client** will need to **approve** the image and may make **additional suggestions** for possible **modifications**.

As such the process of review is likely to be an **iterative process**, going **back and forth between** the client and the designer **until both parties** are happy with the final product.

When this occurs the client will formally **sign** the project off.

Activity

Design a suitable form that could be used to formally check an image when reviewing it.

Ideally this should include both user and client concerns.

Hint: A series of checkboxes could be ideal.

4.3 Legislation and guidelines

The basic purpose of **copyright** is to give the **creator** some say over how their **images** are used by **other people**.

Creative works (such as creating pictures and images) are often called '**intellectual property**' and just as other people should not help themselves to your physical possessions, neither should they use your intellectual property **without** your permission.

For images, copyright covers:

◆ the **copying** of an image
◆ the **modification** of an image
◆ the **distribution** of an image (including **electronic transmission**)
◆ **renting** or **lending** an image
◆ **public exhibition** of an image.

Copyright is **granted** by the creator for **specific** uses. For example, if copyright permission is given so that an image can be exhibited, it does not extend to making a copy or altering it.

Although legislation varies greatly from country to country and is therefore sometimes difficult to apply to resources that are available globally (such as graphics on web pages), the primary UK legislation is worth examining. For the UK this is the **UK Copyright Designs and Patents Act 1988.**

UK Copyright Designs and Patents Act 1988

In simple terms, a **copyright** is the **exclusive legal right** to **use** an **expression** or **idea** (known as '**intellectual property**' or **IP**); it is indicated by use of the familiar © **symbol**.

Generally this is displayed in the order of the copyright symbol, the year of first publication and then the name of the owner, e.g.

© 2008 M Fishpool

In British law, the **initial** owner of a copyright is **assumed** to be the **original creator** of the IP.

However, copyright ownership of any work that is created by an **employee** in the course of their **employment** is automatically transferred to their **employer**. This is usually part of the **employee's contract**.

In addition the **owner** of the work **may not** be the actual **copyright holder**, for example a letter sent from Person A to Person B is **owned** by Person B, but **cannot be published without the permission** of Person A (as the creator, **they** are the copyright **holder**).

The purpose of copyright is to **give** the **creator protection** against **unauthorised duplication** of their IP. IP covered by copyright can include such creative works as books, films, music, photographs, paintings and even computer software. When **copyright expires**, the IP is said to have **lapsed** into the **public domain.**

In 1996, the EU **extended** the period of copyright to **70 years after the year** in which the **creator died** (although there are some exceptions). This is often referred to as *post mortem auctoris* (PMA).

In the UK, a concept called '**fair dealing**' grants some **exclusions** to copyright for the purposes of **academic** or **review purposes**, particularly where the IP is used in a **non-profit making** venture (e.g. in education or for charity). As a matter of courtesy, an **acknowledgement** of the copyright holder's **permission** should be made publicly.

On the WWW, problems occur because it is easy for authors to 'borrow' images from another website in order to incorporate them into products. The use of stolen **images** is particularly awkward since a web-published photograph is typically the copyright of the photographer (or the company who paid them to take the photograph) and not the website owner, so should **not** be used **without** the owner's permission.

You should therefore be careful about borrowing images from other sources (printed or online) **without** checking their **permitted usage first**. A starting point for getting permission is the Copyright Clearance Centre (CCC) at **www.copyright.com**. If the owner is known, they can be contacted directly, **in writing**, explaining **exactly** how you would like to use the image – make sure you specify the **output media** and **method of distribution**.

Activity

Using an Internet-enabled web browser, visit the **United Kingdom's Intellectual Property Office (IPO) resources:**

http://www.ipo.gov.uk/whatis/whatis-copy.htm

http://www.ipo.gov.uk/copy.htm

Unit Links

Unit 24 is a **Specialist Unit** on the BTEC National Award.

It is also a **Specialist Unit** on the following BTEC National Certificate and Diploma routes:

IT and Business

Networking

Software Development

Systems Support

As such it has links to a number of other units, principally:

Unit 2 – Computer Systems

Unit 4 – IT Project

Unit 10 – Client-side Customisation of Web Pages

Unit 13 – Human–Computer Interaction

Unit 21 – Website Production and Management

Unit 26 – Computer Animation

Achieving success

In order to achieve each unit you will complete a series of coursework activities. Each time you hand in work, your tutor will return this to you with a record of your achievement.

This particular unit has 11 criteria to meet: 6 Pass, 3 Merit and 2 Distinction.

For a **Pass**:

   You must achieve **all** 6 Pass criteria.

For a **Merit**:

   You must achieve **all** 6 Pass and **all** 3 Merit criteria.

For a **Distinction**:

   You must achieve **all** 6 Pass, **all** 3 Merit **and** both Distinction criteria.

So that you can monitor your own progress and achievement in each unit, a recording grid has been provided (see below). The full version of this grid is also included on the companion CD.

Assignment	Assignments in this Unit			
	U24.01	U24.02	U24.03	U24.04
Referral				
Pass				
1				
2				
3				
4				
5				
6				
Merit				
1				
2				
3				
Distinction				
1				
2				

Help with assessment

The **Pass criteria** for this unit require a combination of different practical skills that test your understanding of the unit's theme. Practically you will be required to obtain images from a scanner and a digital camera, editing them to meet a users' needs. In addition you will be asked to create and review three original images against user's needs after defining client and user needs for each of them. There is also a need to understand the role of hardware in creating and editing images and you will be asked to suggest two hardware-related upgrades that will provide benefits to the designer.

For the **Merit criteria**, you are asked to make some comparisons between two hardware devices and two graphics manipulation programs; you need to focus on their limitations, especially when considering their ability to capture, manipulate and store graphic images. You will also be asked to practically demonstrate two advanced techniques in graphics manipulation (e.g. changing colour depth, file format etc.).

The **Distinction criteria** revolve around justification, albeit focusing on quite complex concerns: first, you must justify the manner in which your created images have met both client and user needs (e.g. the tools, formats, resolutions you have used); secondly, you must evaluate how developments in output media have impacted on the design and creation of graphic images.

Online resources on the CD

Key fact sheets
Electronic slide show of key points
Multiple choice self-test quiz

Further Reading

Goelker, K., 2006, *GIMP 2 for Photographers: Image Editing with Open Source Software*, Rocky Nook, ISBN 1933952032.

Peck, A., 2006, *Beginning GIMP: From Novice to Professional*, Apress, ISBN 1590595874.

Adobe Creative Team and Dennis, A., 2005, *Adobe Photoshop CS2*, Adobe Press, ISBN 0321321847.

Bain, S., 2004, *CorelDRAW 12*: *The Official Guide*, Osborne/McGraw-Hill US, ISBN 0072231912.

Kay, D. and Steinmetz, W., 2005, *Paint Shop Pro 9 for Dummies*, Hungry Minds Inc US, ISBN 0764579355.

Kelby, S., *The Photoshop Elements 4 Book for Digital Photographers*, New Riders, ISBN 0321384830.

Unit 25

Object-oriented Programming

Capsule view

This unit is best studied after Unit 18 – Principles of Software Design and Development. A 60-hour unit, it is designed to introduce the learner to the concepts and practicalities of working with object-oriented programming (often abbreviated to OOP).

As is usual with most Edexcel programming units, no particular programming language is specified, principally because it could be taught 100 per cent theoretically. However, the better approach that your tutor is most likely to adopt is to work through the concepts by creating practical examples to illustrate them. These days many programming languages follow the OOP paradigm; popular examples being C++, Sun's Java and Microsoft's C#® ('C sharp').

We have decided to focus on C#, a popular and industry-relevant language for the aspiring IT practitioner.

Learning aims

1 Understand the characteristics of object orientation.
2 Be able to use simple object-oriented design methods.
3 Be able to use object-oriented concepts to create and test an object-oriented program.

1 Understand the characteristics of object orientation

1.1 Characteristics of objects

In theory, everything that exists can be considered to be an **object**.

This includes **tangible** things (that can be **seen**, **heard** or **touched**) such as a cat, a drainpipe or a car, and **intangible** things that we know exist but do **not** have the same **physical nature**, e.g. a customer's bank account.

Although objects are clearly vital to the understanding of OOP, the most important concept to start with is that of the **class**.

The methods supported by a class are said to determine its **behaviour**.

For example we could consider a **car** as a type of class and associate the following **properties** and **methods:**

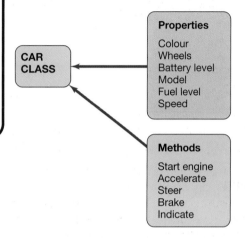

Figure 25.1 Relationship between class, properties and methods

And, of course, there are many more properties and methods that could be listed. In theory, all things that exist in the real world can be modelled in this way. Another point to make at this stage is that the properties and methods are often interrelated; they can **affect** each other, e.g.

| Accelarate **method** | affects | Speed **property** |

(The car gets **faster.**)

| Brake **method** | affects | Speed **property** |

(The car gets **slower.**)

And of course it works the other way too:

| Battery level **property** | affects | Start engine **method** |

(The car won't **start.**)

Although classes are our starting point, we have to move onto objects. An **object** is a **concrete** representation of a class. To make a simply analogy, if the class were a jelly mould, the object would be one of the jellies produced.

For the car class example, there are millions of car objects that exist in the real world. Each one has its **own** registration, model, battery-level, fuel level, speed etc. Equally, unless they are damaged, they can all start, steer, accelerate and brake with varying levels of success.

In Figure 25.2, we've **instantiated** three car objects from the car class.

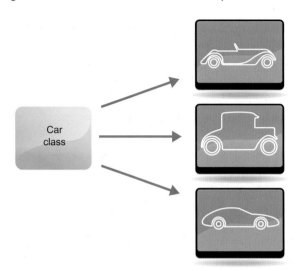

Figure 25.2 Instantiation of three car objects

Each car object would have its **own properties** and be **completely independent** of the others – but they could all be created from the **same** class.

In computing, objects are all around us – users, documents, windows, buttons, scroll bars etc. – these all exist as objects, each with their own peculiar **properties** but, equally, all sharing similar **functionality**.

Successful object-oriented programming relies on the knowledge and use of **pre-written classes** available in such languages as C++, Java and C# and also the programmer's ability to create **original** classes with new functionality.

Braincheck

Complete the gaps below...

1 Classes contain _____ and _____.
2 A class is used to build an _____.
3 The process of creating an _____ from a class is called _____.
4 A _____ is something 'about' the class.
5 A _____ is something the class can 'do'.
6 _____ is the term used to describe the grouping together of properties and the methods that process them.
7 C#, C++ and _____ are all OOP languages.

How well did you do? See page 447 for the answers.

Inheritance

Although a number of classes may be created from scratch, other classes may be built from earlier 'ancestor' or 'parent' classes. In object-oriented programming this concept is called **inheritance**.

Inheritance is a common object-oriented theme.

Inheritance works by a new class being **derived** from the design of a pre-existing class. The pre-existing class could exist in a **class library** (see section 3.3).

For example, if a class called 'Pop-up' was created that performed the basic actions of giving the user a message, it would be possible to **derive** from this a number of '**child**' classes that each built on this foundation to add features, e.g. a warning pop-up, a query pop-up, in the form of new **derived classes**.

In each case, the **basic behaviours** of the **parent** class ('Pop-up') would be **inherited**, for example the ability to display a pop-up window, a title, an icon, text message and an 'OK' button.

In addition, individualised behaviours unique to each class would be available, e.g.

'**User Warning**' class can also display a **warning icon**.

'**User Query**' class can also display a **question icon** and '**Yes**' and '**No**' buttons.

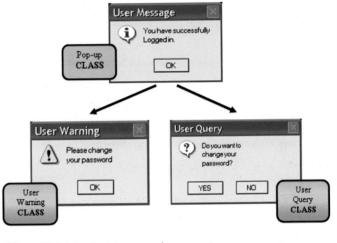

Figure 25.3 Inheritance example

Inheritance allows a software engineer to build on successful (and reliable) program code **foundations**, adding to existing classes to extend **functionality** and **flexibility**. More importantly, any **improvements** to the **performance** or **efficiency** of the parent (or 'base') class would also be inherited by the child classes.

Here is a simple **C# example** of inheritance at work.

```
namespace ConsoleApplication1
{
  class program
  {
    public class shape            // base or parent class
    {
      public void hello()
      {
        Console.WriteLine("I'm a new shape object.");
      }
    }
    public class circle : shape       // derived or child class
    {
      public void greeting()
      {
        Console.WriteLine("I'm a circle!");
      }
    }
    public static void Main()
```

```
    {
        circle myCircle = new circle(); // instantiate new child object
        myCircle.hello();               // call methods
        myCircle.greeting();
        Console.ReadLine();
    }
  }
}
```

The **output** from this inheritance example can be seen in Figure 25.4.

As you can see from the output, the '**mycircle**' object is created from the '**circle**' class, which in turn is derived from the parent '**shape**' class.

As a result, it has access to methods declared in its **own** class ('**greeting()**') and those inherited from its parent ('**hello()**').

The most important line of code in the program is:

Figure 25.4 Inheritance program's output

```
public class circle: shape
```

This line of code creates the '**child : parent**' class **link** that establishes **the inheritance relationship** between the two. In this case, 'circle' is the child, 'shape' is the parent.

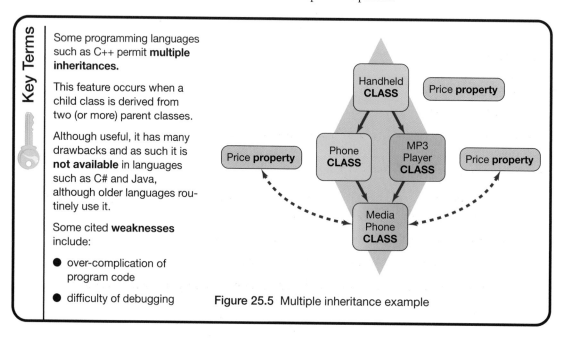

Key Terms

Some programming languages such as C++ permit **multiple inheritances**.

This feature occurs when a child class is derived from two (or more) parent classes.

Although useful, it has many drawbacks and as such it is **not available** in languages such as C# and Java, although older languages routinely use it.

Some cited **weaknesses** include:

● over-complication of program code

● difficulty of debugging

Figure 25.5 Multiple inheritance example

● being used to support poor initial object-oriented design

● creates the 'dreaded diamond' problem (see below).

The 'dreaded diamond' problem is an example of **ambiguity** and is named after the **pattern** formed by a new class that inherits from two classes with the same parent. In the example above, let's imagine that both the **phone** and **MP3 player** classes inherited from **handheld** a property called '**price**'.

Unfortunately as 'price' in inherited by both **phone** and **MP3 player**, which one would be used by the **Media Phone** class? Essentially the property would exist **twice**, both with the **same name**. C++ works around this by introducing the concept of a 'virtual class' but that's beyond the scope of this book.

Polymorphism

In terms of object-oriented programming, polymorphism is taken to mean the ability for a software engineer to use common program code to manipulate **data** of **different types** (e.g. numeric, character, string) in a **transparent** fashion.

In other words, the interface is **identical** (so the programmer doesn't have to worry about remembering lots of different methods) but the operations **behind** the interface are **data type-specific**.

Common OO concepts that demonstrate polymorphism include:

◆ abstract classes
◆ inheritance
◆ operator overloading
◆ method overriding
◆ method overloading.

A simple example of polymorphism using **method overloading** is shown in section 1.3.

Public and private classes

In OOP, **access modifiers** are used to **control** the way in which classes, methods or properties (the data) can be **used**. The term '**visibility**' is often used to describe this feature.

The exact modifier names can vary between different OO languages.

In terms of classes, these are typically either **public** or **private**.

Generally, classes are public (this is what you will see most often), although there are some occasions when a **nested class** (one class **inside** another) can be created:

```
public class outerClass
{
    // members go here
    private class innerClass
    {
        // members go here
    }
}
```

In this C# example, the 'innerClass' can **only** be accessed from the container class ('outerClass'); objects of 'innerClass' would be instantiated by methods of the 'outerClass'. This can be used as a form of **data hiding** but has a mixed reputation with some software engineers.

Public and private methods

Access modifiers can also be used to control the **availability** of the methods in a class.

Class methods can be either **public** (highlighted in green, and can be **freely accessed** from the main function) or **private** (highlighted in red, and be accessed only from within the **same** class).

The following C# example demonstrates this.

```csharp
// Simple quotation system
using System;
using System.Collections.Generic;
using System.Text;
namespace Quotation
{
    public class newQuote
    {
        private float Price;
        private int Qty;
        private float Total;
        private void calcTotal()                 // private method
        {
            Total = Price * Qty;
        }
        public void setPrice(float tempPrice)
        {
            Price = tempPrice;
        }
        public void setQty(int tempQty)
        {
            Qty = tempQty;
        }
        public float getTotal()
        {
            calcTotal();                         // call private method
            return Total;
        }
    }
    class Program
    {
        static void Main(string[] args)
        {
            newQuote Order1 = new newQuote();
            Order1.setPrice(10.0f);
            Order1.setQty(5);
            Console.Out.WriteLine("Order total = {0:F}", Order1.getTotal());
        }
    }
}
```

Any attempt to access the private method from the **main function** e.g. **Order1.calcTotal**() would result in the **compiler** generating an **error**:

```
'Quotation.newQuote.calcTotal()' is inaccessible due to its
protection level
```

Private methods **must** be accessed from other public methods in their **own class**.

1.2 Variables

Public and private variables

As with class members, the variables or properties in a class may be declared as either **public** or **private**. Again, this is simply a matter of **control** and **visibility**.

The concept of **data hiding** encourages an 'only if necessary' approach to making data **visible**. Private variables are **more secure** as they can only be accessed (and changed) by the methods of their **own** class. This helps **debugging** too by **limiting the scope** of where a variable could have been **incorrectly modified** – it's limited to its class.

```csharp
// Simple variable test
using System;
using System.Collections.Generic;
using System.Text;

namespace test
{
  public class test
  {
    private int a;
    public int b;

    public void seta(int tempa)
    {
      a = tempa;
    }

    public int geta()
    {
      return a;
    }
  }

  class Program
  {
    static void Main(string[] args)
    {
      test test1 = new test();

      test1.seta(10);
      test1.b = 20;

      Console.Out.WriteLine("a has the value " + test1.geta());
      Console.Out.WriteLine("b has the value " + test1.b);
```

```
        Console.ReadLine();
    }
  }
}
```

As you can see from the example above, public variables in a class can be **directly accessed** for reading and modification (which is dangerous so is highlighted in **red**). A better option is to use publicly available **accessor methods** such as '**seta**()' and '**geta**()' to deal with the private data (highlighted in **green**).

Many OOP languages use an additional modifier ('**protected**') to let a **derived** class have direct access to its **parent's** variables (even a child class can't access its parent's private variables).

1.3 Software engineering

Software engineering supports a methodical approach to problem solving and program implementation. In particular, a number of concepts are often talked about as being 'best practice'.

These include:

◆ modularity
◆ encapsulation (covered in section 1.1) which could be considered a form of modularity
◆ code reuse
◆ interfaces
◆ method overloading
◆ instance variables vs. class variables
◆ abstract classes.

Key Terms

Although **software engineer** is a title often used to describe a programmer, they are not really the same thing.

Growing in popularity during the late 1980s and early 1990s, the term **software engineering** was used to describe the approach to program development that adopted **industrial engineering concepts** and **practices**. This included a methodical, structured and disciplined approach to the creation, testing, documentation and maintenance of programmed solutions.

The term is defined fully by the **Institute of Electrical and Electronics Engineers'** (IEEE) Computer Society:

http://www.ieee.org/web/
publications/subscriptions/
prod/standards_overview.html

Modularity

In simple terms, modularity is a software engineering approach where a programmed solution consists of a number of self-contained – but connected – parcels of code called **modules**.

Typically, each module is designed to perform **one particular task** but can vary in their length and complexity.

Depending on the actual programming language used, modules are often called **functions**, **procedures** or **subroutines**. Even a **class** by its very nature could be seen as a form of modularity.

The **advantages** of a modular approach to software engineering are:

+ Breaking down **monolithic**, complex solutions (using a process called 'functional decomposition') into smaller modules often makes the development **easier** to **manage**.
+ Modules can be developed separately, by multiple programmers – this can **save** development **time**.
+ Modules can be **tested** separately.
+ Modules can be **debugged** (locating and fixing errors) separately.
+ Modules can be placed in a **library** and be used in multiple programs (they are **reusable**).

Module coupling versus module cohesion

Data can be passed between modules in the form of **parameters**.

This allows the developer to engineer a solution where data is securely controlled; a much better system than having (what is typically called) '**global**' data – data that is declared in a program and which can be altered by **any** line of code.

Coupling is a term used to describe data moving **between** modules.

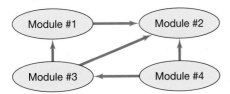

Figure 25.6 Coupling diagram (red arrows = data moving between modules)

In Figure 25.6, module #2 requires data from modules #1, #3 and #4 in order to perform its core task.

Cohesion is a term used to describe modules that **create** and **use** their **own** data.

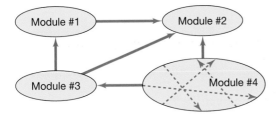

Figure 25.7 Cohesion diagram (blue arrows = data used within a module)

The preferred solution is **high-cohesion, low-coupling**; each module should be as **self-contained** and **self-sufficient** as possible.

Modularity is a key component of code reuse.

Code reuse

Robust and **reliable** software can be difficult to create. The ability for a software engineer to reuse code that has already been **written** and **tested** is, for some, the ultimate goal. Object-oriented programming has reusability as one of its primary **goals**: to create generic, reusable classes that can be used both **within** the application being worked upon and in **future** applications.

The use of a **pre-written software library**, where a developer can select an appropriate module and 'drop' it into their solution, has been a popular approach since the late 1960s. The obvious advantage is that it should **increase** development **speed** and, as a result, **decrease** development **time**.

Software engineers are often accused of '**reinventing the wheel**' – this is simply because developers often **prefer** to use their **own** code rather than reuse code written by another developer. This can be down to **personal pride**, a lack of **information** about **how** the module can be used or simply that they were **not aware** that a pre-existing routine was available that could save them time.

Applications are available that **measure** code reuse in a program using a series of different **metrics.**

Perhaps the most inefficient (and non-recommended) way of reusing code is to simply 'cut and paste' code from an older program. This has the possibility of including **older**, **inefficient code** than might be present in a **distributed** (and **approved**) software library.

Interfaces

As we have already seen, objects interact with each other (and the 'outside world') via their **methods**. It is because of this that we often call this interaction the '**interface**', much like the keyboard and mouse are interfaces between you and your computer system.

In simple terms, an interface is simply a **listing** of the methods that are **exposed** to the world.

However, unlike a class, the interface does **not state how** the methods **work** – there are no **mechanisms** (program code) within each method; the methods are **empty**, e.g. in C#:

```
interface myInterface
{
    void demoMethod();
}
```

Note here that the method within the interface named 'demoMethod' has no C# code to **implement** it. In some programming languages such empty methods can be called a 'stub'.

In order to implement the interface, a fully written class must be created, linked to the original interface. It is the **responsibility** of the class to implement all methods listed in the interface:

```
class fullClass : myInterface
{
    // Explicit interface member implementation:
    void myInterface.demoMethod()
    {
        // C# program code for the full implmentation goes here!
    }
}
```

Why use interfaces?

An interface allows us as software engineers to **define** the **behaviours** of a class without having to worry about **how** it will be achieved; this is clearly a useful **planning** tool.

The most obvious advantage therefore is that it allows us to **separate** the process of **definition** from **implementation**.

Method overloading

Method overloading is a programming **technique** which in some programming languages is one way that the object-oriented concept of **polymorphism** can be implemented.

Let's examine overloading by working through a typical C# example.

```
// overloading.cs

using System;
using System.Collections.Generic;
using System.Text;

namespace ConsoleApplication1
{
  class shape
  {
    private float area;

    // overloaded method, 1 parameter
    public void calcArea(float length)
    {
      area = length * length;        // area of square
    }
    // overloaded, 2 parameters
    public void calcArea(float length, float width)
    {
      area = length * width;         // area of rectangle
    }

    public float getArea()
    {
      return area;                   // return area data value
    }
  }
```

▶

```
class Program
{
  static void Main(string[] args)
  {
    shape square = new shape();      // instantiate 1st shape object
    shape rectangle = new shape();   // instantiate 2nd shape object

    square.calcArea(10);    // call calcarea method, 1 argument
    Console.Out.WriteLine("Area of square is {0:F}", square.getArea());
    rectangle.calcArea(5,4); // call calcarea method, 2 arguments
    Console.Out.WriteLine("Area of rectangle is {0:F}", rectangle.getArea());
    Console.ReadLine();
  }
}
}
```

Compiling this code and running it will give the output as shown in Figure 25.8.

In this example, the class called 'shape' has a **private property** called 'area' and **three methods**:

1 calcArea()
2 calcArea()
3 getArea()

You'll notice that there are two methods with the **exact same name** ('calcArea'). This is **intentional!** This is because it is an example of **method overloading**.

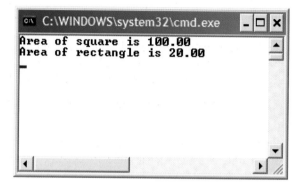

Figure 25.8 Output from C# overloading example

The two 'calcArea' methods are **differentiated** by their signature; they have **different parameters**. When an object calls its calcArea method, the **arguments supplied** are **compared** against each method's **parameter signature**.

```
square.calcArea(10);
                      public void calcArea(float length)
                      public void calcArea(float length, float width)
rectangle.calcArea(5,4);
                      public void calcArea(float length)
                      public void calcArea(float length, float width)
```

Once the parameter has been matched, the **appropriate version** of the overloaded method is executed. These are shown in **green**.

It is the **compiler's responsibility** to perform this task; if a method is used with arguments that do **not** match an appropriate overloaded signature within the class, a **compilation error** occurs and the program will **not** run, e.g.

```
cuboid.calcArea(5,4,6);
```

This would be **illegal** as **no** overloaded method of calcArea currently **has** three parameters (but it may in the future if the code is **suitably modified**, of course).

Instance variables vs. class variables

As we have seen, if a variable is declared inside a class, every object built (or instantiated) from that class comes complete with its **very own copy** of the variable. This is called an **instance variable**.

```
// overloading.cs
using System;
using System.Collections.Generic;
using System.Text;
namespace ConsoleApplication1
{
   class shape
   {
      private float area;
```

In this example, the variable called 'area' is an instance variable – a **copy** of it is made **every time** a shape object is instantiated. **Five shape objects** would create **five copies** of the variable; with each capable of holding a value **specific** to the shape in question (i.e. they can all be different).

This is important because changing the value of the area variable in **one** object will **not** change it in **any other**.

However, sometimes we want to create a variable that is **common** to all objects made from the **same** class. This is called a **class variable**. In C# this is achieved using the **static keyword**:

```
// overloading.cs
using System;
using System.Collections.Generic;
using System.Text;
namespace ConsoleApplication1
{
   class shape
   {
      static private string units = "cm";
      private float area;
```

In this example, **any object** created from the **shape class** will have the same value for the 'Units' variable: cm.

Abstract classes

An abstract class is one that is not **intended** to be used to make objects.

Usually abstract classes are **parent** (or base) classes that are used to build more detailed **derived classes** from which concrete objects can be suitably made MyPlayer.

Unlike an interface however, an abstract class **may** contain **some** basic functionality. The following extract shows the C# notation for creating an abstract class.

```
abstract class MP3player
{
    abstract public void Play();
    abstract public void Shuffle(int numberofsongs);
    abstract public void Listsongs();
}

class MyPlayer : MP3player
{
    override public void Play()
    {
        // code to play a song goes here.
    }
    override public void Shuffle(int numberofsongs)
    {
        // code to shuffle songs goes here.
    }
    override public void Listsongs()
    {
        // code to list songs goes here.
    }
}
```

Notice that because an abstract class's methods are **also** abstract, it is an absolute must for the concrete class to **override them** with properly implemented versions.

This is another example of polymorphism but, **unlike** method **overloading**, the implemented versions of each method must have the same **number** and **type** of arguments, and also have the same **return value**.

Braincheck

Fill in the spaces below:

1 The OO process of creating a new class from another is called ....?
2 The parent class is also called the .... class.
3 The child class is also called the .... class.
4 Deriving a class from multiple parent classes is called ....
5 A nested class is usually ....
6 .... means 'something that exists in many forms'; a core concept for object-oriented programming.
7 A class that is never instantiated into an object is called ....
8 Methods with a different number (or data type) of parameters are said to be ....
9 A method's arguments are also called its ....
10 Abstract methods must be .... by a derived class.
11 A property value common to all objects is a .... variable.
12 An .... is simply a listing of the methods which are exposed to the world.

How well did you do? See page 447 for the answers.

Activity

Frankoni T-shirts Ltd requires a program that will calculate the **production cost** and **projected sales price** of a designer T-shirt.

Frankoni buy blank shirts at the following rates: Small (£3 each), Medium (£4 each), Large (£6 each) and eXtra Large (£7 each).

It costs Frankoni £2.50 to print the customer's design on the T-shirt.

Frankoni aims to make a 30 per cent profit on each T-shirt sold.

Write an **object-oriented program in C#** that will calculate and output production costs, projected sales and the profit of selling a user a specified quantity of each type of T-shirt.

2 Use simple object-oriented design methods

2.1 Simple object-oriented design methods

The software engineer relies on a number of structured design methods and tools in order to **analyse** a real-world problem and **identify** potential classes (and their properties and methods) and how they **interact**.

Common design methods include:

◆ Class Responsibility Collaboration (CRC) cards
◆ UML (Unified Modelling Language) class diagrams

Let's examine each of these in a little more detail.

Class Responsibility Collaboration (CRC) cards

Introduced back in 1989 by Ward Cunningham and Kent Beck, the use of CRC cards is a simple idea that allows software engineers to analyse a real-world problem and discover the classes that can be used to represent its constituent parts, eventually creating a 'table-top' solution that can then be converted into workable OO program code using a selected language.

In CRC cards, a 4 × 6 inch **index card** is used to represent **each** class.

Here is a typical (unused) CRC card:

CRC cards are generated by a team of software engineers through **collaborative discussion**; generally more engineers will improve the opportunities for communication and the free exchange of ideas, with perhaps five representing the most effective number (any more and progress will often be impeded by arguments).

Class:	
Responsibilities:	Collaborators:
....	....
....	....
....	....
....	....
....	....

Initially, the software engineers will nominate a list of **candidate classes**.

Candidate classes can be identified by spotting **nouns** (i.e. 'things') in a problem scenario. These nouns often become the objects in the solution.

These candidates classes will then be developed and reviewed, some being **removed** (and literally ripped up!) through **duplication** or **merging** with, perhaps, some new ones being **added**. This is commonly known as an **iterative process** and often involves the team asking many 'what if...?' type questions to test their understanding of each class, what it needs to do and its relationship to others. The formal term for this is a '**use case**' – the act of **using the objects** to discover what is needed using real-world data and processes.

As a result, and for each class, a full CRC card must be generated detailing what it **knows** or **needs** to do (its **responsibilities**) and the other classes who can **help it** by **collaborating**. The responsibilities are usually identified by the use of **verbs** ('doing words') that exist in the problem scenario.

Classes are kept focused on one discrete 'job' by the very **physical limits** of the index card itself; if a card's responsibilities become **too complex** then perhaps the problem really needs to be **re-examined** and perhaps **multiple** (and **smaller**) classes created instead.

CRC cards scorecard

+ They are cheap!
+ CRC cards are physical so object-oriented systems can be **role-played** with them and the problem **better understood** by the all members of the team.
+ They are **highly portable** and require **no special equipment**; can be worked on anywhere.
+ They encourage **involvement** and **discussion** from all team members.
+ Any classes that are not needed can be **physically** (and permanently) **removed**.
+ They can be used to create OO solutions in many different target languages.
+ Each CRC card can also identify its **parent** (superclass) or **child** (subclass).
- They are often seen as an **informal** methodology, one that is best used in educational circles.

Case Study

The management at **Frankoni T-shirts** have asked a software engineering team to devise a simple object-oriented solution for their ordering system.

Let's analyse an **interview** with one of Frankoni's sales assistants.

We'll flag **nouns** in **blue** and **verbs** in **red**.

'When the customer places an order, the sales assistant records the products and quantities they want and their delivery address and method of payment. This is then used to generate a customer invoice.'

Candidate classes identified (from nouns):

◆ customer
◆ order
◆ sales assistant
◆ products
◆ quantities
◆ delivery address
◆ payment method
◆ customer invoice.

Obvious responsibilities identified (from verbs):

◆ record order details
◆ generate customer invoice.

At this point, the team would discuss each class, identifying new ones, merging existing ones until some agreement was reached. An obvious question would be to ask whether the delivery address is a class in its own right or a responsibility (and therefore a property) of the customer?

After discussion the team might create some CRC cards like so:

Class: Sales Assistant	
Responsibilities:	Collaborators:
Record order details.	Order, Customer, Products
Generate customer invoice.	Customer invoice
Know products.	Products

Class: Customer	
Responsibilities:	Collaborators:
Know products to order.	Sales Assistant, Products, Order
Know delivery address	Delivery Address, Order
Know method of payment	Payment Method, Order

Class: Order	
Responsibilities:	Collaborators:
Know products to order.	Sales Assistant, Products
Know delivery address	Delivery Address
Know method of payment	Payment Method
Know customer	Customer
Know order date	
Know order number	
Calculate Total	

The team would then continue to work through other classes, adding detail to each class through the identification of their responsibilities and collaborators. It is likely that there is no true, single answer to this scenario.

In theory, responsibilities would be broken down into methods and properties for coding purposes within each identified class.

CRC card activity

In a small team, examine a typical **ATM's** (**A**utomatic **T**eller **M**achine) basic components (e.g. keypad) and functions (e.g. withdraw cash) and decide on a list of suitable **candidate classes** that could be used to create an OO version.

Write out CRC cards for **each** of these classes, making note of the **responsibilities** and **collaborators** of each.

Software versions of CRC cards

Although CRC cards are at their best when a manual system is being used, a number of commercial software solutions are available that will help generate the CRC cards virtually.

QuickCRC from **Excel Software** is an example of such a tool (see Figure 25.9).

Excel's QuickCRC is available from http://www.excelsoftware.com/quickcrcwin.html.

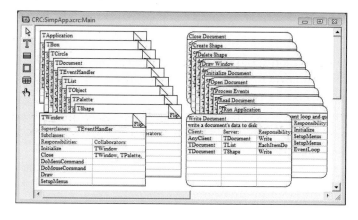

Figure 25.9 Excel Software's QuickCRC

UML (Unified Modelling Language) class diagrams

Unified Modelling Language (UML) is the industry-standard language for the specification, visualisation, implementation and documentation of new software systems. It is a tool used by software engineers to help them **simplify** the process of OO software design.

One element of UML is the **class diagram**, also known in earlier methodologies as the **class schema**.

A single class diagram is broken into three **compartments** showing (from a design perspective): the **name** of the class, its **properties** (**data**) and its **methods** (**functions**).

For example:

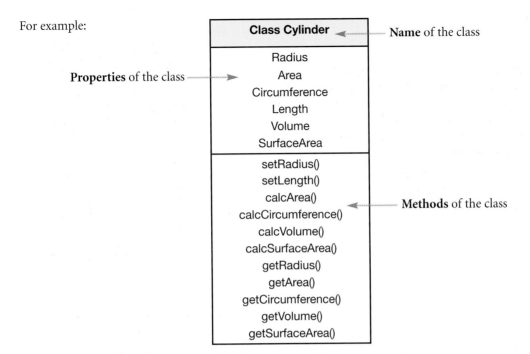

More **conceptual** versions of these diagrams simply state the method's purpose in English, e.g. 'Calculate the Circumference of the cylinder's cross-section' instead of the more program code-like 'CalcCircumference()'.

Class diagrams can also be used to show the **associations** between **different** classes; this is not dissimilar to the concepts of an **ERM** (Entity Relationship Model) as discussed in Unit 7 Systems Analysis and Design in the Core Text.

Building programs the object-oriented way

Using the schema and the cylinder class examples just descibed, design the following class:

Rectangle class

A rectangle has a **long side** and a **short side** measurement.

Its **perimeter** is measured by **adding up** the **two longest sides** and the **two shortest sides**.

It also has an **area** calculated by **multiplying** the length of the **longest side** by the length of the **shortest side**.

3 Use object-oriented concepts to create and test an object-oriented program

This section is ideally suited to a practical exploration of an object-oriented solution from **initial investigation** through to **final testing**.

The following case study has been colour highlighted with identified nouns and verbs.

Case Study

Kris Arts and Media (KAM) require a new application that will calculate the cost of producing a new computer graphic that has been ordered by a customer. Costs are calculated based on the graphic's:

- **resolution** (pixels across × pixels down)
- **colour depth** (how many colours used in printing)
- **number of copies** required
- **paper stock** used (matt, gloss, photographic).

The customer supplies their name and email and is sent a quote for the graphic.

3.1 Classes

The initial step is to identify **possible classes** and how they are **linked**.

Candidate classes identified (from nouns):

- cost
- new computer graphic
- resolution
- colour depth
- copies
- paper stock
- customer name
- customer email
- quote.

Obvious responsibilities identified (from verbs):

- customer orders
- produce new graphic
- calculate order cost
- send quote.

Revising these candidate classes, we can **reduce** the number of classes to just:

- new computer graphic
- customer
- quote.

This is simply because many of the other nouns identified are actually **properties** of the **new graphic** (e.g. colour depth), **the customer** (e.g. name) or **the quote** (e.g. cost).

In addition, the responsibilities 'produce new graphic' and 'send quote' may be considered outside of the scope of the problem as they are **physical actions** rather than the processing required to get the order information and calculate the cost.

Properties and methods

The next step is to identify the **properties** (or **attributes**) and **methods** of each class we've identified.

Class: `Graphic`

Responsibilities:	Collaborators:
Know resolution	Customer, Quote
Know colour depth	Customer, Quote
Know number of copies required	Customer, Quote
Know paper required	Customer, Quote

CRC cards could be used to help us plan these, e.g.

Class: `Quote`

Responsibilities:	Collaborators:
Know graphic details	Graphic
Know cost of graphic	
Calculate cost	Graphic
Know customer details	Customer

Class: `Customer`

Responsibilities:	Collaborators:
Know name	Quote
Know email address	Quote
Know graphic requirements	Graphic

From here it is a short step to generating some class diagrams with some properties and more formal method names.

Class Graphic
graphicPixelsX graphicPixelsY graphicResolution colourDepth numberCopies paperRequired
setGraphicPixelsX() getGraphicPixelsX() setGraphicPixelsY() getGraphicPixelsY() calculateGraphicResolution() getGraphicResolution() setColourDepth() getColourDepth() setNumberCopies() getNumberCopies() setPaperRequired() getPaperRequired()

Class Quote
quoteCost
getGraphicDetails() calculateQuoteCost() getQuoteCost() getCustomerDetails()

Class Customer
customerName emailAddress
setCustomerName() getCustomerName() setEmailAddress() getEmailAddress() setGraphicRequirements()

Control scope of attributes and methods

As we've already seen, both methods and properties can be **public** or **private**.

Generally, methods are public while the properties in a class are private, protecting them from unauthorised alteration.

Let's revisit the class diagrams and denote which methods and properties are **public** (green) and **private** (red).

Class Graphic
graphicPixelsX
graphicPixelsY
graphicResolution
colourDepth
numberCopies
paperRequired
setGraphicPixelsX()
getGraphicPixelsX()
setGraphicPixelsY()
getGraphicPixelsY()
calculateGraphicResolution()
getGraphicResolution()
setColourDepth()
getColourDepth()
setNumberCopies()
getNumberCopies()
setPaperRequired()
getPaperRequired()

Class Quote
quoteCost
getGraphicDetails()
calculateQuoteCost()
getQuoteCost()
getCustomerDetails()

Class Customer
customerName
emailAddress
setCustomerName()
getCustomerName()
setEmailAddress()
getEmailAddress()
setGraphicRequirements()

Some additional information from KAM is needed to calculate the quotes correctly.

Colour depth	Price per page
Monochrome	2p
16 colours	4p
256 colours	6p
65,536 colours	8p
True colours	10p

Paper Stock	Price per page
Matt	5p
Gloss	7p
Photographic	9p

Resolution	Price per page
Small (< 1,048,576 pixels)	£2
Medium (< 2,097,152 pixels)	£4
Larger (2,097,152 pixels or more)	£8

Once the methods have been decided upon, it is necessary to work out the **functionality** of each (what they do in greater detail) and how they work with **other objects** and **their properties**.

A C# solution for this problem follows.

C# solution

```
//KAMquotes.cs
using System;
using System.Collections.Generic;
using System.Text;

namespace KAMquotes
{
  class graphic
  {
    private int graphicPixelsX;
    private int graphicPixelsY;
    private int graphicResolution;
    private int colourDepth;
    private int numberCopies;
    private int paperRequired;

    public void setGraphicPixelsX()
    {
      Console.Out.WriteLine("Image size (pixels X)?");
      graphicPixelsX = int.Parse(Console.ReadLine());
    }
    public int getGraphicPixelsX()
    {
      return graphicPixelsX;
    }
    public void setGraphicPixelsY()
    {
      Console.Out.WriteLine("Image size (pixels Y)?");
      graphicPixelsY = int.Parse(Console.ReadLine());
    }
    public int getGraphicPixelsY()
    {
      return graphicPixelsY;
    }
    public void calculateGraphicResolution()
    {
      graphicResolution = graphicPixelsX * graphicPixelsY;
    }
    public int getGraphicResolution()
    {
      return graphicResolution;
    }
    public void setColourDepth()
    {
      Console.Out.WriteLine("Select colour depth required");
      Console.Out.WriteLine("1 - Monochrome");
      Console.Out.WriteLine("2 - 16 colours");
      Console.Out.WriteLine("3 - 256 colours");
      Console.Out.WriteLine("4 - 65536 colours");
      Console.Out.WriteLine("5 - True colour");
      colourDepth = int.Parse(Console.ReadLine());
    }

    public int getColourDepth()
```

▶

```
    {
      return colourDepth;
    }
    public void setNumberCopies()
    {
      Console.Out.WriteLine("How many copies required?");
      numberCopies = int.Parse(Console.ReadLine());
    }
    public int getNumberCopies()
    {
      return numberCopies;
    }
    public void setPaperRequired()
    {
      Console.Out.WriteLine("Select Paper type required");
      Console.Out.WriteLine("1 - Matt");
      Console.Out.WriteLine("2 - Gloss");
      Console.Out.WriteLine("3 - Photographic");
      paperRequired = int.Parse(Console.ReadLine());
    }
    public int getPaperRequired()
    {
      return paperRequired;
    }
}
class quote
{
    private float quoteCost;

    public string getGraphicDetails(ref graphic customerGraphic)
    {
        String tempString;
        tempString = "Customer wants:" + customerGraphic.getNumberCopies() + "
                    copies of ";
        tempString = tempString + "an image measuring " + customer-
                    Graphic.getGraphicPixelsX();
        tempString = tempString + " pixels across by " + customer-
                    Graphic.getGraphicPixelsY();
        tempString = tempString + " pixels down (totalling " + customer-
                    Graphic.getGraphicResolution();
        tempString = tempString + " pixels) in";
        switch (customerGraphic.getColourDepth())
        {
          case 1: tempString = tempString + " monochrome.";
                break;
          case 2: tempString = tempString + " 16 colours.";
                break;
          case 3: tempString = tempString + " 256 colours.";
                break;
          case 4: tempString = tempString + " 65536 colours.";
                break;
          case 5: tempString = tempString + " True colours.";
                break;
        }

        tempString = tempString + "\nIt will be printed on ";
        switch (customerGraphic.getPaperRequired())
```

```
      {
        case 1: tempString = tempString + " matt stock.";
                break;
        case 2: tempString = tempString + " gloss stock.";
                break;
        case 3: tempString = tempString + " photographic stock.";
                break;
      }
      return tempString;
}

public void calculateQuoteCost(ref graphic customerGraphic)
{
  switch (customerGraphic.getColourDepth())
  {
    case 1: quoteCost = customerGraphic.getNumberCopies()*0.02f;
            break;
    case 2: quoteCost = customerGraphic.getNumberCopies()*0.04f;
            break;
    case 3: quoteCost = customerGraphic.getNumberCopies()*0.06f;
            break;
    case 4: quoteCost = customerGraphic.getNumberCopies()*0.08f;
            break;
    case 5: quoteCost = customerGraphic.getNumberCopies()*0.10f;
            break;
  }
  switch (customerGraphic.getPaperRequired())
  {
    case 1: quoteCost = quoteCost + customerGraphic.getNumberCopies() * 0.05f;
            break;
    case 2: quoteCost = quoteCost + customerGraphic.getNumberCopies() * 0.07f;
            break;
    case 3: quoteCost = quoteCost + customerGraphic.getNumberCopies() * 0.09f;
            break;
  }
  if (customerGraphic.getGraphicResolution() < 1048576)
    quoteCost=quoteCost+customerGraphic.getNumberCopies() *2;
  else
    if (customerGraphic.getGraphicResolution() < 2097152)
      quoteCost=quoteCost+customerGraphic.getNumberCopies() *4;
    else
      quoteCost=quoteCost+customerGraphic.getNumberCopies() *8;
}

public float getQuoteCost()
{
  return quoteCost;
}
public string getCustomerDetails(ref customer customerDetails)
{
  String tempString;
  tempString = "Customer name: " + customerDetails.getCustomerName() + "\n";
  tempString = tempString + "Customer email: " + customerDetails.
                getEmailAddress() +"\n";
  return tempString;
}
```

```
    }
class customer
{
   private string customerName;
   private string emailAddress;
   public void setCustomerName()
   {
      Console.Out.WriteLine("Customer name?");
      customerName = Console.ReadLine();
   }
   public string getCustomerName()
   {
      return customerName;
   }
   public void setEmailAddress()
   {
      Console.Out.WriteLine("Customer's email?");
      emailAddress = Console.ReadLine();
   }
   public string getEmailAddress()
   {
      return emailAddress;
   }
   public void setGraphicRequirements(ref graphic customerGraphic)
   {
      customerGraphic.setGraphicPixelsX();
      customerGraphic.setGraphicPixelsY();
      customerGraphic.calculateGraphicResolution();
      customerGraphic.setColourDepth();
      customerGraphic.setNumberCopies();
      customerGraphic.setPaperRequired();
   }
}

class Program
{
   static void Main(string[] args)
   {
      quote newQuote = new quote();
      graphic newGraphic = new graphic();
      customer newCustomer = new customer();

      Console.Out.WriteLine("KAM Ordering system\n");
      newCustomer.setCustomerName();
      newCustomer.setEmailAddress();
      newCustomer.setGraphicRequirements(ref newGraphic);
      Console.Out.WriteLine(newQuote.getCustomerDetails(ref newCustomer));
      Console.Out.WriteLine(newQuote.getGraphicDetails(ref newGraphic));
      newQuote.calculateQuoteCost(ref newGraphic);
      Console.Out.WriteLine("\nQuote total is: £{0:F}", newQuote.getQuoteCost());

      Console.ReadLine();
   }
}
}
```

C# OO issues

In some methods (e.g. setGraphicRequirements(), calculateQuoteCost() etc.) **an object** is passed as a parameter.

When an object is passed to a method, the method **only** has access to **a copy**. Any changes made to the object will only **change the copy** therefore, **not** the original.

This is called '**pass by value**', e.g.

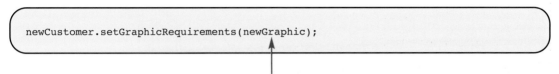

```
newCustomer.setGraphicRequirements(newGraphic);
```

A copy of this object will be passed into the method

Sometimes, however, we want these changes to become **permanent**.

In C# we can make permanent changes to an object by passing it '**by reference**'. In order to do this, the '**ref**' keyword is used to send the original object into the method (not a copy).

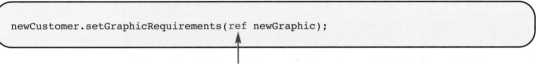

```
newCustomer.setGraphicRequirements(ref newGraphic);
```

The original object will be passed into the method.

The actual notation for 'pass by value' and 'pass by reference' will vary from one OO language to another.

Testing the solution

Although testing is covered in much more detail in section 3.4, a simple **fit-for-purpose** test of basic functionality can be performed by entering some **realistic** test data. Let's select some test data from a KAM customer's email.

To: KAMorders
From: Mr Smith smith@smithhome.co.uk.
I would like to order 400 copies of my company logo. It needs to be printed in 256 colours on photographic stock. The reference sketch I've attached for you to recreate is about 1024 x 768 pixels according to my paint program. Looking forward to a quote! Kind regards Jim
Attachment: Mylogo.gif

A **manual calculation** reveals that this order should cost £860.00.

This is worked out by:

> **Each page** is photographic stock (9p) + resolution of 1024 × 768 = 786,432 pixels (£2) + 256 colours (6p) = £2.15
> **400 pages** × £2.15 = **£860**

Let's enter the values into the OO programmed solution and compare.

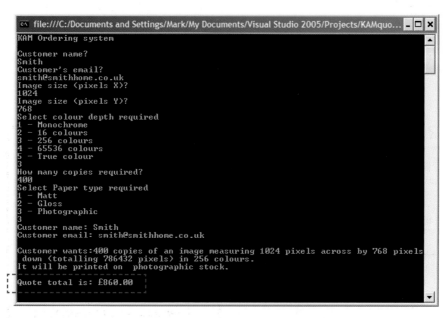

Figure 25.10 Output from C# KAM case study test program

The verdict? It has given an **accurate result**. But as noted, **further testing** is needed.

Alternative approach

It is possible to examine the KAM problem another way, introducing more new OO concepts called **association** and **aggregation**.

In the previous KAM solution, all three classes (customer, quote, graphic) are used to create objects (newCustomer, newQuote and newGraphic) which have one-to-one **associations** with each other.

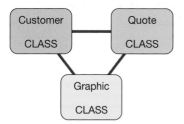

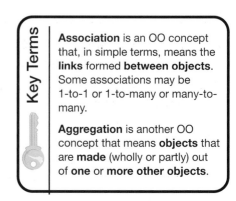

Key Terms

Association is an OO concept that, in simple terms, means the **links** formed **between objects**. Some associations may be 1-to-1 or 1-to-many or many-to-many.

Aggregation is another OO concept that means **objects** that are **made** (wholly or partly) out of **one** or **more other objects**.

An alternative approach would have been to use the **Quote class** as the '**containment**' for the **Customer** and **Graphic classes**. This would have created an **aggregation of classes** inside Quote.

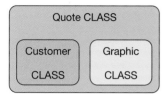

This would have certainly modified the approach to the solution. The Quote class is the **key class**, having need of the other two classes in order to function properly. This aggregation method would have effectively made the aggregated classes **almost invisible** to the main( ) method.

3.2 Objects
Constructors and destructors

In object-oriented programming, **constructors** and **destructors** represent two very important **methods** that exist in a class.

Here is a typical constructor in C#:

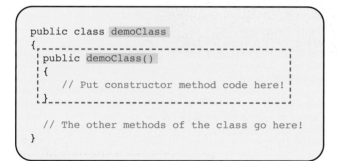

You may have noticed that previous C# examples have **not** made use of a constructor and yet they have still compiled and executed as expected.

How? Well, the simple answer is that C# (like a number of object-oriented programming languages) has a **default constructor** feature.

Constructor overloading

As with any other method, the constructor may be **overloaded**. This would allow its object to be instantiated using a different number (and type) of arguments if necessary.

Here is an example of an overloaded constructor in C#:

```csharp
// Overloaded constructor example
using System;
using System.Collections.Generic;
using System.Text;

namespace Constructortest
{
  public class demoClass
  {
    String message;

    public demoClass()    // no parameter
    {
      message = "***Not Known***";
    }

    public demoClass(String newtext) // overloaded, one parameter
    {
      message = newtext;
    }

    public String getMessage()
    {
      return message;
    }

    // The other methods of the class go here!
  }

  class Program
  {
    static void Main(string[] args)
    {
      demoClass Test1 = new demoClass();
      demoClass Test2 = new demoClass("Hello!");

      Console.WriteLine(Test1.getMessage());
      Console.WriteLine(Test2.getMessage());

      Console.ReadLine();
    }
  }
}
```

As you can see, the two objects ('Test1' and 'Test2') have different 'message' values. 'Test1' has a temporary string, while 'Test2' uses the string passed in from the overloaded constructor.

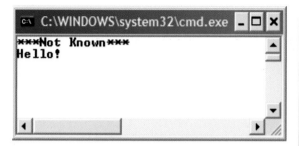

Figure 25.11 Output from C# constructing overloading example

Here is a typical destructor in C#:

```
public class demoClass
{
  public demoClass()
  {
    // Put constructor method code here!
  }

  public ~demoClass()
  {
    // Put destructor method code here!
  }

  // The other methods of the class go here!
}
```

In C#, destructors are called as a part of an **automatic process** called **garbage collection**; this exists in many modern programming languages (e.g. C# and Java).

Garbage collection ensures that the RAM used by objects is **freed** and returned to the 'free' memory heap, making it available for re-use by other programs. This is really a bit like RAM recycling.

When this process **doesn't** work properly, programs can cause '**memory leaks**'. The end result of this is the pool of available RAM getting smaller and smaller until '**out of memory**' messages appear courtesy of the operating system (it may even crash or start to respond very slowly to user input).

If you have experienced such a message before, a faulty program may be the root cause. This was often caused by older programming languages that required the programmer to **manually deallocate** the memory that they had used when the data was no longer required. Unfortunately, they often forgot.

3.3 Pre-defined

As we have seen, classes don't **need** to be written from scratch. Although inheritance remains a popular OO tool, the use of **pre-defined classes** can be quite productive.

Class libraries are generally available as part of the selected programming language, for example C# and Java both provide extensive class libraries that can be used to build comprehensive OO solutions.

In C#, software engineers have access to a very comprehensive library of system classes (as part of the Microsoft.NET **SDK** – **s**oftware **d**evelopment **k**it) which can be used to build any number of Microsoft Windows® applications both quickly and reliably.

Case Study

C# class library example – working with files

The following example shows how to use the C# library of pre-written classes to **display files** in a **selected folder**.

It uses a number of different System **IO** (**I**nput **O**utput) classes. These are highlighted thus:

Blue: System IO classes

Green: System IO class methods

Orange: System IO class properties

Here is the C# program code:

```csharp
// A simple C# class library example.

using System;

using System.IO;

namespace mydir
{
  public class FileLength
  {
    public static void Main()
    {
      String testFolder = "C:/Documents and Settings/Mark/Desktop/marktest";

      // Create a DirectoryInfo object using the correct folder
      DirectoryInfo myFolder = new DirectoryInfo(testFolder);

      // Get a reference to each file in that folder
      FileInfo[] myFiles = myFolder.GetFiles();

      // Display the names and sizes of the files
      Console.WriteLine("Folder \"{0}\" has these files:\n", myFolder.Name);

      foreach (FileInfo file in myFiles) // loop each file in the folder
      {
        Console.WriteLine("{0,-35} {1,-6} bytes.", file.Name, file.Length);
      }

      Console.WriteLine("\nPress any key to continue.");
      Console.ReadLine();
    }
  }
}
```

> This C# namespace must be added to import the appropriate file-based C# classes shown in blue.

Figure 25.12 shows our test folder as shown in Microsoft Windows Explorer®

and through the compiled C# program's output:

Figure 25.12 Explorer view of 'C:\Documents and Settings\Mark\Desktop\marktest'

Figure 25.13 C# program's view of 'C:/Documents and Settings/Mark/Desktop/marktest'

As with many modern **IDEs** (integrated development environment) that the modern software engineer uses, Microsoft Visual C# will make suggestions for **code completion** depending on the preceding **object type**. This makes working with class libraries even easier.

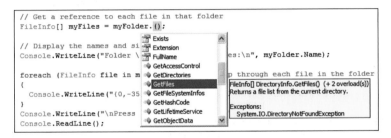

Figure 25.14 C# code completion showing available properties and methods with Intellisense™

Working with class libraries

1 Use the C# class library to display the **current date** and **time**.

2 Use the C# class library to **draw** a '**smiley**' like the one below.

Hint: You'll have to browse through the **C# Help system** to find notes on the various classes you need.

3.4 Testing

Testing is a vital aspect of any object-oriented solution.

A number of processes can be used to **improve** and **simplify** the testing process. Again, although these examples are specific to C#, the principles should apply to any modern OO language.

Indentation and whitespace

As you may have noticed, the code samples in this book use a form of **indentation** (moving code from the **left** margin using whitespace) to illustrate the **underlying structure** of the program.

The following short C# program has **no** indentation.

```
using System;
using System.Collections.Generic;
using System.Text;
namespace indentation_test
{
class Program
{
static void Main(string[] args)
{
int [] numbers;
numbers = new int[10] {3,4,6,-7,3,4,3,2,1,0};
int temp;
for (int outer=0;outer<10;outer++)
{
for (int inner=0;inner<9;inner++)
{
if (numbers[inner]<numbers[inner+1])
{
temp = numbers[inner];
numbers[inner] = numbers[inner+1];
numbers[inner+1] = temp;
}
}
}
for (int output=0;output<10;output++)
{
Console.WriteLine("Data {0} is {1}", output, numbers[output]);
}
Console.ReadLine();
}
}
}
```

This is often called 'flat' code and, as you can see, when shown in this format it's not that easy to tell what the program is attempting to do.

Here's the same program but with an **indentation** of **two whitespace characters**.

```
using System;
using System.Collections.Generic;
using System.Text;

namespace indentation_test
{
  class Program
  {
    static void Main(string[] args)
    {
      int [] numbers;
      numbers = new int[10] {3,4,6,-7,3,4,3,2,1,0};
      int temp;
      for (int outer=0;outer<10;outer++)
      {
        for (int inner=0;inner<9;inner++)
        {
          if (numbers[inner]<numbers[inner+1])
          {
            temp = numbers[inner];
            numbers[inner] = numbers[inner+1];
            numbers[inner+1] = temp;
          }
        }
      }
      for (int output=0;output<10;output++)
      {
        Console.WriteLine("Data {0} is {1}", output, numbers[output]);
      }
      Console.ReadLine();
    }
  }
}
```

Hopefully this is a little more informative. It certainly should be clear to the reader that the program has a **nested for loop** and an **if statement**.

Indentation **isn't mandatory** and has **no effect** on compilation, neither are there any **fixed standards** to the number of 'spaces' that should be used. Some programmers prefer two, four or even six spaces. What **is** important is that it's **consistent** (i.e. two all the time or four all the time) throughout the entire program and that it matches any **organisational standards** that have been laid down.

Another aspect that should be remembered here is that it is **better** to use the **Tab key** rather than using the spacebar. Why? Well, the tab key can be set within the IDE to represent any number of spaces but will only actually store one character (the tab character).
This results in:

+ less typing for the programmer
+ a smaller file size
+ tabs can be instantly changed by another programmer through the IDE menu to their own preference.

Additional whitespace can be used in the form of **blank lines** that are used to separate different sections of the program code (e.g. separating different classes or class methods).

Commenting code

Commenting code is, for some programmers, a laborious and boring process. For those reading code they have **not** written, it provides an **invaluable** peek into the mind of the author and the **inner workings** of the program itself (especially when the code is complex).

Good comments do **not** explain the syntax (rules of the language) but rather the **action** that the code is performing in the **context** of the solution.

As with other modern programming languages, C# supports a number of different commenting formats and these are generally used in a number of different ways.

Multiple-line (or block) comments

Used to comment a block of text or to comment-out (i.e. make the compiler ignore) a section of program code. The block starts with a '/*' and ends with a '*/'.

```
/*  This is a multiple line comment.
 *
 *  Modern programmers don't tend
 *  to use this very much as there
 *  are better techniques available.
 */
```

Block comments like these do stand out in a program and are therefore easily recognised by a programmer as they scan through the code.

Single-line comments

These are used to:

◆ Comment the **end** of a line of code (usually a variable):

```
int password;    // stores the user generated password
```

◆ Comment **before** a section of code to explain its purpose:

```
// The following section of code will verify the ISBN
:
:
```

◆ Or even **comment-out** a **bugged** line of code:

```
Console.WriteLine("Press the return key");
// Console.ReadLn();
```

Let's revisit the mysterious program which we've indented, but this time, let's add some meaningful **multi-line** and **single-line** comments.

```
/* Program.cs
 *
 * indentation test using a simple bubble sort
 * to sort the data into descending order.
 *
 * Author: M Fishpool
 * Date: January 2008
 *
 */

using System;
using System.Collections.Generic;
using System.Text;

namespace indentation_test
{
  class Program
  {
    static void Main(string[] args)
    {
      int [] numbers;      // declaration of array of integers
      numbers = new int[10] {3,4,6,-7,3,4,3,2,1,0};  // initialise array
      int temp;                              // temporary used in swap
      for (int outer=0;outer<10;outer++)     // perform loop 10 times
      {
        for (int inner=0;inner<9;inner++)          // walk along array
        {
          if (numbers[inner]<numbers[inner+1]) // compare elements for swap
          {
            temp = numbers[inner];             // perform swap of two elements
            numbers[inner] = numbers[inner+1];
            numbers[inner+1] = temp;
          }
        }
      }

      for (int output=0;output<10;output++)    // walk along the sorted array
      {
        // output each element
        Console.WriteLine("Data {0} is {1}", output, numbers[output]);
      }

      Console.ReadLine();                       // wait for a keypress.
    }
  }
}
```

Documentation comments

In common with a number of modern programming languages, C# can generate HTML documentation from specially coded comments.

This allows the software engineer to automatically create **hyperlinked documentation** as part of the development process. C# uses XML (e**X**tensible **M**arkup **L**anguage) comments for this purpose.

This is achieved using '///' comments with specific XML tags such as <**summary**>, <**param**> and <**seealso**>.

A sample C# program using XML documentation comments:

```csharp
using System;
using System.Collections.Generic;
using System.Text;

namespace bankaccount
{
  class Program
  {
    /// <summary>
    /// This class creates a bank account with operations
    /// to deposit and withdraw sums.
    /// </summary>
    class bankaccount
    {
      /// <summary>
      /// Store for the account holder's name property</summary>
      string accountHolder;

      /// <summary>
      /// Store for the account holder's balance property</summary>
      float balance;

      /// <summary>
      /// Store for the account holder's overdraft property</summary>
      float overdraft;

      /// <summary>
      /// The class constructor, needs 3 parameters. </summary>
      /// <param name="n">A float representing the starting balance</param>
      /// <param name="s">A string representing account holder's name</param>
      /// <param name="o">A float representing the overdraf limit</param>
      public bankaccount(float n, string s, float o)
      {
        balance = n;
        accountHolder = s;
        overdraft = o;
      }

/// <summary>
/// depositCash method - adds a sum to the account's balance.</summary>
/// <param name="n">A float representing the sum of £ to deposit</param>
/// <seealso cref="float">
/// </seealso>
public void depositCash(float n)
{
```

```
  balance += n;
}

/// <summary>
/// withdrawCash method - subtracts sum from balance, if possible.</summary>
/// <param name="n">A float representing the sum of £ to withdraw</param>
/// <seealso cref="float">
/// </seealso>
public void withdrawCash(float n)
{
  if (checkBalance(n) == true)
    balance -= n;
      else
        Console.WriteLine("Sorry {0}, insufficient funds.",accountHolder);
    }
    /// <summary>
    /// checkBalance method - checks if withdrawal sum exceeds overdraft limit.
        </summary>
    /// <returns>
    /// Return a boolean - true means withdrawal is ok.</returns>
    /// <seealso cref="withdrawCash(float)">
    /// This method is private, used by the withdrawCash method</seealso>
    private bool checkBalance(float n)
    {
      if (balance - n < overdraft)
        return false;
      else
        return true;
    }

    /// <summary>
    /// getBalance method - an accessor method, returns the private balance
        property.</summary>
    /// <returns>
    /// Return a float - true means withdrawal is ok.</returns>
    /// <seealso cref="withdrawCash(float)">
    /// This method is private, used by the withdrawCash method</seealso>
    public float getBalance()
    {
      return balance;
    }

}

    /// <summary>
    /// The entry point for the application (where it starts).
    /// </summary>
    /// <param name="args"> A list of command line arguments</param>
    static void Main(string[] args)
    {
      bankaccount BA1 = new bankaccount(200,"Mr Smith",-100);
      bankaccount BA2 = new bankaccount(300, "Ms Patel", -50);

      BA1.depositCash(30);
      Console.WriteLine("Balance is £{0:f}",BA1.getBalance());

      BA2.withdrawCash(400);
      BA2.withdrawCash(325);
```

▶

```
        Console.WriteLine("Balance is £{0:f}", BA2.getBalance());
        Console.ReadLine();
    }
  }
}
```

To **build** the XML file, it is necessary to change the C# **build options**. This is achieved by **right-clicking** on the solution name in the Solutions Explorer panel (see Figure 25.15).

And then selecting **properties** from the context menu that appears.

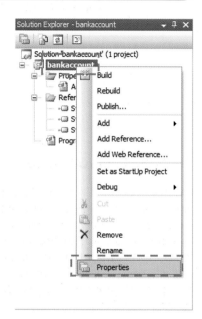

Figure 25.15 Solutions Explorer panel in C#

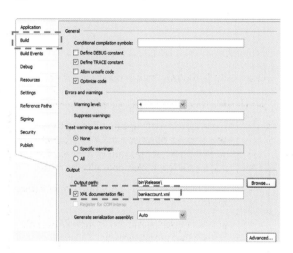

Figure 25.16 Context menu

On the dialogue that appears, choose the 'build' tab and then ensure that (a) the XML documentation file checkbox is enabled and that (b) the XML filename is the same as the name of the solution, i.e. 'bankaccount.xml'.

Another build will now create a **separate .XML file** which can be seen in the project directory and opened in a web browser. Unfortunately, without appropriate formatting it will only appear in a **document 'tree'** format (with the **expandable** and **collapsible branches** that Windows® users are familiar with).

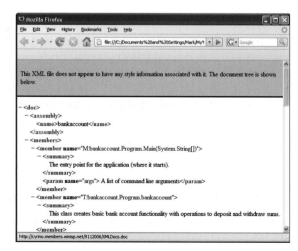

Figure 25.17 C# XML documentation in document tree format, viewed from Mozilla Firefox

However, back in C# we should see that making any further additions to our program will cause the **Intellisense™ facility** to display our **XML comments** as part of its **code completion** facility.

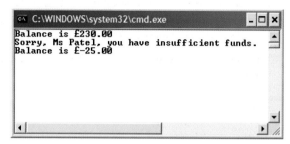

```
static void Main(string[] args)
{
    bankaccount BA1 = new bankaccount(200,"Mr Smith",-100);
    bankaccount BA2 = new bankaccount(300, "Ms Patel", -50);
    bankaccount BA3 = new bankaccount(120,
                      bankaccount.bankaccount (float n, string s, float o)
    BA1.depositCash(30 s:
    Console.WriteLine (| A string representing account holder's name    e());

    BA2.withdrawCash(400);
    BA2.withdrawCash(325);

    Console.WriteLine("Balance is £{0:f}", BA2.getBalance());
    Console.ReadLine();
}
```

Figure 25.18 Intellisense™ code completion

Naming conventions

In addition to identifier names (e.g. variables, classes, objects etc.) being **meaningful**, it was thought that including some kind of abbreviated description alluding to the **type** of the identifier was also useful (it saved the software engineer from having to keep going back to the declarations section of their program if they had forgotten the type of an identifier).

In practice this is as simple as adding a **prefix** that indicates if a variable is a Boolean, string, integer etc.

Hungarian notation

Perhaps the most famous naming convention that uses this principle is **Hungarian notation** which was invented by **Dr. Charles Simonyi** in the 1970s while he was working for **Microsoft®**. It is named after his country of origin. Over the years many other organisations (commercial and educational) have either **adopted** or **adapted** Hungarian notation for their own use.

Here are some simple examples:

`rgStudents`	An array (or **R**an**G**e) of students
`strUsername`	A **STR**ing containing a user's name
`bOverdue`	A **B**oolean value indicating whether something is overdue (or not)

What a great advantage to another software engineer who has to work with our code!

And here's the output from the compiled and executed application:

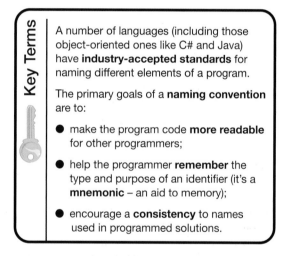

Figure 25.19 Output from bank account solution

Hungarian Notation

A more detailed exploration of Simonyi's Hungarian notation can be found here:

http://msdn2.microsoft.com/en-us/library/aa260976.aspx

camelCase

A capitalisation technique called camelCase is also used which helps to visually identify different words that are 'run together' to form a **compound word** (as program identifiers tend to be). It gets its name from the uppercase letter of the second word appearing to be raised just like the hump in the middle of a camel's back.

CamelCase formatting can clearly be seen in the previously discussed Hungarian notation examples:

```
rgStudents
strUsername
bOverdue
```

camelCase is also used in everyday items such as Apple's **iPod, iTouch, iPhone** and **iTunes.**

PascalCase

A similar formatting standard to camelCase, PascalCase capitalises the first letter of every word. PascalCase appears to be named by the Microsoft® .NET team after Anders Heilsberg (the original designer of Borland's very popular Turbo Pascal compiler) who was a member.

Common everyday examples include Sony's **PlayStation**, international carrier **FedEx**, Video sharing website **YouTube** and social networking website **MySpace**.

It should be noted that the **Microsoft® .NET framework** uses a mixture of both camelCase and PascalCase.

Sun's Java naming conventions state that PascalCase is used for **classes** and camelCase is to be used for **objects** and **methods**.

Underline

In programming, a long-standing alternative to camelCase and PascalCase is the use of the **underline** (or **underscore**) character to separate different words, e.g.

```
rg_students
str_username
b_overdue
```

Activity – Naming conventions

Decide which naming conventions (Hungarian, camelCase and PascalCase) are being used:

1 userPassword

2 strPassword

3 bWorking

4 UserPassword

5 user_password

6 is_it_working

7 rgGolfScores

How well did you do? See page 447 for the answers.

Java naming conventions

A more detailed exploration of Sun's recommendations for naming Java identifiers can be found here:

http://java.sun.com/docs/codeconv/html/CodeConventions.doc8.html#367

Valid declarations

Declarations are a vital part of any program as they **announce the existence** of an identifier to the **compiler**. Declaration syntax varies in different OO languages, but generally they follow a similar pattern.

For C#, the software engineer has only two options.

Simple declaration

This follows the format:

`Type Identifier`

e.g.

`int score;`

`String username;`

In order to compile, the Type must be **valid** and the Identifier **unique** in its scope (the section of code it is in). The C# statement must be ended with a ';' (semi-colon).

Declaration with initialisation

Very similar to the simple declaration but has the opportunity to give the identifier an initial value. And again, the ';' is needed.

```
Type Identifier = Value or Expression
```

e.g.

```
int score = 0;
```

Again, in order to successfully compile, the Type **must** be valid, the Identifier unique in its scope and the Value must be appropriate to the Type selected. For example, the following would **not** compile:

```
int score = 0.5f;
```

This would cause the following **compilation error**:

```
Cannot implicitly convert type 'double' to 'int'.
```

This is because the **Value** being used is **not** an integer (which is what the compiler is expecting to see because of the **Type** being used). In C# a float such as 0.5f represents a 32-bit floating-point number. The lack of an 'f' suffix would have created a double, which is a 64-bit floating-point number. **Neither** could be used to initialise an integer without considerable **loss of accuracy**.

Debugging code

Modern object-oriented programming software such as C# has feature-rich tools to assist the software engineer when they debug a solution.

In a typical IDE, the three most commonly used **debug tools** are as follows.

Trace

A **trace** allows the programmer to **follow** a program **line-by-line** as it executes, walking through the different **logical pathways** as the program progresses.

Tracing is very useful when **conditional statements** (if...else, case etc.) are present. If the **trace** shows **unexpected behaviour** (going down the wrong logical pathway, for example), the programmer will need to **check their logic** to see where things have gone wrong.

In C# this is achieved using **the F11 (Step Into) key** (see Figure 25.20):

```
/// The class constructor, needs 3 parameters. </summary>
/// <param name="n">A float representing the starting balance</param>
/// <param name="s">A string representing account holder's name</param>
/// <param name="o">A float representing the overdraf limit</param>
public bankaccount(float n, string s, float o)
{
    balance = n;
    accountHolder = s;
    overdraft = o;
}

/// <summary>
/// depositCash method – adds a sum to the account's balance.</summary>
/// <param name="n">A float representing the sum of £ to deposit</param>
/// <seealso cref="float">
/// </seealso>
public void depositCash(float n)
```

Figure 25.20 Highlighted line of code being executed during a trace in C#

Watch

A **watch** lets the software engineer **spy** on the **contents** of a variable while the program is running, usually during a **trace**.

One of the most common programming problems is a variable storing **unexpected values**. The watch feature lets the programmer **see the changes in a variable's contents** as different lines of the program code are executed.

The appearance of an unexpected value in a watched variable will allow the programmer to **narrow their search** to just a few lines of program code.

In C#, watches are added using the mouse right-click while the cursor is resting on an identifier (object, variable etc.). The 'Add Watch' option will cause the item to appear in C#'s watch window during tracing (see Figure 25.21).

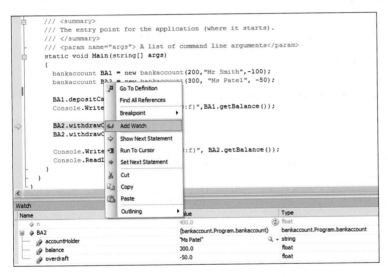

Figure 25.21 The object 'BA2' is added to the Watch window and shows its properties.

More complex identifiers (e.g. an object) can be **expanded** to show all the properties (variables) **inside**.

Breakpoint

A **breakpoint** is a debugging feature that lets the software engineer **mark a line of code** with a **physical breakpoint**. When the program runs it will **halt temporarily** at this point.

From here the software engineer can decide to **trace the remaining code** and/or **inspect** any **watches** they may have set.

The clear advantage here is that parts of the program that are functioning correctly **need not be traced**; the breakpoint can be placed **after** these sections have finished. This can save a great deal of time.

In C#, breakpoints are added by placing the cursor on the required line of code and pressing **F9** (**Toggle Breakpoint**) **key**. The line is then highlighted in red and has a red sphere appear alongside it in the left-hand margin of the code window (see Figure 25.22).

```
        Console.WriteLine("Balance is £{0:f}",BA1.getBalance());

        BA2.withdrawCash(400);
        BA2.withdrawCash(325);

        Console.WriteLine("Balance is £{0:f}", BA2.getBalance());
        Console.ReadLine();
    }
  }
}
```

Figure 25.22 Line of code is toggled as a breakpoint

Pressing F9 again will delete the breakpoint.

White box testing

White box testing examines the **performance** of the program code, ensuring that what has been programmed is generating the **right** results. White box testing takes **much more time** and usually starts **after** black box testing has been completed.

White box testing generally covers a number of different aspects of the coded solution:

◆ **Module testing** – each module or class can be tested separately and in conjunction.
◆ **Dry run ('static') vs actual ('dynamic') testing** – results from manual and automated execution of the program can be compared.
◆ **Boundary analysis** – values are tested below, on and above the upper and lower thresholds of any programmed boundaries.
◆ **Logical pathways** – all branches in program flow resulting from selections and loops are tested.
◆ **Code coverage** – the percentage of coverage provided by a test plan is analysed using this simple formula:

$$\frac{\text{Lines of code tested by test plan}}{\text{Total lines of code present}} \times 100$$

NCover is one of many coverage tools that are available for C# and can be found here:

http://ncover.sourceforge.net/

White box testing scorecard

+ Easy for software engineer to perform tests – they are familiar with the code.
+ Can help to remove **unnecessary** code, making solution **more efficient**.
− As coding becomes more complex the number of **hidden faults** and **unimaginable errors** increases.
− The process is **costly** as a software engineer is needed.

Checking functionality against requirements

Black box testing doesn't **care** about **how** the program was written (i.e. peeking inside). It only wants to see how closely a program meets its list of **functional requirements: does it do what it's supposed to do?**

In order for black box testing to work properly it is important that the tester has **no real knowledge** of the inner workings of the object-oriented solution undergoing quality assurance.

Common black box techniques include:

◆ **Usability tests** – the software is tested from the user's perspective; how easy is it to use? How intuitive are the menu systems and user prompts?

◆ **Functionality tests** – tests to see if the software performs all the tasks that are required of it. How quick and accurate is it? Are there any requested features that are absent?

◆ **Recovery testing** – how well does the program recover from crashes or loss of data?

◆ **Scenario testing** (including **Use Cases** and **Decision Tables**) – realistic data (provided by the end user) is entered into the program to see how it deals with 'live' data.

◆ **Alpha testing** – the program is tested in-house by the end users in an 'early' finished state. It is likely that the end user may request a number of alterations at this point.

◆ **Beta testing** – the program is released to the end users for testing in its final environment; it is likely to be 95 per cent complete at this point. Minor tweaks may still be made as a result of end user feedback. This may also be known as **user acceptance testing (UAT)**. Once all changes have been made, the final version of the software will be signed off by the client, delivered and installed.

Braincheck

Answer the following questions:

1 State two common object-oriented design methods.
2 What is the difference between pass-by-value and pass-by-reference?
3 What is aggregation?
4 What is association?
5 What is a constructor?
6 When does a constructor execute?
7 What is a destructor?
8 When does a destructor execute?
9 What is garbage collection?
10 What problem does garbage collection prevent happening?
11 What is a class library?
12 What is indentation?
13 What is whitespace?
14 Why use comments in OO program code?
15 What is a naming convention?

How well did you do? See page 447 for the answers.

Unit links

Unit 25 is a **Specialist Unit** on the following BTEC National Certificate and Diploma routes:

Networking

Software Development

Systems Support

As such it has links to a number of other units, principally:

Unit 4 – IT Project

Unit 10 – Client-side Customisation of Web Pages

Unit 12 – Developing Computer Games

Unit 18 – Principles of Software Design and Development

Unit 19 – Web Server Scripting

Unit 20 – Event-Driven Programming

In addition this unit has identified direct links with:

Unit 7 – Systems Analysis and Design

Achieving success

In order to achieve each unit you will complete a series of coursework activities. Each time you hand in work, your tutor will return this to you with a record of your achievement.

This particular unit has 11 criteria to meet: 6 Pass, 3 Merit and 2 Distinction.

For a **Pass**:

　You must achieve **all** 6 Pass criteria.

For a **Merit**:

　You must achieve **all** 6 Pass and **all** 3 Merit criteria.

For a **Distinction**:

　You must achieve **all** 6 Pass, **all** 3 Merit **and** both Distinction criteria.

So that you can monitor your own progress and achievement in each unit, a recording grid has been provided (see below). The full version of this grid is also included on the companion CD.

Assignment	Assignments in this Unit			
	U25.01	U25.02	U25.03	U25.04
Referral				
Pass				
1				
2				
3				
4				
5				
6				
Merit				
1				
2				
3				
Distinction				
1				
2				

Help with assessment

To achieve a **Pass** for this unit you will need to be able to describe the characteristics of a typical OO language. From a practical perspective you'll be asked to create a single OO design for a program, document the classes and implement them. Classes have to be created from scratch and from pre-existing ones (but theoretically this could be your own or library classes).

Merit-level performance is dictated by your ability to explain more complex OO topics such as inheritance, association and aggregation in working programs.

In order to achieve a **Distinction** a pair of linked criteria require you to design, test and implement an OO program for a realistic application; after this you can evaluate how the OO approach has supported your attempts at software engineering while solving the problem.

Online resources on the CD

Key fact sheets
Electronic slide show of key points
Sample program code in C# and Java
Multiple choice self-test quizzes
Flash animated tutorials for C#

Further reading

Schildt, H., 2001, *C#: A Beginner's Guide*, Osborne/McGraw-Hill, ISBN 0072133295.

Halvorson, V., 2005, *Visual Basic 2005 Step by Step*, Microsoft Press US, ISBN 0735621314.

Henney, K. and Templeman, J., 2003, *Microsoft Visual C++ .NET Step by Step: Version 2003*, Microsoft Press US, ISBN 0735619077.

Kaldahl, B., 2004, *EZ Flash MX: Animation, Action Script and Gaming for Macromedia Flash*, Trafford Publishing, ISBN 1412006171.

Lemay, L. and Cadenhead, R., 2004, *Sams Teach Yourself Java 2 in 21 Days, 4th Edition*, Sams, ISBN 0672326280.

Schildt, H., 2003, *C++: A Beginner's Guide, 2nd Edition*, McGraw-Hill Education, ISBN 0072232153.

Unit 4 Answers

Braincheck answers – Project management crossword

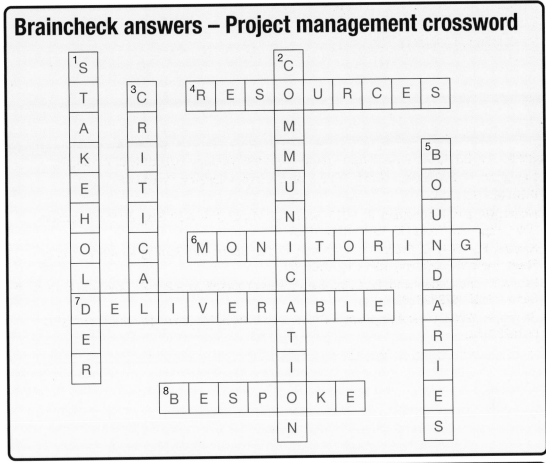

Braincheck answers – Life cycle puzzle

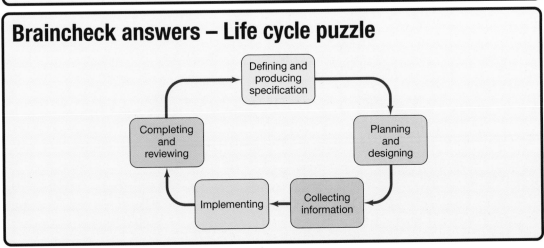

Braincheck answers – Planning word search

```
–   –   –   –   D   A   T   A   –   –   –   –   –   –   –   –   –   –   –   –
–   –   –   –   –   –   –   –   –   –   –   –   –   –   –   –   –   –   –   –
–   –   –   F   –   –   –   –   D   R   O   C   E   R   –   –   –   –   –   –
–   –   –   U   –   –   –   –   P   L   A   N   –   –   –   T   E   –
–   –   –   –   N   –   –   –   –   –   –   –   –   –   C   –   F   –
–   –   –   –   –   C   –   –   –   –   –   –   –   E   N   –   F   –
–   –   –   –   –   –   T   –   –   –   –   –   J   N   O   –   E   –
–   –   –   –   –   –   –   I   –   –   –   –   O   –   O   I   –   C   –
–   –   –   –   –   –   –   –   O   –   –   R   –   –   T   T   –   T   –
–   –   –   –   –   –   –   –   N   P   –   –   –   S   A   A   I   –
–   –   –   –   –   –   –   –   –   A   –   –   –   E   M   N   V   –
–   –   I   N   T   E   R   V   I   E   W   –   L   –   –   L   R   A   E   –
–   –   –   –   –   –   –   –   –   –   –   –   –   I   O   L   –   –
–   –   –   –   –   –   L   E   L   L   A   R   A   P   M   F   Y   –   –
O   B   S   E   R   V   A   T   I   O   N   –   –   –   –   –   N   S   –   –
–   –   –   E   S   A   H   P   –   –   –   –   –   –   –   I   I   –
M   A   E   T   –   –   –   –   –   –   –   –   –   –   –   S   –   –
–   –   –   –   –   –   –   –   –   –   –   –   –   –   –   –   –   –
–   –   –   –   –   –   –   –   S   E   Q   U   E   N   T   I   A   L   –   –   –
–   E   R   I   A   N   N   O   I   T   S   E   U   Q   –   –   –   –   –   –
```

Unit 5 Answers

Braincheck answers – What do you know?

Term	Explanation
Database object	A database object is an independent component that forms part of the structure of a database, and is one that can be manipulated. The term **Objects** is a collective expression to that includes components such as **tables**, **queries**, **forms** and **reports**.
Table	A **table** holds the database data in a **structured** and **organised** way. The data is organised in a grid that contains columns and rows (known as fields and records).
Record	A **record** is series of **data items** that are **linked**, and that are stored in a single **row** in a database table. For example, as a student your name and address will be stored by your school or college. This collection of data about you will form a single record. There will be similar records for your friends and classmates.
Field	So that records are organised, pieces of data that are essentially the same, but which occur in different records, are organised into **columns**, with appropriate headings. Each of these columns is known as a **field**. Examples of fields include, FirstName, LastName, DateOfBirth, HomeAddress, TelephoneNumber.
Format	Each **data type** also has a range of **formats** that can be applied. **Dates** for example can be long, short or customised to suit user need. **Number** fields can be stored with decimal places, without or maybe as currency. As part of formatting, the size of a text field can be changed. By default, Microsoft Access® sets a **text** field size to 50, where the maximum can be 255 and the minimum 1. If the characters in a text field are not used, they will still be stored. Thus it is essential that the size of a text field is suitable for the data it is intended to hold. Leaving the text field size at 50 will mean that a larger input will be truncated (shortened) and, if the input is smaller, empty space will also be stored.
AutoNumber	An **AutoNumber** can be set up and used to provide a **unique** component in a record. With each record that is created using an AutoNumber, the number will be **incremented** without requiring user intervention.
Structure	When we refer to the **structure** of a database we mean how many objects have been created and how they have been created (what their components are); in the case of a relational database it also covers how they interact, and how they are used.

▶

Term	Explanation
Data integrity	Data is said to have **integrity** when it is **valid**. That means that the data is **accurate** and **correct** and has not been accidentally or intentionally **corrupted** through incorrect input for example.
Data integrity *cont*	To ensure that data integrity is maintained, developers use tools that minimise these potential threats such as **validation**, **input masking** and, most importantly, designing the **user interface** in a way that **reduces** the **potential** for data being input incorrectly.
Naming conventions	Database objects should be sensibly named so that users and developers can instantly identify the object type. Tables: these are usually named with the prefix **Tbl** – so a table containing students details could be named TblStudent. Similarly a table of courses could be named TblCourse. Queries are usually prefixed with **Qry**. So QryTutor could be a query listing tutors. **Frm** denotes a Form object and FrmStudent might be the input form that allows users to input data into TblStudent. **Rpt** identifies a Report object such as RptStudentList, which would be a list of all students in the database.
Design View	The **Design View** of an object is the view that allows the developer to **create** and **modify** its **structure**.
Datasheet View	The **Datasheet View** is the view that allows the user to input data.
Form	A **form** is an interface that is organise the way in which the user will input data into the table. It is organised with the user in mind.

Activity answers – Normalisation – Frankoni

UNF	1NF	2NF	3NF
Supplier Name	**Order Number**	**Order Number**	**Order Number**
Supplier Address	Supplier Name	Supplier Name	**Supplier ID**
Supplier Post Code	Supplier Address	Supplier Address	Order Date
Order Date	Supplier Post Code	Supplier Post Code	
[Item Code]	Order Date	Order Date	**Order Number**
[Description]			**Item Code**
[Quantity]	**Order Number**	**Order Number**	Quantity
[Price]	**Item Code**	**Item Code**	Price
[Total]	Description	Quantity	Total
	Quantity	Price	
	Price	Total	**Item Code**
	Total		Description
		Item Code	
		Description	**Supplier ID**
			Supplier Name
			Supplier Address
			Supplier Post Code

Tables identified: Order, Order Line, Stock, Supplier

Braincheck – Crossword

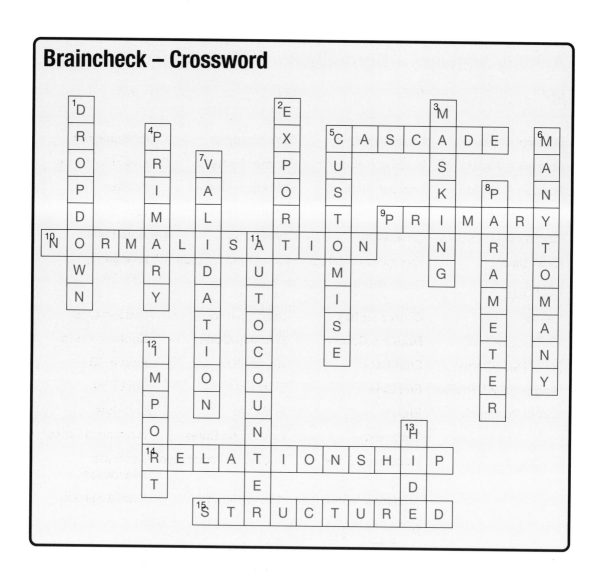

Activity answers – Normalisation – Safe Kitty Cattery

UNF	1NF	2NF	3NF
Customer Name	**Customer ID**	**Customer ID**	**Customer ID**
Address	Customer Name	Customer Name	Customer Name
Town	Address	Address	Address
Telephone	Town	Town	Town
Emergency Number	Telephone	Telephone	Telephone
[Start Date]	Emergency Number	Emergency Number	Emergency Number
[End Date]			
[Breed]	**Customer ID**	**Customer ID**	**Customer ID**
[Cat's Name]	**Booking Code**	**Booking Code**	**Booking Code**
[Inoculation Dates]	Start Date	**Animal ID**	**Animal ID**
[Additional Information]	End Date	Start Date	Start Date
[Kennel Number]	Breed	End Date	End Date
	Cat's Name	Inoculation Dates	Inoculation Dates
	Inoculation Dates	Additional Information	Additional Information
		Kennel Number	Kennel Number
	Additional Information		
	Kennel Number		
		Animal ID	**Animal ID**
		Breed	Breed
		Cat's Name	Cat's Name

Tables identified: Customer, Booking, Animal

If you have applied the rules correctly, this normalisation activity will have had the same results at 3NF as at 2NF. This is sometimes the case with a simple form. If 3NF cannot be applied it is not necessary to do so.

Activity answers – Normalisation – Great Tickets

UNF	1NF	2NF	3NF
Order Number	**Order Number**	**Order Number**	**Order Number**
Order Date	Order Date	Order Date	Order Date
Customer Name	Customer Name	Customer Name	**Customer ID**
Address	Address	Address	Despatch Method
Post Code	Post Code	Post Code	Payment Method
Telephone Number	Telephone Number	Telephone Number	Date Order Processed
Despatch Method	Despatch Method	Despatch Method	Processed by
Payment Method	Payment Method	Payment Method	
Date Order Processed	Date Order Processed	Date Order Processed	**Order Number**
Processed by	Processed by	Processed by	**Event Code**
[Event/Concert Name]			Adult Tickets
[Event Location]	**Order Number**	**Order Number**	Child Tickets
[Date]	**Event Code**	**Event Code**	Concession Tickets
[Adult Tickets]	Event/Concert Name	Adult Tickets	Total Number of Tickets
[Child Tickets]	Event Location	Child Tickets	
[Concession Tickets]	Date	Concession Tickets	**Event Code**
[Total Number of Tickets]	Adult Tickets	Total Number of Tickets	Event/Concert Name
	Child Tickets		Event Location
	Concession Tickets	**Event Code**	Date
	Total Number of Tickets	Event/Concert Name	
		Event Location	**Customer ID**
		Date	Customer Name
			Address
			Post Code
			Telephone Number

Tables identified: Order, Order Line, Event, Customer

Unit 6 Answers

Braincheck answers – What do you already know?

Term	Explanation
Row	A row is a horizontal display of data that is usually displayed left to right. Rows are referred to by their number (in this case 1).
Column	A column is a vertical display of data that is usually displayed top to bottom. Columns are referred to by their letter (in this case A).
Cell	A cell is the data entry point where the row and column meet (in this case A1). When working with data in cells, it is usual to refer to the data by its reference.
Operators	Operators is the collective term for a range of mathematical symbols and abbreviations that define how to process the numbers (or contents of cells referred to) that precede and follow them – for example: $2 \times 10 - 3$ Here the user would multiply two and ten to give an answer, then subtract three. In this instance the answer would be 17.

Term	Explanation
Formulae	The term formula is usually applied to a calculation created by the user using a combination of cell references, numeric values and operators. An example of a formula might be: A3 × F7 − L1 The values in each cell are: A3 = 2 F7 = 10 L1 = 3 The answer in this instance would be 17.
Function	The term function usually refers to a calculation that has a specific operation and purpose. It can be created by the user using cell references, numeric values and operators, or it can be simply extracted from a library of functions and used without modification. Some examples include: SUM AVERAGE MAX MIN COUNT COUNTIF
Parenthesis	This term refers to brackets used to group data together. For example: (3 + 3) − (2 + 2) This calculation could be rewritten as: 6 − 4 The answer would be two.

Term	Explanation
BODMAS	Using parentheses in a more specific way changes the operational processing order of functions and calculations. Let's consider the following example: 2 × 10 – 3 We have already established that, if doing this calculation manually or using a calculator, the result would be the answer of 17. However, if we use parentheses we can change how this calculation is processed: 2 × (10 – 3) In this instance the bracketed data items will be dealt with first, so the calculation would be viewed as: 2 × 7 The answer would be 14. BODMAS stands for: Brackets Over Division Multiplication Addition Subtraction This is the processing order that the computer adopts to ensure that processing is executed as meant by the user.
Condition	A condition is a question point that requires a response before a particular action or actions can be taken. It is checked as part of the processing action. In spreadsheet terms conditions are usually preceded by the term IF. Let's look at a simple example: Condition: Is it raining? If yes – take an umbrella If no – leave the umbrella in the car The simplest example of using a number as part of a condition could be: Condition: Is age > 18? If yes – admit If no – refuse admission

▶

Term	Explanation
Simple Logical Operators	Common examples of logical operators are: AND OR Sometimes it is necessary to test (evaluate) more than one condition. Using an AND operator means that both parts of the condition must be met for the true actions to take place. The OR operator means that if either of the conditions is met the true actions should be executed.
Format	Formatting a cell or spreadsheet means choosing the characteristics of the visual appearance. This could be through changing the colour, size or type of font, **emboldening** the text, using *italics* or <u>underscore</u>, or combinations of different formats. Users can select different number formats including currency and numbers with or without decimal points. It can also refer to changing the background colour of a cell or changing the cell's borders.
Alignment	This is how the text is organised in relation to page margin, or within an object. See the following examples: <table><tr><td>This text is shown right aligned</td><td>This text is shown centre aligned</td><td>This text is shown left aligned</td></tr></table>

Term	Explanation
Merge	As part of organising the presentation it can be useful to merge cells (join them) together to form a larger cell. This is often done to accommodate headings:

Sales of Widgets – comparison of period				
Year	2004	2005	2006	2007
January				
February				
March				
April				

In the example above, four cells have been merged to allow the heading to be spread over a single line, rather than being restricted to a single cell as shown below:

Sales of Widgets – comparison of period				
Year	2004	2005	2006	2007
January				
February				
March				
April				

Term	Explanation
Range	The term range is applied to a number of adjacent cells in either a row or a column that can be referenced: A1:A6 – this is a row of six cells (remember the first number and last number are included) A1:F1 – this is a column of six cells (again the first and last cells are included) The function SUM (A1:A6) will add up the contents of each of the six cells and display the result.

Braincheck answers – Logical operators

1) =IF(A<75,A+B,A+C)	112
2) =IF(AND(A>75,B>30,C>9),A+B+C,0)	162
3) =IF(AND(A<50,B>30),A+B,0)	0
4) =IF(OR(A<50,B>30),A-B,0)	50
5) =SUMIF(A:C,"<=50")	62
6) =IF(A+B=150,"true","false")	True
7) =IF(OR(B=50,C<9),A,0)	100
8) =NOT(7+4=11)	FALSE

Braincheck answers – Spreadsheets crossword

Unit 10 Answers

Braincheck answers

1) CSS – Cascading Style Sheets
2) Separates content and formatting, saves time, consistent formatting
3) Deprecated
4) In-line style
5) Selector
6) Semi-colon (;)
7) 216
8) Italic, oblique and normal
9) Underline, overline, line through and blink
10) Any three from points, pixels, ems, inches, centimetres, millimetres and picas
11) Creating a columnar format

Activity

cm = 6.5 * 2. 54

degc = (98-32) * 5/9

Braincheck answers

True
True
True
False
True
True
True
False
True

Braincheck answers – What do you know?

1) A name representing a value in JavaScript
2) When the web browser is closed
3) Any three from arithmetic, assignment, logical and relational
4) Obtains the remainder from an integer division
5) To give a variable a value
6) Methods or properties
7) If or Switch statement
8) Switch statement
9) Do…while loop
10) Elements in an array

Unit 19 Answers

Braincheck answers

1) WAMP runs on Microsoft Windows platform, LAMP on Linux
2) 127.0.0.1 – used instead of 'localhost', usually for client-server systems or a 'loopback' test
3) A relational database management system
4) SQL keywords used to manipulate a database
5) It's not stored on the client PC so is more secure
6) Environmental data for the server's settings or some client settings
7) Password
8) Posting
9) File size and file type
10) Host, root, no password

Braincheck answers

1) Functionality, user interface, performance, implementation constraints, other factors e.g. security
2) Functionality reflect needs of the stakeholders
3) Comments, self-documenting variables, indentation
4) $ (dollar) sign
5) Yes
6) Name of the PHP file, line number and brief error description
7) Notice, Strict notice, Warning, Parse error and Fatal error
8) Any three from symbol matching, on-line help, syntax highlighting, automatic code completion

Unit 23 Answers

Braincheck answers

1) Hardware is tangible, software is instructions written to control the hardware
2) Firmware is stored on a chip rather than a disk or CD/DVD
3) An update may only be a minor change to an existing product
4) Any three from changing user needs, fix bugs, accommodate hardware changes, organisation policy etc
5) Business case
6) Any three from loss of service, loss of income, incompatibility issues, instability and user preferences
7) Any three from pilot deployment, backups, bookmarking, low-risk installation timings

Braincheck answers

1) Materials, requirements and communication
2) Identification, type of install, collect materials, identify window of opportunity, reduce risks, perform install, test and handover
3) Recommended requirements will get better performance out of the new software
4) End user, line manager, software publisher
5) Aborting the installation and re-instating the previous software
6) User acceptance testing
7) Any four such as personal name, company name, gender, date of birth, email address etc.
8) Any four such as validating the purchase, user information, open communication with customer, bug reporting etc
9) Any four such as discounts, user support, extra downloads, extend warranty etc
10) End user license agreement
11) An encrypted hardware device used to validate a software installation
12) An electronic bookmark for system settings
13) A centralised database of system settings in Microsoft Windows
14) A section of the Windows registry, focusing on a particular aspect e.g. the hardware or the user
15) The 'My Documents' folder

Unit 24 Answers

Braincheck answers

1) Any three from .BMP, .GIF, .JPG, .PNG etc
2) RLE, LZW
3) As a replacement for the .GIF format which uses the proprietary LZW compression algorithm
4) It doesn't lose detail when scaled and can be non-rectangular
5) .SVG
6) A .GIF containing multiple still frames which are sequenced to form an animated sequence
7) Large file size and loses detail when scaled
8) No
9) Rasterization
10) Blending edges using a gentle graduation from foreground to background colour in order to smooth jagged edges

Unit 25 Answers

Braincheck answers

1) CRC Cards, UML schema/class diagram
2) Pass-by-value uses a copy of the data, Pass-by-reference refers to the original data
3) Grouping classes together
4) Connections between classes
5) A method, sharing the same name as its class…
6) … which is automatically executed when an object is built
7) A method, automatically executing and performing housekeeping duties…
8) … when an object is destroyed
9) Release RAM back to the heap when objects are destroyed
10) Memory leakage
11) A collection of pre-written classes for a programmer to use rather then recreate from scratch – saving time, effort and money
12) Use of whitespace to highlight the underlying structure of the program code
13) A non-printable character (a space) or a blank line
14) To explain the purpose of the code, not the syntax being used
15) A standardised method for naming properties, classes, objects etc.

Braincheck answers

1) Properties and methods
2) Object
3) Object, instantiation
4) Property
5) Method
6) Encapsulation
7) Java

Braincheck answers

1) Inheritance
2) Base
3) Derived
4) Multiple inheritance
5) Private
6) Polymorphism
7) An abstract class
8) Overloaded
9) Parameters
10) Overridden
11) Instance
12) Interface

Index

A

ABC Methodology 24
access modifiers 383–84
adaptive maintenance 38
advanced graphics port (AGP) 346
aggregation 406–7
alpha testing 425
analysts 19
arithmetic operators 186–87
ASP render blocks 241
association 406–7
attributes *see* properties
axis scale 105

B

backing up 311, 318
  backup utilities 336–39
  hard drive, imaging 339–40
  registry data, copy of 335
  user data, copy of 335
backout procedures 315, 324
bar charts 104, 143
batch files 237
bespoke solution 8–9
beta testing 425
bitmap images 355, 361–62
black box testing 36, 425
bookmarks *see* recovery points
breakpoint 423–24
business case, making 310–11

C

calendar 224–26
cascading style sheets *see* CSS
cascading updates/deletes 66, 89
cell references, relative versus absolute
  130–31
CGI *see* Common Gateway Interface
  (CGI)
charts 104, 105, 142–43
Class Responsibility Collaboration
  (CRC) cards 393–96
classes
  abstract 391–92
  association/aggregation, using 406–7
  C# solution 401–4
  class libraries 380, 409–11
  CSS 159
  derived 381

identifying 398
  pass by values 405
  properties/methods 379, 380, 399, 400
  public and private 383–84
client/server concept 248
clocks 221–22
CMYK (cyan, yellow, magenta, black)
  printing process 351
colour balance 369–70
colour depth 370–71
Command Button Wizard 93
command line interface versus graphical
  user interface 250
commenting code
  hyperlinked comments 416–19
  multiple-line comments 414
  PHP documentation 297
  single-line comments 414–15
  web pages, client-side 227–28
Common Gateway Interface (CGI)
  241–42
communications 20, 313, 318
conflict management 20–21
cookies
  example script for 181, 183–85
  management facilities 180–81
  security issues 173
  storage prevention 181
  using 182
copyright 373–74
CorelDRAW® 26
corrective maintenance 37
CRC cards *see* Class Responsibility
  Collaboration (CRC) cards
critical path methods 15–16, 18
CRT (cathode ray tube) monitors 352
CSS (cascading style sheets)
  background style 157
  browsers, hiding from older 160
  classes 159
  content/formatting separation 153,
    154–55
  content/padding/border/margin areas
    156
  depreciation 154
  design 207–8
  document trees 156
  external implementation 153, 154–55
  graphical tool 207

headings 209
horizontal menu system 212–13
hover effect 211
ID selector 160
in-line implementation 153, 156
internal implementation 153, 155
lists 209–13
on-screen rendering 156, 157
pseudoclasses, and links 213–16
readability 157
selectors 158
styling list elements 210
unordered lists 210–11
web browser default 153
WYSIWYG editors 207–8
see also formatting (CSS)

D

data capture devices (graphics) 347–49
data entry forms 80
  combo boxes 83
  completeness checks 82
  data consistency 82–83
  data redundancy 83
  drop down boxes 83
  input masking 81–82
  Tab Order 80
  validation routines 81, 84–85
  verification 81
  visual prompts 83
Data Flow Diagrams (DFD) 30
data mining 109–10
Data Protection Act (1998) 302
data types (databases)
  AutoNumber 67, 76
  Currency 67
  Date/Time 67
  Hyperlink 68
  Lookup Wizard 68
  Number – Floating point (decimal)
    67
  Number – Integer (whole number) 67
  OLE Object 68
  Text 67
  Yes/No 67
database creation (MySQL)
  WAMPServer MySQL service, starting
    250
  MySQL console, accessing 250

database creation (continued)
   database setup 251–52
   table creation 252–54
   table checking 253–54
   table population 254, 255
   query, performing 255
   HTML web-based interface creation 255–56
   PHP testing 257
   PHP code review 258
   command line interface versus graphical user interface 250
   HTML source code 257
database skills
   automation 92–94
   customising 90–92
   data entry forms 80–85
   data types 66–68
   errors 79–80
   evaluation criteria 95
   exporting data 88–89
   field properties 66–68
   forms 89–90
   importing data 86
   integrity, ensuring/maintaining 89
   key fields 75–78
   reports 73–74, 89–90
   styles, creating 89–90
   tables 68–70
   testing 95
   see also queries (databases); relational databases
DataX Methodology 24
DCF *see* Design Rule for Camera File system
DCIM *see* Digital Camera Image Movement Folder
debugging code
   breakpoint 423–24
   script debugging 230–32, 298–300
   trace 422
   watch 423
deliverables, project
   product 32
   technical documentation 33–34
   user documentation 33
   user training 33
denary based rgb function 161
design
   CSS 207–8
   object-oriented 169, 393–97
   see also project design
Design Rule for Camera File system (DCF) 358, 359
designers 19
Digital Camera Image Movement Folder (DCIM) 358
digital cameras 347
digital graphics *see* graphics

digital rights management (DRM) 328
direct benefits 5
direct interest 2
Document Object Model (DOM) 169, 170, 177, 178, 222, 224
documentation
   project 32, 37, 41
   scripting languages 227, 296–98
   technical 33–34, 41
   user 33, 42–44
documenters 19
dongles 328
drilling down (data) 109
DRM *see* digital rights management

E
ECMAscript dialect 168
EDP *see* event-driven programming
End User License Agreement (EULA) 327
Entity Relationship Models (ERM) 30, 51–52, 397
Epsilon Project Methodology 24
errors
   data input 79
   data type mismatches 79
   field deletion 79
   inconsistent normalisation 80
   poor design 79
   rectification of 79
   web pages 230, 231
escalation 315
ethical issues
   ethics, definition of 301
   PHP counters 302–3
   privacy, infringement of 302
event-driven programming (EDP) 168
event handlers 169–70, 199
Event Procedure 84–85
Exchangeable Image File (EXIF) information 358, 359
eXtensible Markup Language (XML) 416–19
external hard disks 349

F
file compression 357, 360
file formats
   databases 122–24
   graphics files 355, 357, 361–64
final handover date 10
flash pen drives 349
flatbed scanners 348
flowcharts 219–20
fonts 120, 154, 164
foreign keys 55–56, 68, 75–76
formatting (CSS)
   background colour 161–62
   background images 162

   borders and padding 165
   capitalisation 164
   columns, creating 165–66
   criteria 154
   font size 164
   font style 164
   heading styles 165
   letter spacing 164
   measurement units 164–65
   positioning, of elements 165
   style effects 163–64
   text alignment 164
   text decoration 164
   typeface control 164
formatting (spreadsheets)
   Bold 121
   Borders 121
   Column alignment 121
   consistency 119–20, 122
   Currency 120
   Date 119–20
   Integer 119
   Italics 121
   Real 119
   Shading 121
   Text 120
   user needs 122
formulae (spreadsheets)
   cell references, relative versus absolute 130–31
   complex 117–18
   logical functions 131–35
functional specification 12
functional testing 95, 425
   structured walkthrough 39
   test data 38–39
   test plan/schedule 39–40

G
Gantt charts 13, 16–17, 25, 27
garbage collection 409
generic numbering 358
graphical processing unit (GPU) 346
graphics
   colour, inverting 369–71
   crop 368
   data capture devices 347–49
   editing tools 365–71
   file storage 349–50
   flip 367
   freehand draw 366
   graphic creation 365
   graphics manipulation, stages of 345
   hardware, definition of 345
   legislation 373–74
   output medium 350–52
   process and display 346–47
   resize 368–69
   review process 372–73

rotate 366
tools/techniques 365–71
user requirements 371–72
graphics cards 346–47
graphics files
file compression 357, 360
file conversions 356
file formats 355, 357, 361–64
file management 358–60
file operations 360
file sizes 356–57
filenames 358–59
folder structures 359
graphics software
dedicated bitmap software 353
dedicated photo-manipulation
software 353–54
dedicated vector graphics software
352
embedded graphics facilities 354
file conversions 355
image previewing 354
third-party tools 355
graphics tablets 349
graphs 142–43

H
hexadecimal pair format 161
hives 321, 330
human resources 18–19
Hypertext Pre-processor (PHP) *see* web
server scripting

I
if . . . else statements 191–94
implementation *see* project
implementation
indentation, and code readability
228–20, 298, 412–14
indirect benefits 5
information-gathering
data analysis 28
document analysis 29–30
interviews 28
meetings 28
observation 30
questionnaires 28
inheritance (OOP)
'child:parent' class links 381–82
derived classes 381
multiple inheritances 382–83
inkjet printers 350–51
input masking 81–82
installation, software *see* software
installation/upgrade
intellectual property (IP) rights 327,
373–74
interim review dates 10

Internet Service Provider (ISP) 325
iterations *see* loops

J
Jackson Structured Diagrams (JSDs) 31
Java 168
JavaScript
abstract objects 169
browser actions/appearance 170
cookies, reading/writing 171
document content 170, 171
Document Object Model (DOM)
169, 170, 177, 178, 222, 224
event handlers 169–70, 199
Java applets, interaction with 170
object-oriented design 169
support 168–69
user, interaction with 171
visible objects 169
web page image manipulation 170
see also scripting languages
Job Control Language (JCL) 237
JSP (Java Server Pages) 240

K
key fields (databases)
auto-incremented keys 76–78
foreign keys 55–56, 68, 75–76
primary keys 55–56, 64–65, 68, 75,
264, 270
referential integrity 76
see also relational databases

L
LAMP (Linux Apache MySQL PHP)
packages 244
laser printers 350–51
legislation 20–21, 373–74
licensing
commericial/proprietary 327
open source/free 327
terms and conditions 327
liquid crystal display (LCD) monitors
352
logbooks 34–35
logical design 30–31
logical operators 88, 188
login systems (PHP)
global session variables 288, 290,
291–92, 294
HTML login code 289–90
login process 288–89
PHP login code 290–91
testing 293–94
user table creation 286–87
loops
for . . . in loops 198
do . . . while 197

pre- and post-check conditioning 197
while 198

M
macros
databases 73, 92–94
spreadsheets 146–48
maintenance strategies 37–38
management, project *see* project
management
many-to-many relationships 52–55
media flash cards 347, 350
method overloading 383, 389–91
methodologies
company-specific 24
formal 22
Prince2 22–23
Sigma 24
Microsoft ASP.NET® 240–41
Microsoft IIS® (Internet Information
Server) 240
Microsoft Internet Explorer® 176–77,
210
Microsoft Project® 16–18, 27
milestones, project 10
mobile phones 347
monitors (VDU s) 351–52
mouse movement followers 222–24
MySQL *see* database creation (MySQL)

N
naming conventions
camelCase 420
graphics files 358–59
Hungarian notation 419–20
industry-accepted standards 419
Java naming conventions 421
PascalCase 420
underline 420
National Center for Supercomputing
Applications (NCSA) 241
nested if . . . statements 194–95
network-based solutions 31
network diagrams 15, 16, 18, 30–31
non-key dependency 57
normalisation
First Normal Form (FNF) 56, 59
foreign keys 55–56, 68, 75–76
primary keys 55–56, 68
Second Normal Form (SNF) 56, 60
spreadsheets 62–63
Third Normal Form (TNF) 57, 61–63
Un-Normalised Form (UNF) 56,
57–58

O
object-oriented programming
design methods 393–97

object-oriented programming
(continued)
object-based versus object-oriented
languages 168
polymorphism 383, 389–91
variables, public and private 385–86
see also classes; objects; software
engineering
objects 378
constructors and destructors 407–9
data/functions separation 379
encapsulation 379
inheritance 380–83
instantiation 380
JavaScript 169–70
methods, public and private 384–85
off-the-shelf solution 9
one-to-many relationships 52–55
one-to-one relationships 52–55
operating systems 329
changes 308
recovery points 331–34
testing 232

P
parameters 199–201, 387, 389
part-key dependency 56, 60
pass by values 405
passwords 128
patches 308
PCI *see* peripheral component
interconnector
PCI express (PCIe) 346
perfective maintenance 37
peripheral component interconnector
(PCI) 346
Perl script 241
Personal Home Page (PHP) *see* web
server scripting
PERT (Programme Evaluation and
Review Technique) 14, 25
PHP (Hypertext Pre-processor/ Personal
Home Page) *see* web server
scripting
physical design 31–32
pivot tables 135–38
planning, project *see* project planning
plotters 351
polymorphism 383, 389–91
primary keys 55–56, 64–65, 68, 75, 264,
270
printers 350–51
privacy policy/statement 326
Problem and Requirements List (PRL)
3–4
problem definition 11
product registration
information requested 325–28
licensing 327

pros and cons of 327
protection schemes 328
publishers' privacy policy/statement
326
purpose of 326
programmers/developers 19
project design
Data Flow Diagrams (DFD) 30
documentation 32
Entity Relationship Models (ERM) 30
Jackson Structured Diagrams (JSDs)
31
logical design 30–31
network-based solutions 31
network diagrams 30–31
physical design 31–32
pseudocode 31
storyboards 31
project implementation
deliverables 32–34
monitoring 34–36
plan, updating 35–36
tools 32
project life cycles
completion and review 12
implementation 12
information collection 12
planning and designing 12
specification, defining and producing
11–12
project management
communications 20
conflict management 20–21
corrective action 20
external environment, awareness of
19–20
methodologies 22–24
progress monitoring 20
project outputs, impacts of 21
relevant guidelines/legislation 20–21
resources 18–19
review 40–41
software packages 16–18, 26
see also testing (project)
project managers 18
project planning
activities detail 27–30
critical path methods 15–16, 18
human resources 27
information-gathering 28–30
parallel/sequential processes 27
project plan 24–26
review points 26, 27
software choices 26
tools 13–14
properties
fields 66–68
objects 379, 380, 399, 400

protection schemes
copy protection 328
digital rights management (DRM)
328
dongles 328
Internet-based product activation 328
user name/serial number 328
pseudo code 31, 218
pseudoclasses 213–16

Q
quality assurance (QA) process 308
queries (databases)
Append queries 76–78
data type selection 86
Design View 70–71
expressions, using 86–87
filter criteria, operators for 86–87
logical operators 88
macros 73
parameter queries 88
SQL, using 71–72
queries (PHP)
amending records 276–82
appending records 259–63
deleting records 270–76
performing 264–69

R
Real Time Clock (RTC) 221
recovery points
creating 331–32
restoring 332–34
recovery testing 425
recovery time 26
reducing balance spreadsheets 111
referential integrity 64–65, 76
registration *see* product registration
registry
backing up 335
exploring 330
purpose of 329
relational database management systems
(RDMS) 249
relational databases
benefits of 66
deletes/updates, cascading 66, 89
primary key activation 64–65
purpose of 49–50
see also relationships
relational operators 188
relationships
creating/modifying 64–66
definition of 50
Entity Relationship Modelling 51–52
normalisation 55–63
one-to-one/one-to-many/many-to-
many 52–55